Living Cheaply With Style

by Ernest Callenbach

Ronin Publishing, Inc. Box 1035 Berkeley CA 94701

Living Cheaply With Style
ISBN: 0-914171-61-5
Copyright © 1993 by Ernest Callenbach

Published by
Ronin Publishing, Inc.
Post Office Box 1035
Berkeley, California 94701

This book evolved from these previous works by the author:
Living Poor With Style, Bantam/Straight Arrow, © 1972 by Ernest Callenbach
The Ecotopian Encyclopedia, And/Or Press, © 1980 by Ernest Callenbach

Printed in the United States of America by Hitext - Logistix
First printing 1993

9 8 7 6 5 4 3 2 1

Project Editors: Sebastian Orfali and Beverly Potter
Editors: Aiden Kelley, Dan Joy
Index: Nancy Freedom
Cover Design: Brian Groppe
Page Composition: Ginger Ashworth
Typographic Output: The Bookworks

U.S. Library of Congress Cataloging in Publication Data
Ernest Callenbach
    Living Cheaply With Style
        1. Reference. 2. Consumer.
    I. Title.

Dedication

To all who think for themselves and stay conscious of the
choices that shape their lives . . .

To all who know in their bones that enough is enough, and
want to figure out how much that is . . .

To all who understand that thrift, ingenuity, and resourceful-
ness mimic nature and help preserve the Earth . . .

To all who wish to survive with grace, humor, imagination, and
a little help from their friends . . .

Table of Contents

Introduction

The aim of the book is to equip you to live a better life—more relaxed, more confident, more resilient, more loving, more thoughtful, more satisfying, more genuinely stylish—than you could possibly have with a lot more money. It's not easy to live in America today, and for many of us it's getting steadily harder. But if we learn to live smarter and with less dependence on the money economy, we can tap a rich potential for sustaining healthy, productive, and happy lives—lives with real personal style. This book will both provide you with the knowledge and suggest the change in attitudes that can enable you to escape from the mental oppression of our commodity-crazed society, and to focus on what's really important in life: our human relationships both inside and outside the family, our communities, our physical and mental health, our contributions to the world, and the infinite pleasures and delights life can offer that are *not* dependent on cash.

The chapters that follow do not argue that anybody should have to get along without basic necessities. But if you have traveled in foreign countries where the average cash income is far lower than ours, you have probably noticed that people do not seem unhappier than Americans. In fact, even people who would be considered desperately poor in America often live cheerful and productive lives elsewhere. This contrast tells us that the ability to buy a lot of goods is not the critical factor in making human beings happy.

What is critical is our attitude about what makes us happy. Decades of brainwashing by advertisements have convinced many Americans that happiness results from buying things. Shopping has become our way of life. Commercials tell us, hundreds and thousands of times before we become adults: If you are depressed, go shopping; if you feel inferior, buy something and it will make you more attractive. Many of us have such well-trained reflexes about buying that we could truly call ourselves "consumer zombies." We appear to be alive, but our lives are sustained only by commercial transactions, toward which we march with heavy feet and glazed eyes.

But as you have probably noticed for yourself, life doesn't actually work the way the ads suggest. The satisfactions of most purchases of goods are fleeting. Your house may be full of junk that, when you bought it, seemed to promise some kind of basic fulfillment but then failed to provide it. Even the experience of shopping itself may sometimes make you feel a little queasy, as if you are being exploited by unseen forces. (You are.)

Consumer-zombie attitudes may seem "natural" to people brought up in the television age of heavy consuming, but they are unnatural and temporary aberrations if looked at from an historical perspective. Our forebears knew that contentment comes from feelings of being needed, being valuable to the universe in some way; from a sense of belonging to a supportive community of fellow humans, and perhaps fellow beings, here on our little planet; from the delights of love, sex, music and dance, meaningful work, and spiritual enlightenment. For most of human history, to call somebody a consumer (a person defined by what he or she uses up) would have been an insult. Only for the past few decades have greed and self-interest been enshrined as the goals of American life.

Style.

You live with style when you live in a self-determined and original way that is authentic for you, when you do things you enjoy because you enjoy them and not because you read about them somewhere or heard that somebody famous and rich enjoys them. You live with style when you keep your mind free to invent ways of thinking, feeling, and doing that suit *you*, rather than some corporate marketing department. You live with style when you rely on your own practiced judgment rather than somebody else's pronouncements.

Thus style is a matter of independence, even rebellion; we're not talking here about fashion, which is a matter of commercially fostered fads. America offers a paradoxical living environment, because on the one hand we praise independence of spirit, but on the other hand we are a nation of sheep in our consumer behavior, regularly duped by advertisers. In our commercial life and in our political life, we have become a nation of chronic liars. Living with style means turning away from lies, being your own person—though also realizing that as human beings we are social and sociable animals whose safety and serenity inevitably depend heavily on others. Part of the pleasure of living cheaply with style is to share your tricks and achievements with others, to build a counter-culture in which human beings can live more comfortably and satisfyingly, and to help make American life saner and more humane.

Thrift and "enoughness."

Until recently, America was a thrifty country. People recognized a virtue in doing things economically, in not wasting, in making do with what was available. During the wastrel years after World War II (fueled by a ravenous consumption of fossil fuels), thriftiness temporarily went out of fashion. But in the long run we must rely on this virtue again, and it is time to begin learning how. Much of the information in this book will help you to be thrifty in ways your grandparents would find familiar: re-using things rather than throwing them away and having to buy new; salvaging and repairing; sharing things with others; trading things you no longer need for things or services; keeping only a modest supply of things on hand; using up what you have before you think of buying more.

Some people are fanatics about thrift; there is even a publication called *The Tightwad Gazette* dedicated to showing you, through carefully calculated examples, how much you can save by ingenious re-use of milk cartons, or repairing battered toys found at the thrift shop. (Ask your library to subscribe, if it isn't yet available there.) It's a fascinating challenge to see what is the absolute minimum you can lead a good life on—and it is a lot less than most Americans imagine.

But it is not necessary to be a fanatic, only thoughtful. In *Your Money or Your Life* (Viking-Penguin, 1992), Joe Dominguez and Vicki Robin argue that the essential is to seek honestly to understand what is really "enough." Beyond a certain point, once your real necessities of food, shelter, and medical care have been met, added expenditures bring decreasing returns of satisfaction. After that point, your precious life's time—the only resource you are born into the world with—is being used to procure things that may be halfway satisfying, or may be simply junk. You will be happier if you can find a way to live that keeps better control of your time and relies less on junk.

Competence.

Another virtue our grandparents prized was competence and ingenuity— the ability to understand how things work, to use things efficiently, take care of them, repair them when needed, or figure out alternatives if they broke down. In our consumer society, we have come to depend on artifacts whose workings we do not understand and that we cannot fix when they break down. So a lot of the material in this book simply gives you information you need to cope with the basics of life—all those things that you didn't learn from your parents or in school, but that are essential to survive comfortably on modest amounts of money.

Even questions of diet are covered in some detail. Once we became a nation of fast-food eaters, we lost a sense of proper diet requirements. Recently many people have become conscious of the importance of eating right, but we still need all the help we can get; since doctors are taught almost nothing about nutrition in medical school, we have to be able to provide a decent diet for ourselves without advice from them.

Competence requires confidence, but trusting in our own abilities to learn and cope is the route to confidence. We should try to lean as little as possible on "experts," whether they are plumbers or psychotherapists. Everybody in so-called primitive societies knows how to build houses, dispose of wastes, find and grow food, prepare it, deal with common diseases and accidents, give birth, care for children, and so on. Our goal should be to achieve similar levels of competence in our modern circumstances. All your life you will be picking up pieces of useful information; this book gives you a handy and compact source for a lot of these pieces, and a framework for understanding the bits you accumulate on your own.

A constant theme in the pages that follow is: Think for yourself! Conventional ways of doing things *may* make sense, but often they make sense mainly to the people who profit from them, and you would be better off to find or invent another way. Learn to be critical and analytical about information; even apparently authoritative sources may contain large or small errors, and a wise person is constantly cross-checking and verifying things.

The Green Triangle.

Living an ecologically responsible life doesn't mean self-sacrifice and austerity; on the contrary, it should bring you a richer, more interesting, fuller, longer, and healthier life. But so far nobody has been able to dramatize this on a national level in the folksy, convincing way in which Ronald Reagan and Ivan Boesky made greed respectable.

Does ecological living make *attractive* sense for Americans? It had better, or we can start preparing a suitable tombstone for our nation—and the rest of the globe, which follows our cultural lead. Helpful as they may be, we need more than a cafeteria menu of 50 or 750 ecological good practices to choose among.

Luckily, on the whole it works to assume that the universe displays reassuring regularities that we can rely on. This goes for science almost without saying, since without prediction of regularities it's impossible to devise experiments. But it is also reassuringly true of our daily lives. However chaotic they sometimes seem, they have patterns; we can actually make sense of the ways things work, and react accordingly.

One way we can understand some critical everyday regularities is by considering what I call the Green Triangle. It's a handy means of generating for ourselves ideas for personal and community and national change. (Ecological matters are also inevitably social; we *can't* do it all individually.)

The three points of the triangle are environment, health, and money. The principle that relates these three points is: *Anytime you do something beneficial for one of them, you will almost inevitably also do something beneficial for the other two*—whether you're aiming to or not.

For example, let's suppose you decide to take action to improve your health, by eating less fat-filled meat and dairy products. This will, of course, decrease your chance of circulatory disease and probably prolong your life; it may even make you stronger and give you greater endurance. But since meat and dairy products are relatively expensive, you will also save quite a bit of money; moreover, you will *also* help the environment—since meat production is a very land-intensive and resource-consuming use of our farm productive capacities.

But you can start at *any* point of the Green Triangle. Let's assume you do something beneficial for the environment, like walking or bicycling instead of driving your car. You cut down pollution emissions, you reduce smog and lung damage, you decrease acid rain, and you may help postpone the greenhouse effect. But you'll also help your health, because you get more regular exercise, and you'll save money on gas, oil, and car depreciation.

The third point of the Green Triangle is actually just as potent. Anytime you do something beneficial for your pocketbook, like not buying an expensive gizmo whose manufacturing expends a lot of energy and uses a lot of raw materials, or not taking an expensive trip that turns a lot of petroleum into atmospheric pollution and noise, you're also helping the Earth. But you're probably also doing your health a favor, since you're less stressed out to earn the money to pay off the gizmo or trip; and not pouring a lot of emotional energy into interacting with the gizmo leaves time and attention for other human beings and the kind of spontaneous improvisation and fooling around that our species evolved to be good at. (And don't keep this good news to yourself, or show reinforcing enthusiasm—or envy—toward friends boasting of the latest acquisition. The best way to get somebody to stop doing something is to ignore it, and praise *other* behaviors.)

If you apply the Green Triangle to your everyday life, examples of delightful synergistic effects can be found everywhere; you come out with many useful new perceptions. Some cases: Low- or no-cost fun with other people is almost always more ecologically and financially desirable than hard work and heavy consumption; evidently evolution did not commit an ecological error in making us playful. Exchanges outside the cash economy—trading massages, for instance, or passing on extra vegetables, knowing your neighbor will probably someday help you with a carpentry problem—don't have monetary ramifications you have to worry about, whereas if you pay for a massage, the money may go into a bank, and you know what *they* do with it. Growing or making your own is usually cheaper and healthier, as well as more ecologically benign. Fun, isn't it? So go triangulate!

One last word: even using the Green Triangle, we must still remember that there is no such thing as innocent purchasing, even in countries with eco-labeling programs that guide consumers to "less-damaging" products. Of course, it's good to buy things that do less damage, and we have budding labeling programs in this country, such as the Green Cross and the Green Seal. To keep a sense of proportion, however, the *really* ecologically damaging things we do are to use cars, eat meat, have more than one child per parent, and live in dispersed single-family dwellings (apartment living is something like five times more energy- and materials-efficient). Even the most devoted recycling and conserving will not outweigh the enormous effects of these basic factors. You may not be able to consider change in all of them at once, but how about trying just one?

The other difficult-to-accept green principle is this: *Buy less in general.* There are a few things that we, the rich peoples of the Northern, industrialized countries, can buy that really do positive good for the Earth: photovoltaic cells and solar hot-water heaters, for instance, which move us toward a solar economy. But learning to live more contentedly with less income and less consumption of goods vastly outranks all other things we might choose to do to lessen our ecological impacts. Odd as it may seem, the simple act of consuming less is probably the most radical step you can personally take to save the Earth.

Living Cheaply With Style

Chapter 1.
Buy Cheaply.

There is no such thing as an unmitigated advantage or pure Good Thing, or a free lunch. Any course of action entails sacrifices as well as benefits. If you choose to become an expert typist, your handwriting will suffer through reduced use; if you drive, your legs will be less strong than if you walked. In the course of the day, we all make hundreds of conscious or unconscious trade-off judgments, deciding to do one thing rather than another (or nothing) because we have assessed in some manner the relative advantages and disadvantages, and decided to trade some off against others. Living a sane life is largely a matter of making these trade-offs sensibly.

One trade-off we all make is between time and money. It is tempting to think that working longer hours and thus making more money will improve your quality of life. But this is seldom wise except as a temporary measure. For one thing, by sacrificing even more of your time to your job, you put yourself under greater emotional pressure, and probably injure your relationships with friends and family. For another, by working more you are making your "terms of trade" with the world as a whole less favorable. By increasing your dollar income, you will increase the proportion of it you pay in income tax; you will probably need to spend money on things and services you could provide for yourself if you had more time (plus incurring sales taxes you'd otherwise avoid); the things you buy will mainly be "finished goods" rather than the wood, nails, and other component parts you'd buy if you were doing things for yourself. And, because you would probably not have so much garden produce or other things to barter, you would find yourself paying for everything you consumed.

One of the good things about barter is that it occurs outside the money economy and is thus not feasible to tax. But there are also other ways of emphasizing your private-life productivity, which is not taxed, rather than your job-time productivity, which is. The principle here is that "private" productivity, being untaxed, is actually "paid" at a higher rate.

To obtain a sofa that sells for, let's say, $1,000, you have two choices. If you buy it, you spend $1,000 + sales tax, perhaps a total of $1,060. But to get that $1,060, you have had to *earn* something like $1,300 to $1,500, depending on your tax bracket. The materials in the sofa, however, are probably worth $300. Thus if you build it yourself, even if it takes you longer to build the sofa than it would take in the furniture factory, you are probably being "paid" in savings at much more per hour than you would receive by working and saving your money for the sofa. And you would have performed an enjoyable, productive, satisfying task, and provided yourself with a sofa precisely to your tastes. *buy v. make*

Some people, carrying this logic to its ultimate conclusion, decide to move to the country, where they can do more things for themselves—from building their house to keeping a horse for local transportation. City dwellers are more restricted, but all of us can locate areas of our lives where we could, if we wished, secure more favorable trade-offs both economically and emotionally. Obviously people vary a great deal in their preferences, tastes, abilities, and needs. The person who always cooks at home, vegetarian-style, and eats on about half of what most of us spend on food, may have absolutely no inclination to have a sofa, much less build one, no matter how much could be saved. But you can find applications somewhere in your life for the underlying principle that withdrawal from the money economy generally saves you money. The trick, of course, is to find the areas where it will *also* give you a more relaxed, secure, healthy way of being. The object is *not* simply to pare down your expenses, though that will be a by-product of the process.

Most Americans don't make terribly much money now, and a continuing decline in real per-capita income (purchasing power) is in store for us as a nation. For the vast majority of Americans, therefore, a strategy of minimizing paid employment and maximizing "private" productivity is sound.

But there are some Americans who manage to get high-paid jobs, inherit a house or other assets, or otherwise have money considerably beyond the average income. Does this change the trade-off principle's application? Indeed it does. People with significant disposable capital need to find safe investments for their extra money. People who have enough free capital to make investments can often put it to work multiplying itself at a rate greater than the savings they could achieve through the "minimizing " strategy outlined above. For them, therefore, ever-deeper immersion in jobs or other cash-producing activities makes sense economically. Whether it makes sense psychologically, spiritually, or politically is another question, of course. It may, if you save money systematically toward early financial independence, after which you can spend your energy on activities that benefit the world, whether or not you get paid for them. Lacking such a disciplined plan, it is easy to spend your life making money, until you wake up, at 50 or 60, and realize that you have only one life to live, and that you'd better get on with it, regardless of the economic cost. At this point, many people "drop out"—undergoing an almost religious conversion, often abandoning lifelong marriages and associations. They find to their astonishment that they can get along very happily without most of the goods they formerly strove so hard to buy; they put their energy into new, energy-filled personal relationships with new friends, new lovers, or formerly estranged children; they begin to take risks they would have passed by before, and generally find new excitement and vitality in their lives.

A. Maximizing your buying power.

1. Compare real costs.

Business persons and middle-class people are always trying to estimate whether one way of doing something is cheaper than another. Living this way is, admittedly, a drag; eventually you can become the Economic Wonder, judging everything dryly and arithmetically and seldom having any fun. However, in our society, unless you can calculate comparative costs, you are being had, and frequently. Hence, if our schools were teaching us useful stuff, they would make sure we knew how to compare different courses of action in many real-life situations.

Take napkins, for instance. (Napkins? Well, why not?) You probably use paper napkins, like most Americans these days, and you have probably never thought about it much. If you have, you've probably felt that your grandparents' system (cloth napkins that have to be washed and ironed all the time) is far too much trouble and probably more expensive anyway. You may say that even though you really like cloth napkins.

How to figure which is cheaper? You somehow have to arrive at the average costs. (Average in this kind of situation can mean either cost per meal or cost per week; it doesn't make any difference which.)

The figures that follow may be outdated by the time you read them, but the principles of our calculations won't be affected. Low-cost paper napkins are about 70¢ for a package of 140. (The only cheaper ones are restaurant packages of 500.) That means the cost per napkin is about 1/2¢. If you have four people at a table, that comes to about 2¢ per meal, 6¢ per day, 42¢ per week.

Cloth napkins that don't need any ironing can be bought for about $1, or four for $4. You can also make them, of course, and cut down the cost. They will need to be laundered about once a week. To figure the average cost of something like this, you must spread the costs out over time. How long, for instance, will those cloth napkins last? Obviously, it's impossible to say exactly, but you know it's going to be more than a few months; and you know it's not going to be for years and years. Let's just assume, therefore, that they'll last around a year. (They'll last longer, but what the hell.) The cost of washing them is hard to fix precisely, since they just go into your general washbasket. But you can assign some rough guess to their share of the wash cost.

Now you're in a position to figure a comparative cost. If the cloth napkins last a year and cost $1 each, their average cost per week is about 2¢ each, or 8¢ per week for a family of four. The washing probably adds 5–10¢ per week, so your total cloth napkin costs are around 13–18¢ per week.

Surprised? What you have just realized is that using paper napkins costs three or four times as much as using cloth napkins. This is the great power of knowing how to figure cost comparisons.

Besides, using cloth napkins gives you the chance to make some weird and stylish napkin rings or napkin holders. Clothespins painted different colors will work fine, but you can make much fancier and more elegant items: rings carved out of scrap pieces of beautiful hardwood, metal rings with etched or enameled patterns. These will identify each family member's napkin, in case you worry about germs (though if you really know a great deal about germs, you won't worry much). What our grandparents probably liked best was that each child had his or her own personal thing there on the family table, to use and take care of. Not a bad idea.

The initial cost of something is only a part of its true cost, and sometimes (as with a light bulb) it's only a fraction of what you will pay to use it. To assess the real economic impact of a purchase, a full accounting is necessary and includes: capital cost, i.e., what it costs you to spend your money on that item and not keep it in the bank (or, alternatively, how much you pay in interest to finance it); operating costs, some of which—like berth rental for a boat, or the extra electric consumption on a no-frost refrigerator—may in reality be greater than the investment in the object itself; repair and maintenance costs; and finally disposal costs. These costs must all be assessed over the expected life cycle of the item. Then, dividing by the lifetime, you can obtain a true yearly cost. It is almost certain to be much larger than you expected!

2. Avoid buying brand names.

American industry systematically tries to brainwash us into thinking that brand names hold a kind of magic: that Bayer aspirin is superior to other aspirin (although aspirin is chemically identical), that RCA is better than Zenith, and so on. In fact, this "superiority" consists of a high-priced advertising myth. There are minor differences among products, but the most famous brands are seldom the (slightly) superior ones, and they usually cost more.

Buyers who trust big names like General Electric are buying TV air time with their hard-earned cash, not quality in the goods.

You can usually figure out which brand X, Y, or Z is probably best, because *Consumer Reports* runs elaborate scientific tests and publishes the results, with information on safety hazards, breakdown rates, etc. (Your library has a collection of *Consumer Reports* issues.)

The only rule that makes sense about brand names is: Be especially cautious about the "big brands," whose reputations were probably built some years ago, and are maintained chiefly through advertising. Look for new brands that are getting a reputation by word of mouth from people who know something about electronics, or cars, or whatever is involved. A new, small company, fighting for its life against the giants that dominate its field, may be run by people who take real pride in their product. (Later, if they are successful and expand, they too will pay more attention to financial manipulations than to quality.)

3. Beware of deceptive packaging.

Packaging is a major weapon in the manufacturer's constant campaign to cheat the customer. The companies are absolutely shameless in their attempts to deceive you—and most of the time they get away with it. Breck, for instance, simply changed the size of its shampoo bottles. They used to be simple and round and contained 16 ounces (an even pint). The new bottles were higher, thinner, and shaped funny. They only hold 15 ounces—but the price went up! Presumably Breck discovered that buyers are so stupid that they think a taller bottle always holds more than a shorter bottle, no matter what its shape, and won't bother to check the "unit price" that laws have finally forced stores to display on their shelves.

Packaging is not only deceptive, but also ecologically destructive and remarkably wasteful; sometimes the fancy printing, special shapes, and plastic wrappers actually cost as much as the product. Generally, you are better off buying things in simple packages if their prices are similar. What the fancy packers spend on the wrappings, they often take out in lower quality of the goods inside.

Incidentally, even simple packages are often used deceptively to make things look better: thus carrots are packed in plastic which has thin orange strips printed on it to make the carrots look more orange; green vegetables get the green-ink treatment, apples get the red-ink treatment. Tell your supermarket manager that you think this is cheap deception, and request that the store buy from other suppliers. Similar deceptions prevail in meat to make it look redder. Try to shop in a co-op or natural-foods grocery where such practices do not prevail—and you may even be able to buy many foods "in bulk," with no packaging at all.

4. Beware of deceptive pricing.

Is there any way of knowing what is a "fair price"? Not really, because prices in our economic system (monopoly capitalism) are set by what corporations think they can get, usually colluding with each other to some degree—most blatantly on airline tickets. Today only agriculture and the grocery industry retain any significant degree of price competition. "List prices" are often not real prices, by the way—they are imaginary prices set somewhat higher, so that you can be conned into thinking you're getting a bargain.

a. Check the contents. Beware of items that have labels reading "15¢ OFF REGULAR PRICE!" or something like that. Such labels are often deceiving: check the quantity in the package, compared to other brands—the contents may have been cut down.

b. Do comparisons. There are some ways to tell whether or not you are being fleeced. Fairly standard prices can be found in the catalogs of Sears and Montgomery Ward. If your neighborhood store is offering "bargain" towels, but you see good towels in the catalogs for only half the "bargain" price, you can be pretty sure you're being swindled. These days, to get a mail-order catalog of your own, you have to be a regular customer—but you can find them in the Sears or Ward stores. There's practically nothing, except cars, that the catalogs don't list and describe.

Your library also has (probably in the reference room) the *Consumer Reports Buying Guide*, which rates products on performance, safety, and durability, and lists "suggested" (often fake) list prices. Unfortunately, neither *Consumer Reports* magazine nor the *Buying Guide* makes much effort to suggest whether something is worth buying at any price, or to evaluate its ecological impact.

c. Shop in the better stores. Another way to check prices is to shop around in middle-class stores. Careful surveys have proved that stores in poor neighborhoods charge more and stock poorer goods, on the average, than stores in middle-class neighborhoods. Therefore, when you are interested in finding something, look there, note the different prices and different qualities—and then find what you're after second-hand. If you have a car, you should certainly do your main grocery shopping each week in a middle-class supermarket. Avoid sleazy "bargain" or "close-out" stores unless you are really an expert on what they're peddling; usually their sales are frauds.

5. Be sure it's a different product.

In an economic system dominated by huge advertising programs that often cost more than the product being advertised, you have to be constantly on guard against phony "refinements" to a product that are used to justify higher prices. To add perfume and pink coloring to a detergent may not really increase its manufacturing cost at all; but its retail price will certainly be higher than if the detergent were unadorned. Soap with a fancy label and a special smell doesn't wash you any cleaner than the cheapest soap you can buy, which comes wrapped in plain tissue paper. It's so cheap that most stores won't stock it. There are, unfortunately, many "boutique" stores in which practically all the merchandise is of the fancy, inflated-price variety. Stay out of them!

The industries in which advertising distortion is most extreme are precisely those that advertise the most: cars, tobacco, soap, detergents, cosmetics, beer, breakfast foods, and so on. You can, in other words, be reasonably sure that more effort has been spent in advertising the products than in trying to increase their quality. The differences from one brand to another are minimal; so a lot of money has to be spent to convince you that those differences exist at all.

The basic ploy of the advertisers is to try to make you feel that by buying their product you will somehow feel better: sexier, wiser, handsomer, cleaner, less worried, and so on. But, of course, no product can really change how you feel—even if it did what it's supposed to do.

6. Barter for goods and services.

One reason not to throw things away is that you can probably trade them for something you need. Bartering is an ancient and honorable American custom, and it is particularly valuable for one simple but enormously important reason: Since it doesn't involve money, it can be kept outside the official economy, with its taxed wages, sales taxes, and other methods of siphoning off your resources.

a. Barter services. You can barter items for other items, but you can also barter services. If you know how to do something—how to quilt or bake bread or do carpentry or wiring—the chances are that you know somebody who needs to learn and who can either teach you something in return, provide you some service (gardening? wood chopping? driving you on some errands?), or otherwise "swap" with you. You can even advertise on bulletin boards. (Participation in organized barter "clubs" or services whose membership lists can be obtained by the IRS, however, can expose you to auditing and tax charges, since the IRS views barter as equivalent to money sales and has no compunctions about double taxation.)

Bartering also cements friendships in a way that buying and selling things for cash somehow just doesn't do. You don't even necessarily have to get a return on an item right away. Some experienced barterers know that if they say, "Well, just take it now—you'll discover something you can give me for it," they will seldom be disappointed. Barterers have to take each other's tastes and personalities into account; they have to deal with each other as human beings.

b. Multiply your buying power. If you go into a store to buy something new, you'll pay, let's say, $50 for it. Plus maybe $3 in sales tax. But to get that

$53, you probably had to *earn* about $70 (considering the impact of income tax). On the other hand, if you can find somebody who'll give you the item for barter, you "pay" for it with an item of yours on which you've already gone through the financial preliminaries; you are, so to speak, recycling your previous investment. So your effective outlay for the item you want is probably less than half of what it would be if you bought it new. And, depending on how you value your time, it might be even less if you trade a service for an object.

c. Grow your own products to barter. One of the reasons to grow vegetables, or to keep bees, or to raise chickens, is that they tend to provide you with more than you can use, so that you have surpluses to use in bartering. That can be, in fact, half the fun.

7. Use coupons wisely; avoid trading stamps.

The "29¢ off" type coupon is basically, of course, a device to persuade you to purchase something you had not planned to purchase. Once in a while you will happen upon a coupon at the time you really need something; and on other occasions, though you really don't need it yet, it's for something you're *sure* you will need later. In these cases, but only in these cases, it's wise to use the coupons. At today's high auto-operating costs, it's never worth it to make a special trip to some store just to cash in on a coupon or two, unless you can combine the trip with taking advantage of advertised specials on things you use a lot.

8. Scavenge for free food and products.

There is a particular kind of enjoyment gained in salvaging from a junk pile something whose stylish beauty or usefulness only you can appreciate. A sense of mystery and adventure lurks in scavenging expeditions: You never know what you may find. Sometimes you may even turn up useful objects that you can really never identify—like the four crates made of expanded metal that I once found at the dump, and which I've used for years to support bookshelves or plants.

a. Scavenge at the town dump. In time past, anybody could scavenge at the town dump, and you still can in some towns. Both households and industries throw out an astounding quantity of perfectly usable pans, paper, clothes, appliances, boards, springs, tools, metal, cloth, and glass. People are evidently dismayingly incompetent at simple repairs, leading them to throw out valuable motors, fishing equipment, tires, garden equipment, and chairs whose only fault is a missing rung that you can replace with a dowel in ten minutes. Some of the most interesting objects are discarded merely because they are old: old metal washtubs, old car jacks, old window frames. Frequently these are much better quality than comparable new ones.

b. Scavenge at industrial-waste sites. Even if going to the dump is not your idea of a pleasant outing, you can still be a scavenger. Every industrial establishment has some kind of private dump where it throws things that are later to be hauled away to the main dump, and you can go through it if you make sure the security guards know what you're doing (i.e., not stealing things the company wants). Companies throw away defective products, old machine parts, office furniture, old reference books, a huge miscellaneous collection of stuff. Wander around the industrial section of your town and get to know what goes on there. Sometimes you will also find vacant lots where companies stack crates and dunnage lumber for people to haul away free. Lumber mills sell slab ends (rough but usable slices off the logs) for practically nothing.

c. Scavenge for food. Every day every supermarket throws out wilted vegetables and banged-up fruits. Most of these are perfectly edible—they're just not pretty enough to sell at the prevailing prices. Rather than let this produce rot and be hauled away, some markets will tolerate people dropping by to see what they can use. You'll also find dented cans, leaking detergent boxes, etc. Usually boxes or crates are lying around in which you can put the stuff you want. There are families in this country whose entire selection of fruits and vegetables comes from this source; they use their food stamps or small cash incomes for other foods.

d. Scavenge free meals. The catering services that provide foods for hospitals, nursing homes, industrial cafeterias, schools, and so on are another source of free food: specifically, the daily leftovers of such institutions. Theoretically, they are obliged not to give excess meals away; in practice, by hanging around the kitchens you'll probably meet someone who can't bear to waste perfectly good food and who will pass some on to you. On such expeditions, carry along an innocuous cardboard box to conceal your haul and avoid getting your friendly supplier into trouble. Some restaurants—even very fancy ones—have staff members who will make extra food available to discreet inquiries at the back door late in the evening.

e. Be ingenious. The extent to which you can make use of "waste" material is limited only by your own ingenuity. Given enough of it, you could theoretically construct a whole house, furnish it comfortably and cozily, and supplement your diet wholesomely without spending any money. The key is to learn to look at things without preconceptions. Maybe that funny-looking metal bracket would make a clothes rack. That nice broad piece of wood? How nice it would look as a shelf. And isn't it possible to remove that pair of wheels, which would be fine for a little garden cart or a kid's pushcart?

9. Stock up on bargains.

It is often wise to buy standard necessities in bulk, since that way you can usually get quantity or case discounts. Besides, it saves gas and tedious trips to the store. Many people do this for a surprising number of items: toilet paper, soap, shampoo, canned or frozen foods they use regularly, rice, lentils, and other staples, cleaning materials, light bulbs, and so on.

But of course there is a limit—usually the limit of your storage space. And you only want to stock up on things that don't spoil, rot, or mildew under your storage conditions. Be careful, also, not to overestimate your consumption rate; most preserved foods lose much of their nutritive value if kept more than six months or so. What you need to concentrate on, thus, are mainly nonfood items. Inventory your house and jot down the things to keep an eye out for at discounts: coffee, toothpaste (if you use it), paper supplies, durable goods like towels and sheets, etc.

B. Go buy where they sell cheap.

1. Go to auctions.

If you are immune to crowd psychology, auctions can be a good source for furniture, rugs, clothes, books, and many other things. But you really need to know what you are doing. If you're easily stampeded, you can find yourself paying more for something than it costs new. In many cities permanent auction houses sell furniture and household goods weekly or even more frequently; occasional or weekend country auctions can be found too. Both types are listed in the classified ads of the paper. You can go around beforehand, look at the goods, and find out approximately when they will come up for bids. Then check a Sears catalog to make sure you know what a fair price is. Your game at auctions is to bid only on things you want, and to set beforehand a top limit for anything you want to bid on. I have attended auctions where bidders go completely crazy and bid up an old bicycle that isn't worth ten bucks to $50. On the other hand, working refrigerators may go for $20. But on the whole, auctions are far more time-consuming than secondhand stores. The lure, of course, is that you might turn up something exquisite at a reasonable price (if the antique dealers don't outbid you).

The dedicated auction-goer develops a fine feel for the bidding—when it is petering out, when it will go hopelessly higher, when you are bidding against a determined professional who may have a rich customer lined up, when you are bidding on a piece of junk that nobody else wants, and when someone is bidding against you (a friend of the auctioneer?) just to push the price up.

2. Inspect bulletin boards.

One of the great social inventions is the bulletin board, on which people post notices of things they want to sell or buy. Bulletin boards are commonly found around colleges, in laundromats, in supermarkets, nailed up outside stores, or even on houses. If none exists in your neighborhood, start one—pick a busy, heavy-traffic location, and ask a storekeeper if you can nail up a board somewhere. Seed it with a few cards from your friends and see what happens. A careful buyer can always do better by buying direct from a previous owner than from a dealer. (Obviously you must give a careful tryout to anything you buy anywhere, but especially when you are buying strictly as-is.) People can also advertise rides offered or sought, apartments or rooms to rent or share, things to barter, and so on.

3. Shop at discount houses.

Since World War II there has been a great growth in discount stores; they now exist in every city and sell lots of merchandise of all kinds. Their prices are noticeably lower than the prices in regular stores—though not as much lower as they used to be. Discounters avoid company price-fixing, where this exists in the open, by some kind of membership requirements. This usually means the customer will pay a couple of dollars for a card, but will save that amount on any substantial purchase.

In general, if you absolutely must buy something new, and it costs more than about $20, you will save money buying at a discount house. Still, there are hazards. Since discounters are big-volume operators, they aren't much concerned with honoring guarantees or giving service on defective products. (Many don't even have service departments.) They'll try to stick you with time payments at high rates of interest to get back through the installments what they gave up on price. Also, they may try to sell you inferior brands that look like the more expensive ones but that lack certain features. If you buy a refrigerator because the discounter is selling it for less than an appliance store, you may get it home and discover it isn't the same machine you saw in the appliance store. Check model numbers and descriptions carefully.

This is even more important if you deal with a discount house that operates through the mail—you could end up paying shipping both ways on an item you don't want. And, of course, you can forget any guarantee (not that guarantees are worth much anyhow). But mail-order discounters can be very cheap; they also can be very slow! Generally you become a member by paying for a catalog.

Often co-operatives have "referral" arrangements with furniture and appliance stores that will get you a small discount. Recently co-ops and credit unions have begun to make discount arrangements on new cars, whereby you supposedly get the car for wholesale cost plus a few hundred dollars. However, you will have to sell your old car yourself—and you should still check around to make sure the discounter's final price is fair.

4. Try thrift stores and consignment stores.

The Salvation Army and other helpful organizations maintain stores where, if you have an eye for quality, you can pick up clothes and household items at about a tenth of new prices. Consignment stores, which take in goods from people wanting to sell them but lacking any way of doing so themselves, offer very high-quality items, but be sure they are priced reasonably.

5. Frequent garage sales, yard sales, flea markets.

A major recycling channel, these methods of selling used items can be found in practically any community. Generally you get the best deals in garage sales or yard sales, especially when somebody is moving and is anxious to get rid of stuff before moving day. You have to develop a quick and ruthless eye to avoid spending too much time on any individual collection of junk, and it helps to have a half-formed shopping list in your mind for such occasions. But the main joy, of course, is in finding the things you didn't remember you wanted until you saw them. And then there is also the joy of haggling, which most people seem to expect.

Classified ads in some local community papers are used to announce garage and yard sales; often people put up notices on bulletin boards, as well as on telephone poles on the day of their sale. Beware of "permanent" garage sales, which are really secondhand shops, with correspondingly higher prices.

Flea markets are generally worth the trouble only if they are held by some organization on a very occasional basis. The regularly established ones are mainly filled with secondhand dealers selling the same tired collection of battered tools, old radios, overpriced antique jewelry, and well-worn kitchen implements. (Some of them also offer "hot" clothes, cameras, and electronic stuff.)

6. Don't ignore surplus stores.

These can be another good source of non-new things. Originally, they dealt strictly with leftover war material: uniforms, tents, shovels, and so on. Nowadays many "surplus" stores sell very little government surplus; their chief merchandise is junk—seconds and rejects in clothing, stuff they pick up at fire sales, tools that are often priced as high as (or higher than) in hardware stores. Some things, however, cannot be found elsewhere: beautiful orange-and-white parachutes, camouflage ponchos. Sometimes, if you're careful, you can pick up used mummy sleeping bags or GI clothing at reasonable prices. But in general, treat the surplus store cautiously. It's no place for impulse buying.

Chapter 2.
Eat Cheaply, but Eat Right.

A. Buy good-quality food as cheaply as possible.

There are a few basic rules to follow in shopping for food. (Though as with all rules, it's fun to break them once in a while.)

1. Avoid buying food any place but a grocery store.

Food you buy in a store is usually less than half as expensive as food prepared for you—and it's usually better quality. (If you are dying to try some restaurant, eat lunch, not dinner. You'll get the same food, but usually at a lower price.)

2. Avoid buying in small stores.

The best buys are in the supermarkets in middle-class neighborhoods: Buy your week's food there even if it involves an expedition. However, specialized green-groceries, bakeries, and so on, if run by people who care, can offer higher-quality merchandise than the chains, though often at somewhat higher prices too.

3. Eat before you shop.

If you're hungry, statistics show, you will end up buying more, and more expensive stuff, whether you have a list or not.

4. Never buy pre-sliced meats or cheese.

The slicing and slick packaging can more than double the price per pound.

5. Never buy prepared baby food in cans or jars.

Babies can and will eat all kinds of food if it is simply mashed soft enough for them—which you can usually do with an ordinary fork. If you have a blender you can mash up anything from asparagus to zucchini. Some adult foods, like applesauce, mashed potatoes, and scrambled eggs, are perfect for babies as is. Baby food is one of the worst buys in the entire American supermarket. Some of it is loaded with sugar or salt; some of it contains additives.

6. Never buy soda or candy.

They have little food value; they make you fat; they rot your teeth. But most of all, they cost like hell. If you can't resist your kids' requests, give them fruit juice with a little extra sugar in it.

7. Plan your shopping to last for a week.

Make a list and stick to it. Buy all your basic foods at once; make sure you've got enough to last you the week. The less often you go into a store, the less you will spend.

8. Buy good food in appropriate quantities.

One depressing thing about stretching your food budget is the feeling that you never get anything that's really top-quality. It's better, therefore, after you have laid in your stock of rice, beans, potatoes, and so on, to buy fish, meat, cheese, and other expensive foods with an eye to quality rather than quantity. It will make you feel better to eat a half-pound of good broiled halibut than a whole pound of greasy hamburger.

9. Eat non-standard meats.

Your family may not have prepared kidneys, lungs, spleen, liver, heart, brains, etc., but that doesn't mean they aren't good. Look around in your cookbook and try some out. Heart, cut into quarter-inch slices, can be fried in a few minutes, and tastes delicious in any kind of tomato-and-onion sauce. Brains, which are high-protein foods, can be cooked with scrambled eggs. Some organ meats, however, should only be eaten once or twice a month; brains are high in cholesterol and liver in toxins (unless it is "organically" raised).

10. Avoid buying cans.

Canned vegetables are almost always tasteless compared to fresh or frozen vegetables. Buy vegetables in season whenever possible, of course, when they will be cheap and good. Don't go too much by appearance with vegetables or fruit; sometimes the biggest, shiniest fruit is also the blandest and mealiest, because it's been grown by hurry-up irrigation. Also, most fruit is picked early so that it can be shipped to market before ripening; your best buy is a small quantity of fruit that's on the verge of perfectly ripe. (Don't buy more than a day's supply of ripe, soft fruits such as apricots and plums.) Vegetables and fruits are healthy foods, and you can hardly eat too much of them.

11. Don't be taken in by "convenient packages."

Everything that is pre-packaged or pre-measured costs more than the same thing in bulk. Thus you pay more for tea bags, for cereal in individual-portion boxes, for potato chips in small bags, and so on.

12. Buy house brands.

The cheaper brands labeled by the supermarket chain or co-op chain itself usually are packed by the same companies whose stuff you get in name-brand labels. In canned goods, buy Grade B; it's as tasty as Grade A, just not as perfect in appearance. You pay a lot extra to get all-perfect fruits, especially; and if you can find cans labeled "broken pieces"—of peaches, pears, and so on—they are cheaper still. Some frozen vegetables are always cheaper than their fresh counterparts no matter the season—peas and green beans and corn-off-the-cob, for instance—especially when you buy them in bulk bags rather than the small square cardboard packages.

13. Try to leave your kids at home.

Or shop in a supermarket with some sort of child-care facilities. Otherwise they will be after you to buy expensive sugared breakfast cereal, candy, and so on.

14. Watch for "specials" in the supermarkets.

Most specials, however, just reflect temporary small downswings in costs, perhaps because of fluctuations in crops, or some kind of finagling on the commodity markets. The smarter you are about your food buying generally, the less you feel compelled to watch specials. You may want to save coupons that come in the Sunday paper or in your mailbox, but be selective—throw out all that won't help you buy things you really use constantly.

15. Ask for help.

People who live alone have special shopping problems because the packaging and pricing in supermarkets seems to be done with a family of four in mind.

The temptation is strong to turn to TV dinners and other quickie meals, but these are expensive for the amount of protein and other important nutrients they contain, tend to have a lot of sugar, excess salt, gravies, and other drawbacks, and are also boring compared to simple meals you can fix for yourself. So fight your way through the packages. Unwind the wires and take what you need from the asparagus and broccoli bundles. Get the grocery checker to cut a carton of eggs in half. Ring for the butcher and have him or her package the half pound of meat you need. In time, since so many people are now living alone, such actions will get the message through.

16. Read the labels!

After some decades of prodding by consumer organizations and co-operatives, the food industry has been compelled by government regulations to attach informative nutrition labels to its products. Use these labels to understand what you're eating and what its benefits and hazards are.

The label must first of all indicate what the ingredients are—often very difficult to guess without the labels—and in their order of volume. Thus a prepared food that contains more sugar than anything else (a common occurrence) must list sugar as its first ingredient, followed by water, flour, salt, and whatever else it contains. All preservatives, additives, and colorings must be listed; unfortunately, flavorings (which are often artificial chemical compounds) have been exempted because they supposedly constitute "trade secrets." If you find unnamed "flavorings" listed on the label, therefore, the best plan is to avoid the product.

Food labels must also provide a summary of the nutritional value of the product. This includes numbers (per serving) for the protein content in grams, the calories, and the fat content—not always, unfortunately, separated into saturated and other type of fat. Vitamin and trace-mineral content must also be indicated. For many of these items, the label indicates what percentage of normal daily requirements you get by eating one serving (whose size is specified) of the food.

The sale of irradiated foods (exposed to nuclear radiation) has recently been authorized, though it is as yet unclear whether this process may produce unhealthy by-products in the foods. You can avoid irradiated items by looking for labels with a deceptively innocent-looking flower on them.

B. Catch, raise, gather, or make your own food.

1. Catch fish.

Fishing, hunting, and gathering are primordial survival techniques of human beings, and there is something to be said for staying in touch with them. Even heavily urbanized areas often have good fishing spots quite close by—in rivers, lakes, bays, etc. However, check with your health department about possible pollution hazards in local fish.

Anybody can bait a hook and throw a line in the water, and in small ponds filled with bluegills, the bamboo pole with a string and hook is all you need (and you can do without the pole in a pinch). Bluegills are widespread, and if you happened to be starving in the wilderness, you could do worse than try to catch some. Catching larger fish is something else again, and you need to be instructed by someone who is experienced and actually catches fish. Lots of people have rods and reels lying around the attic unused; you can probably pick up or at least borrow a set for nothing. If the bodies of water in your vicinity have not been rendered entirely uninhabitable by pollution, your teacher will be able to take you to places where people fish who seriously wish to catch fish suitable for eating. There you may find whole families perched on a pier or bank, patiently fishing all day long—and maybe going home with enough catfish to fill a freezer for the winter.

There are other aquatic creatures you may wish to catch besides fish. Crayfish, which are small relatives of lobsters, abound in most streams and in irrigation ditches and lakes. You catch them by wading around and turning over rocks; a small net and flashlight make it easier. (They are most active at night.) As with lobsters or crabs, the standard practice is to kill them by dropping them in boiling water; you shell out the tails, which can be fried in butter or batter. Turtles make a tasty soup and can be easy to catch in some situations. Frogs, which are of course a great delicacy in fancy restaurants, can be speared with a long pole or netted; their legs are the only edible part.

Every state requires a fishing license, and game wardens will appear at heavily fished areas, or on piers where sport-fishing boats dock, to check up. Certain spots, like piers built with federal money, are exempt from licenses. In general, you need to be relatively enthusiastic about fishing to hope to recover the cost of a license.

2. Gather edible wild plants.

Foraging for wild plants is a hobby that can provide you with a great deal of tasty food; wild plants abound in cities as well as the country. It is nice to know which plants that grow in your region are edible. Here are some of the most common and easy to recognize.

Dandelions. This often despised "weed" (a weed is merely any plant growing where humans don't want it) can be eaten in salads or boiled like spinach. It's full of vitamins. The new small leaves are the tenderest. Dandelion roots in the spring can be dug up and sliced and boiled. The embryonic flowers, before they rise up from the crown of the plant, are also edible. And the roots can be dried, ground up, and brewed to make a drink that tastes rather like Postum.

Mustard. A wildly distributed plant that is also grown commercially. Good boiled when young (use the big leaves, not top ones; simmer thirty minutes).

Wild asparagus. Steam like the commercial type.

Cattails. Although gathering cattails can be a tricky and chilly job, this plant offers several edible parts: you can boil the new heads (just before they come through the sheath); you can pare new stalks and boil them; you can pull up the root tubers and mash them in water (giving them several washings) for a starchy mush; you can fry the small top knobs on the tubers; and you can use the pollen as flour.

Acorns. A staple of Native Americans, acorns *must* be leached before they become edible; you do this by boiling them whole for two hours, and then either running water through them for some time or soaking and rinsing them with several changes of water. You can eat them as a meal or mush; you can even candy them. To make a flour that will keep for a little while, you can grind up the fresh acorns, mix with boiling water (to leach), and press out through a cloth; repeat this several times, then spread thinly in a pan to dry, in the oven or in hot sunlight.

Berries. Blackberries are probably the most widely available wild berry; once established, a blackberry patch is practically impossible to exterminate. Blueberries grow wild in many areas; so do huckleberries (which are red, not blue). There are also wild strawberries and cherries. As in eating any wild plants, you need to study identification guides with an expert outdoor person before you eat berries: Some are poisonous.

Mushrooms. Many people have an unreasonable fear of mushrooms. With a good identification guide and some human guidance to alert you to the dangerous types, however, you can make a very good thing out of mushrooms: Some of them are absolutely delectable, and mushroom hunting is one of the nicest ways to spend an otherwise dreary wettish day.

Nuts. Walnuts, hickory nuts, and hazelnuts are all tasty and good sources of protein for the diet; so are sunflower seeds, which grow wild in some areas.

There are many other plants that can be eaten. *Watercress* grows wild by many spring-fed springs; it is related to *nasturtiums*, whose leaves are also a delicacy in salads. *Wild onions* can flavor your dishes. *Chicory* can give you a kind of coffee. *Clover* blossoms and *mint* leaves make good tea (dry them away from heat or sunlight), and *catnip* tea is reputed to be a good sedative.

3. Bake your own bread.

Every cookbook has easy recipes for making bread that is much better than most of the bread sold in stores. It always surprises people how easy it is to make bread: It just takes some mixing, some kneading (working the bread around under the heel of your hand), and some patience—you have to wait for it to "rise" (the yeast you mixed into it will grow and produce bubbles that will make the bread fluffy). Once you get into the basic routine of baking, you will probably branch out into all kinds of delectable (and cheap) pastries, cakes, pies, rolls, muffins—and will discover a good place to buy the many different kinds of flours. Don't be confined by the choices in a typical supermarket; there are lots more, and a health-foods store, though it may be unduly expensive itself, can probably tell you where to find a store specializing in grain products. By doing your own baking you also avoid the additives and preservatives of commercial bread. Homemade bread seldom remains uneaten for very long, but you can store it for a long time in the freezer or refrigerator if you need to.

4. Make your own beer and wine.

You can spend an enormous amount of money on alcohol, even if you're not a real juicer. The price of a fifth of scotch can feed you for a week. But if booze is your thing, or you can't get anything you like better, the best general rule is simple: Drink cheap standard-brand American wine, unless you live in a wine-making region where you can find even cheaper good stuff.

Wine. Wine has been around for several thousand years, but its virtues have only recently become more widely recognized in the U.S. In small quantities wine can actually be good for the health; it relaxes you and provides some vitamins, as well as some calories of food energy. It goes well with many foods, and can make the difference between just a meal and an elegant repast. There are many poor French or Italian households where the absence of wine would be as badly felt as the absence of silverware.

You can make your own wine. It's legal for a household of at least two to make up to two hundred gallons per year for home consumption and not for sale. That's a lot of wine. It takes a source of grapes (or other fruit—plums, apricots, cherries, etc.), a large crock or plastic canister, and a lot of bottles and corks. However, home winemaking cannot reliably produce wine at a significantly lower price than gallon jugs of commercial wine, because of spoilage, wastage, and other factors. Unlike beer, where you really save money, making your own wine is for pleasure and not for thrift.

Beer. Beermaking was formerly frowned upon by the federal tax authorities, for whom booze is a stupendous source of revenue; but now, as with wine, you are allowed to make 200 gallons per year for your own consumption. (No one was ever prosecuted for a little quiet brewing.)

Home brew costs about a fifth of what store-bought beer costs. It contains much more alcohol than commercial beer; it has more vitamins since it isn't filtered to death, and it has a generally richer taste and consistency. You can make draft beer (flat) or fizzy beer, which can have more carbonization than commercial if you like it that way.

What you need for elementary beermaking is a large crock or canister, a lot of clean bottles (screw-top type won't work), bottle caps (soak them before using, so that the cork seals better), and a bottle capper; it also helps to have a hydrometer, and a six-foot piece of plastic tubing (one end stuck through a hole in a scrap of wood so that it floats near the surface in the crock) to use in bottling.

Here's the recipe: Put your crock on a porch or in a cellar where the fermentation smell won't bother you (or suspicious neighbors). Mix some hot water with a can of Blue Ribbon Malt Extract (available in dark or light at most large supermarkets); this takes work, as the extract is very sticky. Then add sugar in the proportion of five pounds to one can of extract (for ten gallons total crock capacity). After you've got the extract and sugar thoroughly dissolved in the hot water, add tepid water until you have the whole crock full of water that feels barely warm to the touch. Into this mixture put some yeast: This can just be ordinary powdery (not cake) baking yeast you buy at the grocery, mixed in a cup of the warm mixture to dissolve it better. But it's better to buy special brewing yeasts. Stir the whole thing to distribute the yeast well. Cover the crock with some polyethylene sheeting, cheesecloth, or other cloth to keep out fruit flies— they love beer! Wait and watch about a week or two, depending on the temperature, skimming off the fermentation scum if it gets very thick. If you live where there are cold winters, you'll have to do the fermenting inside, as the yeast will die in the cold. When the small bubbles from the fermentation (you can see them by looking at the surface from an angle) have almost stopped, or when the hydrometer's red line has sunk to the surface of the mixture, siphon the beer into clean bottles and cap them. (Some people add about a quarter teaspoon of sugar to each bottle.) Don't fill too full; leave an inch or two of air in the neck to absorb the carbonization pressure. Cap securely and mark with the date. (If you have some small bottles, fill them so you can try them as samples to see how the batch is aging.) Beer improves up to six months in the bottle; beyond that there's no point in not drinking it. Generally two months aging in the bottle is about right.

After you've made a couple of batches in this elementary style, you'll be ready for the advanced class. This involves experiments to find which yeasts you prefer (some are top-fermenting, some bottom-fermenting, and they create subtly different tastes in the resulting product), with making ales and meads as well as beers, with using gelatin to clarify the beer before putting it into bottles, and so on. You'll find it best to follow the example of experienced home brewers in keeping careful records, so that when you've done something spectacular you have a way to repeat it. Home brewers are an intensely competitive lot, with their own techniques, their own tastes in sugar ingredients (there's raw sugar, honey, invert sugar, dextrose, lactose, etc.). If you can find one to apprentice yourself to, you'll be assured of a good start.

The chief cautions to be observed are these: Make sure your bottles are really clean, ideally using boiling water as a last rinse, and use a hydrometer, or at any rate don't bottle too early, lest your carbonation become too excessive and explode. (You should not store home-brew bottles where they might get bumped by children or passersby.) If you're doubtful about a batch, put on heavy gloves, cover a bottle with a heavy rag, and open it very gingerly. If the cap flies off and most of the beer spurts out uncontrollably, don't sit around lapping it up; carefully open all of that batch and rebottle it.

There is an art to pouring unclarified and unfiltered home-brew: Open the bottle carefully and pour gently so as not to disturb the sediment. Set it down slowly too. Treated in this way you'll find that your home brew is clear enough to satisfy most people, and it's a real joy to real beer drinkers. Watch out for it, though! It contains almost as much alcohol as wine—about three times as much as commercial beer.

Distilled liquors (whiskeys, gins, brandies, and so on) cost more to make per unit of alcohol, and home distilling can bring stiff prison sentences. However, you may be interested in store-bought hard liquor, even if it is higher-priced. Your best bet is vodka, which is practically nothing but alcohol and water; it's the easiest of all liquors on your system, since it has the fewest "congeners" (oils, sugars, and so on, which are abundant in brandies and whiskeys). There is very little variation in quality from one vodka to another, so buy the cheapest you can get. Often grocery-chain brands are good bargains. One of the worst buys is pre-mixed cocktails, which are fantastically more expensive than the straight stuff.

5. Make your own yogurt.

Yogurt is not the only cultured milk product you might enjoy—buttermilk and kefir are two others to try—but it has the great advantage of being easy to make yourself. It's a delicious and healthy dessert or snack, especially when a little fruit or jam is added.

Basic cookbooks such as *The Joy of Cooking* give easy-to-follow procedures for making yogurt. It's not necessary to buy an expensive yogurt-making rig, though a cooking thermometer will be a big help in getting the milk just hot enough. The essential is a place where the warm mixed yogurt can sit undisturbed for 7 to 8 hours while the culture "works." (Yogurt hates being jiggled. If you disturb it and it doesn't set, you have to do the whole process over again.) You can put a light bulb and thermostat inside an old camp cooler; it should be kept warm but not hot. If you were lucky enough to live at a hot springs, like the Zen people at Tassajara, you could suspend your yogurt culture over the hot water. But simplest of all is to line a box with at least inch-thick insulating foam (including the bottom, and make a piece to lay on top of your yogurt cups or jars). Your yogurt is at 106°–109°F when you finish mixing it, and this heat, if retained in such an insulated container, will be enough.

For "starter"—yogurt containing the microorganisms that turn milk into yogurt—you can experiment with different commercial yogurts, or buy a package of culture from a health-foods store. Save a little of your last batch for starter in the next one. But after ten batches or so, get some new starter.

C. Cook your food efficiently.

1. Steam vegetables instead of boiling them.

Various kinds of metal baskets are available that sit inside any pot with a close-fitting top. Small bamboo steaming racks can be found in Chinese housewares stores. Use only enough water to be sure it does not entirely boil away—usually a half-inch will be fine. Vegetables taste and look better when they've been cooked only just enough—they should be a little crisp and chewy. Light varieties of fish, such as sole, are also good steamed.

2. Avoid frying.

It adds fat calories to your diet even if you use polyunsaturated vegetable oils; adding batter may pose a cholesterol problem and adds still more calories. Your objective, presumably, is to taste the fish or meat or chicken that you're cooking and not the batter; so the best procedure for most such foods is one of the following methods.

3. Broiling.

Broiling adds no fat (or only a little, if you rub some oil on top to prevent charring), allows fat contained in the food to drip out, and produces a tasty but only slightly crisped surface on the food. It is also the simplest cooking method, requiring no special pans, spatulas, or clean-up of the grease that gets splattered around by frying.

4. Pressure cooking.

This is an energy-saving method of cooking tough kinds of meat (such as tongue) in a relatively short time while also conserving food value. But unless you cook such meats a lot, or want to use a pressure-cooker for sterilizing canning jars (a task for which a very large enamel pot is really better anyway), you can probably do most of what a pressure cooker would do by ordinary steaming.

5. Baking or roasting.

In an oven these can be used not only for roasts and poultry, but also for Irish potatoes, sweet potatoes and yams, and casserole dishes. It is particularly nice to do in cold weather, because the heat created by the oven helps warm the house. (Toaster ovens, incidentally, have little or no insulation and pose a fire risk in tight quarters, but they may still be a low-energy way to bake a single yam, or even a turkey breast.)

6. Make soup.

In old farm kitchens a soup pot was simmering on the back of the stove almost constantly. Today, soups are still one of the best ways to provide nutritious and interesting eating at a low cost. A really hearty soup can be the mainstay of the meal, together with a salad and some good bread. And soups can be made from things that are tasty but also low in cost; neck bones, chicken backs, fish, protein-rich beans or lentils, and vegetables such as leeks that are cheap but good. Moreover, a big soup can be one way of using up leftovers without calling attention to them; just toss them in! Soups will keep in the refrigerator for several days. You can vary them easily by adding spices and herbs.

One of the pleasures of soup making is that you can play infinite variations on the basic themes available.

a. Meat soups. You can make your basic broth by boiling soup bones (which the butcher may give you free if you say it's "for my dog"), super-cheap oxtail pieces, or the carcass of yesterday's chicken. Skim off the unhealthy fat. Sometimes you may want to stop there—a clear thin soup may be just the thing if you're sick. Or you can add green vegetables, potatoes, carrots, and onions.

b. Fish soups. If you really want to make a cheap, nourishing soup, buy fish fragments (heads, tails, and odd small pieces), put them in a cheesecloth bag, and boil them. (Or else just toss them in and then strain the resulting broth.) There are many special kinds of fish soups, such as bouillabaisse, which contain several different kinds of seafood. And a fish soup may be turned into a chowder by adding skim or low-fat milk (for white) or tomato sauce (for red).

c. Vegetable soups. A wholesome and filling soup can be made simply from inexpensive vegetables: cabbage, turnips, potatoes, carrots, green beans, onions, and so on. Often you can get these free at supermarket back doors early in the morning. If you have a blender, you can make some really scrumptious chilled soups from potatoes (vichyssoise), broccoli, spinach, carrots, etc.; there is no real line between a drippy purée and a thick soup! Try experimenting with curry or other seasonings.

d. Fruit soups. Yes, there *are* such things, especially in Scandinavia, and absolutely delicious, too. The problem is to keep them from getting too sweet or sticky (which can happen if you boil them too long), and they are eaten chilled.

e. Bean soups. Soybeans are the most nutritious beans, and can be made into many different soups; red beans, white beans, garbanzo beans, lentils, black-eyed peas, and a host of other bean-type things also make thick, rich soups.

To thicken a soup or make it more filling, add various kinds of pasta (macaroni, noodles, little rings, etc.), rice, buckwheat groats, or whatever you please.

f. Don't be intimidated by recipes that start out "To your stock, add . . . " Stock is simply water with juices in it. You produce your own stock when you boil bones in plain water with a little salt. You can also make stock by throwing in a couple of bouillon cubes or using a powder that comes in a jar, either beef or chicken type.

Because of the importance of soups in an interesting but inexpensive diet, you should get soup bowls that really please you; they should be sturdy and big enough for a meal-sized portion. (If you only want a little, use a cup.) Avoid cheap Mexican glazes, which could give you lead poisoning.

7. Eat more salads.

Some vegetables are just as good raw as they are cooked, and you can experiment with them in salads or simply add them to appetizer or dinner menus: peas, beans, jicama (a Mexican root vegetable with a deliciously cool taste), zucchini, carrots, broccoli, cauliflower. Any type of cooking or peeling severely reduces the vitamin and mineral content of vegetables; a large proportion of nutrients lie just below the skin. Like a big soup, salads are delicious and inexpensively nourishing, and are an especially good idea if your diet tends to be heavy and starchy. A vinegary salad dressing will cut through soggy aftertastes, and the green vegetables of a salad are full of vitamins and fiber, which is cancer-preventive and good for your digestion.

A proper salad is mixed in a very large bowl; if you have a wooden bowl you can rub it with garlic first. The lettuce should be dark green and crisp, and it is interesting to use several types. Many other vegetables are good in salads: shredded raw cabbage, cucumbers, carrots sliced very thin, green peppers, green beans, peas, small pieces or raw cauliflower, and so on. (Canned or frozen things are fine too.) Then, when you can afford it, you can add piquant touches with pickles or Italian pickled vegetables, anchovies, avocados, small bits of cheese or chicken, and so on.

Like coffee, salad dressings are an intensely individual question. You should get some good ingredients (olive oil, wine vinegar, pepper, and other spices) and experiment with different proportions and flavorings until what you find suits you best. A little dry mustard and a dash of lemon juice, soy sauce, or Tabasco sauce also serves to liven up a dressing. If you don't particularly enjoy mixing salad dressings, make a whole jarful at once and keep it in the refrigerator. Even with the finest ingredients, making your own is far cheaper than buying ready-made dressings.

There are, of course, many other types of salad that offer tasty possibilities: tuna and chicken salads, salads with gelatin rings, and so on.

8. Teach yourself how to cook.

Some people collect cookbooks; others stick to one basic book and improvise from there on. There are excellent cooks who have no cookbooks at all, but have a head full of recipes taught to them by their parents and grandparents. You will find literally thousands of cookbooks in a big library, and even a small bookstore generally stocks a wide variety.

A beginning cook will want to have instructions available on the fundamentals of cooking: how long you cook the meat, how to make a basic sauce, how to measure ingredients, how to bake bread, and so on. *The Joy of Cooking* by Irma S. Rombauer and Marion Rombauer Becker (Bobbs-Merrill) and *The James Beard Cookbook* (Dell Books) are two good standards of this type. Beyond that, you will want to begin to specialize. The foods of some special cultures may appeal to you. You may want to learn how to make casseroles that can be ready when you come home from work.

You don't have to buy any cookbooks, however; go to your local library and take out a half-dozen promising books; copy appealing recipes onto cards or into a notebook. Or go stand in a bookstore and jot down the essentials of a few dishes that strike your fancy. Most of all, when you eat something you really like at a friend's house, try to get the recipe. Recipe exchanging is a really basic kind of cultural exchange; by helping each other to eat better, we render assistance that is real and stomach-felt.

D. Eat the right foods.

In reality there is no food, not one single food of any kind, that is essential to human health. Even spinach, although it's one of the best green vegetables (along with broccoli, collards, etc.) and good to eat, contains a form of iron that can't be assimilated by the human body—so all those children who had to eat spinach "for its iron" were doing so in vain. Carrots, although they are an excellent source of vitamin A, essential to good eyesight, are not the only source; nowadays margarine is enriched to provide more than enough vitamin A for everybody (butter also contains it).

In short, there is no reason to eat anything you don't like. The world is full of healthy foods, and if you have a varied diet you are probably eating well. Food deficiencies generally occur among people who are so deprived that they eat only a few things all the time. Even a simple regular diet can be perfectly nutritious, but constantly eating only a few basic items raises the chances that you will be missing some of the essentials. (There are forty-three substances, besides air and water, necessary to keep the human body functioning normally.)

Nutrition handbooks and guides and government publications are always coming out with authoritarian rules like "Eat all four food groups every day." These groups are: (1) milk and milk products; (2) meat, chicken, and fish; (3) vegetables and fruit; (4) bread and cereals. You need not eat meat at all (as long as you replace the proteins you would have gotten from it). Nor must you necessarily use any dairy products (a substantial proportion of adult humans are allergic to them), nor fanatically eat the other categories every single day, as long as in the course of a week you are eating a balanced diet. A day is a short time in the perspective of most body processes. Your body doesn't punch a time clock. So what you really have to keep an eye on is relatively simple. (It's also simple to pass good eating on to your children, who will then grow up to eat right and feed their babies right.)

1. Drink and eat nonfat and low-fat dairy products.

Essential proteins—body-building and body-repairing nonfat foods—can be obtained from milk (dried has just as much protein as whole milk), cheese, yogurt, or ice cream (not "imitation ice cream"). Children and nursing mothers need about three cups of milk per day, or about five quarts per week. Although most adults in the rest of the world do not drink milk, it is a relatively low-cost protein source and can now be obtained in nonfat forms almost anywhere. A one-inch cube of cheese equals a cup of milk; yogurt is also an alternative to milk, and frozen yogurt is far preferable to ice cream for health reasons.

The food value of milk is so high that, if necessary, you could subsist for days on practically nothing else, but this is true only for people who, like Western Europeans, have a strong dairying tradition and whose digestive systems preserve the enzyme lactase into adulthood. Cow's milk (which, after all, is adapted to consumption by calves) causes allergic reactions in many children, and sometimes in adults.

If your diet is going to be lean or deficient for a while because you can't afford anything but beans and rice and a few vegetables, try to get together enough money to buy a twenty-five-pound bag of nonfat dried milk—which will last you a long, long time, even if you drink several quarts a day.

There are two kinds of milk, wet and "dried." Each one has special characteristics and uses. Whole milk is fatty or creamy. It must be refrigerated or it spoils. It has to be brought home in heavy containers. It costs about three times what dried milk costs, and low-fat or nonfat ("skim") wet milk is only slightly cheaper. Do not burn wet-milk cartons, incidentally; their inside plastic coating will give off a poisonous gas.

a. Drink dried milk. Dried milk is almost always "nonfat." When you mix it up, therefore, it has a distinctly different taste. Besides being much cheaper, it is more compact to store, because it doesn't need refrigeration until it's mixed; just keep it in a cool cupboard with the container tightly closed to prevent staleness.

Dried milk needs to be colder when you drink it than does whole milk. Its protein or body-building power is equal to that of whole milk; it lacks only vitamins A and D. (Sometimes it is fortified with these vitamins. Check the label. Unless you get a lot of vitamin D from other foods, you may want to take vitamin D capsules.) From a health standpoint, it is much superior to whole milk because of its small amount of fat.

In general, dried milk is a much better deal. If you do drink wet milk, get used to the nonfat type—you can switch to it gently by using "low-fat" milk for a week or two, and then gradually mixing nonfat milk with it.

Most people who have not been brought up on dried milk don't know how to mix and use it. The directions on the package are not always very good. Here's how: Use a big jar, preferably a two-quart pickle jar or something, the bigger the better, so long as it will fit in your refrigerator. Dried milk is like beer: It improves with age, over a day or so; so you want to mix as much up at once as you can. You use about one-third as much powder as water. The best way to get the powder dissolved is to put it in with about half a jar full of water, and then shake vigorously; this is much better than stirring, and also more fun. (Put some music on the record player!) Set it down—in the refrigerator if the house is warm—until the foam settles. Then fill the jar with cold water.

Try to mix up your supply of milk well in advance of when you'll drink it; it takes time for the refrigerator to cool it down. I have found that a good time to mix it is after supper, during the clean-up period; then the next day's supply is ready in the morning.

Cooking with dried milk presents no problems. Where a recipe calls for a cup of milk, use about five tablespoons of dried milk and three-quarters of a cup of water. You can use it this way in soups and chowders, baked foods, stews, omelets, puddings, and so on. To increase the protein in baked foods, you can also replace up to a quarter of the flour in recipes with dried milk powder. (This makes them get a little browner.) You can also strengthen the protein in meatloaf, mashed potatoes, sauces, and hot cereals by adding a little milk powder.

There are even some recipes that *require* dry milk rather than wet. You can get these from the American Dry Milk Institute, 130 North Franklin Street, Chicago, IL 60606.

b. Use milk with imagination. Put added protein in regular milk by stirring some dried milk into it. (This is especially good for pregnant or nursing mothers, or growing children.) Yogurt and buttermilk are not particularly cheap, but they are tasty and provide about the same nourishment as regular nonfat wet milk. Evaporated milk, in cans, is also cheaper than wet milk, but it tends to spoil if kept in the can. (Avoid sweetened "condensed" milk, which has a huge sugar content.) Milk keeps almost a week in the refrigerator. Don't let milk stand in the sunlight—that destroys the riboflavin and changes the taste.

In heating milk for drinks, puddings, and so on, use a low heat. At high temperatures milk forms a film and may scorch, giving it a funny flavor. Acids, such as lemon or tomato juice, may cause milk to curdle.

You can whip canned evaporated milk as well as cream. The secret is to get the bowl, mixer, and liquid very cold (evaporated milk should go into the freezer compartment to chill until ice crystals form around the edges). Never buy pressure-can whipped cream or pseudo whipped cream. It costs a fortune and doesn't taste nearly as good as ordinary whipped cream. You can make whipped cream with a whisk; you don't really need a mixer, hand-operated or electric.

Keep milk and milk products tightly covered, since they tend to pick up odors from other foods.

c. Eat low-fat or nonfat cheeses. Because it is a concentrated protein food and keeps a long time without refrigeration, cheese has been an important staple in European diets for many centuries. (Non-dairying peoples like the Chinese consider it repulsive.) Unfortunately, most cheese except low-fat cottage cheese is very high in saturated fats. Cheese comes in a fascinating variety of types—something like four hundred all together—and is a source of the same kinds of complete protein you get in meat, fish, and eggs. Look around until you find a store with a good variety of cheeses; some stock nothing but cheddar and "process" cheeses.

If you decide to accept their high fat content, there are fancy imported cheeses that can become dear to a real cheese fancier (one of my favorites is a British item called Caerphilly), but you can usually find domestic versions that are excellent. Here are some of the main kinds to try.

Bel paese. A mild, creamy, light Italian cheese.

Blue. Named for its bluish streaks of mold; a very sharp tasting crumbly cheese, often put into salads. (Roquefort and gorgonzola are similar.)

Brie and camembert. Very soft, almost liquid when fully ripened, good for breakfast and dessert. Camembert has a sharper taste. Both have a crust which is edible.

Cheddar. Comes in a range of flavors, from mild to sharp. May be sliceable or almost crumbly, and varies from cream to orange color. It can be used in many recipes.

Cottage (or baker's cheese or ricotta). Lumpy texture and slightly acid milk flavor. Provides the lowest-cost protein of any cheese, with little fat, but is low in calcium compared to other cheeses and milk.

Cream cheese. Very soft, smooth white texture, though the best kinds (without added gum) are very slightly crumbly. Neufchatel is very similar, but it is made from whole milk, not cream, so it's higher in protein and a bit lower in fat. (I also think it is tastier, and it can be cheaper as well.) Avoid Philadelphia-brand cream cheese, which is overpriced because of its expensive advertising.

Edam and gouda. These Dutch cheeses come in ball shapes, covered with red wax. They both taste mellow and nutlike, and are firm and sliceable. The gouda, which sometimes has a faintly acid flavor, also often has small holes.

Gruyere. Sharp, nutlike flavor and very smooth texture.

Liederkranz and limberger. Both these soft cheese have a very strong flavor and smell.

Muenster. Semisoft and creamy white inside, with a mild to mellow flavor.

Parmesan and romano. Usually cured for a year and grated for use as a seasoning in Italian dishes.

Swiss. Mild, sweet, nutlike flavor. Usually light yellow, with large holes, firm and sliceable.

All cheeses keep best for long periods in the refrigerator, but their taste is finest if they are eaten at room temperature. Cheese goes well with fruits and crackers as a dessert, and can be mixed with practically anything else in sandwiches.

Some of the main recipes using cheese (aside from the familiar macaroni-and-cheese) are soufflés, soups, fondues, and desserts (cheesecakes). Chopped up into small pieces, cheese is also excellent in salads.

Low-cholesterol imitation cheeses are available; they resemble Swiss cheese or a rather crumbly Monterey Jack, and have become quite tasty.

d. Avoid process cheese in little jars. This "cheese" is largely water. Also stay away from pre-packaged sliced, cubed, or flavored cheese, which have ridiculously high prices. "Cheese food" is sometimes not too expensive, but may not have much cheese in it—it can also contain dried milk, sugar, corn syrup, and who knows what else.

e. Eat low-fat, sugar-free ice cream, or nonfat frozen yogurt. If you just can't get along without occasionally indulging in ice cream, look around for an establishment that sells first-class ice cream made with natural ingredients and free of additives, artificial flavorings, thickeners, cellulose, and salt.

Generally, the heavier ice cream is, the better, because then you're buying food and not air; but of course the heavier brands are deservedly more expensive. Ice cream really ought to be sold by weight (about a quarter of the ice cream sold fails to meet minimum weight standards, which are lax enough in themselves). Ingredient labeling has also been lax in most states. Happily, therefore, making your own ice cream is an old-fashioned treat that is coming back. Look for a cheap hand-cranked ice cream maker. There are simple recipes in many cookbooks; true ice cream contains cooked syrups, eggs, cream, sometimes gelatin, natural flavorings, salt, etc.

From a health standpoint, low-fat or nonfat frozen yogurt or fruit ices, sometimes called sorbets, are preferable to ice cream. Fruit ices contain no fats or mysterious artificial ingredients—just fruit, fruit juice, and sugar.

2. Cut down red meat intake; eat more chicken, turkey, fish.

Meat is the largest expense in most American grocery shopping lists. Keep in mind that protein is also provided by fish, poultry, eggs, dry beans (especially soybeans), nuts, and peanut butter. Short of becoming more or less a vegetarian, the main problem in eating well but inexpensively is to devise meals that don't use much meat and that avoid the over-priced (because they're over-popular) cuts. Reorient meal planning away from the conventional meat-and-potatoes-and-vegetable rut, and take advantage of the rich, inexpensive alternative protein resources. (In general, poultry is not only your best buy economically, but also less fatty than red meat, if you cut away all skin and excess fat before cooking.) Expense has nothing to do with nutritional value in meat.

It is possible, of course, to have a perfectly healthy diet without eating any meat at all. American meat consumption has been gradually diminishing for a combination of reasons. Even well-to-do people, used to spending about 20 percent of their income on food (and a quarter of this on meat), are needing to trim their food outlays; people with modest incomes, who may spend up to half their money on food, have never been able to spend much on meat.

a. Buy cheaper grades of meat. The cheaper grades (Good instead of Choice) are just as nourishing; surprisingly, tests show that blindfolded people often find they taste better; "lower" grades also have less fat and less waste. Certain cuts—chuck roasts and chuck steaks, for example—are less expensive than others; they are just as tender, however, and the only kind a budgeting cook should use. Rolled roasts have much less waste than rib roasts.

Hamburger is generally the cheapest kind of meat, for its food value, that you can buy. However, its high fat content means you should eat it rarely and in modest amounts; try ground turkey as an alternative.

b. Be choosy about hot dogs. Hot-dog sales are a barometer of economic conditions; when people buy more of them, times are getting hard. But it is no longer easy to know when hot dogs are really a good cheap source of meat. Actually, hot dogs have only about three-quarters as much protein per pound as lean meat; so unless hot dogs cost less than three-quarters as much per pound, you're better off buying nonfatty roasts or other cuts, and still better off if you can find low-fat turkey or chicken hot dogs. The actual contents of hot dogs are ground up so finely that you can't tell what's in them, but they can have up to 30 percent fat ("all meat" doesn't exclude fat). They can have up to 3.5 percent flour, cereal, or dried milk. Nonfat dried milk is a good thing in a hot dog (it's good protein) if the price is low.

There are giant-sized hot dogs called dinner franks, garlic franks, or Polish sausages that have more seasoning than the bland standard dog and usually cost about the same per pound. Regular sausage, however, is so largely fat that it is bad for your health and your budget.

c. Avoid bacon. People sometimes spend more on bacon than they spend on any other kind of meat. This is a big mistake, not only because of the cancer-causing preservatives, but also because it is very fatty and has very little food value. Try to think of other ways to add flavor to your breakfasts: Fry up some hashbrown potatoes with your eggs.

d. Save meat juices. Meat juice is full of vitamins and proteins. Skim off the fat and pour the juice over the meat or other items in the meal, or mix it into gravy, or save it for tomorrow's soup.

e. Avoid "lunch meat." Salami, bologna, liverwurst, head cheese, and other special meat products are generally very high in fats, and they are expensive in terms of their protein content. Dry Italian salami, however, keeps fairly well without refrigeration, and is therefore good for backpacking and camping purposes.

f. Eat more fish. Although the world's fishing fleets are pressing on the resources of the continental-shelf fisheries (where most fish live), fish is still a good low-fat source of high-quality protein and many trace minerals. If you live where good fresh seafood is available, marvelous; if you don't, frozen fish is excellent and not too expensive. (Most people can't tell the difference.) You need less fish than with most meats, because there is little waste from bones; none at all in fillets, which are lengthwise strips; and not much in steaks, which are crosswise slices.

You can also buy fresh fish by the piece, either a whole fish or a part, but usually without the head. The price is lower, but you do have some waste. A whole baked fish on a platter, surrounded by parsley, lemon slices, watercress, maybe little tomatoes, is an impressive meal, and if it is a bass, cod, salmon, or other sizable fish, you can make it go even further with a rice stuffing.

Too many people fry fish, which tends to make it greasy and obscures the flavor. Broiling, actually, is the quickest, easiest, and one of the more delicious ways to cook fish. You can marinate it if you like, or just dab on a little olive oil to keep it from getting too crisp on top. Salmon and some other fish are extremely delicate-tasting steamed or poached, especially with a sauce.

Fish is quick-cooking—broiling takes ten to fifteen minutes, baking twenty minutes to half an hour. Most people tend to overcook fish, letting it get dry inside. It is done when the flesh flakes apart easily with a fork, and it should still look moist.

You may not have tried enough fish to know how much variety there is. The fattiest are salmon, butterfish, and lake trout. Next are swordfish, mackerel, tuna, catfish, buffalo fish, carp, and turbot. And the lightest of all are sole, rock cod, halibut, red snapper, brook trout, and shellfish. The flavor differences between swordfish and salmon, for instance, are just as great as between steak and chicken. You may be delighted to find that your favorite type is among the cheapest—don't be afraid to experiment, even with smelt or shark or sturgeon or fish you never heard of!

Many varieties of canned fish, both water-packed and oil-packed, are available, and can be relatively inexpensive sources of high-quality protein. Tuna is no longer as economical as it once was; if you are looking for something cheaper, try mackerel, a stronger-tasting fish that many people love. Watch for bargains in canned fish—sometimes you will find exotic items that are incredibly cheap and tasty, like the "picapica" one of my friends used to gorge on—a hot-sauce fish of undetermined species, hailing from southwestern Africa; he bought it by the case.

Tuna, swordfish, and other large ocean fish are often contaminated with mercury. These big fish, at the top of their food chains, concentrate contamination in their bodies; so it isn't wise to make them a very large part of your diet.

You can eat as much as you like of smaller ocean fish, such as sardines, herring, or mackerel, and of bottom-dwelling fish, such as flounder or sole.

g. *Try oysters.* The rich consider oysters a gourmet delight. There are elegant dishes with names like oysters Florentine and oysters Rockefeller—delicately seasoned oysters baked in half shells on a layer of rock salt. Some people think oysters are repulsive. Too bad for them! Actually, oysters and their shellfish relatives—clams, mussels, and limpets, along with some other near-shore species like crabs and shrimp—were important in human evolution: They were a reliable high-protein food supply to our ancestors, who lived along the shores of oceans and lakes. Not only were they very tasty, they were also not nearly so dangerous to catch as larger creatures, who tend to be fleet of foot or equipped with fang and claw.

Oysters contain twice the protein of soybeans and about half that of deboned chicken. They also have half the calories of chicken and about two-thirds the cholesterol. Moreover, since oysters are grown in bays—sometimes unaided by nature and sometimes on wires—they don't require gas-guzzling farm machinery to produce, and thus tend to be cheaper than most other animal proteins.

All in all the lowly oyster should not be neglected. You can buy oysters in jars all year round, and oysters in their shells during the season (they're more expensive). Cookbooks are full of delicious oyster dishes. My favorites are oyster stew (with lots of milk and pepper), oysters lightly fried with ginger slices, and most of all oysters baked in the shell on a fire at the beach, with lots of friends gathered round dipping them into butter-lemon sauce, drinking wine to wash them down, and munching on good crunchy French bread. (Remember to take along a stout knife to pry open the shells!)

A worthy bivalve relative of the oyster is the mussel, which you can often gather at low tides. Mussels grow in vast quantities just offshore on cool, rocky coasts, and have been called our single greatest unexploited resource.

Avoid mussels, clams, or other shellfish you catch yourself during the summer months or times when public officials have posted notices warning of contamination.

h. *Eat more poultry.* Chicken, turkey, duck, and goose are excellent and relatively inexpensive protein sources—especially chicken—and contain other important nutrients as well. You can buy them either fresh or frozen; ducks and geese are usually *only* available frozen, except on special order. If you don't intend to use it by the next day, frozen is best, because poultry only keeps under refrigeration a day or two. Avoid pre-stuffed, frozen forms—they cost more, and the stuffing is a food-poisoning hazard.

Because of our mass-production poultry production and insufficient inspection, much of U.S. poultry is now affected by salmonella organisms, which can cause serious illness. Keep a separate cutting board for poultry, and wash it frequently. Always wash poultry as you prepare it, and then wash your hands carefully before touching other foods. Cook poultry thoroughly (juices should run clear, not pink, when you poke it with a fork).

You can buy chicken parts rather than whole chickens, and for some recipes this is a good idea. Cheap parts, such as backs, are fine for soups; delicacies, such as chicken livers, can also be bought separately.

i. Eat eggs, but not often. Eggs are a prime source of protein; unfortunately, their yolks are also a prime source of cholesterol. (Egg whites can be eaten in any amounts you like.) If you are trying to cut your cholesterol levels for your circulatory system's sake, you might want to switch to an "imitation egg" product. However, these contain various additives, so they are hardly ideal.

j. Mix beans and grains to get complete protein. Beans come in a delightful variety of forms and colors, and some of them will *not* make you fart, though there is no general rule about this—you have to experiment to find out which kinds your own digestive system takes to. The best protein suppliers are soybeans, which can be eaten in many different ways, including sprouted (this gives them even more nutritional value than they have as cooked beans).

Some beans really require the lengthy soaking recommended on the packages; others don't. Try different cooking methods and recipes until you find ways of dealing with beans that you really like. Combining beans with corn, as in much Mexican cooking, provides combined proteins that supply virtually all the needed amino acids, and many vegetarians therefore make a habit of eating beans and corn together. Beans and rice also provide essential "complementary proteins."

k. Eat peanut butter. It's tasty, and it's full of protein—but it is also, unfortunately, loaded with fat, and you should keep your consumption modest. (Avoid brands that contain added fat—they will have "partially hydrogenated" on their labels—and sugar.) You can do other things besides make sandwiches with it, too: Spread it on celery, use it to make cookies, or just eat it out of the jar. Four tablespoons plus a cup of milk give you almost as much protein as a quarter-pound of meat.

Unfortunately, in recent years real peanut butter has become hard to find. Proper peanut butter is crunchy (the nuts aren't all squashed up, which makes it stick in your mouth less) and oily on the top (it hasn't been homogenized). If the label is vague, check the ingredients. Real peanut butter is simply ground up peanuts with salt added. Anything else on the label should make you suspicious.

If the separation of oil annoys you and you don't want to stir it occasionally, turn the jar upside down on the shelf part of the time, especially when it's new. Then one good stir when you open it will give a satisfying consistency.

You can make your own peanut butter or other nut butters if you have a grinder or heavy-duty blender. (Walnut butter is actually better nutritionally than peanut butter because it has very little saturated fat; it has an interestingly different taste.) Put in modest quantities of shelled nuts at a time. You may have to add a little oil to get a smooth consistency—use peanut oil or a polyunsaturated, nonhydrogenated oil like safflower oil. And go easy on the salt—it only takes a little.

Once opened, keep peanut butter jars in the refrigerator, to prevent aflatoxin formation.

3. Eat plenty of dark-green vegetables, yellow vegetables, and fruits.

Vegetables and fruits provide essential vitamins, fiber, and food energy. In the course of a week you should include some dark green vegetables such as spinach, collards, broccoli; some yellow ones such as carrots, squash, yellow beans; and some citrus fruits such as oranges, grapefruit; and some tomatoes. Even if you take vitamin pills, you need to eat some of each kind of food in this group. You should, of course, liven up your meals with tasty fresh vegetables when they're plentiful and cheap; but most of the year the basic routine will be buying frozen vegetables and cooking them in as little water as possible. (Their food value is about the same as the fresh ones.) Frozen orange juice is the cheapest citrus you can get; canned tomatoes and juice are fairly cheap all year-round. Raw fruit (apples, pears) with cheese makes an elegant continental-style dessert.

Salads are an especially tasty way of eating vegetables. You can also simply munch on raw carrots, slices of green pepper, celery, cauliflower, tomatoes, cabbage, and so on. Avoid iceberg lettuce, which has almost no food value.

4. Eat whole-grain bread and cereal; avoid rich baked goods and sugary foods in general.

"Cereal" here means grain, not breakfast food, although breakfast foods do come from grains. Wheat, oats, rice, and other grains, along with potatoes and a few other basic carbohydrate foods, are what basically sustain human life on the planet, and along with vegetables and fruits they make up the bulk of a healthy diet. Grains are components of a vast number of food types.

Here is the rundown of the major kinds of available bread:

Whole wheat. Because this is made from the entire wheat kernel, including the skin, where the vitamins and proteins mostly are, whole wheat is the best bread for you. It has a slightly pebbly texture, which makes the most crunchy and interesting kind of toast, and it has enough body that it will hold together a juicy kind of sandwich. Beware of "wheat bread," which is made from mostly unenriched white flour—it doesn't taste as good, and it isn't as nutritious. Some whole-wheat breads are low in fat.

Enriched white bread. To make wheat flour white, the millers have to remove most of the nutrients from it; then they put a little back in and call it "enriched." Though many states still do not have laws requiring even the minimum restoration of nutrients indicated by the "enriched" label, this is an improvement over plain white bread. (Never buy white bread without checking the label.) Most French bread and rolls are enriched, but watch their labels too.

Rye bread (including pumpernickel, etc.). Despite their dark color, most rye loaves are mixtures of rye and unenriched white flours. They are still tastier than white bread, of course, and somewhat better for you; and some responsible bakeries are using all enriched flours.

Raisin breads and similar novelty products. These, often beloved of children, are unfortunately almost never enriched and so not worth buying.

a. Try whole-wheat pasta. Unfortunately, most available pasta (spaghetti, noodles, and the dozens of little round, curly, or shell-like shapes devised in Italy) is made with heavily refined and sometimes unenriched flour. But whole-wheat pasta is slowly becoming available, and noodles are made in green types, with vegetable components—they are both interesting to try and slightly more nutritious. The Chinese transparent noodles called "bean threads," which you can buy in any Chinese market (Japanese stores have a similar product), are made from soybeans and contain some protein.

b. Eat whole baked potatoes. These provide more than starch and possess more protein and other nutrients than most people realize. (There are peoples in the Pacific who subsist almost entirely on yams, which are in my opinion moister and more tasty than sweet potatoes.) Potatoes themselves are not fattening; it is the butter, sour cream, frying fat, gravies, and sauces we add to them that carry the calories. (Nonfat sour "cream" is now available—a real treat for baked-potato lovers!)

You will be happiest with potatoes if you do not treat them just as fillers. There are many delectable potato dishes such as potato pancakes; sweet-potato pies are superb eating. Baked potato skins are nutritious, and delicious with a little butter or margarine.

Potatoes will bake much faster if you stick a big nail through them, to conduct heat into the center. Poke the skins of potatoes with a fork or knife before baking, lest they explode—this is especially necessary when they are baked in a campfire.

Although potatoes keep well in a cool, dark, well-ventilated place, they keep only about a week at normal room temperatures, so don't buy too many.

c. Learn how to cook rice. Of all the basic foods, rice sustains the most people: It is the fundamental food in most of Asia and is widely eaten elsewhere. But many Americans eat it rarely. This is a pity, because rice lends itself to a great variety of tasty dishes that are easier to prepare than many dishes based on potatoes or even pasta.

Americans lack experience with rice partly because we are not taught how to cook it properly, so a lot of people think rice is sticky. There is a surprisingly simple way to cook rice so that it is fluffy and the grains separate properly; it doesn't even require any measuring. Pour enough rice into the pot. Do not rinse unless the original container told you to—that washes away vitamins. Shake it level, and stick your finger down though it to the bottom. Put your thumb against your finger at the level of the rice.

Carry the pot to the sink, and slowly run just enough water so that when your finger tip just touches the rice, the water comes up to where your thumb is. Now put it on the stove and bring it to a boil. Then turn the heat down low and cover. Brown rice, which is the best and most nourishing, takes about forty-five minutes; enriched white rice takes about twenty minutes. Stir the rice every ten minutes or so to spread the water through it and break up the lumps. When it's cooked, all the water will have been absorbed. If you like your rice dry, take off the pot cover toward the end and stir the rice; this will let the remaining moisture escape. (You can cook bulgar wheat, which is equally nutritious and can be used in place of brown rice in many recipes, in the same way.)

This method, besides being easy, conserves all the nutrients in the rice. While the rice is cooking, you can be preparing the other material of your main rice dish. Fundamentally, rice dishes (except for those baked in the oven) are just rice with a tasty sauce containing protein foods and vegetables. Within this general formula you can improvise wildly and still provide excellent nutrition at low cost.

d. Avoid excess sugar. Americans still consume an inordinate amount of sugar, with detrimental effects on weight, teeth, the blood-sugar-regulating mechanism, and probably on psychological moods.

Your body transforms starchy foods into digestible sugars, and a certain intake of sugar, especially if it is the form known as fructose (from fruits), can properly provide some of your carbohydrate dietary energy supplies. But if you are eating both a high-sugar and a high-fat diet, you will probably be overweight, and should attempt to cut down on both.

Sugar sold in stores, whether called "brown," "raw," "white," or whatever, is all refined sugar, made from sugar cane or sugar beets. Honey, which seems to contain non-sugar substances that are good for you and generally tastes more interesting than sugar, might well become your standard household sweetener— but you should still hold down your consumption of it.

5. Minimize use of alcohol and soft drinks; decrease caffeine.

Americans drink literally billions of cans of soft drinks every year—one of the worst features of our diet, because they load our systems with sugar, expose us to additives, and are basically just very expensive flavored water. Don't believe those commercials that suggest your sex life will be greatly improved if you buy Rotto-cola. Remember the healthy alternatives: For a cold tasty drink, make up some iced tea or lemonade; add your favorite fruit juice (and if you insist *some* sugar) to ice cubes and in ice water, as fashionable restaurants do, to make a tasty and practically free drink.

a. Be careful of "frozen juice." "Imitation" juices may be in the same super-market freezer section as frozen juices, but they're really just sugar and water and orange flavoring with a few tiny shreds of orange floating in them. Their sole food value is in a little vitamin C, but you should get that (in much greater quantity) from real oranges, real orange juice, or tomatoes.

Even standard bottled orange juice is not really fresh orange juice; it's made by adding water to concentrated orange juice, usually with some coloring matter. Like the cheaper frozen juice, however, it is extremely good for you. The tastiest way to get orange juice (and some extra food volume as well) is to eat real oranges.

b. Take tea and see. Tea, like coffee, is a mild central-nervous-system stimulant; their active ingredient, whether called caffeine or thein, is essentially the same. (Both also contain tannins.) As drugs go, both are safe—"overdoses" only make you jittery or upset your stomach—but neither is good in excess. Neither drink has any known food value, aside from the sugar, cream, or milk you may add to them, though both contain trace vitamins and other substances in very small quantities.

Tea is the cheapest drink there is, aside from plain water. (Milk combines chemically with the tannin, making the brew distinctly less astringent.) It is cheapest, of course, if you buy it loose by the pound—a pound makes well over two hundred cups of tea. Most tea bags contain enough tea for two cups, so you waste tea if you only make just one—save them. The handiest way to brew just one or two cups of loose tea is with a perforated spoon-with-a-lid that you can buy in good housewares stores. Tea should brew for three to five minutes. Don't judge strength by color—some leaves have more coloring in them.

For larger quantities of tea, use a crockery teapot. Heat it with hot tap water while you're boiling the tea water; that way the tea will stay warm. Bring some fresh cold water to a full boil, and pour it over about a teaspoon of tea for each cup of water. Let it brew in the pot for three to five minutes; then pour. For later cups, it's best to dilute the stronger tea by adding more hot water in your cup. Or you can suspend the tea in a little perforated metal tea ball, dangling inside the pot for three to five minutes.

There are three types of tea. Most tea sold in America is black tea—it gives a smooth flavor and bright color. Oolong tea is partly brownish and partly greenish; it has not been fermented as much as black tea and makes a lighter-colored tea. Green tea, which is drunk by the Asian peoples whose ancestors discovered tea in the first place and probably know more about it than anyone else, is not fermented at all, and gives a very light, sometimes almost colorless tea. It often comes in attractive packages.

The designations "Orange Pekoe" and so on merely refer to sizes of leaf, not quality. Sometimes teas are labeled with the places they come from (Darjeeling, Assam, etc.), but there is no infallible sign of quality in these names.

Most teas sold in supermarkets are blends, as are the coffees, made up by tasters whose job is to produce a uniform, drinkable, but not terribly special product. The real fun of tea, as with coffee, is in experimenting with different types and finding those you really prefer. To do this you have to locate a store specializing in such matters. Such stores now exist all over and are usually delightfully aromatic and friendly places; some of them have bars where you can taste the different types before you buy. These teas have lovely names: Lapsang Souchong, Gunpowder, Jasmine, Keemun, Uva.

You may want to try instant tea if you are a constant iced-tea drinker. Sweetened iced-tea "mixes" are ridiculously expensive combinations of artificial flavor, sugar, and a little tea powder. A healthier and tastier way to fix iced tea is to add a little orange juice to it.

Many interesting mint and herbal teas are now widely available in health-food stores and supermarkets. Most of these do not contain thein or tannin; so they are rather easier on your system. Some of them, like ginseng, are believed to have energizing or medical properties. Fruit teas are also available.

c. Be cautious about coffee. When coffee was first introduced into western Europe, it was attacked as a degenerate substance; its imbibers gathered in coffeehouses, where the brew evidently encouraged intellectual conversation and subversive thought, for the coffee houses served as networks for the transmission of new ideas. Bach wrote a lighthearted cantata celebrating the forbidden joys of coffee.

Americans adopted coffee as our national drink, though we drink it very weak by the standards of most civilized peoples. Only recently have we grudgingly admitted that coffee may not be good for us, especially if we drink more than a couple of cups a day. However, as drugs go, caffeine is certainly relatively safe; just don't abuse it, any more than you would other drugs.

Elegant shops purvey exotic coffees (and teas), roasted in subtly different styles, along with fantastic array of grinders, filters, and devices to make and serve brew in. The search for the perfect cup of coffee can become as obsessive as the quest for any ideal—and as expensive. Most shops dealing in fine coffee will sell you half-pound quantities, so that you can try out a lot of types. People also get into elaborate discussions about the virtues and drawbacks of various coffee-making methods, and of caffeinated versus decaffeinated beans.

Most methods (except for espresso, which uses steam) have the common element of bringing together for about five minutes some not-quite-boiling water and some ground-up coffee, in a scrupulously clean container. You can perk it, filter it in a cone-shaped gadget, drip it, squeeze it through a cylinder of hot water, or even extract it in cold water overnight. The greatest difference is made by the cleanliness of your pot and the kind, quantity, grind, age, and condition of the coffee. You ought to fool around until you find a combination you like. (Boiling a little baking soda will clean the deposits from an old pot.) Store beans or coffee in air-tight containers; if it is ground, use it within two to three days.

The cream or half-and-half you put in coffee also has a great effect; if your home coffee isn't to your ideal taste, it may simply be because you're putting milk in it instead. And be sure you're not putting in too much sugar.

Even if you've developed a taste for really strong coffee, it isn't necessary to turn to instant espresso or yearn for a full-scale Italian espresso maker. A specialized coffee store probably sells "macchinettas," little Italian pots you turn upside down, which make a properly hair-curling brew.

Instant coffee is about half as expensive per cup as real (or freeze-dried) coffee. Since it requires no apparatus but a cup and spoon, it does have advantages for people living very simply. Over the years its taste has improved, and there is some difference in taste between brands, so you may be able to find one that really suits you.

There are now instant-coffee substitutes that taste quite coffee-like and contain neither caffeine nor the methylxanthines that have been connected to benign breast cysts and possibly other health problems. To my taste, the best is Pionier (made from barley, figs, and chicory) and the next best is Bambu. Both are Swiss-made, and cost about as much as regular coffee per cup.

6. Avoid excessive use of salt, fat, and oils.

a. Cut back on salt. You might think that salt is just salt, and that there couldn't be anything to worry about in grabbing for the nearest package. Wrong! Large numbers of people in this country suffer needlessly from goiter (enlargement of the thyroid gland in the neck) because they use noniodized salt rather than iodized salt—which costs exactly the same. Unless your diet contains a lot of fish (which are rich in iodine) or unless you're allergic to iodine (which is exceedingly rare), buy iodized salt.

Many people eat too much salt, which tends to increase blood pressure and may, especially in pregnancy, contribute to needless water retention. Never salt food before tasting it, and try to develop your palate's sensitivity to other than salty tastes—you might be surprised at the delightful delicacies you've been missing by oversalting things.

Prepared or processed foods tend to contain surprisingly large amounts of salt (as well as sugar), which is another reason to minimize your use of them. Bouillon cubes and dried soup mixes are usually very salty. Some things you think of as salty, like potato chips, may actually contain less salt than corn flakes. In general, anything that is pickled, smoked, canned, or frozen will have much more salt than its natural counterpart. Restaurant and fast foods are also usually very high in salt—yet another reason to eat at home.

There is not much difference between "sea salt" and ordinary salt (both come from evaporating water). Some people with high blood pressure benefit from using potassium-salt substitutes.

b. Especially avoid saturated fats. Americans eat a great deal too much fat, and too much of the wrong kinds. Some fat is essential for transport of fatsoluable vitamins, for insulation, and for energy-reserve storage. But only a very bizarre diet indeed would lower your fat intake to dangerous levels. For most of us, the problem is to cut down *saturated* fats (meat fats, dairy product fats, chocolate, coconut, and palm oil fats) or *hydrogenated* fats (as in certain processed peanut butters, etc.), because these tend to raise blood cholesterol levels and thus increase the danger of heart attacks. *Polyunsaturated* fats (margarine, many vegetable oils, nuts, fish) should be substituted whenever possible, but don't overdo them either. Don't use animal fats for frying.

The effect of saturated fat and cholesterol consumption is offset to some extent by exercise, and inherited genetic factors may play a part in your cholesterol level. Still, keep your fat consumption down. Use relatively mildly processed oils, which retain trace nutrients and also simply smell and taste better than oils that have been heated or chemically extracted with solvents, though they will not keep as long. Buy only as much as you will use in three or four months, and keep the container out of sunlight and other hot places.

Experiment with different vegetable oils. Sesame oil is very light and good for sautéing vegetables and for salad dressings. Safflower is another light oil, also suitable for deep-frying. Olive oil is standard for salad dressings and in Italian cooking generally, and poses the least health problems. Peanut oil is a relatively strong-tasting oil.

There is no precise or legal meaning to the term "cold-pressed," which may merely mean "not solvent-extracted." Natural oils tend to be a little cloudy and are not filtered to remove their color.

c. Use margarine, not butter. Butter is a major source of saturated fat; so minimize its use for both weight control and heart-disease reduction. If you do eat butter, the unsalted type is generally preferable, since salt masks off-flavors in butter, and unsalted butter thus has to be of higher quality.

Margarines vary a great deal in composition. Look for those with the least amount of hydrogenated or hardened oils, and the fewest additives. Many supermarkets are now carrying such margarines, and if yours doesn't, phone the buyer and ask for it.

Butter flavorings in shaker form are now available, and can be used on potatoes, yams, vegetables, etc. to get the taste of butter without the fat.

E. Eat the right way

1. Eat a healthy breakfast every day.

America possesses a tradition of hearty breakfasts, and there was once much to be said for this, despite an unhealthy overconsumption of eggs, bacon, and butter. Recently, however, urban dwellers are tending toward a "continental" breakfast—a roll and coffee taken on the run. Unfortunately, we forget that this style of breakfast evolved in connection with an early lunch, as in France, or huge midday main meal, as in Italy. Unless you can arrange your life in some such way (and recent research indicates that the human body *needs* a siesta after lunch!), eat a decent breakfast. There are some relatively painless ways of doing so. Health-food enthusiasts eat tasty, concentrated cereal-nut mixtures that you can also make yourself and save money: They usually contain rolled oats, whole-wheat flour, brown sugar, soy oil, honey, sunflower seeds, finely cracked raw nuts, raisins, raw wheat germ, and small pieces of dried apples or other fruits. You generally eat them with milk poured over them, and small pieces of fresh fruit add to the taste. Most commercial granolas now contain large amounts of sugar and oil; homemade will be better for you.

Since breakfast tends to be a rather regressive time of day, you may like things that you can suck up instead of having to chew: Mix an eggnog by stirring a beaten egg (or egg white or egg substitute) into a glass of milk, and add a little vanilla or nutmeg. Or make a shake by stirring a few tablespoons of frozen orange-juice concentrate into a mashed banana and mixing it into a glass of milk. You can also try jam, coffee powder, chocolate syrup, malted milk powder, or honey.

The traditional bacon-and-eggs breakfast is so heavy in cholesterol and fats (as well as the possibly carcinogenic nitrites in the bacon) that you should indulge in it rarely. Avoid butter in favor of jam, stick to margarine made with polyunsaturated oil, and use decent whole-wheat bread for toast.

Pancakes can be made with egg whites instead of whole eggs, or use "imitation egg" if you don't mind its additives.

Cooked cereals are available in quick-cooking form. They're nutritious, surprisingly inexpensive, and come in many different tastes and textures—from relatively gooey oatmeal to pebbly types such as Roman Meal to really crunchy Irish oatmeal (a cheap equivalent is called "steel-cut oats"). You can sprinkle them with brown sugar, honey, cinnamon, granola, sunflower kernels, and add nonfat milk.

2. Avoid eating out.

The proportion of meals that Americans eat out has been rising sharply (and many of those "meals" are in fast-food places, where the lack of vegetable and fruit foods makes for a badly unbalanced diet). But people living wisely and modestly should avoid eating out whenever possible—for reasons of both expense and nutrition. There are various strategies to avoid it, even if you are not a very home-centered person.

a. Strategy 1: Eat a big breakfast. This will often get you through the day, or else you may need just a small snack for lunch, such as a sandwich you can carry in your pocket, or some cheese and a piece of fruit.

b. Strategy 2: Avoid big meals altogether and, like our proto-human ancestors, have intermittent snacks all day—healthy foods, not junk. You can keep small supplies of food where you spend most of your time, or even make a habit of carrying food around with you (this is easiest if you carry a handbag or a backpack or wear a coat with spacious pockets). Try a bit of bread or hardtack, an apple or orange, maybe a small can of sardines, a piece of cheese or salami: nourishing food that you can if necessary make a meal out of, and not just a snack for emergencies.

The same idea applies when you go out on all-day expeditions. Never go to the zoo or the beach or on a long walk without taking food along. Get to be ingenious at making sandwiches.

c. Strategy 3: Find a grocery store. In most places there is some kind of grocery store within walking distance. For the same money you'd spend on a couple of hamburgers, you can buy a loaf of bread, some cheese, maybe a green vegetable to be eaten raw (spinach or celery), and a quart of milk. For what you'd pay for a slice of pie or cake, you can buy several apples or pears or oranges. Carrying a good pocketknife means you can slice food up, open cans, open bottles, and generally cope with the problems of eating on the move; never be without one.

3. Beware of food fads.

a. Eat many different foods. Any diet that is very extreme and limits your food intake to a few items is likely to be dangerous. Some nutritional safety lies in simply eating substantial amounts of different foods; some of them, at least, will be providing both the basic and the trace substances you need.

Macrobiotic diets, for example, are especially perilous for people with liver damage (from hepatitis or cirrhosis) and can even lead to death. Their claimed purifying effects seem to reflect the calm that sets in from malnutrition. The brown rice in these diets provides a little protein and starch and a few trace elements; it's far better than polished white rice. But eaten alone it will lead to scurvy, and the debilitation of such a low-protein diet will soon lead to other diseases.

To experiment with minimal food intake, do it outright, by fasting. Many Americans eat too much anyhow; so an occasional fast of a day is unlikely to hurt you. After you pass through the stage of feeling desperately hungry, you will get a hunger high. But keep up an intake of liquids (fruit or vegetable juices) to avoid drying out your system. Fasting for more than about forty-eight hours causes substantial changes in your intestinal bacteria and gastric processes, and when you start eating again you may suffer serious indigestion; so begin slowly and with easily digested foods. Always check with your physician before fasting for more than one or two days.

b. Don't use protein supplements. Most Americans consume much more protein than they need. Liquid proteins and other concentrated protein sources are unnecessary for a diet that has normal variety and ample amounts of other nutrients. Severe medical disorders can result if, in hopes of losing weight, you make such substances the major element in your diet for any substantial period.

c. Avoid fast foods and processed foods. Actually, the most dangerous food fad in America today is the fast-food diet: hamburgers, French-fried potatoes, milk shakes. These foods are heavy in animal and other fats and in salt. (They do provide some protein and carbohydrates, but the lettuce in hamburgers can't be regarded as a vegetable.) All in all, the MacDonald's diet is substantially sub-par.

Premixed and prepared or processed foods constitute another commercialized food fad. Almost every element of a standard meal can now be obtained precooked, from the canned or frozen soup course, through the TV-dinner main course, to the frozen-pie or prefabricated pudding dessert. These foods are, of course, generally at least twice as expensive as preparing your own, and they are loaded with additives, sugar, and salt.

4. Try being a vegetarian.

Many vegetarians live to advanced old ages, famous athletes have been vegetarians, and members of vegetarian religions have statistically far better health than meat-eating people. The widespread American belief that you need "red meat" for good health is totally without basis. In fact, in recent decades, with the growth in public consciousness of health issues, more Americans have moved toward vegetarianism, either wholly or partly.

Any dietary change is emotionally threatening, and people generally alter their eating habits slowly and cautiously. Many foods in the standard vegetarian cuisine at first seem strange or even bad-tasting to people accustomed to the standard American diet. Bean curd (tofu) happens to be a superb source of almost "complete" protein, since it's made from soybeans; but unless you have encountered it in Japanese and Chinese restaurants, it may seem formless and alien.

Many excellent vegetarian cookbooks are available. Incidentally, the sole essential nutrient you cannot obtain from a vegetarian diet is vitamin B_{12}, which you should take in pill form. For nutrition, vegetables are a better buy than fruits, though, of course, you should eat plenty of fruit too. Collard greens, sweet corn, black-eyed peas, kale, green peas, turnip greens, parsley, and spinach top the list, followed by asparagus, lima beans, broccoli, mustard greens, okra, and—red peppers!

F. Keep it clean and safe.

1. Keep your kitchen clean.

You will wash your dishes, of course—because it's unpleasant to eat off dirty ones, not because dirty ones breed microbes. You'll wash washcloths and towels because otherwise they get musty and mildewy. You'll scrub down your table and food-preparing area because otherwise they get encrusted with old juices and crumbs and attract cockroaches. These practices are pleasant as well as healthy. But there are some other considerations to be aware of.

Building code regulations, in providing a handwashing place next to the toilet, are intended to interrupt the cycle of feces-to-hand-to-mouth by which certain serious diseases, like typhoid, and certain annoying things, like worms, can be transmitted.

The kitchen ought to be a comfortable room and as pleasant to look at (and be in) as any other room. Indeed, there's a good case for making the kitchen the central room of the house, as it used to be. It's warm, a family with children spends a good deal of time there, and eating is a central family activity; it's silly to have food preparation locked away into a separate room out of sight.

There's no reason to try to make your kitchen "spotless." A kitchen without any spots is a place where nobody can feel at home. You have to pay *some* attention to cleaning up your kitchen, but not too much. The following are the essentials:

a. Wash the dishes efficiently. The more one-bowl or one-plate meals you cook, the less dirty dishes you wind up with. You will also cut down on dish washing if you get into the habit of washing out bowls and pans you use in food preparation as soon as you're done with them, while you're waiting for a pan to heat up or something. Use a dish pan rather than washing dishes under hot running water—it saves much water-heating energy and also much water. Certain things should not be washed at all—heavy iron frying pans, for instance, should only be wiped or rinsed to preserve their "seasoning." And don't dry your dishes—dish towels just spread bacteria around.

b. Take out the garbage regularly. Fancy garbage pails are a perversion, in my opinion, designed to conceal from you the existence of slops. This concealment soon leads you to forget to empty the pail, which in a few days becomes genuinely foul. The best solution I know is to use grocery bags, stood in a corner somewhere, for nonrecyclable and noncompostable items, and have a series of cardboard boxes for recyclables: glass, aluminum and tin cans, and newspapers. Compostables can be accumulated in a sink strainer and/or a bucket with a top. Peelings, skins, rotten leftovers, and so on should go here. You can compost them in a special bin or just bury them in a trench in an unused part of your garden.

c. Clean work surfaces diligently. A kitchen needs a good chopping block or other cutting surface for cutting up meat, vegetables, and fruit. Very beautiful handmade hardwood cutting boards can be bought, or you can make one of your own. It's a good idea to disinfect any cutting board occasionally, with some bleach in water, followed by a thorough rinsing. Direct sunlight is also a disinfectant; so when you get into a new place, wash the cutting board and lay it outside for an hour, which also will give it a good smell. (As noted earlier, keep a special cutting board for poultry.)

Sunlight and air are natural allies in keeping a kitchen sweet-smelling and comfortably clean without making it your life work. Use open-front cabinets, with things stored in attractive jars rather than advertisement-laden boxes; most boxed foods last much better if air is kept away from them. Don't pile up fruits in a deep basket where the ones underneath may get rotten without your noticing it. (Keep fruit out of sunlight, which makes it mealy and *doesn't* hasten ripening.) Bread and vegetables, however, keep better in a damp atmosphere, as in the refrigerator.

d. Use simple, basic disinfectants, cleaners, etc. Most households have enough cleaning agents to clean a hotel. In reality you need very few: soap or detergent of some kind for washing dishes and clothes; a cleaning powder for removing greasy spots on dishes, pans, and floors; and ammonia for washing floors, toilets, windows, refrigerators, stoves. (Clorox, another washing compound, is ridiculously expensive—other brands of the same substance can be bought if you don't like ammonia. Never mix ammonia and bleach, by the way, they produce a deadly poison gas.) Try natural cleaning agents, such as baking soda, vinegar, salt, etc.—these are cheaper and also nontoxic. If you really need a more powerful cleaning compound, buy "TSP," which is the working ingredient in most spray-on cleansers. (Be careful: It's a caustic, and dangerous to eyes.) Cleaning agents are often colored, perfumed, and advertised as containing fake "secret new ingredients" as a way of selling them at double the price.

2. Avoid food poisoning.

We are surrounded (and indeed inhabited) by bacteria of many kinds, and no matter how stringent food-inspection practices are, some of them come along with or get into our food. They can multiply and cause food poisoning if we allow certain conditions to exist. Surveys have found, for example, that about a third of our refrigerators are set above 45°F (7°C), whereas 40°F (4°C) is required to keep bacteria from multiplying. Put a thermometer in your refrigerator occasionally, and if necessary adjust the temperature setting.

Meat and poultry kept at room temperature after cooking will support rapid bacterial growth in an hour or two. This goes for chicken salad, ham salad, and tuna salad, and sandwiches made from them for lunchboxes as well. Our digestive systems cope pretty well with moderate amounts of foreign bacteria, obviously, or we would never have survived at all.

The most dangerous kind of food poisoning is botulism, which can arise from dented or damaged canned goods. Don't buy such cans, and if the contents of an opened can look or smell funny, throw them out; don't taste them, since botulinus toxin can be fatal in very small amounts.

Staphylococcal contamination of food can occur if you prepare meats while you have an open cut on your hand. Try to keep the preparation of meats and poultry separated from work on vegetables and salads, since cross-contamination can otherwise occur.

As will be clear from all of this, cutting down your use of meat also cuts down the need for certain kinds of safety precautions in your kitchen, and thus simplifies your life.

3. Use your freezer right.

Freezers, those trophies of the appliance-mad society, are drastically over-rated. A freezing compartment in a refrigerator is a convenience; you can preserve frozen foods in it that you bring home from the store, freeze bread to keep it for a week, keep ice cream for a while, and make lots of ice. However, a separate freezer is worthwhile only if you grow large amounts of your own food or have access to really cheap sources. Otherwise, since a freezer takes lots of current to operate and much capital to buy, unless you get one very cheaply, you will probably be losing money all around.

Also, you may tend to *waste* food: Only a freezer that goes down to 0°F (–15°C) will preserve foods for more than a few weeks without losing most of their nutritive value. It takes a good deal of planning and care to use a freezer efficiently. You have to constantly put the new stuff on the bottom, so as to use up the older first. You have to be very careful about wrapping and packaging foods, which will quickly dry out if not in airtight containers. You have to mark everything so you can tell what is inside the wrapper. Frozen foods deteriorate rapidly once thawed, and should never be refrozen unless they have been thawed in the refrigerator.

Finally, "half a side of beef" deals are often swindles, and almost never save you money. Even if they're honest, you don't need to eat that much beef.

Chapter 3.
Handle Your Legal & Financial Affairs Better.

Dealing with money is an area in which you really need to think hard and carefully, no matter how much you hate it. Money won't take care of itself; it will only disappear.

A. Live by a realistic budget.

If you have some kind of regular job that just barely covers your expenses, there is only one way to make sure you stretch your money until your next check: by dividing it into weekly amounts, and then spending only that amount. Moreover, if you're trying to save some money, the same principle applies: You have to put aside the savings at the beginning and then divide what remains. Otherwise it will be impossible to get through to the end of the period with enough to eat, and you will end up borrowing, which will only make the next period harder.

Assuming you have a checking account to store your money (so you don't spend it too early, or get robbed), here's how to do it:

- When you get your check, deposit it in the bank; but hold back enough cash to live on for the first week.
- Pay your rent, utilities, telephone, car payments, and any other regular bills right away. If you're saving up, put that away too.
- Divide up the money that's left, in the bank and in your pocket, into the number of weeks you're budgeting for. The result is the number of dollars you have to spend each week. It will seem discouragingly small, and remember this has to cover everything: food, car repairs

and gas, clothes, medicines, bus fares, children's lunches, and so on; so try to spread these expenses out over the month as evenly as you can.

- Buy your staple supplies (flour, rice, beans, spaghetti, dried milk, bread) in large quantities at the beginning of each week. That way you will have enough food to get through the week if you need it. Buy more perishable things, such as vegetables, meat, cheese, eggs, and fruit, only after you've made sure you can last the week.

- Never "borrow" from next week's money. If you're going to need something that can't be covered by your weekly amount, save up by scrimping this week, so that you can buy it next week.

- If you can be thrifty or lucky enough to come out at the end of a week with any money left over, you deserve to be able to spend it thoughtlessly—buy some luxury you've been wanting, or just blow it! The puritan minds tell you to carefully stash it away and get your fun out of counting it or something. That's not a very enticing sort of pleasure—and besides, the time to do your savings is at the beginning of the month, when you put a little aside in a credit union or savings account.

B. Saving.

Even people on low incomes can save surprising amounts of money by means of thrifty living. In fact, *Your Money or Your Life*, by Joe Dominguez and Vicki Robin (Viking-Penguin, 1992), explains how many people can achieve "financial independence" in less than a decade by working very hard, saving everything they can, steadily decreasing foolish expenditures, learning to live better on less, and putting their savings into safe investments like long-term U.S. Treasury bonds.

Checking accounts do not normally pay interest, so you also need to open some other kind of account—a bank savings account or "money-market account"—to store your savings in, though they will probably earn only enough interest to keep up with the rate of inflation. Once you have $5,000 accumulated, you can buy bonds, through a stockbroker. Treasury-bond income is free of state income tax; "municipal" bonds are free of federal income tax. Buying bonds is not a perfect way of getting income from your money (it shrinks in value as the years go by), but it is the least troublesome.

Conventional financial advice says you should invest in some stocks as well as bonds, since stocks may grow in value over time (especially a *long* time). You can do this by buying shares in a mutual stock fund. It's risky, but less risky than taking flyers on individual stocks yourself. In my opinion, it is unwise for people who don't have the time or talent to become real experts to put their spare money into the stock market. Other ways of storing money, such as CDs (certificates of deposit), need constant attention to be sure you are getting good rates. Some people invest in gold coins, gold itself, jewelry, art works, or rare collectable items; these investments are particularly risky, earn no interest, and are really a form of gambling. If you want a cache of money that could be used if the entire financial system crashes, you could buy some old, genuine (but not collector-quality) silver dollars, but your time would be better spent learning to grow vegetables.

C. Make your money work.

1. Buy real estate.

Tax policies favoring real-estate investment mean you can, for your own residence, deduct from your income tax the interest portion of your mortgage payments (which means almost all of them); for rental property you own, you can deduct depreciation as well as operating expenses. Property taxes are also deductible.

In computing your possible financial picture if you buy real estate, remember that you should usually "leverage" as much as possible—that is, use a minimum of your own money (in down payment) to get the use of the lender's money during the period you are waiting for the property to appreciate (and, for rental property, "depreciate"—in tax terms). If you have excess cash beyond your down payment, you might consider buying another property. But the amounts you put into down payments are, by that fact, not drawing interest; this lost interest is, in a sense, one of the costs of owning the property.

2. Build a crooked house.

If you simply wish to buy or build a house and live in it for the rest of your life, you are badly out of step, and will be penalized, or at least not helped, by the tax laws, which work in favor of speculators. Nor are tax-assessment policies favorable to the thrifty, handy owner-builder. If you manage by hard work and ingenuity to build a wonderful dwelling for a fraction of the cost a contractor would charge, you will be assessed the market price, and your taxes may be so high you can't afford to live in the house. If you build a house, and intend to live in it forever, consider making it so weird-looking that assessors will give it a low figure.

3. Pay debts at the last minute.

Do not pay any debts until you absolutely have to, since this allows your money to sit in the savings account as long as possible. Don't use a higher than necessary tax-withholding rate to build up a refund with the IRS; this is simply giving the government the free use of your money all year, and depriving yourself of the interest it would earn. If you are self-employed or have outside income, make sure you do not overpay your quarterly estimated income-tax payments. And where possible postpone deductible expenses—medical outlays, charitable deductions—until late in the year, allowing the money to work for you as long as possible.

D. Establish credit—and don't use it.

Credit is the ability to borrow money when you need it. But the best time to establish credit is when you don't need it. Then later it will be available if you get stuck or suddenly decide to make some purchase for which you can't find the cash immediately. (Remember there is both the credit you obtain from banks, stores, credit-card companies, and loan companies, and also the informal credit you obtain through friends.)

If you have had a regular job for some time, a checking account, a listed telephone number, and some local references, you can easily establish credit with an oil company (inquire at a gas station). The next easiest is often a high-priced clothing store. Since such stores are generally approached by high-income people, they are used to issuing credit readily. Use your card for a couple of small purchases (everybody needs socks and handkerchiefs!) and pay the account promptly when you get the bill. Once you have these to list on your credit application, you can ask to have your credit limit raised. This may mean filing a new application (which is why you should keep a copy of the original one; so you can be consistent), but it is a good idea from time to time. Whether you will get it will depend on your job and address stability, your income, and whether you have overdrawn your checking account or had credit disputes; avoid both during the period you are establishing your credit.

It is now illegal to deny credit to women on the basis of sex, marital status, part-time employment, or their husband's lack of credit. If you are refused credit, in most states you are entitled to know why, but the procedure of applying to the local credit-rating bureaus is cumbersome and must be carried out in writing. If a blot is laid on your credit, however, it is worth the trouble to find out why and either correct errors in the records or settle whatever dispute is responsible for the refusal. If you are billed incorrectly on a credit account, question the billing in writing; until the matter is settled, not paying the amount in question will not affect your credit rating. Such disagreements must be resolved within 90 days after your complaint.

You can now obtain a free copy of your credit report from one of the major rating companies, and others may follow suit. Write to: TRW Consumer Assistance, P.O. Box 2350, Chatsworth, CA 91313-2350. They will need your full name (and your spouse's); a verification of your address, such as a photo-copy of your driver's license or a phone or utility bill; your social-security number; and your year of birth. They will tell you how to get errors corrected, which can usually be accomplished within a month.

Once you possess credit cards, use them as little as possible; they give some people the illusion of money-free purchasing. A simple rule is to buy some small thing on credit every six months and pay the bill promptly to avoid the otherwise staggering interest charge. Then your credit will continue to be available in case you do need it sometime.

There are several real uses for credit cards. One is to help in cashing checks; unfortunately, many merchants have taken to using the ownership of a credit card as an index to your general financial state, though this may be technically illegal. Another is to is to enable you to rent cars, which is now virtually impossible, no matter how much cash you offer as a deposit, without some kind of credit card. (You don't have to pay for the car rental with the card; you just have to possess one.)

If you are on the road a lot, obviously there are other ways in which a credit card can come in handy, though it's not essential—you can carry less cash and don't have to bother with traveler's checks. In ordinary life, however, the credit card and charge account are dangerous items. You may think you are strong-minded about not spending money, but restaurant owners with a business interest in human behavior have found that people spend about 30 percent more if they charge their bill rather than paying cash. Also, once you use a card in an emergency, you tend to get hooked.

Credit-card companies and banks offer many different terms (and more or less dubious inducements) to get you to choose their credit card rather than somebody else's. You simply want a low yearly fee, low interest rates (in case you *can't* pay something off immediately, but if this happens it's a danger signal), and a normal monthly billing cycle.

Even if you don't actually spend more personally, the credit-card system causes customers to pay more, for two reasons. First, because it costs a merchant money to honor credit cards (about 3 percent of your bill), he or she naturally raises prices enough to cover the costs. So everybody who patronizes credit-card establishments, whether by cash or charge, pays more than if the establishment did a strictly cash business. Second, and more important, the interest on late payments of credit cards is outrageously high (sometimes even more than 20 percent)—it's left unregulated by legislators, who get fat campaign contributions from the retail interests. In a money economy, everything costs money—even collecting money. Despite the computers, mistakes are often made; so a secondary bureaucracy must be set up to handle complaints and irregularities and to police disagreements and frauds. This, of course, adds to the expense of the whole system and helps to drive the prices higher.

A Dictionary of "Credit" Shucks and Tricks

Easy Credit Terms! = We will give you a loan to buy our inferior goods at outrageous interest rates.

Low Interest! = The highest interest that the law allows (varies by states—may be 36 percent per year or even more).

Low Carrying Charges! = Charges that may be as great as the interest, or even higher, and cannot be legally limited.

No Payments for 60 Days! = We will charge you interest on the entire loan several months longer than usual, so your goods will end up costing you even more.

Save Now! = Buy now, and end up paying more later.

Nothing Down! = If we don't get it from you at the beginning, we'll get double from you in the end.

E. Borrow money as cheaply as possible.

Sooner or later everybody gets into a position of having to borrow money. You may be undertaking some project that requires materials you can't finance yourself, or you may get clobbered by medical bills, or you may just run out of cash before you get paid on a new job. The problem is how to borrow on the least disadvantageous terms. Renting $100 for a year may cost you $10–12 from a bank, $12 from a credit union, $18 if it's part of a time-payment plan, and $36 or more if it is from a finance company.

What follows rests on the assumption that you have previously established your credit in the community, which takes some time to accomplish.

Your strategy is to find a loan at the rates at which large loans are made for ordinary business purposes. Anything higher than that is an extra, and you are paying it because they think you are a "risk." You must therefore make yourself look like as good a risk as possible.

1. Always try your bank.

(Secretly you may wonder whether they possess good judgment if they would lend money to anybody like you—nevertheless, give it a try.) If you've kept a checking account there for a couple of years and haven't yet welshed on any bad checks, they will at least consider your application. Make sure you have what is called a constructive purpose to declare when they ask why you want the loan. Paying off or consolidating a group of high-interest time payments is a constructive purpose. So is buying appliances, furniture, a car, etc.—though a bank will not normally lend you anywhere near the total cost of an old used car. Repairing your house or buying equipment and tools that will help you earn money are also considered very constructive. Buying a new wardrobe or buying records are, regrettably, not constructive in the bank's eyes.

2. Belong to a credit union.

Credit unions are co-op banks; their members pool their savings so that they can (through a paid professional staff) lend money to each other. Their loans are generally competitive in interest rates and sometimes better than those of banks (not to mention auto dealers) as well as easier to get, especially if you have been a member for some time and have a stable job. (Most credit unions will lend up to $5,000 on your signature alone.) Credit unions are usually limited in their membership—to government or company employees, or grocery co-op members, or teachers—but you can probably find one you're eligible to join. (Some 36 million other Americans have.) It's good insurance against a sudden need for cash, either in a emergency or for some large purchase. Try to apply well before you need a loan, however, since credit union loan committees often meet only once a week.

Credit unions can now issue "share drafts," which look like checks and work like checks: They enable you to draw against your savings, but until it's actually paid out, your money continues to sit there and pay interest. Loans from a credit union are often insured; if you die, the loan is paid off and your family is not obligated for it.

3. Try finance companies.

Finance companies (or loan sharks, as they are often known to their unlucky customers) will rent you money even if you are not a good risk or have a bad credit rating—but they will charge you plenty for it. Different companies may rate your riskiness differently; so shop around and see if you can get a better deal. Watch out for service charges and other extras; look in the contract to find the annual interest percentages and the total financing cost. Be wary of contracts that give the company a claim on your property if you have any. And find out what happens if you miss a payment.

4. Try pawnbrokers.

Pawnbrokers, though you can sometimes buy from them at decent prices if you really know the merchandise in question, are a last resort for borrowing money. Their interest rates are utterly unregulated and can be astronomical. And of course if you can't scrape together the money to redeem your goods by the due date, you lose them. A pawn broker will seldom lend you more than about 10 percent of the actual value of an object—or give you more than that even if you offer to sell it outright.

5. Try friends.

Friends who have accumulated savings that they're not likely to need for a while are another possible source of loans. To avoid endangering the friendship, it is best to be businesslike: Write your arrangement down on paper, so that you each can have a copy, and plan a definite repayment schedule. Most friends will not expect interest, at least on a short-term loan, but it's a generous gesture to offer it anyway; after all, you'd have to pay it if you got the money in the bank. If you borrow money from a friend to put into some business venture, be clear about whether you simply pay back the money loaned or pay a share of the profits.

6. Don't borrow from the mob.

Underworld lenders connected with rackets of one kind or another circulate in depressed neighborhoods. If someone on the block offers to lend you money, especially in connection with some kind of deal, say thanks but no thanks. The terms may sound tempting, but in case of a dispute you may end up dead.

7. Don't co-sign unless you're willing to pay it off.

A person who is borrowing money—from any source—may sometimes be asked to get a "co-signer." A car-purchase contract sometimes calls for a co-signer, and so may installment-buying contracts. When you co-sign a contract, or "sign a note" as it's sometimes called, you are just as liable for it as the other person is. You are, in fact, guaranteeing that he or she will pay, and promising to pay yourself if the other signer doesn't. This is very different from just "signing a reference," as people sometimes call it. It might put you in debt for hundreds or even thousands of dollars. It is wise, therefore, to sign notes only for members of your family or very good friends—people you'd really be willing (and able) to pay up for if necessary.

8. Understand the terms of installment plans and contracts.

Considering the variety of things available secondhand or through scavenging, bartering, or repairing, there are really not many items that you need to buy new, and the hazards of installment buying should make you hesitate even more. Time buying is unwise for people with irregular or low incomes. Even when both halves of a couple are working at decently paid jobs, they can find themselves desperately tied down by time-payment debts.

a. Don't buy anything new if you can help it; and try to save up the money for purchases beforehand. This isn't easy—but making payments isn't easy either.

When a merchant offers to sell you something "on credit," he is really offering you a loan. In the payments you make, you will not only have to repay this loan money, but also have to pay a bigger chunk of interest than if you had borrowed that amount of money elsewhere. You always pay more when you get credit from the seller than when you borrow from a bank or credit union.

There is a great temptation to ask only one thing about an installment purchase: Can we afford the monthly payment? For people with no money at all in reserve, it's hard not to get focused exclusively on this question, but you then get taken for much more than you would spend if you had the cash or could save it up.

Businesses make bigger profits from you through installment buying. For one thing, people buy things they would never buy if they had to save the cash. For another, if somebody walks into a store and plunks down cash for a color television set, the store makes only its markup—maybe half the purchase price. But if you walk in and buy that same set on time, the store makes its markup and also collects interest charges.

b. Never carry more than one time payment, if you must carry any at all. This way you keep down the hazard of getting overextended, minimize the amount of interest you lay out, and can vary the way you spend money from month to month.

Remember that when you sign an installment contract, you are promising to pay *all* the installments due. If you miss payments and the store repossesses, you *still* owe most of the money, probably not to the store, but to the big finance company the store sold the contract to. You may be confronted by a creditor with expensive lawyers, not to mention debt collectors who can follow you to work, bother your employer, endanger your job, and finally garnishee your wages. In short, the chances are that you can lose a lot more through time payments than you gain.

c. Never sign anything before you read it. Any paper a business or salesperson asks you to sign is probably a contract, no matter whether it says "receipt" at the top. Say firmly that you want to sit down and read it. When you sign a contract, you are promising to do everything it says—or take the legal consequences. If a salesperson is over-anxious for you to sign, there are probably parts of the contract he or she doesn't want you to see, which means you are almost certainly being swindled. Whenever any part of a contract is not clear, take it to a Neighborhood Legal Service office, or some reliable friend or relative, and talk it over. Never trust salespeoples' interpretations: They will say anything to make a sale and can guess what you want to hear. But in case of trouble, you will have no way of proving what the salesperson said—all that counts is what's down on paper.

d. Look at the total cost. A contract will usually indicate the price of the object, your down payment if there is one, and the remaining price to be paid.

Then the interest charges must be spelled out, as well as any carrying or service charges. Federal tax and sales taxes may be added. The seller may try to make you buy insurance, especially in buying a car—but you should arrange your insurance elsewhere, since the seller's is almost certain to have small coverage and high cost. Finally, the contract should show the total cost you will be paying. Look at this figure carefully: It will probably seem much larger than what you expected from the salesperson's pitch. If it is too high, say you have changed your mind and walk out.

Time-payment contracts will show the size, frequency, and due dates of payments. (The quicker you pay off a loan, the less it costs in interest.) They will also spell out what happens if you should miss a payment or stop paying. Usually this includes repossession, additional interest charges, garnisheeing of your income, and so on.

e. Never sign a contract where some of the blanks have been left open. If a blank doesn't apply to your deal, fill it up with Xs. The seller should sign the copy he has shown you, right in front of you. If the contract papers disappear into a back room with the salesperson "to check" or "to get the boss's OK," they may come back with changes. Make sure all the copies read right and are the same. Then take yours home and store it in a safe place. If you ever have any dispute with the seller, the contract is the only legal weapon you have.

Contracts for work to be done around your house (if you own it) are especially dangerous, since they are often really mortgages on your property. Even where a small sum is involved, never sign such a contract. If you miss payments, your house can be taken away from you. Borrow the money from a bank or credit union if necessary, and pay by check. Many swindlers thrive in the field of home improvements—roofing, aluminum siding and storm windows, termite work, and so on.

If you absolutely can't say no to a home-repair salesman and find you have signed a mortgage on your house, the Truth-in-Lending law now gives you three days of cooling off during which you can notify the contractor (in writing) that you wish to cancel the contract. This cooling-off period, however, is widely misunderstood: It does not apply to house purchases, or indeed to most purchases; the law was passed to curb abuses in door-to-door sales, especially things like memberships in camps or health clubs.

9. Use your right to file for bankruptcy wisely.

Businessmen and businesswomen go bankrupt all the time—when a new venture fails or an old one crumbles. But most people tend to think that "bankruptcy" is a terrible thing, like cancer; so they don't think of taking advantage of it as a businessperson would. (Some large corporations have escaped liability for injuring masses of people by going deliberately bankrupt, and managers sometimes loot a company into bankruptcy.) You are "insolvent" in the eyes of the law if your liabilities (debts, including installment debts) far exceed your assets. But you aren't bankrupt until either you or your creditors file a legal petition (which requires a modest fee) and a court officially declares you bankrupt. The petition must be filed in U.S. District Court, and often legal aid is needed. You will also have to appear in Bankruptcy Court.

Although the "trustee" appointed by the court will pay off part of your debts by selling some of your property (like your car, or any property you may own but don't live in), each state has a list of things that can't be taken away from you. Generally, this includes your "homestead," at least up to some fixed value, and personal items like clothes, tools, and some furniture; you can also specifically ask to keep certain other things. If you have been in business, you can often keep the last month's wages due you from the business. Everything considered, it is sometimes to your definite advantage to go bankrupt and start over fresh.

You can go bankrupt only once in six years. You can also be prevented from "discharge" (release from debts) in bankruptcy if you conceal assets, refuse or fail to answer questions to the court, disobey a court order, obtain credit with false statements, or commit other frauds.

The moment you file for bankruptcy you are protected from your creditors, who must then deal with the court or trustees.

"Chapter 7" bankruptcy is the usual type for individuals. There is also "Chapter 13" bankruptcy, which sets up an arrangement for repayment. This is a good idea if you are in some kind of small business, however unorthodox, and don't want to injure your credit or reputation.

Our bankruptcy laws are sometimes criticized as unduly liberal. (In medieval times, you went to "debtors' prison," often for life—a practice frowned upon by our founding fathers.) They actually function as a kind of national insurance system for individuals and small businesses that do not make it, spreading the creditors' losses around in as fair a way as possible, and getting the individuals involved back to some kind of productive work. Moreover, many types of debt are not dischargeable through bankruptcy.

F. Minimize your income taxes.

If your income is entirely wages subject to withholding and your medical expenses are no more than average, you have no way to improve your tax situation, and may as well fill out the "short form" and forget it.

On the other hand, if you have other kinds of income that are reportable (i.e., *not* from Social Security, tax-free bonds, or illegal sources), there will be ways you can reduce your taxes if you are willing to file a "long form." It means a rigorous habit of saving receipts during the year, keeping an expense diary, and an evening or two of mind-twisting work with figures; but most families can come up with enough deductions to make it worthwhile. A tax expert will probably be well worth the fee you pay—in organizing your information for the highest tax advantage and in telling you what limits to observe in claiming deductions. Certain amounts are regarded as legitimate by the tax auditors, and if you stay within those you'll probably get by. The fee of your tax preparer is itself a deduction for the following year.

What happens if the Internal Revenue Service questions your tax return? Around 3 percent of all returns are audited. First, they will get in touch with you, informing you that they think you owe them more money. This may be said on some kind of mass-produced form, rather than in a letter. Like any businessperson, you are free to proceed as if an honest mistake or difference of opinion is all that is at issue. You or your tax preparer will write back or go to the IRS office and argue with them, using whatever evidence you can muster. If that doesn't work, they send you a "ninety-day letter," which is another form saying you have to pay up. You can, however, appeal this decision to a higher-ranking auditor by writing or calling at the office. And if that doesn't get you anywhere, during your ninety days you can still appeal to the Tax Court of the U.S., which has branches all over the country. It costs only a small fee to argue your case before the court, and you can find out how to file by asking at the IRS office. If you lose, you have no alternative except to pay up—though businesspersons with a lot at stake can go into appeals court. To the amount the IRS says you owe, they will add an interest charge.

Don't be shy about itemizing deductions. Deduction possibilities are put into the tax laws (for things like house interest) to gain middle-class support for the giant tax rip-offs of the corporations. A business manager who did not take total advantage of such possibilities would quickly be fired. As long as this attitude dominates our society, you are foolish not to claim everything you reasonably can. Nor do you necessarily have to keep elaborate records to justify your deductions; there is less than a one-in-eight chance you will be asked to show records. If you are audited, you may not be able to substantiate some of your claims and will have to pay up. (But always save the checks by which you've paid medical bills and other major deductible expenses.)

Incidentally, you may be able to take advantage of depreciation allowances yourself. If you have bought any tools or equipment that produce income, you can deduct part of their cost each year. You can also deduct the operating costs of your car if you are required to own it for your work, or use it for income-producing purposes. In general, since the tax laws are written to help business, you are best off if you can set yourself up as some kind of small business. Then your expenses for transportation, publicity, phones, office, rent, and so on are all deductible. You can even give yourself an expense account if you're careful about it, and take customers out to expensive dinners like the high spenders do. You can also buy at trade discount. But you must make sure there is some real business involved somewhere in the enterprise. This may not be as hard to arrange as you think; some of your favorite activities can sometimes be set up as business.

Businesses also know that in cases of special hardship the IRS will extend the date of your payment of taxes at modest interest. There is a special form you have to fill out, but this is a lot cheaper and simpler than borrowing money from a bank or credit union.

G. Have quick access to your own lawyer.

If your income is no more than 125 percent of the official federal poverty level, you can get legal help from agencies such as Legal Aid that are supported by federal funds. Legal Aid societies operate in almost all cities and counties. They cannot deal with "criminal" charges (if you have been arrested), but they can help in "civil" matters such as rental disputes, child support and visitation rights, name changes, problems with banks or collection agencies, food stamps and Social Security, education, and immigration. If you cannot find such an agency, write to the Legal Services Corporation, 750 First Street N.E., 11th floor, Washington, DC 20002-4250 (phone number 202-336-8800) for a list. For help with criminal law, you must find a private lawyer or turn to the public defender's office.

1. Know when you need a lawyer.

If you're under the illusion that reasonably smart people can handle all their affairs without ever needing a lawyer, forget it. You could need legal help if:

- Someone serves a legal paper on you, indicating that you are being sued.
- You are arrested for an alleged crime (serious or not).
- You are involved in an injury or property-damage claim as in an auto accident. (Don't sign anything or talk to anybody until you've seen a lawyer.)
- You buy or sell real estate without a realtor.
- You sign a contract, deed, will, or other legal paper.
- You are involved in a contested divorce or one involving property or children. (You can "do your own" uncontested divorce.)

However, in recent years a great deal of self-help law information has become available, in both book and software forms. To educate yourself about legal questions, and find out what areas you can handle yourself, ask for a catalog from Nolo Press, 950 Parker Street, Berkeley, CA 94710 (phone number 800-992-6656). Nolo can not, however, give you specific legal advice.

2. Negotiate the fees.

Even just a half-hour discussion of your case with your lawyer will cost something, since most lawyers don't give free advice any more than doctors give free treatment. Relatively standard fees have been developed for most legal services.

On the other hand, lawyers get "contingent fees" for many kinds of work—personal-injury cases, will breaking, and other little chores. On this basis, if the lawyer wins for you, he or she pockets a third to a half; if he or she loses, you aren't out anything at all. (Make sure of your liability for court costs in a written agreement with the lawyer.) Such agreements are required by some states. You can negotiate a "cap" on a lawyer's fees, incidentally.

"Minimum" fees are usually arbitrary and may be far less in the town or county next door. If so, you can probably dicker with a lawyer to go down somewhat. Lawyers are free to advertise, and they do, though the prices they advertise are solely for routine work. This competition, and the fact that people have been coming out of law schools in huge numbers, has reduced the cost of certain legal services. (We have about ten times more lawyers per capita than England, a much less suit-prone society.) Also, it is at last possible for lawyers to practice in prepaid groups the way doctors do; they can, for instance, serve groups like unions and co-ops. Since this promises better and cheaper legal service to people with little money, look around and see if any organizations in your area have group legal services. But beware of some "legal clinics." If sponsored by a law school, they may indeed resemble a low-cost medical clinic. Others are simply law offices specializing in easy, standard jobs like uncontested divorces, but charging high fees for everything else.

Some unproblematic legal matters can be handled by paralegal offices, which are usually listed in the Yellow Pages under "Legal Typing Services," "Services for Attorneys," or sometimes "Divorce Assistance."

3. Choose your lawyer carefully.

It is not easy to find the right lawyer for you. As with any service, begin by asking around among your friends, including small business owners. They may have a lawyer they can recommend. The local bar association will give you the names of several attorneys active in the kind of work you need, but will not make recommendations; and there is no screening of the attorneys on the list, who may simply be the hungriest in town. When you make an appointment, ask in advance about the consultation fee. Some lawyers have a special initial consultation rate.

As with doctors, it is okay to "shop around" for a lawyer—but each consultation may cost you. Never get into a relationship with a lawyer without getting clear on the financial deal. (And don't be panicked into retaining a lawyer you don't feel comfortable about; legal emergencies can usually wait 24 hours.) Even people with middle-class incomes often cannot afford to undertake a legal action, because it will cost more than they could expect to win. If you do use a lawyer, examine the bill carefully; a company called Legalgard, set up to do that for you and operating in a number of states, claims that 80 percent of legal bills contain "irregularities," and you can guess how often they are in your favor.

Honest lawyers will never promise to win a case for you. They can't get you out of a legal contract you have signed, like an unfair settlement deal, just because it's ridiculously unfair (and you shouldn't have signed it in the first place). They can't change the laws just for you—though in recent years, when Congress has been badly constipated, much of our social progress has been achieved through the courts. But they can help you skim by with the least legal trouble possible, as wealthy people's lawyers do.

A good lawyer will try to keep you out of court, incidentally. A trial, even if you are unquestionably in the right, is a game of chance (the judge or jury may not believe you, despite the evidence), and will be extremely expensive. A good lawyer, who knows how to use threats and how to negotiate settlements, can often get you most of what you would get if you won in a trial.

Just having somebody who is "your lawyer" is an immense psychological advantage in your life. It makes you feel you aren't entirely alone and helpless; if you get in a jam your case will be argued correctly; you have somebody who can explain the system to you and prevent it from screwing you. But the less you have to do with lawyers, the better off you will be. Remember that many personal and neighborhood disputes can be settled through some kind of informal (or, if necessary, formal) mediation process—using a trained, impartial third party rather than risking the complications, expense, and bitterness of the legal process. Many cities and counties maintain dispute-resolution services, and there are also private organizations (including the Society of Friends) that provide mediators. You can even locate mediators through the Yellow Pages. People might agree on a respected neutral member of their community to serve as a mediator. In contemplating mediation, keep in mind that what you are after is not so much to win as to restore peace and respect between you and your antagonist. This usually involves some compromise and flexibility on both sides, and the emotional clearing-up involved will have good results for both you and your community.

H. Use the small-claims court.

This is a special court (sometimes called by other names) where claims involving small amounts (generally $1,500 to 5,000, varying by state) can be decided. You probably can't have a lawyer represent you, and you can't appeal if you lose—though the person sued can appeal if he or she loses, and in some states can have your suit transferred to another court, where you will need a lawyer if you pursue the matter. The virtue of small-claims court is that it is cheap, relatively easy, and relatively prompt. If you have a good case, and especially if you have good witnesses, you are likely to win.

You can probably obtain a pamphlet from your local small-claims court that will explain its procedures and rules. If you decide on small-claims court, you should then send a registered letter to the person or company you plan to sue, stating your case and informing them of your plan to sue if they don't give satisfaction by such and such a date.

If they don't come across, you must go to the courthouse to ask the clerk for advice and to file your suit. (There is sometimes a special clerk's office for small-claims cases.) You have to fill out a form giving the exact business name and address of whomever you're suing, and pay a filing fee of several dollars. Usually you must also pay a small fee to have a marshal "serve the papers" notifying the people you are suing and requiring them to appear if they want to defend themselves. A date will be set on which you must appear in court to personally state your case.

Prepare for your appearance by getting together whatever documents you possess that are relevant: work orders, purchase orders, canceled checks, written estimates. Jot down an outline of your story, with dates in order, so you don't get mixed up in telling it. Bring along any objects that might be useful in making your case (damaged items, etc.) and also any witnesses who can support your story. A person with some expertise on auto repair makes the best witness in suing a repair shop, for example, so long as he or she is not your friend or relative.

The judge will ask you to describe your side of the argument and why you think you are entitled to "damages"—payment by the other party. State your case factually, without making emotional accusations. It usually helps not even to look at your opponent while you're talking. Try to present your story logically and as briefly as possible. Then the other side will have the chance to answer your case. Sometimes the judge will give you the chance to question each other, or make additional arguments. Then usually he or she will send the decision to you by mail.

If you win, the judge's decision normally causes the losing party to pay up immediately. At the worst, you might have to pay another couple of dollars to get a court "writ"—a paper that forces the loser to pay.

Pushing a case in small-claims court will cost you a small fee and time away from work. But that is far less than a lawyer would charge.

Landlords and storekeepers can also sue you in small-claims court, and you must then show up on the appointed day in court or you will lose the case automatically.

Chapter 4.
Buy & Operate a Car as Cheaply as Possible.

If you do not own an automobile, and are considering whether to buy one, you should be aware of exactly how much you will have to spend in order to operate and maintain it. You may discover, if you live in a large city, that you may be better off not owning a car, and instead using other forms of transportation as demanded by each specific occasion.

A. Know how much it costs to operate a car.

Even if you got a car free as a gift, it would cost huge sums to operate. And you must think of the purchase price in two ways to be economically realistic: First, if you borrow the money, add on the interest to the original price of the car; second, consider that the money you are putting into the car (as down payment or total payment) could be in the bank earning interest, whereas if you put it into the car it immediately begins to "depreciate." (Because of depreciation, as well as to minimize risk of a new car turning out to be a lemon, you should plan to keep a new car for around 100,000 miles. It is also the depreciation factor that makes it generally more cost-effective to buy a used car, so long as you check it over thoroughly.) You need to think of a car's cost in terms of cost per person per mile. If you want a car for a carpool, a comfortable large car may actually be more economical than a four-person car, and you may find a used one really cheap.

Insurance. In most major cities these days, your insurance bill will run as much as the average cost per month for the lifetime of the car itself, even if you have an old clunker, even if you carry nothing but the liability many state laws now sensibly require.

Repairs. You can't ignore these, though they're erratic. They certainly cost you more than gas, oil, and tires. Some, like regular tune-ups, are essential to avoid spending even more on gas. You'll go a couple of months without spending anything, but then you'll come to a job that'll eat up a hundred bucks. (If you can do your own work, of course, you can cut down such expenses by maybe half. But don't kid yourself if you're not an experienced mechanic.)

Gas and oil. People who have cars drive around a surprising amount—they tend to put in at least ten thousand miles a year. At current prices, this can mean a great deal of money; figure your expenses out on a monthly or yearly basis. To cut gas consumption:
- Drive at lower speeds;
- Avoid or turn off air conditioners;
- Cut out unnecessary short trips;
- Accelerate gently;
- Do not idle the engine for more than a minute if you can turn it off.

Licenses and fees. Even if your car is so old it's down to the minimum rate, licenses cost you something. Your driver's license has to be renewed periodically.

Parking and tolls. These include parking meters (and parking tickets), bridge and highway tolls, parking-lot fees.

Theft. You may also have things stolen from your car (car thieves can open a locked car in about fifteen seconds) and, of course, the car itself could disappear. Or vandals may crack windows, tear off the radio antenna, remove hubcaps, or steal tires. You can insure against such losses, but you can't escape the aggravation.

The minimum operating costs of a car are thus probably much more than you suspected, and alternatives to driving one make economic as well as ecological good sense.

B. Buy a car carefully.

For many people, emotional and status factors are the critical determinants of what kind of car they buy. Others are more concerned about good mileage and low maintenance costs. Minimization of lubrication and other servicing requirements is also a selling point that many people find important—though this is a two-edged "improvement," because it often leads to infrequent checks of the car's operating components.

Before you get close to buying any car, go to your local public library and study the ratings of both new and used cars in *Consumer Reports*. No matter what decision you finally make, you will learn a lot by doing so. Talk to friends who have cars of the kinds you're thinking of, especially about their service problems; the availability of good and reasonably priced service is probably the single most important factor in owning any car. (An experienced and trustworthy neighborhood mechanic with low overhead is the ideal.)

If you have learned how to give a car a thorough checking over, and utilize a mechanic to diagnose its engine, brakes, etc., you will always be wisest to buy used cars, and from private parties. Unstylish though it may be, a small, clean, used car, bought after careful inspection by someone more knowledgeable than your friends, will give you the most transportation for your money, and the least aggravation about repair frequency and adequacy.

1. Dealers' tricks to beware of.

Buying a car from a dealer is like wading through a swamp full of crocodiles: Some of them (the big new dealers) are fat and a little lazy, but they can still bite your leg off; the smaller, hungrier ones (the used-car dealers) will chase you over a three-foot wall. Here are some auto-sales tricks:

The bait and switch, commonly used in TV, radio, and other commercials, is luring the customer in with a very attractive low-priced deal that's really unheard-of—like a practically new car for half its original price. When you get to the lot, the salesman or saleswoman confidentially tells you that you can have it for that price, of course, but the block is cracked and the front suspension was wrecked in a crash. But over there in the corner is a real deal. . . .

Inflated, fake asking prices are commonplace in selling practically everything, but because so much more money is involved in cars, they're more likely to impress you. The dealer simply puts a price on a car that's a couple of hundred dollars more that he expects to get for it. Unless you've been studying the *Blue Book* prices on cars, you may not know this—and when the salesperson tells you he or she can knock off $150, you may think it's a big favor. You should never buy a used car without checking the book (*Blue, Red,* etc.) price on it. Don't just peer over the salesperson's shoulder either: Get a friend or service-station attendant to let you look at a copy—or try the library—so you can be sure you're looking in the right place and know what the numbers mean. Both "high" (retail) and "low" (wholesale) prices are given and assume that a car is in good saleable condition.

Although theoretically new-car prices are firmly fixed, in reality they're inflated prices too, partly because the manufacturers post inflated tickets, and partly because the dealer (unlike many used-car lots) will sometimes take your old car in trade. (It would be absurd to pay the ticket price for any new car.) But the amount of "discount" or allowance the dealer gives you on your trade-in is only one part of the calculations. Different dealers will give you different prices on new cars, and it pays to shop around; you may save several hundred dollars, except on very popular foreign cars that are in limited supply.

Once in a while a dealer will actually sell a new car at near cost—to win a bonus from the manufacturer, to meet pressing debts, or because financing the deal will bring a kickback on the financing. But auto selling is not an occupation that naturally develops one's generosity. Most "bargain" deals should be handled only with a forked stick, like a rattlesnake. The only ones I would trust are from co-ops, which can sometimes get you a new car for only a little more than the "official" (and probably fake) wholesale price.

Altered contracts. Much of the trickery of car selling comes in the paperwork. The salesperson will make you some deal on a scratch pad and then go in "to sell it to the manager." Well, it turns out the manager makes a few little changes that the salesperson passes off as unimportant—but the contract is put in front of you to sign anyway. The salesperson will try to pretend to be your friend; the manager will even come out and "let" the salesperson beat him down to your price, in return for some slight changes in the financing—which, it turns out later, will cost you several hundred dollars extra.

Bushing is when the salesperson dickers with you, agrees on a price, and then before you sign writes a higher price into the contract without your noticing it. Make sure you look at the written price and make sure all blanks on the contract are filled in or X'd out—especially the trade-in allowance.

The highball is when the salesperson gives you a phenomenally generous trade-in allowance, gets you drooling over the good deal you're getting, and then suddenly notices a mistake. By that time, probably you're so set on the new car that you won't back out or will accept a lower trade-in allowance. Oddly enough, lots of people will fall for this, losing hundreds of dollars by a moment of confusion and hesitation.

The lowball is the same trick but working from the price—offering you a car at a very low price, and then at the last moment substituting a higher price.

Road-testing. Salespeople will try to discourage you from *road-testing* a car. In two-thirds of car sales they get away with this, ridiculous as it may seem. Any car you're discouraged from testing is probably a turkey. Don't even look at it.

Guarantees. Big dealers will often offer a *guarantee* of some kind (thirty or ninety days) on used cars. This means little unless they are also new-car dealers with their own shop where they can actually have the car repaired—usually not very speedily—when something goes wrong.

Whenever salespeople ask you to sign something, it is some kind of contract. Read the contract; get a cup of coffee from the machine, sit down, and tell them you'll see them in fifteen minutes. If they put on pressure, tell them you want to take it home and study it, or show it to your sister-in-law who's a lawyer.

The contract must contain the *serial number* and motor number of the car, and you should insist on comparing these with the actual numbers on the car before you sign. Not having these exactly right can cause you lots of legal trouble later and maybe even loss of the car, or you might not be able to get it registered. (Even a fancy-looking car can have a stolen engine put into it.) The contract should also include all the extras, services, and repairs the dealer promises to make, spell out the guarantee if there is one, and contain all other elements of the deal. Anything not written in the contract is just hot air.

There are dealers who will fiddle with a car after you've signed the contract but haven't yet picked the car up. They'll put on worn tires, switch to an older battery, even pull out a radio or other accessories. If you suspect you're dealing with a real crook, make a list of the tire numbers and note down all other equipment, so that they realize you're prepared for trouble.

2. Inspect used cars carefully.

Unless you're really experienced with cars, it pays to have a mechanic look over any used car you're thinking of paying more than $100 for. It's hard to find a good or totally honest mechanic these days, but most mechanics will give you a reasonably accurate opinion for a modest fee. Don't even consider buying a used car whose present owner won't let you consult a mechanic. (If the owner or dealer is afraid to let you take the car yourself, ask him or her to go along.) A mechanic can make tests you can't do yourself. A compression test will show how much power is being wasted by worn valves or rings. The condition of the spark plugs and oil will give clues to the motor's condition (water globules in the oil mean real trouble). The mechanic can check the brake linings and wheel bearings, and spot frame welding or other signs that the car has been in a crash. If some repairs are needed but you're still interested in the car, get the mechanic to write down exactly what they are. A dealer may offer to fix them, or you can use such a list to beat down an owner's price.

If you are an AAA member you can also use the AAA diagnostic service in major cities. However, this checkup, despite the fancy electronic equipment used, is probably not as useful as a checkup by a good mechanic who really knows the kind of car you're considering. And stay away from other "auto diagnosis" shops—they may try to sell you a new motor when the old one is fine.

Naturally, you should only spend money on expert advice after you've narrowed down the possibilities to one car that seems your best bet. Before that, check out all the lots to make sure you know what's available. There are lots of things you can check yourself, and many of them will remove a car from serious consideration—unless you can get it at a rock-bottom price:

a. Check the transmission. It's wise to avoid cars with an automatic transmission. They eat more gas and wear out brakes faster (especially in city driving) than cars you shift yourself. They have more costly repair jobs, can get wrecked by being carelessly towed, and can't be started by pushing or rolling downhill when the battery is dead. Also, they're less fun to drive—they put a mechanical decision-making system between you and the road, decrease the "feel" you have for what the car is doing, and prevent certain kinds of quick actions (like downshifting in the case of brake failure) that might save your life.

b. Check the tires and wheels. There should be enough tread on the tires to last you a year or two. That means the tread depressions should still be at least an eighth-of-an-inch deep. Check for spotty wear patterns, or wear that's worse on one side than on the other (except on VW beetles and older buses—they're built to wear that way). Make sure there is a spare tire, and that it holds air; it doesn't have to have much tread. There should be a jack and a lug wrench for changing tires. Grab the tires at the sides and twist them; if they move more than a little, the steering rods or other parts may be worn. Look for oil and grease leaks around the rear-wheel hubs.

c. Check the shock absorbers. Jump on the bumpers, then off. If the car bounces up and down, the shocks are gone. This means the wheels won't hold the road properly.

d. Check doors and windows. Open and shut all of the doors and run the windows up and down. Damage to doors may mean the car has been wrecked. Anyway, you need to know if all the doors work. You don't necessarily need to have them *all* working: It's a bargaining point if they don't. Some states make you replace broken, cracked, or pitted window glass, which is *very* expensive. (You can, for rear-door windows not essential for driving safety, put in a piece of plastic sheet or plywood.)

e. Check the lights, etc. Turn on the lights and walk around the car to see if they all work; try both low and high beams. Have someone push the brake pedal and see if the brake lights work. Check turn signals, dome light, defroster fan. Try the windshield wipers. If there's a washer control, try it. Does the horn work?

f. Check the starter. Does the starter turn the engine over briskly? If it doesn't, the battery may be weak, or connections may be loose, or the starting motor may be developing trouble.

g. Check the motor. An engine naturally has some oil in it, which doesn't mean anything, but is there any oil on the ground where the car has been standing? This might indicate oil leaks. Does the motor run smoothly at a fast idle just after it's been started? If it doesn't, there may be ignition, choke, or carburetor trouble. At moderate idle, do you hear fairly loud clicking from the valve action? Does the car make a big cloud of blue smoke just after being started, or when you give it a shot of the accelerator? If so, it's probably burning a lot of oil and may need engine work on the piston rings, cylinder walls, and valves—all of them expensive. Engines with fuel injection and electronic ignition tend to run cleaner and give better mileage.

h. Check the choke. Most recent cars have an automatic choke, which is supposed to give the engine a richer mixture of gas and air when it's starting up cold. Then after the engine warms up, a normal mixture is supposed to return. Automatic chokes very often got out of adjustment, however. They interfere with starting, or they make the engine stall, or they keep it running too fast after it's warmed up. The automatic choke is one more device to make cars "simpler to drive"—and more expensive and troublesome to maintain. Count yourself lucky if you find a car with a manual choke—but learn to use it right, or you'll waste gas.

i. Check the clutch and bearings. Does the car move off smoothly, without chattering in the clutch? Does the pedal have to come all the way out before you begin to move? If it does, the clutch needs adjustment and may also need an expensive repair job. To test further, put the car in high gear, put the hand brake on tight, give it plenty of gas, and let the clutch out slowly; this should stall the engine right away if there's some clutch left. Also listen for rattling bearings when you accelerate or decelerate—these mean transmission bearing trouble. Listen for knocks and clicks in the transmission.

j. Check the gears. Will the shift go smoothly into all gears? Do you hear funny noises when you're shifting? Does the car jump out of gear when you accelerate or decelerate? Does the reverse gear work OK? Can you shift down from higher to lower gears without any clashing noises? Any trouble with the gears may mean expensive transmission work.

k. Give it a road test. Does the car accelerate well? Try it at highway speeds as well as on the streets. Does it shimmy? (Tire trouble.) Does it tend to drift off to one side or the other if you lift your hands slightly off the wheel? This would indicate front-end misalignment; but it might be due to road slope or wind—try it going in several directions. Does the car rattle a lot? Try the brakes gently: Do they pull in one direction, indicating bad brakes on that side? Do they brake evenly at high speeds? Loud squeaks probably show the lining is worn down; this can be serious if the drums get scratched, but most brake work isn't terribly expensive. You should never drive with faulty brakes, even just around your neighborhood. Most people who get killed in cars are within five miles of home.

l. Check the steering. Is there play (looseness) in the action of the steering wheel? If you can turn it more than an inch without resistance, the mechanism is probably worn or out of adjustment and may endanger your control of the car. Turn the wheel from one extreme position to the other extreme position, feeling for "bumps" or hard-to-turn places. Power-assisted steering may seem like a nice luxury, but it wastes energy and gives poorer road "feel."

m. Check the instruments. Naturally, never believe the mileage shown on a car! (And lube stickers may be phonies stuck on by a dishonest dealer.) But check the speedometer to see that it operates and also the fuel gauge and any other instruments. Unfortunately, the "idiot light" trouble indicators of some modern cars can make it impossible to tell whether the gauge is really working—the absence of a danger light may only mean that the bulb is burned out, the sensor is defective, or a wire is loose. But most cars have their idiot lights wired so that when you first turn on the switch, but haven't yet started the engine, all the trouble lights go on. Make sure this happens; if it doesn't, there may be something seriously wrong (such as no oil circulation).

Since many recent American cars don't have full instrument panels, you might have to do without some useful gauges. But you *can* install them yourself; auto parts stores sell kits that contain: (1) a temperature gauge, so you can tell if the engine is overheating—a common problem of old cars whose radiators have slowly clogged up over the years; (2) an ammeter, to tell you if the generator is charging the battery, or if some unexpected short circuit has occurred; (3) an oil-pressure gauge, to warn you if the engine pressure fails—which is about the worst thing that can happen to your engine, as it will ruin itself quickly without oil.

n. Check the safety belts. For many people, driving a car is the most dangerous thing they do, and every car ought to have safety belts—all around if possible, but certainly in the front seats. Safety harnesses (across the shoulder and lap both) are better still, because they keep your head from banging into the car in case of an accident. Wearing a shoulder belt in combination with a lap belt at least doubles your chances of surviving an accident. (If some fit of madness compels you to buy a new car, make sure it comes with air bags, which are even safer. Use the waist belts that supplement them.)

o. Check on alignment and balance of wheels. Wheels that aren't aligned properly cause tires to wear unevenly. Look for flat spots or tires where one side is worn down much more than the other. Correcting alignment isn't expensive, and is usually worth it for the money you save on tire wear. If the car shimmies, especially at speeds around fifty to sixty miles per hour, it probably means one or more tires are unbalanced—that is, heavier on one side than another. This is easily fixed by adding balance weights; most service stations can do it.

p. Check the direction of travel and levelness. A car that's been wrecked may have its whole frame bent out of line so that the rear wheels don't exactly follow the front wheels, but run off to one side a little. This makes the car unsafe and also causes terrible tire wear. You can spot this by having someone drive the car straight away from you, or by following it in another car. A car that doesn't set level probably has a broken spring—a dangerous condition.

q. Check the radiator. When you get back to the lot after your test drive, check the radiator with the motor still running. Can you spot any fluid leaks anywhere on the radiator surface? Any bubbles coming to the top inside the radiator (which probably means a blown head gasket)? Has the radiator lost fluid since you started out?

r. Check the muffler and tailpipe. Hold a heavy rag over the end of the tailpipe and see if any smoke comes through the walls or seams of the muffler, or through cracks in the exhaust pipe. Leaks cause the engine to make more exhaust noise, and they can poison you with carbon monoxide (a deadly gas) if engine fumes get into the passenger compartment. If you can't check this yourself, ask the mechanic to do it. A new muffler and pipe isn't expensive on most cars.

s. Check the body. The condition of the body is the last thing to worry about in an old car, but you should take a look at it anyway. Repainted parts tell you the car has been in at least one wreck. Are there rusted-out parts around the lower edge of the body, where winter road salt has eaten it away? This can get so bad that air—and exhaust fumes—will leak into the car. Are the fenders on tight so they don't squeak and wiggle if you shake them? Are the bumpers still intact?

t. Check the upholstery and interior. You'll have trouble if springs are beginning to pop through, but otherwise worn seats can always be covered with an old blanket. Make sure you feel comfortable in the car. Does it have enough leg- and headroom for you? Can you see well enough? Are the seats at a comfortable height and tilt? Surprisingly, many large, expensive cars are more cramped inside than smaller, cheaper models.

As a general rule, you're likely to be better off buying from a private party, at least if you know anything at all about cars. You won't be taken in by guarantees or promises, because there aren't any. You won't be up against a stream of fast talk and fancy figuring. And there's seldom any difficulty about taking a test ride and getting the car checked by a mechanic.

C. Know how your car works.

A car is not complicated as modern machines go. Moreover, car engineering and design have moved with astounding slowness, considering all the fuss made yearly about "new" features. In reality the current stick-shift car is the same machine as Henry Ford's Model A, except that it's bigger, more powerful, and extremely more expensive. All its major components are the same, though in a front-wheel-drive vehicle or a rear-engine vehicle a few of them are arranged differently.

Here are the basic parts:

The heart of the thing is, of course, the motor (1). Inside it, rapid explosions made by a gas plus air mixture drive pistons back and forth. The engine gets its air plus gas mixture from the carburetor (2). The carburetor gets gas from the fuel pump (3); it sucks in air from the outside. Because the engine makes a great deal of heat as it works, it needs a radiator (4) to get rid of the heat. To start, the engine is cranked by the starting motor (5), which draws electric power from the battery (6).

Cars use electricity for several other purposes besides lights. The explosions inside the engine are triggered by spark plugs; their current comes from the coil and distributor (7), which get it from the battery when you are starting the car; after the car is running, the generator (8) makes electricity for the plugs and also recharges the battery—which gets a little run down by the effort of starting the motor. The motor's energy gets to the wheels through the transmission (9), which is a box full of gears controlled by the gear-shift lever (or automatically in automatic-transmission cars). From the transmission, power is carried back to the rear end, sometimes called the differential, a set of gears that turns the wheels. (Front-wheel-drive cars and rear-engine cars transmit power directly from the transmission to the wheels.)

You should also know that the engine, transmission, and differential contain oil, to keep the parts from heating up and wearing out. The dipstick that the gas station attendant shows you indicates whether the engine oil is at its proper level.

D. Learn to minimize your operating expenses.

Anyone wanting to work on his or her own car should get the shop manual for it, not just the owner's manual. (Sears sells them if you can't find one free somewhere.) Cultivate friends who are good with cars; help them out and see what you can learn from them. If you know somebody who has the same make of car you do, hang around and find out how he or she manages, what tricks he or she has learned. Or if you're still in school, take a course in auto shop. No matter what kind of life you end up living, you'll probably have to cope with cars sometime or other; so be prepared!

1. Save on gas.

Fuel costs are a small component of the overall costs of running a car, unless you drive a great deal. For ecological, health, and financial reasons, you should try to cut down on your driving. But there are a few other ways you can cut your costs. The smaller, lighter, and more streamlined a car, the less gas it will use. So don't carry around a lot of heavy stuff, and avoid roof racks, whose air resistance takes a heavy mileage toll. Air conditioners cut mileage about 15 percent; either disconnect yours or avoid using it.

If you live on something you can officially call a "farm," or if you own a boat, you can buy gas for nonroad purposes and thus escape paying that part of the price which goes to taxes for highways and roads. The ideal situation is to have your own buried gas and private pump, as many old farms do; then you can get one of the local oil distributors to come around and fill it up from time to time, at a price considerably lower than you pay in gas stations. When you buy gas and put it in your boat at a marine fueling station, you get a receipt that you turn in as part of your income tax and get a refund. It is, of course, illegal to siphon gas out and put it in your car (it is also illegal for the oil companies to do some of the things they do). If you do siphon gas, for this purpose or in emergencies, use a pump, not your lungs, to get the siphon action started; many people don't realize that gas is a toxic substance (as well as tasting terrible!).

Cars with diesel engines get much better mileage than gasoline-powered cars, and at one time diesel fuel was much cheaper than gas. The price advantage has diminished steadily, however. It has also been discovered that diesel exhausts, though they contain less smog-producing pollutants, have more fine particulate matter in them, which is cancer-causing.

2. Give it regular tune-ups.

Regular tuning of your engine will increase gas mileage about 10 percent. Checking and, when necessary, replacing spark plugs and distributor points (like much other minor routine maintenance) is easy to learn; get a friend to show you how. You can also easily clean or replace dirty air filters, and replace oil filters. Adjusting carburetors takes some skill, as does setting the engine's timing, but millions of drivers do it themselves, and so can you.

3. Learn good driving habits.

You can save a lot of gas (and aggravation) by avoiding stop-and-go traffic. Aim to keep your speed steady—no jackrabbit starts, no sudden braking. Avoid unnecessary idling. Keep your top speed down to 55; beyond that, pushing air out of the way consumes extra energy and your mileage plummets. Don't open windows unnecessarily; it creates drag and cuts mileage, sometimes as much as an air conditioner does.

4. Conserve on oil.

Unless your car is already burning great amounts, it is worth spending a little more to get good oil, because oil is what keeps the engine from wearing itself out. It's also worth it to change the filter. Ironically, the short-trip driving done by most cars is absolutely the worst way to treat an internal-combustion engine. Oil doesn't lubricate well until the engine is really hot—which takes up to half an hour, and many town-driving trips are only ten minutes long. Heat-control valves and automatic chokes tend to get stuck (experts estimate that half the heat-rise valves on American cars are out of order). This increases the tendency of old engines to drip gas down into the crankcase, where it dilutes the oil and forms corrosive acids. Cold engines also give lower mileage. We will never get free of these inherent drawbacks until electric or other motor systems are adopted, at least for city driving.

Engine wear will be cut down if you use "multigrade" oil. These are marked "10-30W," etc. They lubricate better in cold engines, still work in hot ones, and don't congeal too badly in cold weather. If you have a fairly new car, "extended service" oil is required when you are supposed to change oil only every six thousand miles. (If you read nothing else in your car-owner's booklet, read the section on lubrication and oil changing; it may double the lifetime of the car.)

Standard oils today contain many substances intended to control gumming, foaming, acid formation, and so on. Stay away from other additives, and from stuff you add to the gas—they won't save as much as they cost you. Reused oil, which lubricates even better than new oil but has lost its additives, used to be cheap and easily available (it was standard for the army). Now drained oil is no longer recycled and filtered; so it is practically impossible to find reused oil, either for cars or other machinery. This situation is both a technological and ecological absurdity. (If you change your own oil, look around for a station that will accept it for recycling. Don't pour it in the gutter to end up at your local beach!)

Various novelty oils have been introduced in recent years, and may increase your mileage very slightly (though not as much as buying radial tires). There is even a very high-quality oil made from vegetable sources; as petroleum gets scarcer, such oils will doubtless become more common.

5. Use the right tires.

Most of the small amount of innovation in the auto industry in the last thirty years has come from European research. Radial, steel-cord tires were used in Europe for twenty years before finally reaching us. These tires last about twice as long as nylon or rayon tires. They hold the road better in turns, they are more resistant to heavy impacts, and because they take low air pressure they have a large "foot-print" to hold better on the road. (Do not mix radials and bias-ply tires on your car or handling instability will result.) Radials also roll easier and can thus give you several miles more to the gallon. Their disadvantages are that they cost more (though not twice as much) and that they make a little louder hum on the road. Because of these terrible drawbacks, supposedly, the American auto and tire industries kept them from us for two decades! Instead we were and are still offered the standard rayon tires, nylons tires that develop annoying flat spots at night, and fiberglass tires.

You cannot tell what kind of a tire you are buying by the name and price. Until strong government standards are enforced, the only sane procedure is to buy tires at Sears or Montgomery Ward—dependable sources with straightforward descriptions in their catalogs. Pay no attention to labels like "premium," "first-line," and so on. These are just words; one brand's premium tire may be another brand's cast-off third-quality tire.

Most people on a low budget will put retread tires ("recap" is the better term) on their cars. A recap should run almost as long as a new tire before it wears out, but it costs only half to two-thirds as much. Buy recaps only through a mechanic or shop you trust; cheap retreads tend to wear rapidly, may throw off the new rubber entirely, and can otherwise cause trouble. A good recapping house will give you a written guarantee, usually for something like ten thousand miles.

Tires wear a little differently on different wheels; so rotating them is often recommended. This is a waste of money unless you do it yourself, because switching costs more than you save in rubber. (Don't rotate a new spare—save it, so that you'll only need three new tires). If you notice one tire wearing badly, it might be worth the expense needed to realign the wheel—but you might be better off just to let it wear. New tires also need to be balanced, since they are often a bit heavier on one side and may cause annoying bump-bump-bump as well as spotty tire wear.

6. Use the right battery.

Auto-battery prices and quality vary enormously: Never buy a new battery from a service station—it'll probably cost much more than at Sears. Unless you have an automatic transmission, you can probably get started by having someone push you, or letting the car roll downhill, or by stopping somebody and running jumper cables from his or her good battery to your dead one.

Unfortunately, intermittent short-trip driving in town never gives a battery much chance to get recharged. If that's your main kind of driving, get a high-quality battery.

The strength of a battery is measured in "ampere hours." Sears has a chart that tells you which of their batteries has the right rating for your car. In cold-weather starting, you'll need the full rating power.

E. Save money by doing your own minor repairs.

The going prices for auto repairs, especially in established dealerships, have become so astronomical that once a car is out of warranty, it is essential to find a good independent mechanic to work on it. But you can also gain skill at diagnosing what is wrong with your car, and you can learn how to fix common small troubles that require no special skills or expensive equipment. Many evening schools now offer do-it-yourself auto-repair courses, some of them especially set up for women. (People who don't understand the fundamentals of cars are easy marks for unscrupulous repair shops.)

Any car needs a tool kit, but an old car even more. You should carry, besides the usual tire-changing tools and flashlight, pliers, and screwdriver, several items that will often be useful:

- a pair of jumper cables to start your own or other people's cars;
- a piece of three-quarter- or one-inch rope to use in towing;
- a tarp;
- some old gloves for working in cold weather;
- some electrical wire and tape;
- a set of extra fuses;
- some road flares to lay out in case of accidents;
- an eight-foot piece of clear plastic tubing with a squeeze pump to siphon gas and some kind of can to catch it in;
- miscellaneous old ropes for tying on cargo too big to fit inside;
- an old windshield-wiper blade for cleaning off dew;
- and a scrap of rigid sheet plastic for scraping off frost and snow without scratching the glass. If you live in snowy country, you'll also need chains and an old shovel for digging yourself out.

Acquiring all these things will obviously take some money—another seldom-remembered expense of owning a car.

The best way to learn how to do minor repairs and maintenance is to work along with friends who have the same make of or a similar car. But you can also get a repair manual from the library that will explain many repair operations, both generally and specifically, for most common cars. You should periodically replace spark plugs, and clean and gap them in between changes; this is easy to do. Fixing worn wiring and leaky water hoses are other common, easy jobs. You can change the oil if you have a way of disposing of the old oil without causing pollution; you can use a hand grease gun to lubricate some cars. If you have generator trouble, you can pull it out and take it to a generator shop for rebuilding. When switches go bad, brake cables need tightening, or taillight glass gets broken, you can almost always cope. And once you get used to working on your own car, you will probably gradually get more confident and skillful until you are doing everything but major motor work. And even that is within the competence of the ordinary person if you study the relevant manuals carefully, get any necessary machine-shop work done by a capable outfit, and have good general tool skills. It is a wonderful feeling to have torn down your motor and rebuilt it: Now you *really* know what makes it go!

1. Be able to identify problems.

In driving around in a car you need to be able to tell whether it's running all right. Here are some common, obvious danger signals and what they mean.

Heavy, thumping noise; car may also bump up and down. A tire has probably gone flat or blown out. Don't brake suddenly; slow down and then pull over as far off the road as possible. Stop at a level place where the tire can be reached for changing. Open the hood, which is a sign you need help. Driving on a flat tire will ruin it and may damage the wheel rims as well.

Grinding noises, especially when you shift gears. Something is giving way in the transmission. If the car will run without making a really awful noise, put it in second and drive slowly and carefully to your repair shop.

Weak turning over, then nothing, when you try to start the motor. Battery is probably "dead" (run down), unless wires are loose or broken. However, this does not usually mean you need a new battery. If a battery runs down because of a short or because the headlights were left on, it will usually work fine once it's charged up again (and any shorts fixed). A dead battery can usually be charged up temporarily in a service station, and this should get you to a trusted mechanic. (Never try to have anything serious done to your car on the road—use makeshifts and stopgaps to get it back home to someone you know.) Stick-shift cars with weak batteries can be parked on hills, where you can coast down a bit to start them; this may stretch an old battery's life a couple of months. But prepare yourself for the shock of buying a new one. If you like to keep old cars around, a cheap battery charger is a handy thing to have.

Steam coming out of hood when you stop; probably hissing noise too. The engine radiator fluid is boiling over. Drive into the first gas station. Keep the motor running and drive to the water hose. Open the hood carefully, and uncap the radiator *only* with a heavy rag protecting your hand and with your face turned away. Then very slowly run cold water into the radiator until the motor cools down.

Motors overheat for two main reasons: The cooling system is clogged or it has a leak. (Some heavy new American cars boil over simply from going up long steep mountain grades.) Incidentally, if the steam disappears before you get to a station, it may just be blowing away before you can see it. You need more water anyhow.

Brake pedal goes down slowly to floor when you push it. You've got a defective master cylinder in your brake system. Sometimes pumping the pedal will give you more braking power temporarily, but get it fixed right away; defective brakes cause many accidents. Often, especially if you're on the road, you can get a gas station to fill up the brake-fluid reservoir, and then you can limp home, pumping the pedal when you brake—but drive cautiously, and use the engine to slow down (by downshifting) as much as possible.

Brake pedal goes quickly down to floor. Your hydraulic brake system has failed completely, probably because of a bad leak. Instantly shift into the next lower gear, even if the gears clash as you do so (into "low" or "first" gear on automatic transmissions). The engine will then help you slow down. Try the emergency brake, but watch out, as it may make the car jerk or swerve. American cars really have parking brakes rather than emergency brakes, but they can save your life going down a hill if you use them. If this doesn't stop the car, and you're on a hill or about to hit people, run into a hedge or parked car or wall or small tree. It's better to ruin the car than kill yourself—or others—at the bottom of the hill!

Burning smell. This may just be the odor of air pollution, but it can also come from electrical wires heating up and burning their plastic or rubber covers, or from leaving your hand brake on, or from tires that are badly out of alignment and twisting against the road as they turn. Stop and see if you can see the source of the smell. Hot wires need to be replaced promptly.

Smoke. If you smell or see smoke, stop and get out of the car immediately. Collected oil may be burning, or a gas leak may have caught fire. Unless you have a good fire extinguisher handy (*not* water) and really know what you are doing, get at least fifty feet away from the car. Don't go back till you're sure the fire, if there was one, has burned itself out.

Grinding, sandy noises, or a slight shimmy felt through steering wheel. These may indicate trouble in the bearings. Get a mechanic to listen.

Whining, shrieking sounds. These can come from fan-belt slippage, or from normal operation of some power-steering mechanisms.

Chattering of clutch when you start off. This may be annoying, but it doesn't hurt anything. Unless your clutch slips, which makes the car dangerous to drive, leave it alone.

If all this sounds like a lot to worry about, think again about whether you really need that car!

2. Buy your own parts.

Every auto company spends a lot of money advertising that its parts are better than other companies' parts. This is a big joke at the customer's expense. Many parts in a car are manufactured by small feeder companies anyway—and the big companies seem to think they're all right then. Never buy "original" parts if you can help it. Parts for all U.S. cars and for many foreign cars are available through Sears, Ward, and many small-parts suppliers. In any case, make some phone calls before buying any parts—prices vary a lot.

Auto parts and accessories stores sell a lot of junky accessories, but their basic parts are pretty standard. If you know cars, you can save money by buying from wrecking yards, whose prices are usually just a shade under wholesale. They buy totaled-out cars, in which most of the parts are often perfectly sound and undamaged, for maybe a hundred dollars. Thus, although they're sharks and you have to know what you're doing, you can often get a good battery (take along a hydrometer to check it), radiator (make leak checks), tires, and specialized parts. However, wrecker prices on small parts are often more than from stores; anything that costs less than one or two dollars, buy new.

3. Get the best deal on collision repairs.

One important reason to drive an old car is that you will not be motivated to spend large sums keeping it in mint body condition; if you collect some insurance when somebody hits you, you can hang onto the money. Despite the great national campaign to strengthen bumpers against minor crashes, they are still very fragile. A crash at 10 m.p.h. will totally ruin many cars from a safety standpoint and may cause dollar damages into the thousands.

Finding a good, trustworthy mechanic is the single most important necessity when you own a car, especially an old one. Keep looking around. They do still exist. Ask your car-owning friends.

When you're dealing with a mechanic you don't know well, be very careful. The auto-repair business is full of incompetents and swindlers who will "repair" things that have nothing wrong with them, damage things that were working OK, and charge you for things they didn't do. When you take your car in, get a work-order sheet filled out that says what is to be done. Never sign a blank order sheet, or you may find yourself paying for jobs you didn't want done. Ask beforehand how much a job will cost. Experienced mechanics have standard estimates for all common jobs and can tell you within a few dollars.

Try to find a mechanic who isn't a "rulebook mechanic" determined to put everything in factory-fresh shape. What you want is to keep the crate running at the minimum possible expense. You need a mechanic who is reliable, but who knows what is really necessary and what can be put off or not done at all.

If you have a serious disagreement with a mechanic about the work or the bill, you'll have to go to small-claims court. Your state may have an agency intended to police abuses in auto-repair shops, and a complaint to them may solve your problem without your having to go to court. (It may also help to eliminate an incompetent or crooked mechanic.) There is also the federal toll-free number of the Bureau of Automotive Repair: 800-952-5210.

Chapter 5.
Travel Cheaply but Well.

The automobile was invented as a mechanical replacement for the horse and carriage. It introduced a degree of freedom and movement unprecedented in human history, and set in motion a profound transformation of our society. But the car, delightful as it might have been in a nineteenth-century land of wide open spaces, is really not appropriate for urban living patterns. It is, in fact, in that class of things known as "positional goods": things that are undeniably good to have, if only a few other people have them too; if they're too common, they interfere with everybody's enjoyment. We therefore need to become aware when we can travel more cheaply or enjoyably in something other than a private automobile.

A. Travel in someone else's vehicle.

1. Try carpools.

People trying to save energy (and money) but who dislike ordinary forms of public transportation should explore the possibilities of car- or vanpooling, which began to expand dramatically in the late seventies. In most cities, there are phone numbers posted near toll bridges or other concentrated points of auto traffic, so that people stuck in rush-hour traffic jams will notice and remember them; these numbers are for offices where you can enter your name in ongoing carpool programs or obtain names of people like yourself who are interested in setting up a carpool. Pooling works only for people who have regular work schedules that they stick to, since the vehicle has to operate on a definite schedule. Carpools are especially advantageous for people who live in outlying areas and commute downtown, where parking costs add to the other costs of owning your own car. But they are also used by people working in suburban or small-town jobs.

See if your employer's personnel office sponsors or organizes carpools (if it doesn't, it might save a lot of parking-lot space by doing so).

Government grants are sometimes available to finance purchase of vans, if a suitable nonprofit umbrella organization can set up a scheme. A van makes it possible to carry substantially more people, of course, but an ordinary car will get your carpool started; later on, you may want to invest in a more comfortable van. (Or, if your group tends to expand, charter a full-sized bus.) In many small carpools, driving and use of car is rotated among members. In some, a driver is hired. There are carpools where snacks and drinks are shared on the way home, and hot coffee provided in the morning. Like buses, carpool and vanpool vehicles are entitled to use special or "diamond" lanes through congested points, which often makes your trip to work substantially faster than if you used your own car.

Special hazards to decide about before your pool goes into effect: how long to wait for tardy members, and your policy on smoking, radio-playing, and eating.

2. Try a small plane.

Although small-plane travel is not as safe or fast as commercial air travel, it is probably as safe as highway transportation, and of course you get to see the Earth and what we have been doing to it from a totally new perspective. Most pilots seem to charge considerably less than commercial air prices. Sometimes they will have to land in airports where ground transportation is not easy to get; inquire about this aspect of your trip.

3. Try taxis.

Few American cities with taxi service approach the ideal, as Londoners know it. Even in these few cities, the taxis are standard American cars, and so are clumsy and inconvenient to get in and out of, and lack the baggage compartment and driving agility of London cabs. (The Museum of Modern Art held a competition to design a better taxicab for us, but none have yet appeared on the streets.) If our cities were intelligently managed, the city councils would spend on subsidized taxis at least half of what they are spending on streets and parking lots, and everyone would be a lot better off. Taxis cut down congestion, decrease the need for parking space, and move people around faster than cars, since they don't need to find parking spots. In short, they eat up less of society's resources and produce less smog. Besides, they're fun to ride in. Let someone else do the driving and enjoy yourself with your friends in the back seat, or watch the world go by.

Taxis seem expensive. The question, however, if you're trying to develop a sane style of life, is whether they're really more expensive than other ways of getting around—in particular, whether you're better off using taxis or having your own car. Of course, if you drive around a lot on little trips all the time, you may find it hard to get cabs quickly enough to suit you, even in New York, which has more cabs than any other U.S. city by far.

But let's consider a person who doesn't have to drive around all day. If you calculate what your car really costs you to operate, the amount per month would buy you a surprising number of taxi rides, even at today's rates per mile. And except in very spread-out cities like Los Angeles, taxis can also be cheaper than rental cars.

Moreover, if you use taxis, you don't have to worry about whether your car is dependable for an important trip. And you're not worrying about $75 for a repair bill, or where to park. You're not worrying about the tires getting slick, the brakes jerking dangerously, or somebody stealing your mag wheels. You're not even worrying about whether there's enough gas to get to the store and back.

Taxi service might well be a public service, just as the transit companies are. If the government was serious about cutting unemployment, it could buy fleets of taxis and use unemployed youths to drive them. Even if they made nothing but tips, the fun of driving around would appeal to many young people. Or there could be self-driven taxis—city-owned small cars that were legal to drive only in a restricted area downtown, that you would leave for the next user, and that turned on when you inserted your credit card in the slot. (Later you would be billed for the mileage.) Such short-haul taxi systems could readily use electric vehicles, cutting down on metropolitan smog production.

4. Try public transportation.

The degree to which you can use public transit, and either use your car less or get by without one entirely, depends on your location; but many people who actually live quite near frequent bus service don't realize it is there. You may just be in one of those well-served spots that has frequent, rapid service in all the directions you usually go. If you are a sociable sort, you may find riding the bus rather more interesting than sitting all by yourself in your car. So call up the main office of your transit system and ask them to send you a free map of their lines, plus schedules for those lines you plan to use, if you know their numbers. Once you have the map, study it. Mark the location of your house, your job, and wherever else you go a lot—clinic, school, supermarket, downtown—or would like to go. Now try to figure out from the map whether there are direct lines that run from near where you are to near where you want to go. (With parking the way it is these days, a comparison with car travel makes "near" anything within about six blocks.) If there's no direct line, what's the next best way to go—the one that involves the least changing? In the central areas of most cities, you should be able to get most other places with one or two changes. If the best way to go is still not clear, sit down at the phone with the map in front of you and call the information office of the transit system. The line will probably be busy; keep trying. Tell them where you are and where you want to go, and be ready to write down what they say.

In most cities, bus or streetcar service is so infrequent that you need a schedule if you want to avoid standing on the corners waiting. Drivers carry schedules, or if there is no printed schedule, they know how often their lines run at different times of the day. Systems that have printed schedules will usually send them out if you ask by phone.

Don't get the feeling that you can't get around if you don't have a car. One of the secrets of living an interesting, vital life is to not let yourself get restricted to your own neighborhood. Get out and circulate. Don't be ashamed to carry large objects onto the bus. Parents wear papoose-type baby carriers or take on baby strollers; shoppers carry on big bags or little two-wheel carts; hikers wear knapsacks; travelers carry on luggage. It's a public service, and you're the public. Also, if drivers give you any difficulties, or are unpleasant, note down exactly what time it is and what bus line you are on, then write a tough letter to the transit authority, giving this information and describing the incident. Bus driving isn't exactly a joy to the soul, but drivers owe it to the public to be civil.

And even if you do have an occasional bit of discomfort in using public transit, remember that parking meter and parking fees alone would cost you more than you're paying.

5. Try motorcycles, motorbikes, mopeds, and scooters.

Some people ride motorcycles for economy and convenience, but many get hooked on the sheer excitement of it: You're in direct contact with the rushing air, so that it seems more like flying than driving; you're in direct command of the machine, which won't even stand up without you. (You are also, of course, in more peril of your life, and have something like four times more chance of accidents than in driving a car, which is the most dangerous activity that most people engage in.) You can ride on dirt tracks, over hills, through trees, even through creeks—where only a four-wheel-drive car could go. You can park between buildings, between cars, under stairways or porches, usually (though not always legally) on the edge of sidewalks. And, unlike riding a bicycle, you can carry a passenger with you.

A light motorcycle is by far the cheapest motorized transportation around. Used cycle prices, however, may not be as low as you'd hope—you can rarely get a cycle that's in safe operating condition for the amount that will some-times get you a working car. Gas expenses, on the other hand, are far less.

Hundreds of thousands of people even now ride small Japanese cycles, for pleasure, to work, and around town. A light machine with an engine displacement of 125 cubic centimeters or less will easily keep up with town traffic. A slightly larger machine will handle anything you'll encounter on the highways. (In learning to ride, make sure you have an experienced teacher, and develop a healthy respect for the power in even a small engine, or you may quite literally flip out.)

a. Learn to repair your own bike. In the past, motorcyclists tended to be mostly mechanical types who loved to putter with their cycles. Nowadays repair service is widespread enough that you don't really have to do your own work—though it will give you a sense of security in remote places if you learn how to handle basic repairs. (Although cycle repairs are generally cheaper than auto repairs, doing your own work can still save you a great deal of money.) The engine and transmission of a heavy cycle are as complex as those in cars. One great advantage of the light new machines is that they have two-cycle engines: removal of cylinder heads is simplified, and so is transmission work. However, this simplicity of construction is paid for by faster wear, since their moving parts move faster. They are also noisier and smellier.

People who entrust their lives to a cycle should learn how to check it over carefully for worn parts. A frayed cable or loose nut could cause you to lose control at a fatal moment. Check your tire pressures often: Low pressure can allow a tire to rotate on the rim and cause trouble when you least expect it—in fast accelerating or braking. Make sure your brakes and lights are always in perfect working order; a motorcycle is a small, light, and difficult-to-see object in heavy traffic.

Riders of really big bikes, whose engines have more than a thousand cubic centimeters and may develop more horsepower than a light car, say there is nothing like them for speed, comfort, and the pure joy of movement. But a tiny Yamaha or Honda 50 will get you around, and at far less cost than a car. Mopeds, which can usually be pedaled to start them up or if the motor fails for some reason, get fantastic mileage. They require no driver's license, can be parked in bicycle racks or on the sidewalk, and will keep up with street traffic. They are generally user-repairable. Their operating costs are around a penny a mile. Such light bikes are safer than scooters, which were developed in Italy for dodging through foot traffic—they're very maneuverable but have small wheels and high motors and are thus not so stable.

Once you are an experienced rider, you can not only borrow cycles but also rent them, if you need transportation briefly or in a distant city.

b. Be a good passenger. The rider of a motorcycle steers and controls it by small movements that redistribute the weight slightly. As a passenger, you should not try to anticipate the movements or "help" steer. Keep your feet on the pegs and keep your body like a rigid part of the bike, your weight squarely on the saddle, with as little wiggling around as possible. Hang on tight to the rider or the hand grip; a hunched-over posture may be the most comfortable on long rides. (Frequent rest stops are a good idea in cars, and even better on bikes.) Wear shoes and heavy clothing for protection against the wind and in case of a spill. Women should not let long hair loose—it will fly up around their faces and may flick dangerously across the driver's face as well. For safety, passenger as well as rider should wear good crash helmets. It's hard and distracting to talk on a bike; so develop signals for stopping, warning of cops, giving road directions, and so on.

B. Travel by muscle power.

1. Try bicycles.

Though some misguided souls still regard them as kid stuff, bicycles have outsold cars in the United States since 1973, and their place in our national life will surely continue to grow. The days of driving around the corner for a loaf of bread are over, and for many short trips the bicycle is becoming an increasingly common replacement for the car. This is true, astonishingly enough, even in places like New York City, as well as in small cities and towns; many people's lives are organized so that most of the trips they make daily are less than a mile or so. This is easy range for a bicyclist, even if he or she is totally out of shape, which few regular bicyclists are, since riding not only develops your leg muscles but also gives your heart and lungs a workout.

For the rest of the world, bicycles are a prime smog-free means of adult transportation. In some compact cities like Amsterdam, they not only outnumber cars, but are faster, easier, and incredibly cheaper as a way to get around.

The best bikes are made of very light metal. You can pick one up with one hand and hoist it on your shoulder; so you can easily carry it up steps, into buildings, and so on. Two designs now predominate: "mountain bikes," which are fine for riding on pot-holed streets, and touring bikes, meant for long-distance and high-speed riding on roads.

Most bikes have gearshifts (and usually hand brakes instead of coaster brakes). In flat places, a three-speed shift is enough. Where it's hillier, you may want a ten-speed bike, which will get you up a steep hill with ease and allow you to adjust your pedaling to the terrain: You get the farthest with the least work if you keep your pedaling rate even. These are the bikes favored by the cycle enthusiasts you see zooming around in parks or on country roads. They're magnificent, colorful machines. Since a good bike should last you forever, the cost per month is still very low even for a seemingly expensive model. But a three-speed with coaster brake is the best and easiest-to-ride bicycle to start with, and usually fine for commuting.

Bikes need very few repairs. (In taking them apart, some axle and pedal nuts unscrew "backward.") You can easily fix everything except gearshift problems, and even these are cheap to have fixed in a shop. Buy yourself a bike-fixing guidebook, and you will spend virtually nothing on repairs—a pleasant change from car ownership. Oil everything about once a month, except ball bearings, which should be coated with grease every few months. If the chain picks up dirt, take it off and soak it in oil.

Some people prefer to ride an old and beat-up bike because it is less likely to be stolen. There are plenty of car thieves around, of course, but stealing a bike is easy work for anybody with a bolt cutter that can nip off your chain and lock. Even the fantastic new locks can be defeated by a well-equipped thief, so removable wheels and seats are available to make your bike less attractive (but always lock all wheels and seat to the frame). Police in smaller cities have a good record of recovering stolen bikes that have been previously registered with them, but you're still wise to keep your bike inside, especially at night, or at least out of sight of passersby. Europeans have ingenious hooks or pulley systems that suspend bikes by their front wheels in hallways or other unused corners; you can probably find a safe convenient place by adopting this approach.

Racks can be bought that clamp onto car bumpers and support a bike; you can make such a rack with a few boards and bolts. It gives you a drive-then-ride flexibility that can be very useful if you have a parking problem near your job. Folding bikes also exist that fit into a car trunk or a closet.

There's a good secondhand market in bikes, especially on the bulletin boards around colleges and universities, where thousands of students own bikes and sell them when they leave town. Bike dealers often have used bikes, though not so cheap. Sears sells solid three-speed jobs for a reasonable price; so if you can't do better than their price secondhand, get one of those. For many years I have ridden an old Sears bike that is plain and durable, and doesn't look as much worth stealing as one of those fancy Italian models. It also has handlebars designed for upright riding, rather than the curved-down handles, which give more leg power but require you to lean forward.

You may feel that bicycles are all very well, but how do you haul anything with them, and what do you do about children? You'd be surprised what can be carried on a bicycle. In European cites you may see a man balancing a heavy load on what seems a frail bicycle. But actually a bike can support a hundred pounds in addition to the rider. And for a small child, you can bolt a seat on the back, complete with a safety belt. These cost only a couple of dollars, and kids love them. If you also have a carrying basket on the front, you'll be able to haul at least one bag of groceries. Baskets, big enough to hold four bags of groceries, are used on downtown delivery-service bicycles, if you really need hauling capacity! Bike stores, too, sell backpack bags for carrying books, clothes, lunch, and other small items.

In many cities you're required to have a bell or horn in order to get licensed. Bells are best because horns' rubber bulbs are soon torn off. It's a good idea to register your bike (the fee is usually nominal) as insurance against theft. Real insurance can be bought, but it's expensive.

Even if you lose a bike to thieves once in a while, you'll still be saving money. After I had my Sears bike for two years, for example, I calculated that compared to taking the bus to work I had saved five times what the bike cost me (not to mention health benefits, saving on parking fees or tickets, etc.). At this rate I could have the bike stolen twice a year and still be ahead.

A couple of safety notes: Although it may make you feel like a truck-driver at first, wear a sturdy bicyclist's helmet. Even in a minor spill your head can easily strike the ground (or a nearby car) with enough force to fracture your skull, merely by the action of gravity. Since car drivers sometimes don't notice bicycles as fellow occupants of the public streets, you could even get into an accident where you get banged against a car or thrown from your bike. In any such encounter, a helmet greatly increases your chances of coming through with only minor injury. (You should always ride defensively, of course, just as you drive a car, only more so—never get into a position of depending on a car driver seeing you. Be aware that there are drivers who maliciously threaten bicyclists for the fun of it. This is a form of criminal assault, and if you have evidence and witnesses to prosecute such a driver, you will be doing every rider a great service.) If you ride at night, get a light that straps onto your leg and moves up and down as you pedal—calling attention to your position better than a fixed light. They're also small enough to fit in a pocket, so they can't be stolen. A white reflector pointing forward or a headlight is also an important safety precaution, along with reflectors on the wheels (making you visible from the side). Keep tires inflated to the pressure called for on the sidewall; low pressure makes a bike harder to pedal, and too much makes it bouncy and gives a less firm grip on the road. In rain or snow, you'll need a snugly fitting coat, parka or poncho, and gloves.

The real triumph for the bike rider comes during rush hour, when the cars are stalled in long tangled lines, or crawling bumper to bumper down crowded streets, looking for parking spots. Then you zip along freely, watching for drivers who open car doors without looking back, between and around cars. At such times the bicyclist gets home faster than the car driver, and it doesn't cost anything. Nor does the bicyclist worry about parking spaces, parking tickets, driver's licenses, gas shortages, hubcap thieves, or people who like to scratch automobiles' shiny paint.

A postscript on kids' bikes. The balloon-tired, low-framed, small-wheeled, big-seated bikes are strictly toys, as your child will soon discover if he or she tries to follow you for more than five or six blocks on your full-sized bicycle. With their chrome, fancy upholstery, and stick-type gearshifts, they are really just junior car substitutes, useful only for messing around on the block. They are also tippier than regular bikes. If you want your kids to be able to go anywhere, get them real bikes.

A child's first bike should have a coaster brake, which is easier to learn to use than hand-operated brakes, where braking more strongly in the front wheel than the rear one can give you a spill.

2. Try walking.

Dedicated walkers make up a kind of secret society, and if you meet some members they will tell you their favorite haunts. Meanwhile you can start out simply by walking to a few of the places you usually go to by car or bus. Then the next time you go, try a slightly different route. You'll probably be surprised at all the things you notice. Don't be in a hurry. Do your first walking when you can afford to stroll and loll a little, so that you don't resent the fact that it takes longer to "get somewhere" than if you were on wheels.

Check out your own "walking range." If your present comfortable range is only a couple of blocks, extend it little by little. In countries with better public health (which means most of the industrialized world), people normally walk distances up to a mile every day.

Then look around to see if there aren't some really fascinating parts of your city where you've never been on foot before. Try to find a foreign neighborhood that has interesting stores and people. Or look in your parks for pleasant places you've never been. Is there an arboretum, or garden for exotic plants? Is there a lake you can walk around? Is there a beach or river you can walk along? Check out local newspaper columns or books that give pointers on interesting nearby walks.

After a while, you'll probably realize that you have your own special style of walking. Some people walk fast; some walk slow. Some stop a lot; some keep going. Some walkers like best to walk in the rain, or at night, or with their dogs. Some only like to walk where there are trees or water. Some find "nature walks" dull and walk only on busy city streets. You'll never discover your own style unless you try out the different possibilities.

The point of walking is to give you pleasure. It's what a philosopher might call "activity in accord with true virtue"—the virtue of using your body for what it evolved for. With our American concentration on "practicality," we have come to think of walking only as a means to an end—the end being to get somewhere, whether we know why or not. But walking is also an end itself: the enjoyment of your body's potentialities.

Brisk walking is also one of the best forms of all-around exercise. It tones up your body, without putting severe strain on joints or ligaments, as running can do, and it's especially good for tired backs. Walking briskly only half an hour three days a week is good insurance against heart attacks, and reduces your cholesterol level. See whether you can get in this walking time as you run errands—this may help you feel you are not "wasting time." Walking may also help your appetite for wholesome foods and aids in weight control. It develops your breathing. (Many city people take very shallow breaths—which is perhaps understandable considering the quality of their air.)

In short, even if you have a car, make a point of walking whenever and wherever you can.

C. Travel where cars don't usually go.

Getting out of town once in a while is refreshing to the spirit; even if you don't have any money, you don't have to feel permanently stuck where you are. You can't expect to travel in the middle-class way without a great deal of cash. But—especially if you're by yourself—you can travel light and travel far. The secret is to provide your necessities outside of hotels, motels, restaurants, and so on. If you are traveling by car or truck or camper, arrange to sleep in it. Take along a stove to cook on and try to eat restaurant or fast food only for special occasions. Use state and national park campgrounds occasionally—plan your route so that you hit one when you need to take a bath and do the wash. Plan your route to avoid interstate highways as much as possible—find the old roads that wind around through interesting little towns.

1. Try the train.

Air travel is heavily subsidized and is, unfortunately, more convenient for long trips than the train. In time, our train system will have to be restored, because trains consume far less energy and money for all except very long trips. Amtrak is a feeble attempt in this direction, hamstrung by foot-dragging incompetence from the railroads that actually operate the trains. Probably a whole new train system, using novel technology such as magnetic-suspension, linear-motor trains now being built in Japan, will ultimately be adopted. Meanwhile, you can sometimes find a train going where you want to go, and if getting there on time is not too important to you, give it a try. Be sure to bring along sandwich makings, fruit, and other food to keep eating expenses down.

2. Try long-distance buses.

Greyhound and other bus lines reach most places in the country, and they are cheap. Long-line buses now have more spacious seating than airplanes, clean restrooms, and non-smoking sections; they provide a soft, comfortable ride and bus stations are usually in convenient central locations. Take along food, since most places where buses stop are greasy spoons. In planning a bus trip, find out whether there are express buses to where you want to go—they make far fewer stops and are usually bigger. You can stop off repeatedly on a bus ticket; so it can be a fun way to travel if you want to see some places along the route.

A great alternative to Greyhound service is the Greentortoise Adventure Bus travel. Like their motto, "Arrive inspired, not dog tired," the Greentortoise provides clean, comfortable, and fun busing—often they stop for communally cooked meals, a dip in the creek, or a long sauna. The buses convert from two tables, padded benches, and back bunk into bunks for all, so that everyone brings a sleeping bag and stretches out for a comfortable night sleep. Although Greentortoise is based in San Francisco, it has main routes up and down the west coast, to Yosemite, Yellowstone, the Baja peninsula, Alaska, and even to the East coast. This is not for the pampered traveler! Greentortoise is adventurous travel for those who want to pay less and enjoy the trip more—and get friendly with those they're traveling with. For more information, call 1-800-227-4766.

3. Try hitchhiking and bicycling.

Hitchhiking is, of course, the cheapest and in some ways the most interesting way to travel; so it is unfortunate that it has gotten increasingly dangerous in the U.S. With a pack on your back and a sleeping bag, you can be as footloose and fancy-free as it's possible for a human being to be. And if you have time, bicycling is a healthy and exciting way to travel; you won't go so far, but you'll see more and learn more. In the words of a wise old geographer, Carl Sauer, "Locomotion should be slow, the slower the better; and should be often interrupted by leisurely halts to sit on vantage points and stop at question marks."

4. Try a drive-away car.

If you have a driver's license and seem responsible, you can often get cars from a drive-away agency (see the Yellow Pages or ads in newspapers). Sometimes you have to pay for the gas, but often not. Ask about the insurance situation. This can be the fastest cheap way to get from one major city to another.

5. Try air courier travel.

Companies need passengers to accompany packages to places all over the world, and so offer anyone over eighteen an opportunity to fly at a greatly reduced fare. The packages take the place of your luggage; so while your own baggage may be limited, this gives you the chance to go to places you never could have afforded to go before: Paris for $99, or Hong Kong, Madrid, London, Sydney, Rio de Janeiro, and so on. For the full details on courier companies, telephone numbers, and flight destinations, write for the *Courier Air Travel Handbook*, published by Thunderbird Press. To order a copy, call 1-800-345-0096 or send a check or money order for $10.70 (which includes shipping and handling) to Thunderbird Press, 5930-10 W. Greenway Rd., Suite 112 N, Glendale, AZ 85306.

D. Try unconventional places to stay.

Taking a conventional vacation may cost so much that you spend the rest of the year recovering from it financially. This tends to cast a pall over the whole operation. So the problem for most people is to find ways to get out of their usual surroundings and still spend no more money that they would if they stayed home—or maybe less. Well, there are ways.

1. Try camping.

There are many public camping grounds in this country, especially in the West. Those in the state and national parks have two disadvantages: They cost money and are crowded, with the camping spots strictly regulated and jammed together. In many, advanced reservations are essential, and in some especially popular places, such as the Grand Canyon, these are given out by lottery! There is actually less privacy in such campgrounds than at home. And they are sometimes noisier because people run transistor radios, get drunk and boisterous, and generally ruin any wilderness feeling in the park.

Your best bet, therefore, is in the national forests, where camping away from the roads is usually permitted anywhere you can find a suitable site, and the only regulations concern fire permits—which are altogether reasonable and may help keep some inexperienced camper from burning down half a county. (You'll do your cooking on a portable stove anyway, and burning scarce wood is not advisable ecologically; so you'll seldom want a fire permit.) Detailed maps showing established campsites with toilet and water facilities are available from National Forest Service offices in Washington and in many other cities, and at forests' headquarters. These maps also show the many dirt roads and trails that lead off into remote regions where only hardier backpackers penetrate—and where you will be free of the clusters of pickup campers, generator rigs, and other perils that infect popular campgrounds.

Astonishingly enough, walking about a mile is plenty to get away from such "campers," and may well bring you to some idyllic lake, meadow, stream bank, or other pleasant spot. Your best plan is to buy the U.S. Geological Survey "quadrangle" map of the general area you're interested in; study the dirt roads that lead into the wilderness in interesting directions. Be willing to use up some time exploring an area; if you get to know it, you may find places you want to come back to next year, and the year after that. Your map will also enable you to strike out across country to campsites further away from the roads, and to other points of interest—lookouts, hot springs, etc.

There is something exhilarating about carrying everything you need for a week on your own back and being free to go wherever your feet take you. But for such a venture you need proper equipment and some experience in overnight camping. It's best to borrow the equipment for your first try: You may not like it. The minimum you need for fair weather is a backpack to carry stuff, sleeping bag and a waterproof ground cloth to go under it, food (sporting-goods stores or mountain shops carry dehydrated types), a cooking pot and spoon, compact portable stove, matches, compass and map, a canteen, insect repellent, and a strong knife. You may also want to take along some luxuries, like a fishing line and hooks, a few band-aids, a fork. Take a complete change of clothes, including fresh socks. A broad-brimmed hat and sun-screen preparations will prevent sunburn. Remember that temperatures outdoors can plummet at night and get very high at midday. If showers are likely, a thin poncho can cover you and your gear. If rain is possible at night, take a tarpaulin to suspend over your sleeping bag. (A backpacking-weight tent is, of course, a lovely luxury in bad weather.)

It is surprisingly easy to get lost when you are a beginning hiker. Learn to rely on your map and check your bearings frequently. Better yet, go with experienced hikers and learn their tricks. Living outdoors is invigorating, but if you don't learn how to do it right, you will wear yourself out and irritate everybody around you. The great thing about camping is the utter lassitude that settles over you once you have laid out your camp—and you want to be able to enjoy that to the fullest.

A pleasant variation on camping by car or on foot is the boat trip, which can take you through country literally inaccessible by any other means and often extraordinarily lovely (sometimes, too, horribly polluted). For this, of course, you have to build or rent or borrow or buy some kind of small boat, and make sure (by talking with experienced boaters) that it will serve on the waters you plan to travel on—some small lakes can get very rough, and even small rivers can have tricky rapids. Special needs for boat living are: ways to keep sleeping bags and other dry gear dry despite splashing; cover from the sun's heat (big hats, tarps); a waterproof container for matches; life preservers. On some river banks, it's very hard to find sleeping spots; it helps to have a boat large enough to sleep on comfortably if need be. Tie up along the bank; don't count on just drifting. You'll also need paddles, oars, sail, or motor. Learn the essentials of water safety, and abide by them. On navigated bodies of water, learn the routes of the barges, freighters, or other heavy traffic before you get into any situation that could be disastrous.

2. Try exchanging your car for a van.

Since vans get low mileage, you might be able to make a deal with a friend for a couple of weeks. Few restrictions now exist to prevent you from stopping and sleeping in a van near beaches, lakes, and other attractive spots.

3. Try exchanging houses.

You can sometimes arrange to switch houses with friends who live in nearby towns or in the country, thus giving both sides a change of environment. It's also possible to do this with strangers, usually by placing an ad in some publication read by the kind of people you'd like to exchange with, or in the local paper of the place you want to go. Be prepared to furnish good references.

In an exchange vacation you may be able to get near a beach, river, forest, or some other naturally pleasant place; you might get to live in a city you've always wanted to visit; you might live in a houseboat, or just on the other side of town. In any case, it's a change—but without all the hassle of picking up household bag and baggage, and without the expenditure of energy involved in keeping a pack of children on the move. It's the next best thing to the old pattern of a family cabin owned by rich relatives.

4. Try work vacations.

Young people, especially, can sometimes arrange to work at ranches, orchards, resorts, and other establishments that have a heavy need for seasonal help. The best way to find such possibilities is through personal contacts—parents, friends, relatives—but employment agencies and ads sometimes help, and you can also talk to people in ski-equipment stores, for example, if you want to spend some time working in the mountains during the ski season. If such inquiries don't turn up anything, just go to the area well before the season you're interested in, and nose around, asking advice from the permanent residents. "Eco-tourism" arrangements are developing, where you travel to another culture and do ecologically useful work; check ads in environmental magazines.

When you drive, especially on vacations or other leisurely trips, try to explore back roads rather than sticking to interstate highways. You will discover interesting little towns, see a lot of scenery that's usually far more interesting than the built-up areas along major routes, and get some sense of how people live in nonurban settings. You will also find eating and lodging cheaper off the main routes.

5. Try hostels.

Although the hostel movement is not as well-developed in the U.S. as in Europe, there are still a surprising number of hostels available (also in Canada). These are generally stripped-down accommodations offering a bed, toilet and bath facilities, sheets if you have no sleeping bag, and sometimes shared cooking facilities, for a very low cost. Hostels are often run by YMCAs or similar organizations, but some are privately operated. They can be found in cities and in beautiful rural settings, surrounded by forests, beaches, and hiking areas. While some are sexually segregated or feature restrictions, others offer family rooms, pleasant communal living rooms with fireplaces, and are generally looser now about who sleeps where and with whom. A greater variety of people use hostels now than in earlier times, when their clientele was mainly penniless students on backpacking tours. For further information: American Youth Hostels, Building 240, Fort Mason, San Francisco, CA 94123 (phone number 415-771-7277).

6. Always bring a sleeping bag.

The sleeping bag or bedroll is an invention of far greater implications than you might guess. It liberates you from the idea of bed, the nest, as a permanent structure to which you must return every night; it makes the whole world a possible sleeping place. With your bag strapped to your back, on your bicycle rack, or thrown into the trunk of your car, you can camp anywhere: at friends' houses, in parks, in the country, in your car, at the beach—in short, anyplace where the police leave you alone.

Moreover, getting children used to sleeping bags makes them far more portable than children used to sleeping only in cribs or beds. You can take them with you to parties, on visits, on long drives: as long as they're in their familiar bag, they'll be able to sleep cozily.

There are many forms and qualities of sleeping bag: the "mummy" bag, GI and other; the standard bag, which can be zipped onto another one to make a bag big enough for two people, and can also be used unzipped as a quilt; the double-size bag. The cheapest and easiest to get are made of heavy cotton and filled with synthetic stuffing. These cost less than a good quilt. They are all right for indoor use or warm, dry weather. But if the temperature goes much below fifty degrees, you'll be cold, and if they get wet and soggy, you'll really be uncomfortable. Any bag you plan to use outdoors should have an inner weather flap along the zipper to keep out drafts.

The best sleeping bags are filled with goose down and covered with (very light) nylon or (heavier but sturdier) a super-tight-weave cotton cloth. Some good bags also now have a thin sheet of plastic foam, whose air bubbles make excellent insulation. Because a down bag loses its insulating value when wet (and can be quite hard to dry out), some people prefer synthetic bags, even though they are not quite so warm; they maintain their insulating qualities even when soaked, and dry out readily. You can find descriptions of really good bags in the catalogs of expedition outfitters such as Recreational Equipment, Inc. (a co-op that gives out straight information and also a dividend at year's end in Sumner, WA 98352-0001; customer service phone number 800-828-5533), the Eddie Bauer Company (Box 3700, Seattle, WA 98124), and Sierra Designs (2039 Fourth Street, Berkeley, CA 94710). A good bag costs money, but if you can afford a down bag, it's a smart investment and should last a long time if you take decent care of it. Most kinds of bags need to be dry-cleaned, not washed, but you can cut down the frequency of cleaning if you use a detachable liner, or pin (or tie) a sheet into the bag.

A down bag "breathes" especially well: as you sleep you give off a lot of water vapor as well as heat, and the down lets this escape. (Don't throw a waterproof tarp over your bag at night—it traps the vapor and will make you colder, not warmer. If it's raining, string the tarp a few inches above the bag, with an air space between. Otherwise you will get drippy and thus clammy.) Remember that sleeping on the ground requires a watertight ground cloth under your bag—without one your bag will suck up moisture from the earth. An inch-and-a-half-thick foam-rubber pad makes a good mattress, but a camping pad of Ensolite is warmer, and waterproof besides.

The best down bags have their seams sewn so that there are no thin patches. If you're going to spend money on a down bag, get one that's made properly.

Camping out in deep snow or at very low temperature is a special problem. Don't try it unless you have proper gear and are with people who really know what they're doing.

7. Bring a portable stove.

If you do a lot of camping or are otherwise on the move, a portable stove can be a blessing and save you a lot of money. (I used to keep mine in a VW camper, but it was easily removable to take to campsites.) The new propane stoves are as easy to use as a stove in a house—but it only costs a few cents to cook a meal on a small backpacking stove using white gas, and about eight or ten times as much to cook it with propane.

If you are going backpacking, you will need a really small, light stove. There is a Swedish model called the Svea that burns white gas, has a self-contained cooking pot, and is reliable. (Practice starting and cleaning it before you go out with it; it's tricky.) Primus makes a good alcohol-burning backpacker's stove. These tiny stoves generate a surprising amount of heat, but you would not want to do regular home cooking on one.

The Coleman brand name is one worth paying attention to; they make better car-camping stoves than anybody else and cheaper than most. However, don't be misled by their expensive "Coleman fuel." The stoves run perfectly well on ordinary white (unleaded) gas, also sometimes called naphtha. The procedure of pumping up the pressure in the tank may seem complicated at first, but it soon gets to be second nature. And unless you do something dumb like trying to pour new fuel into a hot tank attached to a hot stove, they are perfectly safe. (Cool all gas-burning appliances and take them to a safe place for refilling—away from people, tents, clothes, leaves, grass, or anything inflammable.)

White-gas lanterns are also the best kind of intense light where electricity is not available. Their disadvantage compared to kerosene is that they make a constant hissing noise.

Chapter 6.
Find the Best Place to Live.

After the mess made of our cities by redevelopment and "renewal," some planners have finally realized that lively street life is the essence of cities. We have to arrange things so that the streets are interesting and safe, or people won't go into them. When they get the chance they will move out to the suburbs, leaving their old neighborhoods to rot.

As it happens, interesting streets are also safe streets, because they bring a lot of people out to them. No city can have enough police to patrol everywhere; in the end, a citizen's safety depends on fellow citizens being around, keeping an eye on things, taking a hand if somebody is getting roughed up or robbed, and so on. Neighborhood Watch organizations are a good way to get people cooperating for mutual safety; if one is lacking in your neighborhood, call the police department and find out if they will advise you how to start one.

In looking for a place to live, whether to rent or buy, you should find out what street life is like. Avoid neighborhoods where people turn the streets over to drug dealers and muggers at nightfall. The best streets tend to be a little noisy, a little crowded; you're always running into neighbors and passing the time of day as you go to the store or the bus or subway. Places where people are on foot a lot are better than places where everybody drives. Streets that are full of little shops are livelier and safer than streets occupied by huge stores or by office buildings. Streets with children on them tend to be occupied by people who care about the neighborhood. And streets with trees are generally cooler in summer and more pleasant all year round.

Let's say you have never looked for a place to live before. How to go about it?

Once you have some idea of a couple of neighborhoods you want to consider, do a little exploring. It's best to be able to use a map. But just wander around—on foot, or on a bicycle, or by some other slow-moving way of travel. Use a criss-cross pattern to be sure you don't miss anything. Stick your head into the stores; try to get some feel for "how people treat each other around here." Do they sit on their stoops or porches, do the kids play in the street? Ask people questions—about public transportation, about stores, about the school—whatever concerns you. And above all, ask everybody whether they know of any places for rent.

Give yourself as much time to look as possible, so you can take advantage of informal leads. It takes weeks of steady looking to find anything you'll really like.

The best deals in housing are always gotten by word of mouth. You hear from relatives or friends that a good place is going to be vacant. Or you're talking to a storekeeper and he or she mentions that a relative has a place for rent.

Places advertised in the newspaper or listed with realtors may be all right, but they will usually be more expensive and not as satisfactory as things you hear of by word of mouth. There's another reason to try to find places directly: Owners who advertise tend to treat their properties as businesses; so they add in all their expenses, may have tax lawyers and other expensive overhead, and end up charging more for a place than a small landlord does. Watch for "For Rent" signs as you walk—these are usually used by small owners, or by people who rent out part of their building and live in it too.

Be careful of landlords or landladies who live there. They tend to keep their places in good repair, which is an advantage, but they also tend to be nosy, which is very unpleasant for tenants. Some old people, who haven't yet realized the sexual revolution that has taken place since World War II, will even object to overnight visits from women friends or men friends or just friends—though this is now permitted even in college dormitories! Best of all seems to be an owner who is retired and lives out of town, but who comes around occasionally to check on the building or fix things.

Always pay your rent by check (so you can prove you paid by showing a copy of the canceled check) even if the owner offers to give you a receipt.

If existing apartments do not fit your tastes or budget, you can live in places like lofts, warehouses, or former stores—which artists and others have been converting to dwellings in many of our central cities. It takes some competence in carpentry, plumbing, and wiring—but it can get you space, convenience, and style.

A. Buying a home.

In the late seventies, houses (and other real estate) became so expensive that relatively few people are now likely to generate the down payment and income required to buy one. Buying a house has become possible mainly for those folks who already have one that has risen in cash value, so they can sell it and then put the money into another house. This situation is already forcing people to consider purchasing houses jointly, usually by forming a mini-corporation for that purpose. If you find yourself in a position to buy (perhaps a condominium), here are the elementary facts about it (but also discuss the process at length with friends who have done it).

Real-estate agents work for the *seller*, not you; so when you go to an agent's office and say you'd like help in finding a house, keep in mind that the agent's friendliness has a perfectly business-like basis: He or she makes that juicy commission only if you can be persuaded to buy. A competent agent can help you calculate what effect buying a house at a given price will have on your tax situation; can tell you how to verify the property taxes that have been paid on the property (but generally *not* what taxes may rise to once you have bought the property, usually much more than was listed on the tax rolls before the sale); and how different methods of financing will affect your payments. Financing is extremely important, because a small difference in interest percentage (or "points," interest paid in advance to persuade the lender to give you the loan) can make a serious difference in monthly outlays. It is even more important if you stay in the house for more than a few years and pay off a substantial part of the mortgage. (Generally, by the way, there are interest penalties if you sell within five years. For that and other reasons, such as loss of your "closing costs," you should not buy a dwelling if you don't plan to remain in it for a long time.)

In the early years of a mortgage you are paying almost nothing but interest charges, and building up a very small "equity" in the property. (After a few years, your mortgage may allow you to pay off the principle—the amount you still owe—faster. This can save you more in the long run than you lose by foregoing the full tax deduction.) Home ownership is generally advantageous from a tax standpoint, since you can deduct all interest charges from your income at tax time. (It is mainly this tax policy, really a subsidy of owners by renters, and not some mysterious propensity toward house ownership in the American heart, which has made house ownership so common in this country.)

You must, of course, maintain a house after you buy it, and this takes considerable time, money, and work. It helps to be handy with tools and mechanical matters generally, and to enjoy spending a certain portion of your free time fixing up your abode; if you don't, a house can become a real burden.

Stay away from "land contracts"—widely used in the Chicago area and elsewhere—which soak you with enormous interest charges, make you vulnerable to instant foreclosures, and leave you without the advantages of FHA guarantees. Study the situation carefully. Check with the city to find out whether a highway is planned to go through your property or nearby. Check the schools, the street lighting at night, the garbage, and other public services. Look into the tax bill— don't take the realtor's word for it (call the assessor's office). Before you sign anything, talk to your lawyer. (A paper innocently called a "bid," "offer to buy," or "deposit receipt" may really be a contract to buy.) Check the fire-insurance situation. This is now a difficult problem in many central-city areas. Many insurance companies have "red-lined" such areas and refuse to write policies there. The rule here is either get the policy before you sign to buy the house, or (as is usually easier) insert a clause in the house contract that makes it conditional upon your getting insurance. That way the seller's real-estate agent will have to help you get it.

If you already own a house and are thinking of selling it, it is essential to get a tax accountant or tax lawyer to help you. The tax laws provide capital-gains loopholes intended for rich people who sell property and want to keep the money they get from it; here, for a change, little people can usually use the same loopholes—but only if they get expert help.

However, beware of relying on a real-estate agent for such needs. In fact, you can sell your house yourself through advertisements in the local paper; hire a lawyer to go over the sales contract for a few hundred dollars, instead of the thousands you as a seller would "normally" pay a real-estate agent. It is one of the best-kept secrets of the real-estate game that the 6 percent commission is not sacred or fixed in law; you can negotiate with potential agents, and set either a low commission or a set fee in dollars. Realtors have been in effect skimming an enormous tax off real-estate transactions, and in fact contributing very little that the multiple-listings service (a cheap enterprise to operate) doesn't do. Shop around for a selling agent, if you feel you need one, who will give you a favorable commission or agree to accept a fixed sum.

1. Consider a co-op.

Apartment buildings are not always owned by private or corporate owners. In "condominiums" you buy an apartment (or duplex) from the builder or owner, and contribute to a building operation and maintenance fund that is supposedly managed by you and your fellow owners. (In New York, such apartments are traditionally called "co-op apartments.") Condominiums are being created by many owners of rental properties because they can be sold for very high prices.

But there are also true co-op housing developments—organized, built, and operated by co-operative societies, sometimes newly set up, sometimes offshoots of existing co-ops.

It is hard to get a co-op housing development going, and most recent ones that have succeeded have been managed by experienced co-op housing foundations. For more information, contact Brad Caftel at the National Economic and Law Center, 1950 Addison Street, Berkeley, CA 94705 (phone number

510-548-2600). Although co-ops cannot produce low-cost housing in high-cost central-city areas (only government subsidies can accomplish that), they can build cheaply and well in the surrounding gray areas. Their advantages are that they have no investors who skim off profits; they can build on a scale to take advantage of skillful architectural design; they create a sense of sharing and community among the people who live in them, thus have few vacancies, and have low maintenance, utility, and recreation costs; they build equity for owners and give tax savings over renting; they have lower closing costs and financing costs than ordinary mortgages do; sale is generally easier; and because of co-operative maintenance, they preserve a high value in the property.

Another option is co-housing—like co-ops but with communal areas and activities designed by an architect *and* the people who will live there. From Europe but arriving here. For information write The CoHousing Company, 1250 Addison Street, Berkeley, CA 94702.

2. Check out condominiums.

Apartment renters generally resist the conversion of their buildings to condominiums, since it almost always increases their monthly outlay on housing by a substantial amount. (If you have a lease, you can probably stay until it runs out.) However, as with house ownership, the ownership of a condominium gives you access to the great American tax shelter: the fact that interest payments (which make up most of your monthly payments) are tax-deductible, along with your local property taxes. On balance, therefore, if your income is high enough to be significantly taxable, you might be at least as better (or as well) off after condominium conversion—assuming that you have the necessary down payment and don't have to borrow it too. If your building "goes condo," obtain (with your fellow tenants) an independent engineering report on the structure, its wiring and piping, its heating system, its roof, and so on. As a condominium owner, you will share responsibility for all repairs that may become necessary. The owner of the building should be expected to provide in writing substantial warranties of the building's major components. Have a lawyer working for you (not the owner) in a condominium conversion; the documents are complex, the issues treacherous—far more so than in the ordinary house-buying contract.

Some condominiums are sold before they are built. It is risky to participate in such ventures, for you don't even know what standards of construction will prevail. In an established condominium you can inspect what you're buying—and have a structural engineer or house-inspection service look it over—and see what kind of community you would be getting into. Some condominiums cater to singles who do a lot of partying. Some have families with children; some don't. Some have good, cooperative relationships prevailing; some are hostile. Some may have restrictions on hobbies like ham radios, on pets, or on renting out your unit if you are away. Ask whether the condo board is involved in lawsuits—they could cost you plenty, both emotionally and financially.

Condominiums may be harder to sell than detached houses, and they have not risen in value as fast as houses. Operating costs in condominiums are very often higher than predicted. If your total costs, square foot for square foot, would be nearly as high as those of house owners in the vicinity, it's a bad deal.

But condominiums do offer amenities you would probably have a hard time providing for yourself: pools, saunas, squash courts, golf courses, boat docks. (Often these remain in the hands of the developer, who can and will raise the rent to the condominium owners association.) They may be attractively designed and landscaped—with less cost to you, and no maintenance and gardening duties to perform.

Before you get serious about a condominium, obtain the free booklet *Questions about Condominiums* from the U.S. Department of Housing and Urban Development, Washington, D.C. It explains possible legal pitfalls, dangers posed by unscrupulous developers, and critical financial factors.

In some cities, tenants-in-common ownership has become popular, because it enables people without much money to buy part of a house or apartment building. TICs are attractive, but risky—if one partner goes broke, or leaves, you may get stuck with a share you don't want and have trouble selling.

3. Investigate mobile homes.

At present, few families of average income can afford to buy a house of any kind, and they are therefore turning to mobile homes. Many towns that formerly turned up their noses at mobile homes (or "manufactured homes") are now beginning to allow them on ordinary town lots.

Financing for mobile homes has increasingly come to resemble that for conventional houses, with VA and FHA loans available for 12- to 20-year terms. Construction and fire-safety requirements have been formalized, so that the structures increasingly resemble a cheapened standard house.

People planning to build a house themselves in the country often find it a good idea to live in a mobile home while they're doing it. In town, if you plan to do a serious remodeling job, you might park a trailer in the driveway and live in it while the house is totally torn up. Generally urban trailer "parks" are depressing places, though some of the new ones (which usually have only around 150–175 sites) have trees, green areas, and a spacious feel. Since many parks provide a central recreation area where laundry, playgrounds, and other common facilities are located, they often generate quite a feeling of community. Traffic inside generally moves slowly (if road bumps aren't installed, they should be) and children are safer than on ordinary streets. Check out a possible park on a hot day, however; the expanses of asphalt and close proximity to other people's windows (and radios and TVs) can be hopeless disadvantages.

Although most mobile homes are owner-occupied, there are usually some for rent. There is a brisk market in used mobile homes, which are available for much less than any kind of fixed house. Lot rentals for space to park them on often cost more than the monthly mortgage on the mobile home itself, but vary widely.

4. Make your own Gypsy wagon.

The modern equivalent of the Gypsy wagon is the converted bread or mail truck or school bus, painted in cheerful colors and sporting chimney pipes, stained-glass windows, decorative carved woodwork, carpets, hangings, and all the comforts of home.

Ingenious and restless souls have discovered anew that a moveable house has its advantages. For one thing, it makes it easy to get out into the country for indefinite periods; you aren't hung up with paying a steady city rent. You can rove around visiting your friends, in the country or in the city, without necessarily having to ask them to put you up. (They might like to come out and sleep over in your truck instead.) You're never forced to eat out—your kitchen is always with you. If you find a spot you like—and can find a place to park your rig where the locals won't bother you—you can just stay there for a while. (Offering to pay a little, like a dollar a day, and a friendly attitude will soften most country suspicions.) When you feel like moving on, you move on.

In this era of homelessness (brought on by government neglect of our housing) people of many class backgrounds can find themselves without resources to rent an apartment or even a room, but they may sometimes be able to get a hold of an old truck and make it into a cozy home. If you have a small but regular source of income, you can remain mobile, avoid conflict with police, and have a safe place to store your goods while you pursue jobs.

If you're actually going to live in your rig, you have to make it tolerably comfortable and appealing. Otherwise you'll soon find yourself retreating into a house existence. This means the basic essentials: heat, sleeping place, food-preparing place, washing place, and toilet. Most van-type vehicles are simply tin boxes.

Insulate. Line the inside with insulating board, insulation batting covered with old carpets, or something similar.

Install a stove. The best is a gas space heater that runs on bottled gas; vent the heater exhaust out the roof or side to get rid of fumes. (A cheap kerosene heater isn't much fun in a small space. Never sleep with any kind of oxygen-burning heater going—it could use up all your oxygen and kill you!) Trailer supply houses sell bottled-gas equipment and other things you may not be able to build or find in junked vehicles.

One sizeable bottled-gas tank can feed a heater, a gas hot plate (though a

Coleman or even Sterno will do for light cooking), and a "flash heater" to heat water. Such a heater is, admittedly, a luxury—but it will probably mean the difference between living in your truck and just camping in it. You won't always be parked outside a friend's apartment and able to use their shower.

Put shutters on the windows; this may avoid calling attention to your presence in situations where sleeping in campers or trucks is prohibited.

Mount your water tank sturdily at the highest point on the vehicle, so that the water will flow into heater and faucets. The gas tank can be mounted anywhere outside the living quarters. You'll need a convenient way to climb up to attend to both tanks.

There are many kinds of portable toilets designed for campers and trailers. Aside from the ordinary bucket, the cheapest and simplest are just toilet seats with plastic bags hanging underneath. You seal them up tightly after use, and dispose of them in a garbage can. But there are nowadays various portable toilets that are relatively inexpensive and hold the excrement in a compartment that unhooks and can be carried unobtrusively to a toilet and dumped. (They use a chemical disinfectant and deodorant fluid.) Fancy recreational vehicles, of course, have built-in holding tanks for their toilets, which you have to find a camper discharge connection to empty.

You may want to wire in electric lights from the truck's electric system, but these run down your battery; so kerosene or butane lights are better. You can even get refrigerators that run on butane. For obvious reasons, make sure you have a fire extinguisher.

You can live in smaller vehicles, so long as you arrange them right. People have lived in VW campers for months, and in delivery trucks and station wagons too. A friend of mine (and his big dog) once lived in a VW sedan; he took out the passenger seat and the rear seat, and laid a padded sleeping board the length of the car. (To remove the front seat, you generally must detach some kind of sliding device under it. The back of a rear seat usually comes loose by sliding it up toward the roof, which unhooks it; the seat itself then just pops upward.) By taking out the rear seats in ordinary American cars, you usually get full-length sleeping room, with your legs stretching back into the trunk.

An alternative to curtains (which require rods or strings or wires) is to paint the inside of the glass in back with thinned white paint. This gives a nice glowing light during the daytime and privacy both day and night. Then you need to string just one curtain across at the back of the front seat.

In a really small space you have to keep everything super-compact: a sealable coffee can for a toilet, a sterno or some other small stove, only one pan and one bowl, and so on. But it is amazing how much gear you can cram even into a VW if you have to. Regard it as a challenge to your ingenuity.

B. Apartment hunting.

Sometimes an apartment can seem so appealing when you first walk in that you forget to check it thoroughly to see whether it will really suit you. Here, therefore, is a handy checklist to run down when you're considering an apartment or house.

Space. Most people try to have one room per person—four rooms for a four-person family, and so on. (The strong American preference for this ratio is now causing our rooms to get smaller on the average.) But this standard is hard to find for large families; so members have to double up. Both for biological families and for extended families each member needs a private space for sleeping, entertaining, reading, thinking. But these private spaces can be small (only a bit bigger than a bed) if the common-use areas are spacious— say, a good-sized kitchen and one very large main room (or pair of rooms connected with an archway or sliding doors). The higher the ceilings, the more spacious a place will seem.

Light. Sunlight falling into a room can brighten it up enormously, and give you a place to grow indoor plants. Sunlight is warming to sit or lie in. And if some of your windows look out on trees or a yard of some kind, better still. Skylights are often beautiful, and even if they leak (as they often do) they're a delightful source of additional sun.

Air. Especially in places that get hot in summer, you need cross-ventilation—windows at opposite ends, so that air will move through .

Heating. Check and see if all of the radiators actually work. In many parts of the country, you'll be paying for heat in your rent, so make sure there is some! If there's a gas heater, be sure it's vented, so that it can't asphyxiate you.

Plumbing. There should be a sink in the kitchen; try both hot and cold water faucets. Look under the sink to see if the drain leaks. Go in the bathroom and try the toilet. Turn on the cold and hot water in the basin. Try the faucets in the tub or shower too. You can fix many small plumbing defects, but serious leaks mean trouble, and living without hot water is like camping out all year round.

Security. Everybody gets burglarized sooner or later these days, but you can help make it be later by having a strong door on good hinges, with a proper lock. (You might even want to invest in one of the new pick-proof locks.) There should be a window-locking device on all the windows, especially if they look out on the ground or on fire escapes.

Fire escape. On the second floor or higher, you need another way out if the hallway is in flames—a fire escape or a window out onto a porch roof. If a room is at the end of a long corridor, you might want to tie a heavy escape rope onto a stout hook near a window—and train children to use it if they sleep in that room.

Vermin. Check around for rat turds, stain marks on walls that show where rats or mice have been passing by, cockroaches, and so on. Most central-city areas—and many fancy neighborhoods—harbor these unwelcome visitors. You can get rid of the rats, and most of the cockroaches, but it pays to know if they're there before you move in. Garbage cans should be the snap-top-type, so they're ratproof and dogproof.

Amenities. Many old buildings have pleasant additions that make life nicer. If there's a fireplace, find out whether it works. If there's a roof you can get out onto, that helps in the sticky summertime, and might offer space for gardening. Some big apartment buildings have garbage-disposal chutes, which are handy. In smaller places, a car-parking spot may be included. If there is no shower, and you like one, ask the landlord if he'll pay for the parts if you put it in.

Safety. One of the dangers of old buildings is peeling layers of old paint. Small children eat paint flakes, which give them lead poisoning—leading to mental retardation and other illnesses. Check both walls and floors. Other common dangers are rickety stair railings or porch railings, gas leaks in stoves or heaters, cracked windows whose pieces may fall in onto children, elevator doors that don't work right, and areas that don't have working hall lights. It's also wise to check for places that make it easy for purse snatchers or other unsavory types to hide and pounce on people going in or out.

Chapter 7.
Fix It Up and Furnish It Cheaply.

Your quality of life can often be increased enough to become comfortable, even pleasant, if you can apply some ingenuity to the place where you live. Given that rather few Americans can now afford to buy a house, and that good apartments are becoming rarer and more expensive, it can make a great difference in your life if you can transform a tiny, ugly apartment into one that feels spacious and looks lovely.

Here are some strategies for doing that.

A. Fix up your apartment.

Generally the person who lives in rented places faces a sticky problem in dealing with owners. If you complain and get the owner to fix things up, the result may be a raise in your rent. And if the owner won't fix up and you go to the city health department, which investigates and forces the owner into making repairs, you may find yourself facing an eviction notice. Supposedly protective laws may not be much protection in such cases.

So many tenants tolerate broken plaster, leaky pipes, dirty garbage facilities, missing window panes, and other such problems rather than run the risk of being evicted. After all, even a beat-up house is better than no house at all—or a slightly fixed-up house at a higher rent.

There seems to be only one way to get around this vicious circle, and it won't work with all owners. Some of them evidently like to see people live in bad surroundings. But most are not really crookeder than the rest of us; they're just reacting to tax laws that make it positively desirable to let their buildings rot.

Here's why. First, owners generally make the most out of their money by buying a building, creaming off the depreciation allowance from their income taxes, selling in five years, and then buying another building and doing the same thing all over again. The value of a building doesn't drop very much if it gets run-down, and unless it gets hopelessly dilapidated it can always be rented because of the housing shortage. (If the housing department declares it unfit for human habitation, many owners will just walk away and leave it; there are thousands of such abandoned buildings in any major city.) Second, if an owner makes any visible improvements or any outside improvements that the city finds out about, the building's property taxes will be raised.

You have to approach your landlord or landlady, therefore, with a deal that won't cause tax trouble, and might even make a little more money when the building is sold. Basically, you offer to fix up the place yourself, if the materials needed are provided for you, in return for a written lease that keeps the rent where it is for a significant period (at least a year and if possible two). If you paint a sizable apartment, you are saving the owner in labor costs at least a month's rent. So the owner is ahead, and so are you, since you've got a newly painted place but at the same old rent.

Or suppose there's broken plaster in your walls. To get a plasterer to fix them is expensive and might lead to a hike in the rent. But you can plug up the holes yourself, usually by getting the owner to finance about a dollar's worth of plastering compound.

Generally the owner will be distrustful at first of your ability to carry out such jobs. Tell him or her you can understand this, and that you'd like to do a small job first, like painting the bathroom, to show you want to do it right. Then get the owner in to look at the results, and ask for the paint for the other rooms.

B. Turn waste space into living space.

How can you live better in cramped quarters? We can take some tips from the Japanese, who have learned how to live in more jammed-in conditions than Americans will face for many years, if ever. Most Japanese can't afford to devote any one space to just one function. So they don't have a dining room, of even a stationary table—they store a light table on top of a cabinet and only bring it down for meals. Their walls are lined with storage cabinets—sometimes mounted high enough to keep the floor underneath free. Then what space there is can be used for anything. You can bring out sleeping quilts and any space in the house becomes a bed. You can bring out pillows and any place in the house becomes an area where friends can sit and socialize.

We can also learn from boats, whose designers have become extremely ingenious at compressing things and combining them. In boats, there is a storage place for everything—if there wasn't, things would roll all over the boat in a storm. And the tiny living spaces in boats are enormously appealing.

Sometimes, if you own your house or have a permissive landlord, you can actually change the arrangement of space in your house. Many walls are nonbearing—they don't hold up the roof or the storey above—and can be removed without weakening the structure. Or you can knock the plaster off the studs or make an archway. It makes a house feel comfortable and interesting if you can see more than a few feet into it. This is why a big mirror or a large window makes a small room much more tolerable.

Outside spaces can be rearranged too. You might turn a flat roof into a roof garden or sunbathing area. If you can get a rooftop to yourself, you can construct a little outdoor sleeping shelter. By building a fence out of recycled lumber or driftwood, you can make a small private garden or play yard; sometimes you can enlarge a window into a door to give better access to the outside.

Moving costs money as well as trouble and work, and it disrupts your neighborhood friendships and contacts. It is always better to rearrange your present dwelling rather than move—even if you have to put a little money into it. Beware of moving too often for too little advantage.

C. Decorate to suit yourself.

Once you have finally found a place to live that suits you, and it has at least the bare essentials, how do you make it home?

In our commercialized society people quickly get into a stereotyped pattern of thinking about their houses, and begin to imagine they must fill up their houses with all manner of junk that some ad writer has said will make them happier.

Obviously, you can't be happy following somebody else's guidelines; you have to find your own. And the way to begin this is, simply, take it easy. Instead of hurriedly throwing into a new apartment all the things you could possibly "need," try to concentrate on bringing into it only those things you really love and absolutely must have. Give the new place time to develop its own spirit—don't try to make it look like the last place you lived, or your friends' or parents' houses, or something in a magazine.

When you've taken a new place, go over with nothing but a cushion, and just sit quietly for a while in each room. Look around at its windows, walls, ceilings, floor. Notice how the light falls, and what you see out the windows. Listen to the noises. Feel how the air circulates. Don't be in a hurry to fill it up in your imagination; just concentrate on the spaces and their feel. You should never fight a house, you should fit into it. See if you can judge what the place "wants" you to do with it. Is its light made gruesome by a coat of pea-green paint? Would a little painting of cabinets or door and window trim give some life to the interior and link one room to another? Can you provide special places for the furniture you're bringing in, so that it will feel at home and not crowd you?

It is easiest to make a house express you, and thus suit you, if you take a simple-living approach: We should dominate our goods, and not let our goods dominate us; in arranging dwellings we should strive for elegant simplicity, for lightness, for grace. We should be aesthetically economical—which usually means financially economical too. In the long run it is better to have a few really good things in your house than a hodgepodge of cheap stuff; the good things will serve you better. A simple-living approach should not mean austerity or denying yourself pleasures; it means making sure that your pleasures are really satisfying, and that they are your own, not castoffs from television and magazines.

Real luxury consists in having about you the things you need and love, and nothing that interferes with or cheapens them. If you treat your dwelling with this kind of careful respect, it will repay you with a sense of repose, shelter, and peace.

Here are some ways you might begin inhabiting a new place in good spirit.

Once you have done any painting you have in mind, consider repainting some of your furniture, even if it isn't strictly necessary; a little paint of similar or related colors can make it look like it really belongs there. If the windows have good shapes, you might avoid putting drapes or curtains over them; you could paste on rice paper or other decorative paper, which transmits a soft, delicate light but gives you privacy. If there are places where it would be nice to sit on the floor (like in front of a fireplace, or in a corner), try to find a soft secondhand rug; on it you could also keep some pillows, with covers of cloth whose colors work interestingly in the room. Cover up any bare hanging light bulbs—the cheapest way, and an attractive one, is with big paper-lantern globes you can find in Chinatowns or import stores.

Try to bring into your house reminders of the natural world outside, so that you remember the house is, after all, a part of nature. You may be sick of driftwood or shells, but the world is full of strange leaves, sticks, rocks, moss, and so on; if something strikes you as having some mystery or beauty about it, bring it home.

Don't be afraid of "bare walls." A plain wall, if it's a tolerable color, can be a restful and surprisingly interesting part of your house—no wall is utterly without subtle variations in texture, color, light reflection. Some people like to plaster their walls with magazine-clipping pictures, calendars, posters from travel agencies (which you can often get for free), outrageous newspaper headlines, stolen placards from the streets, and so on. You also need a place for tacking up messages, reminders, unpaid bills, funny or gruesome tidbits. You can easily devote one wall for such a purpose, by putting up either a big sheet of wrapping paper to tape things on, or a piece of plywood or corrugated cardboard to tack things to.

Scrounge or buy cheaply many unusual kinds of coverings for bare floors that can often give a luxurious feel to a run-down apartment. The most sumptuous is outdated carpeting samples from places that specialize in wall-to-wall jobs. They come in squares about eighteen inches on a side, and in many thicknesses, textures, patterns, and colors. You can sew them together in a super-crazy quilt, or you can cut them up into irregular shapes and glue or sew them onto a piece of heavy backing.

Uneven floors, or floors with a lot of cracks in the wood, can be covered with masonite, which is the cheapest possible covering—cheaper even than all but the sleaziest linoleum. But by looking hard you can find rugs and carpeting of passable appearance in thrift shops. If they're small, and not too heavy and stiff, they can be dyed. They can be cut to fit in small rooms, or even laid one on top of another to give a softer surface. If you find an especially beautiful rug, it can be tacked on a wall that's hopelessly cracked or peeling. Burlap, or any other kind of inexpensive cloth, can also be used as a wall covering or hanging.

Japanese tatami mats are the most attractive cheap floor covering, but they wear through easily if you push chairs around on them. They have a good smell, being made of rice straw, and they feel pleasant to the touch when you lie down on them. They are warm to the feet, and absorb dirt less than a rug.

But don't be so sure you need floor coverings. If your place has good wood floors, treasure them! Many old houses have either beautiful patterned hardwood floors or worn softwood board floors. It is worth a lot of work to restore such floors to good condition, for they will be a pleasure to look at and walk on. You can rent big powerful floor sanders from equipment rental places, and then varnish or oil the sanded wood. It's hard, dusty work, but satisfying, and cheaper than anything else you could do with your floor.

Never try to remove old linoleum—it's practically impossible. Cover it up with new linoleum or some other surface.

D. Control the temperature cheaply.

1. Cooling.

Many dwellings are not well-insulated, and in hot weather they get pretty unbearable. For both economic and ecological motives, any habitation that's likely to remain standing for more than ten years is well worth insulating these days. The result will be less heating in cold weather, and a more comfortable dwelling in hot weather, very possibly enabling you to avoid an energy-hogging and health-endangering air conditioner.

Besides, there are other ways of cooling your house. In the Southwest, people use an air cooler mounted at one of the main windows. It ought to be used in the tropical summers of the East Coast and Midwest as well. It is essentially a large cube-shaped box about the size of the lower half of the window, fastened to the house so that air can flow through it into the house. Then inside the box, at the top, a drip system is installed, usually fed by just a garden hose: The hose is connected to several rows of pipes (plastic pipe is cheapest) with rows of tiny holes in them. From these holes the water drips onto some kind of porous matting: the traditional southwestern one is made of aspen fiber, but you can also hang cheesecloth or burlap, string, dense twigs—anything that will let both air and water pass through will work. The excess water is just left to drip down onto the ground. These contraptions will not, of course, cool air as much as an air conditioner, but they help a lot, don't cost anything to speak of, and use virtually no energy.

Sometimes one side of your place will face the sun, and get hot on that side. This can be pleasant and a good source of solar-heating energy in the winter, but for the summer, you need to build an overhang of some kind—check a solar architecture book at your library to figure the proper angle and how far it should go. Shades inside won't help, because once the sun's rays get through the glass, their heat will spread around inside the house. If you can't manage a permanent overhang, put up some kind of bamboo shade or awning over the windows, or paste aluminum foil over the windows on the outside. Epoxy glue or rubber cement will hold pretty well if you clean the glass first and make sure to glue the edges down firmly. Face the shiniest side of the foil toward the sun, so that it reflects better. (Aluminum foil inside the windows will help some, but it still lets the glass get hot and radiate heat into the room.)

Sheet aluminum is excellent roof insulation; in the Sierra foothills, where the summers are ferociously hot, every building has a bright shiny aluminum roof. Aluminum roofing is surprisingly cheap, too. If you can't stand the shine, paint it; the coating won't cut down its heat reflectance much.

It is also possible to make hot weather more tolerable by paying attention to the air circulation in your house, and by having a big fan to help circulate the air when you want it circulated. Houses cool down during the night; therefore, during several hours in the morning, the inside walls and air are cooler than the outside walls and air. So keep your windows shut until the temperatures are about the same inside and outside. Once your house walls and ceilings have heated up thoroughly, it's likely to be hotter inside than in the shade outside, so it's to your advantage to draw the outside air in with a fan. Keep this up through the evening hours, perhaps even after bedtime. (Better yet, go sit outside in the shade, listening to the breeze blow or watching the clouds.)

The way to get a fan to push air through a house is to close all the windows but two: one where the fan is, and one at the other end of the house. Houses differ a lot in their natural air-circulation patterns; two-storey houses are especially tricky. Sometimes you get the best results by the fan in the upstairs room, pointing outward, and opening a first-floor window that's in the shade and not over hot concrete. At any rate, if you point the fan in, remember you have to open something somewhere else so that the air can flow through the house; otherwise the fan only stirs up the air right in front of itself.

Many old houses, and houses built by people who pay proper attention to environment, are laid out so that shade trees protect them from the southern (noonday) and western (afternoon) sun. If you live in a very small house and in a very hot spot, you might consider a Sierra trailer-dwellers' trick: Build a "tree"—an extra aluminum roof over the house, so that the sun's rays can't hit it, and air can circulate. This can be cheaper (and quieter) than buying and running an air conditioner, and of course it keeps off rain; so it might avoid a reroofing job on the house. But try to relate the "extra" roof to the existing roof as a kind of echo—not just a flat platform over it.

As Bernard Rudofsky points out in his fascinating book *Streets for People*, the poorest Italian or North African town has streets that protect people from the sun in a way unknown in our American cities. Sun-filtering lattices and vines cover the Arab market streets; the Japanese use sliding cloth curtains to cut the sun's heat. But Americans just fatalistically accept broiling on hot asphalt and concrete as a natural part of life. We too could build shade-producing arcades like those built by the early Spanish settlers in the Southwest. Short of that, we can put up awnings or lattices made of inexpensive wood strips—in heavy snow country these can be made demountable for winter.

2. Greenhouses and solariums.

If you think greenhouses are only a rural possibility, think again. Even if you are a high-rise dweller, if you have a balcony with southern exposure you could convert it into a greenhouse. If you live in a house, of almost any kind, the chances are that you can add on a greenhouse that will help heat your dwelling and provide you with a place to grow vegetables.

In new construction, architects are slowly becoming smarter about taking advantage of the sun's energy though both "passive" designs (arranging windows, overhangs, and heat-storing masses of concrete or masonry to catch heat when it's needed and keep it out when it isn't) and "active" designs (arrangements that pump heat from one place to another), as well as hybrid designs. But in any remodeling of an old structure, you should consider carefully how to incorporate greenhouse-type features. The essentials: To allow heated air to rise through the house, the greenhouse should be at the lowest possible living level; to store heat efficiently, it must have a strong enough foundation to support not only earth containers for plants but also a concrete floor or row of water-filled barrels. To control hot air movement and buildup, it must have ventilation openings to let outside air enter, and doors into the house living areas that can be closed. To prevent excessive heat in summer, the greenhouse needs shades or overhangs or a deciduous tree, and often a steep angle of the double-glass walls, plus openable vents up high.

Rows of planter boxes, even in a small greenhouse, can support a surprisingly productive vegetable garden. The plants will also help to humidify your air, which is especially healthful in winter.

3. Insulation.

Insulation (and other forms of energy conservation) would enable us to save—and thus in effect produce —far more energy, at much less expense, than we could produce by nuclear technology.

It is relatively easy to calculate the pay-off times of spending X dollars on insulating your ceiling or walls; even at current fuel prices it usually works out to be three to five years. Considering what else you might do with any money you happen to have, this is a sensationally profitable investment. Merely insulating your attic will save about 8 percent in your heating bill. Moreover, tax credits are available to motivate you even further. And some utility companies, finally beginning to see that they can't expect publicly subsidized nuclear power to rescue them, will even come out to look your place over and give you advice. (It will not necessarily be very professional. If a really big job is in prospect, try to find an architect or engineer with substantial solar-design experience.)

Insulation comes in basically two forms: loose and in batts. The loose form is sometimes a spun rock material, which is fireproof, and sometimes recycled paper in shredded form, which has been fire-treated. Unfortunately, the borates that are used to coat the paper particles tend to come off after a while, and the paper shreds will then burn. This is a hazard mainly around electrical connection boxes in the walls and ceilings where heat can build up, or over ceiling lights that are mounted flush. It may be some faint comfort to know that trouble from such sources will almost certainly happen in the first few days after installation; so if your house doesn't catch fire by then, you're probably okay. But the sensible procedure is to build little boxes around these hazard points and keep insulation outside them.

Loose insulating material has the great advantage that it can be blown into already constructed walls. Fiberglass in batt form is fireproof, but can be installed only over ceilings or in walls under construction. Since tiny glass fibers come off the material and can be drawn into your lungs, where they are carcinogenic, you should always wear a mask and minimize your exposure to fiberglass. Don't tear or pull at it any more than necessary, and wear gloves (the fibers can enter your skin and are irritating).

Batt insulation is given ratings according to how much heat it will keep in (or out). The higher the R number, the more insulation value you get. Your city building department can advise you on what level is wise for your climate; if you are planning a sophisticated solar-heating system, find expert solar-experienced people to advise you.

With suitable insulation around the north side of a structure, and large double-glass windows on the south side (with insulating shutters to cover them at night), a house can derive much of its space heating from the sun, especially if the sunlight hits a large mass of concrete, stone, or water (say, rows of metal barrels) after it comes through the glass.

It is as important, in older houses, to seal cracks as it is to insulate ceiling and walls. Install weatherstripping around doors, and repair or replace sills that allow air passage. (A lighted candle or incense stick will show where air is flowing in.) Seal up cracks around doors and windows where they meet the plaster of the walls. If you have a fireplace, make sure the damper shuts tight when it's not in use; if it won't, use a piece of metal to cover the fireplace opening (plywood might catch fire if you put it on before a fire is entirely out).

Double windows, or even just plastic sheeting tacked over the windows, result in remarkable fuel savings. Installing or improving ceiling and wall insulation generally pays for itself very quickly at today's fuel prices. So will insulating shutters, especially over large areas, that you close at night. And, perhaps most important and easiest of all, wear a sweater and get used to an air temperature of around 68°F/20°C during the day (drop it to 55°F/13°C when you go to bed). This is healthier for you, keeps the air from feeling so dry, and saves far more fuel than would seem possible, because those last few degrees of warmth are "bought" at a very high price in energy. The same is true of air-conditioner cooling; try to get used to a 78°/25°C level.

E. Introduce water sports.

1. Put in a Japanese-style tub.

Most Americans conceive of bathing as a solitary occupation, like praying, aimed at making you as nearly antiseptic as possible. This is nonsense, because our skin is normally inhabited by millions of microbes. In fact, since skin is rather like bark (soft and porous), scrubbing its surface only reveals a fresh crop of microbes further down. The body is marvelously equipped to deal with microbes on its surface; tears, for instance, contain antibiotic substances. Too much washing with soap can remove the skin's natural oils, making it dry and stiff, or disrupt its natural acid-base balance, making it a prey for fungi. All you really need is to remove sweat residues and any actual dirt you may have picked up. So the less soap the better. What you mainly need for joyful bathing is plenty of hot water. You also need friends: If warm water is pleasant for one body, the pleasures can rise geometrically when several bodies are added. Unfortunately, the standard American tub will barely accommodate two people. You could bathe in streams or lakes, where the water is often too chilly for much lounging about, or in hot springs or hot baths; or else build your own oversize tub-pool. It ought to be something like three feet deep and perhaps five feet on a side, or round, like many commercially available hot tubs. Build it on solid ground or over a reinforced part of the floor; filled, it will weigh two tons, more than enough to break through an ordinary floor and flood whatever is below.

The Japanese have thought most seriously and poetically about baths. When you arrive at a Japanese home after a long journey, you are first of all offered a bath; the Japanese know that a hot bath (in a deep tub) refreshes the weary spirit and soothes the tired body. The traditional Japanese bathtub is made of fragrant-smelling wood; you scrub with soap and a dipping basin, outside the tub; then after rinsing off the soap, you soak up to your neck.

Most Americans take deep, hot tub baths only when they're sick and on doctor's orders (or in romantic movies, with lots of soap bubbles). But in the seventies a hot-tub craze swept California middle-class households, and in that state you can still buy wood or fiber-glass tubs in a wide range of prices, and with various types of heaters. (One ingenious system hooks up to your regular hot-water heater, and can be further linked with a solar-heat source.) It is important to have a way of covering your tub with an insulating material, to cut down heat loss and thus minimize your water-heating costs.

These hot-tubs have now spread to other areas with warm climates (they are best for outside use), but if you live in a colder place you could still build yourself a smaller Japanese bathtub. (As far as I know, they cannot be bought in this country.) This isn't particularly tricky, except for the heater. Build a box out of two-inch-thick lumber. (It need not be finished lumber; the roughness of sawed timber feels good.) You will have to design it carefully and put it together with large screws ("lag screws") because the weight of that much water will push apart a box that's just nailed together. Seal the cracks with caulking compound. It'll probably still leak a little; and because you will need to drain it, put it in a laundry room, converted garage, or other room with a waterproof floor and a drain.

You can connect it into your house hot-water system by use of a heat-exchanger and pump, or you simply buy an old water heater and let the hot water recirculate through it naturally. (For this system the heater hot-water outlet must be lower than the tub; otherwise you must install a small pump to circulate the water.) The heater thermostat may require some adjustment to avoid making the water too hot (most people like it at less than 110°F/43°C).

As with any bath system in which the water is retained, you must take health precautions against waterborne bacteria. Swimming-pool supply houses can provide you with a chlorine compound. And from time to time the tub needs draining and scrubbing.

After the kitchen, the bathroom is the most important room in the house. It's ridiculous that bathrooms are built hardly bigger than closets; see if yours might be enlarged by knocking out a wall, or perhaps adding a big bay-window alcove. A proper bathroom not only has a comfortable, deep tub (and a shower, if you like showers) but should also have plenty of room for taking off clothes and for sitting around and reading; it should have a big window that looks out on trees and green things, or a view of some kind. An ample supply of clothes hooks (which can be simply short dowel rods glued into a board) makes it easier for several people to use the bathing facilities at once; a good supply of large towels is also desirable. (You can buy toweling fabric by the yard.) A bathroom should have a slatted wooden bench, comfortable for damp bodies to sit or lie on, and big enough to double as a massage table. Make sure there are some plants—ferns generally love the moist air of a bath area. There's no reason for a bathroom to be all white enamel and antiseptic like a hospital. (But avoid colored or flower-printed toilet paper; it may cause inflammation.) If you wish to bar commercialism in your bathroom, remove the wrappers from soap and toilet paper before you store them. Whether you prefer natural wood or brightly painted walls, a soft rug or a cool smooth floor, consider the bathroom a meditation chamber. From water came all animal life on earth; the act of taking a bath is not only to get clean, but to restore contact with our primal element. A bath ought to be a joyous occasion.

2. Install a shower.

Although a lot of old houses have only bathtubs, with a little ingenuity you can always add a shower. You need two things: a spray for the water, and a curtain to keep it from going all over the bathroom. Here's the simplest and cheapest way to do it.

Find some kind of ring-shaped or squarish tubing for the shower-curtain rod. A hula-hoop will work; so will old water pipes. The opening needs to be at least thirty inches across, so that there's enough room inside. Now look around your bathroom and see how the rod can be suspended. The easiest way is usually to use wires running to screw eyes set into the ceiling and the wall next to the tub. That way you can usually suspend the rod at four points, which will make it hang firmly.

Now find or buy some kind of curtain. The plastic kind sold in dime stores work fine, and you need two of them to go all the way around. This is one use where nylon fabric is a good idea, because it sheds water and dries quickly. Be sure to make the curtain is big enough to go entirely around you as you stand in the tub—you must keep the wall and floor from getting soaked.

Plumbing-supply, hardware, and variety stores sell various spray attachments. The main consideration is whether the attachment will fit the spout on your tub. The rubber press-on type will jump off some spouts. Take along a little drawing of your spout, and make sure you can return the attachment if it doesn't stay on.

Some sprays come with a bracket that screws into the wall at neck level—you can hang the spray head there for a shower, or take it down to spray yourself in the tub. Other kinds you'll need to suspend from a wire or a homemade bracket.

Of course you can also let your imagination run wild in a shower. Since bathing is such a pleasant thing, make your shower curtain big enough for two people to get inside. Embroider designs on the curtain. Build a translucent portable shower stall of fiberglass. The spray fitting can be a complicated water sculpture made of gracefully bent flexible copper tubing, or plastic transparent tubing, or who knows what. You can arrange it to spray you from above, below, and sideways. . . .

F. Furnish it innovatively.

1. Sleep well, but creatively.

The "bedroom" is a waste of scarce space. It is generally used only about eight hours out of twenty-four; its floor space is generally far too big to be justifiable in terms of how much use is actually made of it. The only time a bedroom is really worthwhile is when it is used as one person's private space—where he or she retreats to read quietly, watch TV, talk to a friend, make love, sew, and so on. This kind of multiple-use bedroom makes sense in large households, where privacy is hard to come by. But even then relatively little space is required.

a. Try sleeping alcoves. Look back on two contrasting traditions. In the old Dutch farmhouses, beds were built into the walls as special alcoves, separated from the main room (in which cooking, eating, visiting, and everything else went on) by a curtain that could be drawn when you went to bed. These alcoves seldom had windows to the outdoors, because glass was very expensive; modern counterparts usually do, partly for ventilation and partly because it's nice to be able to lie in bed and look out. To save further space, the bed was not low like ours, but high enough that cupboards or drawers could fit under it. Thus both sleeping space and clothes-storage space were provided in an area of about four by six feet; even a modern bedroom is around ten by twelve feet, plus a closet. Such alcoves can be built with doors, of course, and with a little

strip of floor space along the front where you can stand to dress. Such "room-
ette" bedrooms would, if we had a rational building industry, be available
through a catalog order service; you could build only your main room, with its
kitchen, bathroom, heating, and other facilities, and then bolt on a series of
roomettes around the sides where you wanted them. You can sometimes adapt
this approach to existing bedrooms by constructing an alcove around your
bed. It should have a lower ceiling than the rest of the room, to mark off its
special role (a hanging cloth of some kind will have the same general effect).

   b. Try movable beds. The Japanese have traditionally not had separate
sleeping rooms. They sleep in a bedroll: Mats and quilts are kept in a cabinet
by day and laid out only at night. While this seems to lack privacy to most
older Americans, especially where sex is concerned, societies that have lived in
this manner have evidently developed ways of getting along; some Americans
who live communally have also found that sex is not necessarily always a
private activity.

   Anyone who has done any amount of sleeping-bag living will realize that
this system has many advantages. For instance, so long as the floor is dry
everywhere, you can pick your sleeping spot according to your mood: sometimes near the fireplace; sometimes on the veranda to listen to the rain; sometimes on a couch. Where a number of people are all bedding down in a large
room, you can drift over to be near people you are feeling good about—you're
not tied down to a piece of furniture.

   Curiously, Americans have always been a lot more ingenious about sleeping arrangements in their cabins or summer houses than in their regular houses.
All that's really essential for a sleeping place is a mattress or foam pad of some
kind lying on a firmly supported piece of plywood. (Springs are expensive,
usually bad for your back, and take up space.) Hence beds can be placed
practically anywhere. You can hang them by chains or heavy ropes or wires
from the roof. You can build them as little high-up balconies (surrounded by
curtains if you like). You can make double-deckers or triple-deckers. One
clever friend of mine put his bed over his sink; he realized that any airspace
high over a fixed object like a sink is just going to waste—so he built a two-by-
four frame, nailed up a plywood sheet and a railing, built a little ladder, and
had a bed without wasting any floor space at all.

   In the future more and more people will be doubling up in houses and
apartments. Families with many children have sometimes had three or even
four kids sleep in a double bed. But this system doesn't really let the kids get
the sleep they need, especially if one of them gets sick or is wakeful and keeps
the others awake. The cost of plywood, foam-rubber mattress pads, or recon-
ditioned mattresses is low enough that you can build a bed for everyone. (You
need a piece of five-eighth-inch plywood, two-by-fours for a frame to hold it
up, a piece of one-by-three for a railing, and a mattress.) Often, too, you can
find a corner of your house or apartment that isn't being used, where a bed can

be built—sometimes all you need to support it is some boards nailed into the wall studs. The addition of a skylight can often make a high-up space delightful for a bed-platform.

Beds can sit in alcoves, roll up, fold up against the wall, or go back into a closet like the so-called "in-a-door beds." Or you can have a bed platform that also serves as an eating or studying table or as a workbench.

In short, you need not be trapped by the orthodox idea of a bed. A bed is the nest of leaves or pine needles where you curl up for the night. It can be any place you like, and made in any way you like. It can have any kind of bedclothes you like—from a sleeping bag to a down comforter to the conventional two sheets, two blankets, and a bedspread.

c. Try a water bed. Water beds are interesting, whether you are concerned with backaches, the floating sleep-inducing gentle rocking they give you, or sex. (They are not to everybody's taste in any of these departments; try to get invited to sleep on one for a series of nights before you contemplate buying one, or rent one for a month.) Very expensive, deluxe water beds are being made, but here are the minimum requirements: a strong floor (a water bed weighs up to a ton and a half); a sturdy frame of two-inch lumber, smooth inside and reinforced at the corners (to keep the vinyl bag from stretching and breaking); a thin plastic liner to catch water if the bag should be punctured or spring a leak; and either an insulating pad on top of the bed or an electric heater under it.

Heaters are still the main problems with water beds. Cheap ones are not safe against possibly dangerous short circuits, and they all use a lot of electricity; keeping a ton of water heated up to 85° or 90°F will add plenty to your electric bill. They also (like electric blankets) expose you all night to electromagnetic fields that may pose a health hazard.

A few suppliers offering super-cheap water beds are using too-thin vinyl; it should be twenty mils thick (twenty thousandths of an inch, that is). Fixing a leak caused by a puncture is possible with repair kits sold by dealers.

Water beds are hardly adapted to a mobile life, but for many people who stay put they have become a standard form of bed. They are cheaper new (if you look around, and build your own frame) than an ordinary bed.

If a water bed is too wavy for you, filling it more tightly with water may help. Some beds are also being filled with a gel that floats you like water but doesn't slosh around.

2. Make your own bookshelves.

Most apartments and houses lack bookshelves, though they may have incinerators, dirty-clothes chutes, special silverware drawers, linen closets, and other storage facilities. The near-universal student solution is the board-and-concrete block system, in which you can use any kind of boards you can get hold of; they don't all have to be the same type, length, or even width. Variety and interesting wood is half the game: driftwood, used construction lumber, old pieces of shelving. With a half-dozen boards and about eight blocks (which you may have to buy at a building-supply firm), you can change the arrangement whenever you get bored with it. Large concrete blocks are more stable and cheaper than the small red bricks; and the holes are useful for holding pencils, letters, chopsticks, rulers, and many other little things that won't fit into your drawers.

Always build more bookshelves than you think you will need. You will soon fill the extra space with radio, stereo, disks, and boxes of small objects.

Board-and-block bookshelves can also be turned into benches for extra guests, or supports for one end of a table made from a flush door. If worst comes to worst, you can burn them for heat, as Mozart had to do with his furniture when he lay dying in poverty in Vienna.

3. Make your own things to sit on.

The Japanese say of Westerners, "They live on chairs," whereas in Japan people sit either directly on the soft tatami-mat floor or on large flat cushions. Enormous amounts of our time are spent sitting in chairs of one kind or another: office chairs, kitchen chairs, easy chairs, car seats. . .

This is, obviously, not essential. You could, if you wanted to, furnish your place Japanese-style and live very comfortably. It might take your friends a while to get used to it (and to taking their shoes off at the door), but it would be a simpler and more healthful way of living than perching on chairs: Getting up and sitting down would give your overall body muscles more exercise, and it would not crunch your internal organs as does sitting in ill-designed chairs. Let's assume, however, that you are not prepared to go that far, at least not yet. You should still be thoughtful about your chairs and try not to have any around that are ugly; sitting in an ugly or uncomfortable chair will not do your state of mind any good.

Comb the secondhand stores very carefully. Couches are pretty much hopeless. Even new ones force your back into a couch-potato slump. You can find good old kitchen chairs, often with a rung or piece of back missing, but still sturdy and beautiful. Don't try to find a set; be happy with an assortment of beautiful different ones. Many old chairs have been coated with layer after layer of paint but are good solid wood underneath; see if you can find a chipped-off place where the wood is visible. Paint remover will take the paint off, if you have patience.

Easy chairs can be very nice to curl up and read in, but it is hard to find inexpensive attractive ones. The old leather chairs that our grandfathers sometimes had have all worn out, and new ones are ruinously expensive. Chairs of a more recent vintage are mostly covered with cloth or plastic, often in ghastly colors. (A dark vinyl leather-like covering is now available that doesn't feel so clammy and is softer than most plastics. In dark brown or black, it can be tolerable.) The easiest and cheapest solution to the easy-chair problem is an old armchair whose upholstery is worn out, but whose springs aren't sticking out; throw an attractive large piece of cloth over it.

If you come across a really beautiful, heavy chair of simple design, you can, though it requires careful workmanship, reupholster it yourself—even in leather, if the shapes do not require complex fitting. Study it carefully first, however; the more of the covering that can be attached with tacks, rather than by fitting and sewing, the easier the job.

a. Try unusual couches. There are many drawbacks to an ordinary couch. It is often so bulky that it gives a small room a crowded feeling. A full-sized couch supposedly seats three people, but actually the middle person makes an obstruction so the end people can't talk to each other. (The old-fashioned two-person "love seat" is better for conversational purposes.) Many couches are either too narrow or too lumpy to sleep on comfortably, and their pillows don't make satisfactory sleeping surfaces even if laid down on the floor.

Couches that fold out to make a bed can be convenient, but they are almost always ugly, are either too stiff or too saggy, and cost a fortune unless you can find a battered one secondhand. Futons, which are cotton mats sewn together so that they fold up either into a pile or (with a wood frame) into a couch, are a healthier alternative—and save space too.

"Studio couches" are really low beds with some extra back cushions thrown in. They tend to slide away from the wall the minute you lean on the cushions, but they are comfortable to sleep on.

In short, few if any really satisfactory cheap couches exist, and if you want one, you will probably have to make your own.

Luckily, this is not difficult, if you liberate your mind from the conventional ideas. What you are after, presumably, is something that you and your friends can sometimes sit on, sometimes lounge on, and sometimes sleep on: In short, a largish, more or less flat surface, probably with a back along one side to lean on. This, like a bed, can be achieved with a large piece of plywood, some two-by-four lumber to support it, a slab of foam rubber or an old mattress, an attractive large piece of cloth, and some odd pillows to lean on.

You can make it freestanding and thus moveable, or you can build it into a corner—which is easier, since you don't need so many legs. It's nice to do this near a fireplace, so that you can lie on it to watch the fire. You can make it practically on the floor, or higher. You can also hinge it at the back so it will tilt a bit for more comfortable seating but go down flat for sleeping. If you can locate the ceiling joists, you can even suspend your couch on ropes or cables, so that it can gently swing back and forth. You can make a storage box under it, or even drawers.

One paradoxical reason to build your own or buy furniture (and rugs) secondhand is that new ones are now impregnated with insecticides (as are many building materials). These smell peculiar and may be carcinogenic. Let somebody else live with them until the chemicals have dispersed.

b. Try pillows. A supply of large pillows and cushions can substitute for bulky chairs, and make couches or sofa areas more comfortable, colorful, and appealing. Elegant Japanese-made flat cushions are available in more and more stores now. You can also make cushions or pillows yourself from pieces of surplus-store foam rubber, pillow stuffing bought in sewing stores, old rags, or whatnot.

Some people sleep without pillows, but most of us sleep better with a pillow that suits us. It is, in my opinion, a necessary luxury to buy a pillow you really like. My own taste runs to feather-filled pillows of a moderate firmness; foam tends to be too bouncy, and other stuffings tend to sag down into heavy, lumpy layers.

4. Make your own eating and work surfaces.

Eating is the one activity that all people in a house usually do together, so in a way the table is the real center of the household. Therefore it ought not to be just some cheap piece of formica-covered plywood with chrome-plated legs, but a true "board," as in bed and board. The best, most ceremonious tables are made of heavy solid wood, fastened firmly together and mounted on stout legs or a base. In general, veneered tables are to be avoided; although sometimes elegant, they will begin to peel in time. If you cannot find a solid table big enough to feed comfortably all the people you like to feed, make one. Prefabricated bases are available inexpensively in finish-it-yourself furniture stores; you just have to worry about the top.

Round tables have the great advantage of equally integrating everyone in the conversation. Their shape naturally tends to make people feel more together. But it is hard to find round tables big enough for more than six people, and they are harder to build than square or rectangular tables.

A table should be of hardwood, and it should be finished carefully with nonglossy varnish or oil to bring out the natural beauty of the wood. If the wood is attractive, you don't need tablecloths or placemats. All that will be needed to preserve it is wiping off with a damp cloth, and an occasional re-oiling to keep it liquidproof.

5. Paint or varnish your furniture yourself.

Don't be too eager to paint things, especially wood things. There is a terrible compulsion in America to keep things freshly painted—whereas in fact houses, furniture, shelves, utensils, and many other things can often look more interesting with a certain patina of age on them. Wooden shelves, chairs, tables, cabinets, and so on are often best left uncoated; leave the wood to face the world, and it will take on a soft luster, a pleasant variation in surface tone; it will feel good to the touch. Even houses are doubtful for painting; paint may protect the wood somewhat, but probably the cost of paint is not balanced by longer life of the wood. And weathered wood has a special soft beauty of its own.

If you do decide to paint, remember that a good painter almost always spends more time preparing the surface than in actually painting it. You need to scrape off the old paint where it's loose, fill the holes with putty or spackle, use a piece of sandpaper wrapped around a block of wood to sand off the irregularities, and generally make the surface clean and free of grease (which keeps paint from sticking). Then give it two coats. The ad on the can probably says "covers in one coat," but don't kid yourself; look at the dry first coat in the light of day. For light colors over dark, especially, you can't do a decent job with one coat.

Varnishing needs even more careful preparation, because there the wood itself will show through. Hardwoods will stand an incredible amount of scuffing, chopping, cutting, scouring, dripping, and general abuse, and will often get more beautiful in the process. You can give them some protection by soaking linseed oil or sealer into them, which won't make them shiny. But if you want to give them a tough coating, either spar varnish or one of the plastic varnishes like Varathane is best; they can be gotten in dull as well as shiny finishes. Try to do varnishing in a dust-free room—varnish picks up dust as if it was flypaper.

There are basically three kinds of paint: water-based ("latex," rubber paint), oil-based, and plastic-based (acrylic). Water-based paint is the easiest to use, because it can be washed off fingers, brushes, rollers, and floors with plain water (if cleaned off before it dries). White latex wall paint is the easiest for hiding your predecessors' peculiar choices in wall colors. Oil-based paints are usually the most feasible for outdoors, where sun and water give surfaces a tremendous drubbing. Acrylic paints, which are quite expensive, have intense, long-lasting colors that endear them to artists; and they are resistant to weather. Most modern paints contain chemicals that are injurious to health. Keep as many windows as possible open while you paint, and for several days thereafter; try to sleep somewhere else for a few days if you can. (If something has a penetrating "chemical" smell, it will surely not do you any good. Trust your nose!)

Any kind of paint can be put on with a brush or roller, but rollers are useful only when you're covering large flat areas. Even if you use a roller, you must have a brush too to do the corners, moldings, and edges. Some people like foam painting pads; they don't speckle you with paint the way a roller does, but they can drip on your arm.

A gallon of paint covers about 500 square feet—which is the ceiling and wall area of a room ten feet square and ten feet high. Thus, painting a whole apartment can get expensive. If you're not too fussy about exact matching of shades, you can find paint in surplus stores and other low-cost sources. However, it won't last as well as better paint, and it may not cover up the underlayer quite so well. A discount paint store is your ideal source.

It is possibly to use whitewash, the ancient covering for many country fences, barns, and whatnot. It washes away very slowly and irregularly, leaving an extremely nice weathered effect. To make it, buy from a paint store some lime, fine-ground casein (the main ingredient in white glue), ground kaolin (white clay), and sodium carbonate (if you intend to use it outdoors). Approximate ratios for outdoor use: 32 ounces lime, 8 ounces casein, 6 ounces kaolin, and 1 ounce sodium carbonate. For indoors: 30 ounces lime, 20 ounces kaolin, and 3 ounces casein. Precise measurements are not essential. You mix all the ingredients dry, very thoroughly, then add about half their volume of water. Stir until dissolved, and let stand half an hour before application.

There are other alternatives to paints and varnishes. Pretechnological societies found other ways of giving wood a finish, and you can sometimes find ways of doing similar things. The soft, lustrous surface of the veranda planks in traditional Japanese houses comes from their being wiped down by hand over the years, so that a mixture of sweat oils gradually protects them; linseed oil, rubbed in, will give wood a similar beautiful soft glow. Sculptures in some New Guinea areas were polished with animal fats rubbed thoroughly into the wood, and in fact practically any kind of fat or oil will tend to give wood a protective gloss. Any kind of hard rubbing down tends to close the surface pores of wood slightly, making it a little less water-absorbent. If you don't like the raw look of newly sawed wood you can "paint" it with a mixture of earth and water; this darkens it and makes it look a bit weathered. Painting new redwood with water with baking soda mixed in it will give the raw wood a pleasant old look.

Professional painters buy very good brushes and use them for years, but they have gallons of solvent, paint thinner, or other cleaning agents handy. For the person doing an occasional small paint job such as a chair or table, it is cheaper to buy a "throwaway" paint brush, since you would spend at least as much buying the cleaning stuff. (For very small jobs, you can make a temporary "brush" by rolling a little piece of thin rag around the end of a stick and tying it on; it isn't elegant, but it works.) But if you like to do painting, it is a pleasure to have two or three really good brushes; they put the paint on much easier than a cheap brush. A good brush has soft, dense bristles. To take care of such brushes, clean them immediately after use by working them in a container of thinner and hanging them up to dry (drill holes in the handles if they don't have them already), so that the bristles don't get deformed. Don't rub a good brush on the lip of the can when you load it; tap it against the inside of the can. Don't use a natural-bristle brush in latex paint.

You can clean a brush on which paint has hardened, but it isn't easy and is hard on the brush. First scrape off all the paint you can with a putty knife or other dull scraper, then soak the bristles several hours in diesel oil. You can also use paint remover, but it's so expensive that doing this is worthwhile only if you happen to inherit a really superb brush and want to restore it to good shape. For work you're going to continue next day, you can make a little rig to suspend the uncleaned brush in a can or bottle containing linseed oil (so the bristles don't lie on the bottom and get bent). If you're putting away a brush for a long time, soaking it with linseed oil beforehand will help it stay supple.

Latex (water-based) paints give the least trouble in the cleaning of brushes and rollers. Wash them in rapidly running plain water as soon as you're finished with them. If you stop work for a while, wrap them in waxed paper or plastic film to keep them damp and flexible.

Chapter 8.
Grow Your Own.

The more you become independent of the commercial system, the better off you will be, and this can even be applied to your food. Growing some of your own can save you money; it can assure you that no pesticide residues are on what you eat. But perhaps even more important, growing productive plants as part of your life connects you to the underlying biological realities of the planet. It teaches you (and your children) about nurturing other living things. Once you get some experience in gardening, you may even feel like branching out to keeping bees and raising chickens or fish.

A. Plant your own garden.

City people, as well as those in smaller towns, are turning increasingly to gardening as a source of wholesome and inexpensive food (not to mention pleasant recreation). Many city dwellings have backyards, balconies, or roofs where food can be grown either in the earth or in planter boxes, tubs, etc.

1. Find free materials.

You can probably borrow or pick up free a spade, rake, hoe, and watering hose; you can probably find scrap lumber to use for constructing planter boxes; and a vacant lot somewhere will provide a source of soil—though it may need plenty of compost, steer manure, and other conditioning materials to bring it up to a standard your plants will like. Your local sewage plant probably has fertilizer sludge (usable on all but root vegetables) available for the hauling; dig it in during the fall. You may also be able to find free mulch material, which greatly decreases watering and garden care: sawdust, lawn clippings, rice hulls, etc.

2. Get good advice.

Good gardening books abound; look in your library. Also talk to some experienced gardeners in your area to find out what kinds of vegetables thrive best in your locale and soil type, and which are prone to diseases or insects. Limit your first growing experiments to plants that are good bets.

3. Try easy plants first.

Some plants, like zucchini and other squash, are virtually indestructible and produce unbelievable yields. Most people have success with tomatoes, peas, beans (though these may need dusting with rotenone or other natural-source pesticide), carrots, lettuce, and corn. All these foods taste immensely better fresh. Even if you use no pesticides on them, wash before eating, since city air contains toxic materials.

4. Dig digging.

You should like digging to be a successful gardener (even though, once you get your garden soil in good condition, mulching can greatly decrease the need to disturb the soil). This is especially true for soil that hasn't been worked for years, which will be packed down so solidly that nothing much can grow in it. To turn unworked earth into a garden, you have to spade it over thoroughly, down as deep as your spade can reach. Throw on some fertilizer or manure and some compost (rotted leaves, twigs, etc.) or peat moss to keep the soil from packing down again, and rake it before you plant. Notice whether it has worms: Numerous active worms are a sign of good soil (worms provide aeration and drainage, and their castings are superb fertilizer; in fact, worms are being used to treat sewage wastes). Get started with composting as soon as you start thinking about gardening. A small, inexpensive soil-testing kit is useful to check the acidity of your soil. You might also save some room for a spice garden.

5. Plant fruit trees.

Fruit trees are a nice thing to plant, too. They take some years to produce any fruit, so others may reap the benefit of the trees you plant (just as you are reaping the benefit of trees planted by earlier generations). But the cost of a bare-root fruit tree is hardly more than the price of a bunch of cut flowers, and there's something particularly satisfying about planting a tree.

Your trees are likely to produce more fruit than you and your friends can eat ripe, so you should lay plans for drying some of it. Wire racks laid in the sun on a roof, and protected by screen or cheesecloth from birds and insects, will serve, but more complex devices and methods also exist. Again, check your local library for more information.

6. Learn modern techniques.

In recent years, great advances have been made in productivity on small plots, using techniques of deep digging (two feet deep!), raised beds, and close planting to keep down soil temperatures and conserve moisture. These techniques are sometimes called the BioDynamic or French Intensive methods.

B. Grow plants indoors.

Even the drabbest apartment looks better with flower pots on the windowsill, and green plants will make any space more livable. Living plants always make people feel good. Plants also give off oxygen during the day; that can't hurt either.

1. Start with easy plants.

It's not hard to grow most indoor plants. Ask advice at a garden-supplies place (some stores have garden departments), and start with the easiest, cheapest types. Avoid the conventional rubber plants and philodendrons—try ferns, ivy, or others. If you have kids around and worry that they'll knock the plants over, hang the plants on wires or brackets (you can put them in hanging baskets); you can also improvise containers from large painted tin cans or wooden boxes. Most plants need to be near windows but not in hot sun. (If they need more light, paint the wall behind them white, or put a mirror there.) If you have no good soil available, buy potting soil from the garden-supplies place.

2. Give them enough water.

In a heated apartment or house, plants need a surprising amount of water. Some that most willingly grow in damp places, like the beautiful ferns, need daily watering. Start with only a few plants, so that you can study how they behave, and you'll learn what they need.

Most vegetables won't grow in a heated place in winter, but you can grow hardy things like peas in a window box during the summer; they have beautiful, delicate flowers, and fresh peas taste much better than frozen or canned ones.

3. Grow trees indoors.

You can even plant small trees indoors if you pick the right kind of tree, and trees are surprisingly cheap—sometimes less than a big potted flower plant. They will need quite a lot of water, and do best if you don't keep the temperature terribly high. Ask at a garden-supplies place or nursery. Some nursery salespeople refuse to believe trees can survive indoors. Keep looking around until you find one who has tried it and knows what he or she is talking about. *Ficus benjamina* is one species that grows well indoors.

Nowadays many people are buying small live evergreens at Christmas instead of chopped-off trees. That way you aren't encouraging the killing of trees, and you get to plant your tree after New Year's in your yard or in a park or along the street somewhere. Evergreens can stand a week in a moderately heated house if you put them in the coolest spot—usually next to a big window—and if you are careful to keep their roots thoroughly moist at all times. (Even a three-foot-high tree can give off a quart or more of moisture a day, and this must be replaced through the roots.) A live Christmas tree smells nice, and accords with the reverence for life that many of us like to think we are expressing at Christmas time. Nurseries can give you detailed advice about planting the tree. The essentials are to dig a big hole and provide some soft earth in it for the tree's roots to penetrate—and to make sure the tree gets enough water in its early months in its new home. Remember that a small tree will someday be enormous, with powerful roots; don't plant it right next to your house.

4. Grow food plants indoors or for decor.

Traditionally, people have been reluctant to mix decorative with edible plants. This prejudice is now luckily being overcome. Asparagus, for instance, makes an attractive shrub after you have your fill of its springtime shoots. Artichokes and rhubarb are dramatic garden accents. Beans, peas, and some squash can be trained on trellises to give privacy or shade. Strawberries and New Zealand spinach provide ground cover plus edibility. Nasturtium leaves give a tangy taste to salads (as, of course, do dandelion leaves when young). A row of bush beans will make an attractive backing for low-growing flowering plants. Alfalfa is a hardy, pleasant-looking plant that you can use in planting strips and also to feed your rabbits—as well as sprouting seeds for yourself.

C. Avoid pesticides and herbicides.

In your personal life, you should minimize exposure to all pesticides and herbicides, as well as other suspicious chemical compounds. Natural pesticides (rotenones, pyrethrins, soaps, etc.) are available for your garden. Take proper precautions when using anything in spray or dust form, of course—wear a paper mask, or at least a dampened handkerchief over nose and mouth. A few bugs should be tolerable; they take a kind of natural "tax bite" out of your produce, and most of them have predators (lady bugs, birds) that keep their populations reasonable.

Herbicides have no acceptable place in home gardening or indeed in any urban land maintenance. Manual mowing or removal of undesired plants is always preferable.

You can not only seek out occasional "native plants" for your yard (species that are adapted to your climate and soils because they grew wild in the region for thousands of years) but attempt to recreate "wild" associations or communities of plants. Unless your neighbors complain that lawns are the only decent way to cover earth, a natural-looking yard can be very satisfying.

D. Create your own fertilizer by composting.

The fertility of our gardens would be greatly increased if we diverted most of our biodegradable kitchen wastes back into the earth. (Animal products, including bones, will biodegrade, but tend to attract scavengers.) The process is simple, and the results can be astonishing.

1. Dig a trench.

The easiest procedure is to establish a trench in some part of your garden that needs soil improvement. Dig a trench about a foot deep and a couple of feet long. When you have accumulated a basket full of kitchen scraps (a closed-top bucket enables you to accumulate them longer without decomposition odors) you deposit them in one end of the trench, then extend the trench a foot or so, shoveling the dirt you dig up onto the garbage you have just deposited. This process will cover quite a lot of area in year, and the deep digging produces great improvement in the garden soil. A drawback is that certain items (grapefruit rinds, for instance) may attract skunks.

2. Build a bin.

A composting bin can be built of any kind of sturdy salvaged or scrap lumber. For a four-person household, a bin three feet square and three feet high will accommodate kitchen wastes, grass clippings, gathered leaves, animal or chicken manure, dried-out annual plants, etc. A plastic sheet used as a cover will prevent the development of a fly population, increase the compost's temperature, and thus speed decomposition; but you might prefer a tight-fitting wooden lid.

Composting requires dampness; sprinkle some water onto the pile occasionally. An openable panel at ground level permits you to shovel out the finished material, which will be soft, loose, and pleasant-smelling. Otherwise you should build the bin without a bottom, and remove finished material by blocking it up slightly. (In a warm climate, composting is rapid—only a couple of weeks.)

3. Use a garbage can.

The same result can be obtained by using an old metal or plastic garbage can. Cut off the bottom, so you can remove finished material later, and punch a few holes near the bottom, to provide air. You can do composting in a cylinder made of wood slat fencing, inside a wall of old concrete blocks, or even in a plastic trash bag. (Add a couple of quarts of water to leaves, clippings, kitchen refuse, and some soil; tie the bags and shake them up every couple of weeks.)

Composting wastes can be mixed into soil, or simply spread on your garden and dug in. They improve soil quality. In time, fertilizer from the composting process in dry toilets will probably be legalized for use on food-producing gardens. This would permit a household with a large garden to become virtually a self-sufficient stable-state system for food production and recycling; it has been calculated, for example, that four persons' urine produces the nitrogen required as fertilizer for growing the vegetables they will eat in a year.

E. Raise chickens.

Considering that chicken-raising is perfectly legal in many towns and even in cities, surprisingly few people take advantage of this as a source of low-cost protein—both meat and eggs. It can also be a pleasure, and highly informative to children; and if you produce too many eggs for your own use, you can barter with them or give them to friends.

Raising a few chickens takes very little cash, or time, and can use up kitchen scraps that you wouldn't want to compost (chickens will eat meat scraps, oyster shells, and various other kinds of refuse). Six leghorn hens can keep the average family in eggs most of the time. If you have a yard with long grass, they will consume quite a quantity of bugs, and some grass and weed seeds, and will probably be sleek and beautiful, with an interesting social life. Like people, chickens do not seem as happy in small cages.

To get started in chicken raising, you need a sheltered warm place for the chicks, which you'll have to buy from a hatchery. (In cities a pet store can sometimes supply them, but at a higher cost.) A large wooden crate or even big grocery carton will do for a dozen or so. In cold climates you will have to keep them indoors; if you keep them outdoors, make the box dog-proof and rat-proof. The easiest warming system is to get a 150-watt flood-lamp bulb and suspend it over the floor of the crate—try about three feet above in ordinary weather. Make sure there is some shadow the chicks can get under if it gets too hot. Give them a constant supply of water and chicken mash; they eat more or less all the time. The water is especially important; if it runs out, the chicks will quickly die. Scatter wood shavings or some other absorbent material around to soak up the moisture from droppings. Chicks make a contented peeping sound when they are all right; if you hear them squealing piteously, they may be cold or hungry. They are normally very active and run around a lot; then they lie down in a huddle to sleep for a bit.

As they get bigger, you can gradually raise the lamp, since they need less warmth. By the time they have a more or less full set of feathers, they can take spring, summer, or fall weather—but get them used to the outdoors gradually; don't just toss them out. You should start feeding them some mixed grain or cracked corn, about the time they get wing feathers. Strewing a thin trail of corn is a good way to get a chicken to go where you want it to. (Chickens are not very bright, but they are not as hysterical as turkeys. The one thing you can count on is their pecking at all small, shiny, or moving objects.)

In order to raise chickens in town, you need to provide a securely fenced yard, to keep out marauding dogs and raccoons, and you need to avoid keeping roosters, whose crowing will probably be considered a public nuisance by your neighbors. Chickens need a place to roost at night off the ground. They will sometimes adopt a convenient tree, or you can provide a roost made of two-by-two boards.

When the hens are nearing laying age (about five to six months), provide some comfortable nesting boxes. These should be well off the ground, and have an entrance hole just big enough for a hen. Throw some straw or dry grass inside (make sure the boxes are protected and will stay dry). Collect eggs daily. The ideal system is to have an opening in the back of the nesting box through which you can quietly put your hand to remove the eggs, even when a chicken is sitting there. To encourage beginning layers to lay in the boxes rather than under a woodpile somewhere, some people put a darning egg (or a real egg) into the laying box when they think the hens are about ready. Early laying is irregular, by the way; it takes some weeks or even months for a hen to get into the almost-one-per-day rhythm that a good hen can achieve.

The quality of eggs chiefly depends on a hen's diet. If she is getting plenty of grass and bugs, they should have lovely orange yolks. Hens need cracked oyster shell as a source of calcium for the egg shells, once they begin to lay. Refrigerate your eggs; they keep better when cool.

There are several varieties of chickens available from hatcheries, and a great deal of special hybrid breeding and genetic research has gone into them. The leghorn is the standard all-white chicken, the workhorse (so to speak) of the poultry world. It lays white-shelled eggs, in case you suffer the delusion that they taste different. The leghorn's disadvantage is its dull appearance, especially if it is kept in bad surroundings so that its plumage gets raggedy—which normally happens with good layers. Leghorns also tend to escape over fences, being light and better fliers than heavier birds. Hatcheries now have their own types of chickens developed for meat production, and these carry names given by the hatcheries. Most of them are white too, though they are developed by crosses from such attractive forebears as the New Hampshire (a chestnut-colored, dark-reddish bird; the rooster has iridescent blackish tail plumes; his neck feathers tend to be a lovely mixture of reds and golds), which you may still be able to buy if you look around.

Even in a large enclosure, chickens are prone to a poultry disease called coccidiosis, which is transmitted through wet droppings, and is thus most likely to spread in damp chicken houses or crowded pens. Birds with this disease droop and die; their livers have small yellowish pockmarks. Your county agent will probably be willing to come over and tell you if your birds have it, or you can leave a dead bird with him for analysis.

Vegetarians sometimes keep chickens just for the eggs, but most people want to eat the birds too. You may not find killing them easy, if you grow fond of them.

The best way for an amateur to kill a chicken is the old hatchet on block. Make a quick, clean job of it—which means making sure the chicken's neck is laid out flat on the block. (Get a helper the first couple of times you try it.) Then hang the flopping bird up by the legs on a previously arranged rope. It will swing around wildly and spray blood a considerable distance; hang your rope out in the open somewhere. The flopping helps to drain the body of blood, which is a good thing.

There are several ways of removing feathers. The easiest for general purposes is to dunk the whole bird into a large pot of almost boiling water for a minute, shaking it around to get the water into all the feathers. Then hang it up again and pull out the feathers, largest first. They will come out in great gobs, but underneath you will find "pinfeathers" which refuse to come out so easily. They don't hurt the cooking any, but they do look unsightly, and you'll probably have to get out the worst ones with pliers, since they're slippery. A good scald usually means you have only a few to deal with, however.

To remove the bird's innards, you should cut off the neck as short as possible, then reach in and loosen the organs accessible from the front. Then make a cut around the anus, reach into the body cavity, and pull everything out—intestines, gizzard, lungs, liver, and everything should come out pretty much in a clump. Feel around to make sure you got everything: Wash out the cavity, then feel around some more. Trim off the waste from the edible innards; skin the neck. (This whole process is known, for some weird reason, as "dressing.") Your bird is now ready to cook.

Chickens sold as "fryers" are generally young roosters. If they've been well-fed, they are best eaten at about six to ten weeks old. A pullet that has been laying for six months or so is still pretty tender, but an old hen is chiefly good for stewing.

F. Keep bees.

The term "busy little bees" is not just a joke: Bees are incredibly industrious, and if you provide them a decent home they will forage ceaselessly for you and provide surprisingly large amounts of delicious honey for practically no cost, in almost any region except heavily pesticided agricultural areas. Bees are legal to keep in many towns and some cities; if they are not legal in your town, you could probably organize a successful campaign to change the situation.

Besides, bees can be raised in indoor hives, as schoolteachers sometimes do for children's benefit. A hive can be attached to sit on a windowsill, so long as the bee entrance is a bee-tight pipe; it can even have a glass wall (coverable with a flap—bees don't like light in their hives), so that you can check up on them. And of course a beehive will fit on many urban balconies. Beware, however, of locations near other people's balconies or windows, since bees returning at dusk are attracted by light. Rooftops are also good possibilities, but on hot asphalt roofs you must provide ample shade to keep the hive cool, and mount it on an elevated platform where breezes will also help cool it.

Bees not only produce honey, a delicious and relatively healthy sugar substitute and food-energy source, but also fertilize many plants, including fruit trees, which are common in towns. People sometimes have an unreasonable fear of bees, but in fact if a hive is in a backyard away from pedestrian traffic, it poses no danger to residents or passers-by; your dog, if you have one, will soon learn to keep away from it. A careful beekeeper rarely gets stung, but it does happen.

Your local college may offer a course in beekeeping, and your library certainly has useful books about it. Best of all, however, is to find a beekeeper who is already doing it and apprentice yourself for a while. You can keep only a few bees, just enough to provide honey for yourself and friends, with very little work. But you may easily be tempted to get more bees, to learn the intricacies of the field, and to start extracting honey and selling it in jars—at flea markets or through stores—as a handy extra source of income. With sugar prices high, and many more people conscious of the pleasures of honey, the demand is likely to continue strong.

G. Have a fish pond.

Bees have a short lifetime; around any busy hive you will have a lot of dead bees, and fish happen to love dead bees. Some people, as in the Farallones Institute Integral House in Berkeley, dig a fish pond (theirs is about ten feet square, maybe five feet deep, lined with black plastic sheeting to prevent water loss) and put their beehives next to it. The Integral Urban House also has a small home-made windmill that runs a pump to aerate and filter the fish-pond water. Bluegills will grow in such a pond, but you may want to experiment with more exotic species—tilapia, carp, etc. Even if your county is urbanized, it should have a county agricultural agent who can give advice on ponds. If a fish pond is more than you want to undertake, you can always feed dead bees to your chickens!

Chapter 9.
Live Well in Your Home.

One key to having a high quality of life is to own *only* those things that you yourself need or want, and *not* to own anything else, no matter what your neighbors may think. If you don't waste money on buying or maintaining things that are of no essential use to you, then you will have more money or, better yet, more time to spend on what you truly value.

In this chapter we will think about *things*, the kinds of things that people have in their homes. We will ask whether you really need or want them, how to get the best use out of them, and how to repair them as cheaply as possible.

A. Do you really need that appliance?

People trying to live cheaply will want to minimize their dependence on appliances as well as their energy consumption. What is a reasonable minimum? In my experience: refrigerator, stove, stereo, blender, toaster, and iron.

The energy consumption of new appliances varies widely, and you should compare carefully the labels that most of them now carry. Over a five-year lifetime, you will spend more than the purchase price of most major appliances on the energy they take to run; so their energy drain is probably their single most important feature. Frost-free refrigerators, upright freezers, and air conditioners are particularly heavy energy users. Since most appliances, like American cars, are constructed to last at least 10 years (refrigerators and freezers up to 20), on the whole you will get better value for your money—and in many cases more energy-efficient appliances—if you rely on secondhand sources. It takes some knowledge and care to be sure of what you're getting, or at least to minimize the risks.

1. Is the warranty worth anything?

You may on occasion buy something new, and be asked whether you wish to buy extended warranty or guarantee coverage. Should you pay any attention to such questions? Obviously the local reputation of the dealer's repair department is an overriding consideration. But if you do not know the people you're dealing with, remember that guarantees and warranties are usually intended to protect the company that manufactures the appliance, not you. They promise to "replace defective parts" or something like that, but they protect the company from any other liability. So you will probably have to pay not only for shipping your appliance to the factory, but also for the work of replacing the defective part. This usually costs far more than the part itself.

Second, a guarantee is only as strong as you are in enforcing it. If the manufacturer is two thousand miles away, you don't have any real chance. The local dealer will often disclaim any responsibility, unless you are a steady customer or look like you can cause real legal trouble. The Better Business Bureau, which is a kind of mutual-defense-league of local businesses, will tell you that all their members are respectable firms who always treat their customers fairly, and that they're sure nothing is wrong. Your only recourse, therefore, except in rare cases where you might sue in small-claims court, is public exposure, and you don't have much chance unless your local paper carries a public-service feature.

If you are thinking of buying some appliance new—like a washer or refrigerator—you should consider Sears or Montgomery Ward. They maintain their own repair and service departments, and many people give good reports about their handling of breakdowns during the guarantee period.

Appliances are, unfortunately, still being designed so that repair by the user is very difficult. One sensible criterion for whether to buy something is whether it looks like you could get in to see what's wrong if it develops trouble.

Modern manufacturers take a great deal of trouble to make sure that things don't last too long; so you can count on breakdowns. Insist on a dated sales slip with any appliance you buy new and keep it with the guarantee paper (you don't have to send in the guarantee postcard as directed). Then if trouble occurs within the supposed guarantee period, it can't hurt to check with the dealer.

Whenever you buy an appliance, new or secondhand, insist that its serial number be written down on the sales receipt. Otherwise the store may deliver another model, an older or defective one, etc., and without the serial number to prove your point, no lawyer can help you get your money back.

2. Do you need an air conditioner?

The air conditioner was a virtually unknown appliance at the end of World War II. It is now one of our greatest consumers of household energy.

People have become so convinced they cannot live without air conditioners that they keep their dwelling windows closed, with their conditioner running full blast, even when they would get cooler faster by opening a couple of windows.

New buildings, even in hot climates, can be constructed so that mechanical air cooling is very seldom desirable. In old buildings, money spent on insulation will quickly be repaid in lower air-conditioner operating costs (or in not having to rely on one at all). If you feel you *have* to have one, wire up a simple outdoor thermosensor to a dial set at the temperature you are asking your air conditioner to achieve, in such a way that when the outdoor temperature is lower, a bell rings or a light flashes. (A good hardware store can sell you the parts and give you a wiring diagram.) Wire it so that the only way to stop the signal is to turn off the air conditioner. In one experiment, householders with such devices cut their electricity consumption by 16 percent.

3. Do you need a blender?

The blender is probably the small electric appliance most worth having around your kitchen. You can do everything an electric frying pan will do in a heavy iron skillet; you can do everything a toaster oven or microwave oven will do in your stove. But you can't make juices out of vegetables without a blender, and you can't make milk shakes easily. A heavy blender will chop up and purée practically any kind of fruit or vegetable. So you can produce mixtures as fantastic as those offered by a "juice bar"—celery and cabbage juice, plum and apple juice, apricot and pineapple juice. You can also make cheap baby food, puréed broccoli soup, carrot cake, zucchini bread, walnut butter, sauces to pour over ice cream, and lots of other things. Blenders are simple machines that either work or don't; so they are relatively safe to buy secondhand if you try them out first. The new ones have variable speeds and other refinements, but all you need is one whose motor runs, whose top stays on, and whose bottom doesn't leak. (Ask to try it with a little water in it.)

If you do a lot of cooking, especially for large groups of people, you may find a *food processor* worth the money (and clean-up time). It will do many things that a blender can't, since it is strong enough to handle meats, nuts, and other relatively tough foods. If you like Oriental dishes, you might be especially interested in a processor, since it will chop, slice, and shred things much faster than hand chopping. On the other hand, such work is a good way to take out aggressions.

4. Do you need a microwave oven?

There are some appealing aspects to microwave ovens: They cook or warm things rapidly and with some energy savings. But many of them leak microwave radiation into their surroundings, and the dangers connected with them have not yet been satisfactorily measured. Microwaves cook flesh (the eyeballs are particularly sensitive, and people working at radar stations have sometimes developed cataracts) and they may well have other, subtler effects; scientists in Eastern Europe have set safety standards 10,000 times more stringent than ours, and they may know something we don't—perhaps about the effects of microwaves on the delicate electronic patterns of the brain.

The wisest personal strategy is to avoid microwaves whenever you can. Keep your children (who love to peer into oven windows) away from any microwave ovens in your friends' houses. Be aware that certain kinds of ceramics are unsafe in microwave ovens because dangerous substances leak out of their glazes into your food. Don't sit near the microwave oven in restaurants; don't have one in your house; if your apartment neighbor has one next to a shared wall, try to cut down on your use of the area next to it. (Microwaves pass through ordinary wall construction; metal screens or even aluminum foil will obstruct them.) Commercial and military radar installations, along with television stations, are other major sources of microwaves in our environment; try never to live close to one, especially in their "line of fire."

5. Do you need a refrigerator?

According to the research chief at *Consumer Reports*, it is not true that everything is of inferior quality today. Refrigerators and wringer washers, he says, are definitely better today than in years past.

Actually, any refrigerator less than five years old can be expected to give many years of service, and many older machines still have plenty of life in them. So simple and sturdy are the compressor-pump units that do the actual work that they outlast the springiness of the rubber gasket around the door.

Aside from the greater energy efficiency of some newer models, there is no overwhelming reason to buy a refrigerator new, in spite of the "Look, no defrosting" advertisements. (Frost-free models cost 40 to 100 percent more to run, besides costing more to start with. They also have complex circuitry, fans, heaters, and so on that break down.) Defrosting a refrigerator merely requires turning a switch and removing the water as the ice melts; why so many people regard it as a fearsome chore is beyond me. (If you don't like to lift a tray full of water, use a little piece of plastic tube to siphon it into a pan or bucket.) But make sure you turn on a secondhand refrigerator for a while before buying it to see if it also freezes ice; and listen to the motor to see if it labors, especially when starting up.

There are three main ways to save energy and money on your refrigerator.

1. Keep it no colder than 40°F (5°C). (Put an ordinary household thermometer in the middle of the box for 10 or 15 minutes.)

2. Buy a new door gasket for it, so the cold stops leaking out. (Check the

gasket's tightness by putting a sheet of paper against it and shutting the door; if the paper slips out without friction, the gasket is probably shot. Try this at several places around the door.)

3. Make sure your refrigerator is no bigger than you really need. A big box loses more cold than a small one; it may also waste food that gets hidden in the back. In recent years small "apartment-size" boxes have come on the market. They stand counter-high, so that you can prepare food on the top, and they have a freezer compartment for temporarily keeping frozen foods.

6. Do you need a toaster?

Almost all toasters fall into the class of Needlessly Shiny Objects, and take a lot of useless attention to keep clean. Some are now made of stainless steel or aluminum or enameled like old fashioned pots. But you can always cover up chrome plating—especially if it's begun to flake off or rust through—with some bright-colored enamel. Unplug the toaster, get all the grease off before you paint, and be careful not to let drips of paint go down inside.

If you're buying a toaster secondhand, insist on plugging it in to see if it works. The handle should stay down, then pop up briskly. All the heating element wires (the flat wires inside that turn red) should heat up on both sides of each piece of bread. Check for a dangerously worn or frayed cord, and see if the adjustment for darker or lighter toast works. (For darker toast, the bread stays down longer.) The bottom should open so you can clean out crumbs that collect. When you clean a toaster, unplug it and use a small rag—never put a toaster under water to clean it, because electric wires will get wet and may short out or give you a shock.

Some recent toasters don't have a push-down handle; you put the bread in the slot and the toaster lowers it automatically. This fancy feature, like most extras, is likely to break down and cause expensive repairs. The same goes for "humidity-control" features. A toaster is a simple machine designed to do only one thing, reliably. Get a simple one.

Even simple toasters are not always worth repairing, since the repairs may cost more than a new toaster (or another secondhand one). If you're good at repairing, or have a handy friend, it's worth opening up the toaster to see what's wrong. But first just hold it over the sink with the bottom open and give it a good shaking: The most common troubles are due to crumbs or raisins clogging the works. Other likely troubles are loose electrical connections and misadjustment or failure of the bimetallic strip that moves in response to the heat and lets the toast pop up.

A safety note: If a piece of bread sticks inside the toaster, unplug the machine before you poke anything down the slot to pry it out. You can get a nasty shock if you touch the heating elements with a metal knife or fork.

7. Do you need a vacuum cleaner?

Probably the easiest way to keep house floors clean is to have no rugs and to vacuum every couple of days. A lightweight upright or "vacuum broom" cleaner will usually serve such purposes, though it won't clean rugs as well as a regular heavy cleaner. However, there's not much that can go wrong with a vacuum; you're likely to get a fairly good deal on a secondhand vacuum as long as you let it run a while when you try it out and make sure it really picks up dust. (Try it on a little sand—that takes good suction.) Holding your hand over the hose isn't a good test—it's how well the nozzle sucks stuff from the floor that counts. Don't be impressed by "attachments," which just clutter up your closet. You can vacuum anything except tight corners with a basic nozzle. If you have rugs or carpets, a heavy upright vacuum with rotating brush will beat the most dust out of them. If your nozzle scratches things, put a little adhesive tape on the bottom edges.

No vacuum will work right unless you keep emptying the dirt collector. So when you buy one, try emptying it to see how much trouble it is. "Disposable" bags add substantially to the cost of operating a vacuum; try to find a model where you simply dump the dirt onto a piece of newspaper and wrap it up. Also check to see whether there is a narrow neck that will clog up easily. (A clogged hose can usually be poked clean with a broom handle.)

If you do carpentry or other messy work, you may want a heavy duty or "shop" vacuum with heavy motor and bigger pickup tube. It costs no more than the ordinary vacuum, but takes up a little more space.

Vacuum cleaners are among the noisiest of common appliances, and responsible for a good deal of noise pollution. Ironically, companies that built quieter machines found that most people wouldn't buy them, because they associated loud noise with good suction; so the companies built them noisier again. But you may still be able to find a relatively quiet model secondhand. Pay attention to its cleaning ability, not its sound!

8. Do you need a washer and dryer?

These are expensive appliances, and when breakdowns occur, they can cost half of what a new machine does. Unless you have a great deal of washing to do, therefore, you may be better off to use the laundromats—or, even better, to share a washer and dryer with a couple of neighboring houses. (These machines are not harmed by being outdoors unless it gets so cold that water can freeze in their piping; so sometimes they can stand on a covered back porch or in a shed, for easy access by all. This also keeps the noise level down in your house.)

Try not to do small loads, which are wasteful of water and energy. If you have a washer that adjusts for larger or smaller loads, don't forget to adjust it.

Under the impact of higher gas and electricity prices, the clothesline is making something of a comeback (solar-powered drying!). Sun drying disinfects diapers, incidentally.

Watch out for expensive bleaches, fabric softeners, and other laundry gimmicks. Clorox, in particular, is far more expensive than identical products under different names. Dry bleaches are also expensive, including the (weaker) oxygen bleaches.

9. Do you need an electric can opener?

As in most other areas of the house, a lot of the single-purpose utensils commonly found in kitchens are not really necessary. You can cut out cookies with a glass instead of a cookie cutter. You can roll dough, as our grandmothers did, with a broomstick or wine bottle rather than a rolling pin. You can poach eggs in any frying pan. If you are eating right, you will seldom need a can opener—but you will open a can occasionally, especially in the winter in cold climates. There's no need to junk up your kitchen with an eyesore chrome-plated can opener. Get a simple can opener from the dime store, or—if you really want to keep the signs of cans as inconspicuous as possible—a GI can opener from the surplus store. There are fiendishly ingenious gadgets hardly bigger than a nail clipper, but quite capable of opening cans if you have reasonably strong fingers. Be glad if it makes can-opening slightly unpleasant—that will motivate you to use more fresh and frozen vegetables, which are better for you (and frozen vegetables are generally cheaper than canned anyway).

B. Save energy and money.

1. Insulate your water heater.

Your domestic water heater accounts for more of your home energy consumption than anything but your furnace. Wrap it with an insulation jacket (which many hardware stores can now supply) or use ordinary fiberglass wall insulation, taping it loosely around the tank (remember to wear a mask or handkerchief over your nose and mouth), and you will cut heat losses 30 to 40 percent.

An electric ignition system is no advantage for a hot water heater, since the pilot light does useful work in helping keep the hot water hot.

Your water heater will consume much less energy if you use less hot water—by not letting it run while you wash dishes, by installing flow restrictors in shower heads, by washing clothes with cold or cool water (and washing things requiring hot water in a washer that can handle small loads with less water).

Gas-burning water heaters and clothes dryers are much more economical to operate than electrical ones. There is less difference with stoves, but expert cooks generally prefer gas, because it can be quickly turned up or down.

Especially where state tax credits apply, the installation of a solar water heater will generally pay for itself in a few years. The possibilities range from very simple pre-heaters suitable for warm climates to relatively sophisticated designs involving heat exchangers, nonfreezing collecting fluids, and small pumps, which can provide your entire hot-water supply in any climate.

2. Maintain your furnace.

Old furnaces clogged and coated with soot inside may become inefficient and need cleaning. A new fuel-injection nozzle (many oil furnaces have wrongly installed ones) might cut your heating energy consumption in half. A "retention head" burner can significantly increase the efficiency of an old furnace and is much cheaper than buying a new furnace. Remember to close off the heat from unused rooms and close their doors.

3. Eliminate pilot lights on stoves.

You can save much energy by eliminating pilot lights on gas stoves, which burn a surprising amount of gas, since they run 24 hours a day all year. Matches are fine if you don't mind the trouble; electric lighters now come in most new gas stoves and can be fitted into old ones. If you do a lot of baking, you may be able to improve the insulation in or around your oven.

Fireplace flues can carry away huge amounts of heat; close the damper whenever you don't have a fire going. (Better yet, replace the fireplace with a wood stove.)

4. Use a wood stove.

Even in cities, wood for fuel is often available at prices that (per unit of heat) beat oil or gas—assuming, of course, that you have a really efficient stove, and aren't just using a fireplace or an open Franklin-type stove. Generally a fireplace is a net *loser* of heat—you suck more warm air out of the room and up the flue than the fire provides. Close the damper whenever you don't have a fire going.

A good stove is expensive. Moreover, it requires a commitment of energy and care, or it will not keep you warm, and may burn down your house. Nevertheless, wood stoves have spread through the country in great numbers. (In some places they cause noticeable air pollution; check on the situation in your locality before buying one. Also, sophisticated "new generation" stoves burn more cleanly and are less likely to cause flue fires.)

Wood stoves appeal to people partly for economy's sake, partly because they use a renewable energy source, and partly to provide a secure back-up against future heating-oil shortages, which are likely to be severe and, in harsh climates, can be dangerous. A good wood stove will warm an average-sized house quite satisfactorily if it is used right and is equipped with a blower to circulate warm air to distant rooms (sometimes, but not always, ducting is a good idea for this purpose). Stove dealers will generally be willing to visit your house and recommend a stove appropriate to it. However, there is a wide range of experienced opinion about wood stoves; do a lot of checking before you decide on one. People's recommendations vary widely, depending on their expectations and habits.

To maintain a fire for a long period during the night, a stove must be of the airtight type, so that the draft can be closely controlled. Some airtight stoves have glass holes in their doors, so that you can see the fire, but this is never like being in front of a fireplace. Some stoves have flat tops, so that you can cook on them. Some have water-heater attachments, on the back or in the stove pipe, which preheat water going into your regular water heater. Some are designed to be used with a small motor-driven fan to increase the draft. Some have heat jackets to confine the air they heat, which can then be sent through ducts. Some will hold long logs, and some only short ones.

All wood stoves pose fire hazards and should be installed in conformity with your local building codes and regulations, or your house fire insurance may become invalid. There are three main safety requirements for stoves, as follows.

1. They must stand on a fireproof base (ideally fire brick) and be a specified distance away from walls; if closer, the walls must be covered with a protective metal sheet set out from the wall surface.

2. They must have a properly designed stove pipe to insure smoke passage, maximize heat diffusion into the room, and minimize creosote deposits. (Creosote builds up from smoke particles, especially those from green wood; in time it becomes flammable, which can cause chimney and stove-pipe fires that are terrifying and dangerous. Stove pipes can be installed so that they are easy to clean, with an openable T to catch creosote behind the stove as it runs down inside the pipe.)

3. The stove pipe must pass through walls or ceiling or roof within fireproof collars, as prescribed by your local building code. In areas where wood stoves are common, building department personnel have much valuable experience with stove installations. They share your interest in not having your dwelling burn down; so you should follow their requirements. A stove draws in a certain amount of air from the room, which it then sends up the stove pipe and/or chimney. New houses are sometimes so tightly sealed that a stove cannot get enough air, and will smoke. (The same can happen with a fireplace or Franklin-type stove.) You must then allow a little air to enter somewhere.

Every stove has some idiosyncrasies, and it takes weeks of breaking in before you and your stove will fully understand each other's performance requirements. But having a stove you know and love, especially if it saves you immense amounts of money, can be a gratifying experience.

Before investing in a wood stove, explore the availability and price of firewood in your area. Lay in a supply of wood in the spring, so that the wood can be well-seasoned by the time you need it. Store it where rain or snow cannot dampen it. Plan your delivery and storage to minimize the work of picking up the logs and hauling them around; wood is heavy. The best stove wood is from modest-sized logs, so that the burning surfaces are at least half round (rather that split sides all around). Oak, hickory, and fruit woods burn the best and give the most heat. You need some soft wood around to use as kindling in starting fires, of course. But green wood and soft woods should be burned only as last resorts; they give relatively small amounts of heat, and large amounts of creosote—which, sooner or later, you must clean out of your stove pipe and chimney.

If you are near woodland areas, a chainsaw and pickup truck will enable you to gather your own firewood. Don't underestimate the sheer labor this involves; but of course it can reduce your fuel costs to very little (unless you have to rent the truck). In national forests, with a proper permit, you can usually cut firewood for yourself; send for a brochure called *Firewood for Your Fireplace*, to Forest Services, U.S. Department of Agriculture, Washington, DC 20013.

Tightly rolled newspapers can be used for fuel in fireplaces or stoves, though they're quick-burning. You can buy a device to help, but a piece of broomstick will do fine. Fold sections of paper so they end up about 12 by 15" and a half-inch thick or less. Soak in water with a little detergent in it; this assists in wetting. Roll the papers onto the rod, squeezing out water; slide out the rod and stand your "log" on end to dry. It will take some weeks, even if you dry them on wire mesh to let air circulate. A daily paper makes a couple of logs, the Sunday maybe a half dozen, and they burn about half an hour.

5. Save water.

- During such processes as shaving, brushing teeth, washing dishes, etc., turn off faucets when you don't actually need them running.
- Fix leaky faucet washers promptly; a slow drip can waste hundreds of gallons (besides making an annoying noise!).
- Buy a low-flow shower head (or your water company may give you one free). Or install a little disk called a flow restrictor in the shower head (hardware or plumbing-supply stores sell them—they cost very little).
- For decorative plantings, choose species with low watering needs.

- For vegetables, plant closely in raised beds, and use a drip watering system rather than over-all spray watering. Cover exposed soil with mulch (which also minimizes pests).
- For lawns, minimize evaporation losses (and do your grass a favor) by infrequent deep, long watering. Water in the evening.
- In washing your car (if you really *have* to!) use a bucket of soapy water, and hose the car off only after you've scrubbed it.

6. Save electricity.

Electricity savings are possible by avoiding electric heaters, by not overlighting rooms, by turning lights off when nobody is using a room, and by avoiding high-wattage appliances like electric broilers, frying pans, hair-dryers, and irons.

Most light bulbs are made to burn out in 750 hours. There are some bulbs produced that burn much longer: 1,500, 2,500, even 10,000 hours. The catch is that the longer the life, the less light a bulb puts out. (There is no way around this: It follows from the physics of lamp filaments.) Moreover, the cost of lighting your house is mostly in your electric bill, not in the cost of bulbs. During its 750-hour life, a bulb eats up electricity worth five or six times what the bulb costs you, depending on where you live. Research has shown that even if companies have to pay for labor to have a bulb changed, they are better off using standard-life bulbs. The ordinary user is also better off buying standard bulbs. You get more light output from one 150-watt bulb than from two 75s, by the way.

It is not getting easier to find standard bulbs. Many retailers have switched over to "soft-white" or other novelty bulbs that have a special inside coating and carry a higher price, though they give off no more light. (Generally they give less, in fact, though their diffuseness may be an advantage for a few special close-work situations.)

If your bulbs are burning out too fast (and especially if several of them burn out at once), it is probably because the voltage in your area surges above the standard 120 volts frequently. If this happens, bulb life is seriously shortened. You may need to use bulbs rated for 125 volts instead, although they will give somewhat less light; you can find these at electrical stores. But the so-called "long-life" bulbs will cost you far more money in your electric bill than many early burnouts.

Compact fluorescent lamps have little fluorescent tubes curled up close together but operate in the same way. They produce pleasant light frequencies, and though they cost more initially, they use about a quarter of the electricity of an incandescent bulb, and last more than ten times longer; so they actually save you a lot of money. Unfortunately, they will not fit in many fixtures (or reading lamps). Recently a new type of efficient fluorescent bulb, shaped like an incandescent bulb, developed and should be on the market soon.

Fluorescents produce less heat—businesses use them to prevent internal heat gains that mean more air conditioning, and incandescent lights use more electricity. There are new fluorescents now that have better color/light rendering, and less hum.

To save money (and energy) on lighting, turn off your lights when they're not in use, and keep the general illumination level down to what is really essential—your house doesn't need the bright lights of a hospital operating room! You can probably cut 15 percent off your electric bill simply by developing the habit of turning off lights when you leave a room.

The appeal of tube-type fluorescents is, of course, that they produce more light with less current than do incandescent bulbs, and as a result they've spread wildly through our homes and businesses. But they have so many disadvantages that I decided some years ago not to use them in my house. Unless they have electronic ballasts, they make an annoying hum. Some of them flicker. But more important, their light output is not spread out evenly over the spectrum like sunlight and incandescent light, but instead is concentrated in small "peaks" of intensity—lots of pink, then nothing much until you get to blue. (This unnatural character may explain their hypnotic effect in supermarkets and department stores.) Full-spectrum fluorescent tubes are now available, and though they cost more, they are what you should use if you don't mind the hum and flicker.

There is some inconclusive but frightening evidence that all fluorescent light is somehow harmful. It certainly is to plants (though there is a type of fluorescent tube, including the Gro-Lux and other brands, specially developed for indoor plants), and it has been vaguely connected with various human ills. Light can be thought of as "ingested." It passes quite readily through human tissue—as you see by holding your hand up to a strong light—and directly affects the nervous system through the retina. On the whole, therefore, it seems wisest to avoid fluorescents, and to make sure you get a modest amount of natural sunlight. Getting up with the sun and going to bed no longer after it than possible may make sense at home as well as on camping trips.

7. Try to qualify for "lifeline" rates.

Some states have required utilities to establish "lifeline" rates for those who use little gas or electricity (including many old people living alone) who formerly were forced to pay higher rates than industries gobbling up enormous amounts. If your state doesn't have such laws, let your representatives know that it's about time it did. If it does, you may be able to cut your energy outlays substantially by cutting your usage a relatively small amount—enough to get under the lifeline maximum, and thus getting the lower rates.

C. Save on household goods.

1. Buy cheap clocks and watches.

I am constitutionally dubious about "disposable" goods—things that are made to be unrepairable, and which you throw away when they start giving you trouble. But in time-keeping devices this is now the only reasonable kind for most people to have. Mass-produced timepieces keep better time than many expensive jeweled ones; yet they cost very much less. (There are only two or three kinds of insides; so you can buy the cheapest with confidence; they all run.)

If you happen to have an expensive watch and something goes wrong with it, a watchmaker will charge you a good bit just to open it up, blow on it, and find out what's the problem. So the lesson is clear: Buy cheap watches and throw them away—usually they will keep time for five years or so. The same is true for alarm clocks. Avoid luminous dials—they give you a daily dose of radiation that can't do you any good. (Dials illuminated by a tiny orange bulb are okay.)

If you find alarm clocks ugly or just want to simplify your possessions, you may want an arm wristwatch. Small battery-powered travel alarms are available. There are also solar-cell-powered wrist watches, which never need batteries—the first real mass-market application of solar power!

Watches are a necessary evil at best. They interrupt and distort the normal passage of your own biological time and rhythms, and impose mechanical standards that have no real meaning. The watch, like the time clock and the business suit, is usually a symbol of servitude. Try "losing" your watch once in a while—put it away out of sight somewhere. You'll probably find that you get through the day just as well without it—and it might be relaxing.

"Digital" watches are a good example of technological hypertrophy, incidentally. Our actual experience of time is not second-by-second but in lumps or chunks, and usually when we need to know the time, an approximation within five minutes or so is plenty accurate. A watch with hands provides us with an "analog" representation of time, which corresponds fairly well with our experience of it. A watch with numbers gives us superfluous digital precision—which our systems then have to translate back into the analog terms we live in.

If you have an electric alarm clock, it probably generates a surprisingly powerful electromagnetic field. Keep it at least three or four feet from your body as you sleep.

2. Buy inexpensive dishes.

The Western European ideal was white china or porcelain dishes, shiny glassware, white linen napkins—and if you're lucky enough to inherit such stuff, don't be foolish and get rid of it: It's beautiful, like old jewelry. But for most of us, the problem is what to eat on day by day. Secondhand stores abound with plastic dishes and mass-produced dark china dishes that might as well be plastic, and old plates decorated with little flowers and tinted a faint pink. How to avoid them?

The first thing to keep in mind about dishes is that they don't all have to be alike. A table will, in fact, be more intriguing if every place is set differently. So don't trudge through thrift stores looking for "a set of dishes." Look for good individual items that really interest you. If they genuinely hit you, you'll almost always find that they also go together nicely—they may be different sizes or weights, but they'll have a common spirit.

Second, there's nothing wrong with a chip or two. A beautiful old plate is still a beautiful old plate, even if it's nicked. (Cracks, however, seldom stay mended, even with epoxy glue.)

Third, stay away from plastic, for dishes and glasses both. Eating is one of the most personal, intimate things you do; so don't corrupt it by eating from things that have a plastic look, feel, or smell.

People with small children may want to consider a new type of dishes; these are actually glass, but virtually unbreakable—they won't break or chip even if dropped on a wooden floor. Unfortunately, they have a slightly glassy surface, but they do come in plain colors or reasonably attractive patterns.

3. Buy practical knives.

A few of our essential artifacts go back to the beginnings of human history, and knives are among them. Peoples have used knives (first stone, then metal) as long as they have been human. And we use knives constantly, many times a day. (Not to mention the intense symbolic role that knives play in our fantasies and dreams.) You might think, then, that people would insist on having really beautiful knives that could aptly assume their important place in our lives: After all, it is well within the capacity of modern designers and factories to manufacture elegant, inexpensive knives. But most stores sell junky knives and most people use junky knives, or knives that look fancy but can hardly cut butter. If you are used to seeing knives only in ordinary hardware or variety stores, you should visit a specialty knife store sometime. This will give you a new perspective on knives and prove to you how awful-looking most people's knives are—which is too bad, since an ugly or unbalanced knife is a constant nagging annoyance, whether we realize it or not.

Although the variety of shapes, sizes, and styles in a big knife store will seem bewildering, there are just two kinds of knife that the average person needs: a pocket knife, and a fair-sized knife with which meat, bread, leather, rubber, small pieces of wood, vegetables, and other things can be cut. A knife with a blade about eight inches long can be used in the kitchen and also carried around with you in a sheath on your belt, for camping. The well-known Bowie-type sheath knives are very strong; they have a protective hilt and usually a six-inch blade, although an eight-inch version exists which is known as the "Arkansas toothpick." A knife made of a good carbon steel can be re-sharpened for years and will retain a keen edge. Carbon steel can discolor from food acids like tomato juice, and it can rust if left wet. But this doesn't hurt its cutting ability, and you may like the irregular dark patina that develops; or you can keep it burnished with metal polish or steel wool. In recent years, however, stainless-steel knives have become virtually as good.

To carry around with you, a pocketknife is practically a survival tool. Some will do any light mechanical job, except hammering. Knives are made with screwdrivers, bottle openers, can openers, corkscrews, augers, files, saws, scissors, tweezers, and even toothpicks. The Swiss army knife, which is available in a wide range of sizes and complexities, is solidly made, although expensive. Being a stainless-steel job, the one thing it can't do terribly well is cut. It's red and has "Officier Suisse" stamped on the blade, but there are many cheap imitations.

What you need in the way of knives, of course, depends on many factors of taste, and some people just like to have a lot of knives around—there's no denying that a wide assortment of beautiful knives is lovely to have in your kitchen. The shapes of knives are like the shapes of boats and other artifacts that have been around the human scene for a couple of thousand years: They have been varied and refined over the centuries to the point where very elegant knives indeed are available, along with the commercial junk. Knives vary in balance (how their weight is distributed), heft (their total weight), and handle and balance shapes, which affect how they fit your hand and working habits. You should not settle for a knife that doesn't look and feel right to you. The manner in which the handle is fixed to the blade needs special attention. Is it firm enough to take heavy stresses? Is the metal binding around the handle ends, if there is one, flimsy? If there is no hilt, is there a rounded, projecting heel on the blade so that your wet hand can't slip onto the blade? Are there places where cracks may open up to catch food particles and moisture? Does the brass or bronze or other metal of the handle go well with the color of the blade?

Price is not a reliable indication of the quality of a knife, although no really good knife is cheap. You can pay a great deal of money for a practically useless stainless-steel knife, but you can get a carbon-steel knife that will last you for decades for only a few dollars.

Sharpening knives is important to keep them in good health and serviceable to you. Do not use wall sharpeners or other grinder-type sharpeners unless you are experienced with knives and can tell if they are in proper adjustment; otherwise you may grind away your blade and never get it sharp. Anyway it's better to get a sharpening steel—one of those long, thin, rodlike devices. Or you can use a small stone—they are cheap and come on wooden handles, making them convenient to hold in the hand so you can strop the blade on them. Buy one in a specialized knife store, and use it as they tell you to.

There's more to using a knife than just hacking away. Peer into the kitchen of the next Chinese restaurant you're in and study their technique of chopping vegetables with incredible speed and precision; if you are a real vegetable eater you may want to get a chopper as well as a knife. Get somebody who really knows how to carve to show you the joints in chicken and things like leg of lamb. One secret of carving an odd-shaped piece is to slice off one side to give you a flat side; then put that on the bottom.

4. Buy a good mirror cheaply.

Every house needs a more or less full-length mirror—women and men both like them, and it's also important for young children to get some idea of what they look like. New mirrors are expensive, but secondhand stores sell mirrors at reasonable cost, especially when they have a cracked corner or a little patch of the silvery backing flaking off. But check that the mirror is really flat—stand back at least ten feet from it and see if it gives a true reflection. A wavy mirror is madness-making. It's best to have a good flat mirror, even if it has small defects or an unaesthetic frame (you can always take a frame off or replace it).

5. Buy an inexpensive wet mop.

One of the jolly little swindles that keep American businesses going is in mops. The old string-type mops are a mess to handle, and you really need a bucket with a wringer to dry them between swabs at the floor. Hence someone invented the mop with a sponge and a little lever to squash the sponge and get the water out. This was so clever, in fact, that many mop companies started making them. But each mop company shaped its device a little differently, and each company designed a slightly different replacement sponge, with a different method of attaching it to the handle. This ensured that nobody could replace a Brand X sponge with a Brand Y sponge, and since Brand X ones are likely to be out of stock at any given time, this means that you can chase around a long time before finding one that matches. Worse still, you may try to make the Brand Y sponge fit. By drilling new holes, you may be able to use the new type. But then again you may not.

Your only possible recourse is to march into the store with your mop and ask the clerk to put a new sponge on it. The chances are about 99 to 1 that clerks won't be able to do it, even if they are willing to unwrap the sacred cellophane packages. You then ask to see the manager, pointing out that you bought the mop less than a year ago, paying a hefty price for it, and how come its sponge can't be replaced? (You talk in a loud voice in scenes like this and wave the old mop handle around, and complain about stores not standing behind their merchandise.) If you're lucky they will simply give you a new mop to stop you from discouraging sales to other customers.

When you come back for a replacement sponge next year, of course, you'll find that there is another crop, none of which fit either. This is known as progress. Maybe it explains why American Indians got along with dirt floors.

6. Buy inexpensive pots and pans.

There's almost no reason to buy pans new. Secondhand stores have a good supply of heavy old frying pans and pots of many sizes, discarded by people who have gone in for Teflon-lined pans, electric pans, and other "gourmet" ware. (Teflon, when it gets overheated, gives off a poisonous gas; don't let it in the house.) In a general way, the heavier a pan is, the better, because it will conduct heat more evenly. Thin aluminum pans conduct heat all right, but they dent easily and have a tinny feel. There is some evidence that constant cooking with aluminum pans introduces small but unhealthy amounts of aluminum into your system. In any case, stainless-steel pots are the easiest to keep clean and are very durable. The best contain copper or aluminum bottoms, which aid heat distribution. Get pots with tight-fitting lids, because they save a lot of heat and also help in cooking vegetables quickly. It may be worth it to buy a brand-new lid to go with a cheap secondhand pot, even though you spend more on the lid.

You don't need an expensive pot rack to hang pots from. Use nails or dowels in an attractive board (or the wall) or wire hooks made from coat hangers.

7. Buy inexpensive, stainless-steel utensils.

These days "silverware" usually means either silver plate or stainless steel. There are two reasons why stainless steel is better: It is generally made in simpler designs, and it doesn't peel the way plate does. Secondhand stores usually have big boxes full of assorted cast-off knives, forks, and spoons. (Don't worry about uniformity or you'll get nowhere.) Learn to spot used stainless by its soft gray color and its hard feel (silver plate tends to be a bit yellower, and often you can see brass or rusty steel peeking out where the plate has begun to wear through or peel off.) Then pick out items that have plain lines and a good heft to them. Watch out for knives with loose handles. Bent fork tines can usually be straightened, but they'll never be completely straight.

New stainless steel in pleasant and sometimes elegant designs can now be bought fairly cheaply in import outlets and some hardware stores.

If you eat oriental style, you should have chopsticks. Bamboo ones (not plastic) are best, and can be bought very cheaply in Chinatowns. They simplify table setting, not to mention dish washing, and are fun to eat with. Incidentally, when spoons or forks slip down the sink drain, you can often fish them up with a pair of chopsticks.

8. Use string or cloth bags for shopping.

The standard European shopping trip is accomplished not with heavy double-thickness brown paper bags (for which many trees die daily) but with the traditional string bag—which, these days, is also available in colorful (and perhaps here excusable) plastic. You can routinely carry a string bag in pocket or purse just in case you need it, since it folds up to practically nothing. It is a good idea, of course, to save and reuse brown bags; but you can't carry them with you very easily.

Sturdy cloth shopping bags have also become available, as a means of avoiding the impossible choice between "paper or plastic" at the checkout. Carry a couple of these in your car, and you will save many trees. It will help you remember to take them into the store if you hang a little reminder card on the door handle of your car.

If you live near enough to a big-enough store to do your major shopping there, consider a small hauling cart big enough to hold a couple of grocery bags. It will give you some exercise and reduce air pollution.

D. Fix it yourself.

Every home needs to have a drawer or box or cabinet that is its toolbox. There you should keep a small but basic supply of fix-it materials. You'll have a certain amount of money tied up in these things; so you'll want to accumulate them slowly, but every item you can make last a little longer saves you the cost of replacing it. Often a minor repair, which costs nothing except the use of a pliers or some glue, will extend the life of an object for years. Some people never have any repairs done outside the house; they allow into the house only things they know they can take care of. Most of us, though we admire such firmness of character, like to have at least some things around (such as a stereo) that we know we can't deal with entirely. But we can cope with many of the minor problems that arise.

Here are the basic household tools: hammer (a full-sized one, not a tack hammer); screwdriver; pliers; wood saw; pipe wrench; crescent wrench; a small wood plane; medium-sized file; hacksaw (for metal); wood chisel; putty knife; paintbrush; oil can.

The basic household repair materials should include: electric tape; some jars of assorted-sized nails; a jar full of assorted screws; another full of assorted nuts and bolts and washers; a box of spackle to patch holes in walls; paint thinner, diesel oil, or linseed oil to clean brushes. Also you'll find a collection of several kinds of glue useful: epoxy glue (for difficult gluing jobs, even glass, and where moisture may be a problem); Duco cement (for small objects—quick drying); white glue (Elmer's, etc.—for wood, paper, and similar materials); Barge Glue (a flexible, strong, waterproof glue for practically anything—hard to find, but worth the hunt). There are several other useful kinds of glue to have around, such as contact cement (for things you can't hold or clamp while they dry), silicone-rubber cement (for joints that must flex), plastic-mending cement, and waterproof resorcinol glue (for use on furniture that may get wet or steamy).

You should also have a can of lightweight oil to lubricate small motors or hinges; a spray can of silicone lubricant for sliding doors and drawers; and a penetrating oil for unfreezing frozen nuts, locks, and hinges.

Once you have a set place where you keep working materials, you will slowly accumulate more—leftover pieces of wire, steel, hunks of rubber tire or inner tube, bits of leather, partly used cans of paint (hammer the top back on tightly, or the paint won't keep), and lots of other fascinating things. Don't let anybody shame you into throwing any of this stuff away; you'll need it the next day! (If necessary, store it in boxes to save space.)

Beginning do-it-yourself repairers often get discouraged, because they manage to get something apart, find nothing wrong with it, and then can't get it back together. There are two tricks you can use to make sure this doesn't happen. But also take comfort from the fact that often merely disassembling, oiling, cleaning, and reassembling a device or appliance will make it work again—you may not have noticed it, but in taking it apart you removed some dirt that was fouling a contact, or loosened a shaft that was binding.

The first trick is to provide near your working place a big surface on which you can lay parts out strictly in the order you remove them, and so far as possible in the relative positions they occupied. That way, even if you get confused as to what does what, you can always just blindly put everything back in order, if necessary. Be especially careful about washers, spacers, and other small and apparently trivial parts: They may have to be in just the proper order for parts to move properly, or even to stay together at all. As you remove each part, notice if it has grooves or keyways or special-shaped holes or pins, and how they fit.

Second, you can code parts by marking them. This is essential in many gear mechanisms, for instance, where worn teeth must run just as before or they will bind; you mark them by putting small punch marks on two teeth of one gear and on the tooth they meet on the opposing gear. With wires, you can attach little bits of colored yarn, or small tags, pieces of masking tape with colored markings. With wooden objects, you can write corresponding key letters or numbers on the part of each piece where it meets another piece, so that in reassembling you bolt A back onto the other A, and B onto B.

Most mechanical devices turn out to be full of old, gummed-up oil and dust that needs to be removed by soaking or wiping and dabbing with alcohol, paint thinner, or some other solvent. Avoid over-oiling when you reassemble. And in devices with small, delicate parts, such as clocks, you need special, very light instrument oil or sewing-machine oil, used sparingly. Sometimes you can clean such devices without disassembling by using a straw and blowing hard, and then dabbing solvent on the end of a toothpick or a piece of heavy string.

1. Rent special tools.

Most cities now have many rental companies that will rent you anything from a small electric drill to heavy equipment, such as a cement mixer. Their prices vary a good deal; so try phoning a couple from the Yellow Pages to locate what you want. (Most items require a deposit; ask how much.)

Often being able to get the right kind of heavy tool will make the difference between being able to do a job yourself or having to hire a professional. Sanding and refinishing a floor is a good example—you can rent a heavy sander for a day and do a job that would literally be impossible without it.

Renting tools is not second best to owning them unless they are tools you use constantly. Even contractors seldom own all the tools they need; they rent them occasionally, and so don't need to worry about theft, repairs, upkeep, or paying off the purchase price. The more expensive the tool, the more advantageous is renting.

When you are checking out something from a rental outfit, be sure you know how to work it. Also verify that it's in working condition—otherwise you may be liable for repair costs. A good way to make sure of this is to ask them to "show you how to use it."

Rentals are usually for twenty-four hours, but some items can be gotten for a shorter time at a cheaper rate. You can also rent things by the week— even vacation trailers.

A few public libraries have now begun to loan tools; your city may have a public tool-rental service.

2. Do minor repair.

Around every house there are things that drive you crazy because they won't work right. Often this is a sign that you should get rid of them; but there will be times when you don't want to, or can't.

Cabinets that won't shut or stay shut. Scrape off the bumps of paint that have accumulated around the edges of doors and around hinges and latch. Unscrew the catch and soak it in paint remover, or at least scrape it and squirt some penetrating oil into it. Better yet, throw it away and replace it with a cheap magnetic catch (one of the few modern household inventions that is a real improvement over what it replaced). If the cabinet is no longer square, you may have to unscrew the hinges and plane the edges of the door (or the door hole).

Can openers that won't cut or turn the can. Soak in hot soapy water, then clean the working parts with an old toothbrush, toothpick, etc. If the handle doesn't turn easily, put a drop of oil where the handle or shaft passes through the frame.

Handle loose on knife. If the blade is simply extended down the handle, pull it out, fill the hole with epoxy glue, and force the blade back into place. Let it dry for two days to cure the epoxy fully, or wetness will loosen it again. Big knives usually have riveted handles that can be pounded to tighten.

Bed squeaks. Get rid of the springs (better for your body anyway). Lay a panel of plywood over the slats and sleep on that. If the frame of the bed squeaks, try gluing the loose joints. Or maybe now is the time to think about doing away with your bed entirely.

Electric fan doesn't go back and forth. Clean the oscillating mechanism under the back of the fan with alcohol, paint thinner, or even a small rag with soap and water. Put a little oil on the moving parts. Oil the fan motor—just a few drops—if you can find an oil hole.

Electric iron sticks. Irons get fouled from starch, soap residues, etc. Washing when cool (and unplugged) with soap and warm water will usually remove the stuff, or use very fine emery cloth or steel wool. Then coat the iron with candle wax, beeswax, etc., and wipe off the excess.

Stove pilot light won't stay on, or burners won't light. Since grease is probably the culprit, clean the whole thing thoroughly first, or you don't have a chance. Warm water and ammonia works. Poke a needle through all the gas passages. Adjust pilot gas at the little screw where the tube begins that goes to it. Remove tubes to burners and make sure they are clear. They also need to be level. Sometimes blowing gently will light a stubborn burner. You will save energy and money by installing an electric ignition system (or by using a laboratory-type lighter and turning the pilot off for good).

Screen door bangs. Tack several layers of inner-tube strips along the door frame to cushion bang. Or buy a door closer (tubular gadget) or a snap-shut device that flips over as the door closes.

Window blind snaps up, or won't stay down, or won't go up. On the whole, shades aren't very attractive. But the lightproof kind are the best way to make a room dark during the daylight hours. If you have them, you should understand the clever little ratchet mechanism inside one end of the roller. A shade that won't stay down can usually be fixed by oiling that little ratchet. It has a spring that enables it to rewind the roller just as much as it's pulled down, but no more and no less. If the shade is dropping loosely, you wind the spring up by pulling the shade down and then taking it out of the brackets and rolling it up to the top by hand. If it's snapping up too fast, reverse this: Take it off the brackets and unroll it by hand. A shade that rubs against one of its brackets all the time may not be mounted level, or you may be pulling it sideways as you reach for it. If the edges get frayed, trim them with a scissors.

Electric plug won't stay in receptacle firmly. Sometimes you can get it to stay by bending the prongs of the plug outward slightly, and then reinserting it. In very old receptacles, however, you may need to turn off the house current, remove the receptacle from its box, and put in a new one.

Electrical trouble. When you move into a new place, make sure you find out where the fuses are. The most common trouble with electricity is that a fuse blows out because too many electric appliances are turned on at once. If that happens, all the lights on that fuse's circuit will go out. Turn off most of the light switches and all the appliance switches, and go with a flashlight or candle to replace the fuse (it screws in just like a small light bulb) with another of the same amperage rating (usually 10, 15, or 20 amps). Keep a box of fuses on hand, since fuses almost always blow at night when stores are closed. A blown fuse has its little window blackened by the melted fuse metal inside. If the replacement fuse also blows, you've got real trouble, and an electrician is needed. Never put a penny into a fuse hole; if there is a short circuit in the walls, you may burn down the house. Replacing a low-amperage fuse with a higher amperage one enables you to operate more lights or appliances, but decreases the safety factor in your wiring, especially in old houses with their original wiring. If your trouble, however, is sudden surges of current from the starting up of a furnace or refrigerator motor, "delay" fuses will tolerate these surges without blowing.

Old houses tend to have too few electrical outlets; so people get multireceptacle plugs to stick in them, and run extension cords all over the place. There is nothing wrong with extension cords, but most of those sold in ordinary stores are too light; they get frayed or worn and short out, or pets or children chew through them. The best thing is to build your own extension; measure to where you want it go, and buy heavy-duty wire, a good solid plug, and a multireceptacle outlet for the other end. Staple the wire to the baseboard as it goes around the room to keep it from getting mashed by furniture, vacuum cleaners, etc. But be sure to use the padded type for this, and don't puncture the wire.

Keep electrical cords and devices away from sinks, bathtubs, and pipes, since water conducts current, and you might get a nasty or even fatal shock.

If you are really short of outlets (or blow fuses often), you may have too many electrical devices in the house.

3. Fix small electrical appliances yourself.

Many simple devices like hot plates, waffle irons, toasters, hand irons, and hair dryers are basically just heating coils (or strips) in some kind of case. They have a thermostat to keep them from getting overheated. Hair dryers and room heaters also have a fan to circulate the air they warm. Aside from cord trouble, the most common problem with these appliances is a break in the heating element. Over the years the heating coils or strips literally evaporate; also they get more brittle, and a jolt may finally break them, so that the current can't pass anymore.

To deal with these devices, first check the prongs on the plug and the cord to see that the wire is OK. Also check to make sure there is current in the receptacle you're using. A simple test is to plug the appliance into some other outlet.

If you have to open it up, be sure the appliance is unplugged. Sometimes screws or bolts are under the nameplate or handle, which comes loose. Once it's open, shake it and look for places where the heating elements seem loose. They may also be loose at the terminals. You can reconnect broken ends by twisting them around each other firmly and squeezing with a pliers. (Make sure the twisted ends don't touch the metal case, or they'll short-circuit and give somebody a nasty shock.) This procedure won't last as long as a new element—which an electric shop can probably sell you if you have the model number—but it doesn't cost anything.

Lamps and other nonheating-type appliances have several things that may go wrong with them. In order of likelihood: plug not making contact in receptacle (bend prongs a little); cord broken (replace); bulb not touching the bottom of socket (unscrew bulb, unplug lamp, and pry up tab at bottom of socket); switch broken (take apart and put in new one).

4. Improvise instead of buying.

It is nice, of course, to be able to repair and build things "like a professional" —to buy the right replacement parts or hardware, to fit and machine things to fit exactly, to attach them with the best screws, clamps, and brackets. But this can be expensive; so the home fixer, who is trying to make improvements while still not spending any money, must be ready to improvise at every level.

The key is to be bold. You will get nowhere by trying simply to cut corners—you'll end up with tawdry results. What you need to do is to think big, and you may come up with something really beautiful. There is always more than one way to do things, and sometimes the usual way is not the most attractive or interesting. It is possible, by developing a sense of innovative design, to build and fix things without a great deal of the usual money-eating expenses.

Here, for instance, are possible alternatives to some basic hardware items.

Hinges. You can use a nail or dowel coming from a frame into the swinging door, window, or whatever. Or combine big staples and nails. You can also use pieces of inner tube, leather, or other flexible and durable substances, tacked on like hinges. Better yet, use a sliding door—a piece of plywood running between strips of wood—that doesn't need hinges.

Latches. In parts of the country where wood is used for everything, like the Pacific Northwest, door and gate latches are made with wooden bolts sliding in wooden guides.

Clothes hooks. If you have a wooden wall, or a wooden strip running along the wall, drill holes in it and glue in dowels.

Toilet-paper holder. Find a small Y-shaped branch; carve it to shape with a pocketknife and screw onto the wall (the same idea, but with a bigger stick, works for paper towels).

Cupboard doorknobs, and other hand grips. Use small, odd-shaped pieces of driftwood or weathered wood.

Broken windows. In places where it makes a burglar's entry easier, broken glass should be replaced. But in other locations you could preserve the old glass by taping the crack (outside and inside) with some fiberglass-reinforced wrapping tape. A whole roll of this is expensive; try to beg, borrow, or steal a few feet of it. (Package-wrapping stations in warehouses, stores, and offices have it.) No other kind of tape, except Mystik tape, which won't let light through, will stick to glass for any length of time. Clean the glass carefully where the tape will be; make sure it's dry before you stick on the tape.

Best of all is to get the owner to pay for the glass and putty if you do the work. It takes only a few minutes to learn—the essentials are to clean the frame carefully and measure the window dimensions exactly, so that the glass shop cuts the pane to fit precisely.

Curtain rings. With a pair of pliers you can improvise rings out of clothes hangers; they can even be made to spring shut on the cloth, so that no sewing on is required. Generally rings are better than sewing the cloth into a wide hem and then sticking the rod through—even if the hem is very big, it tends to bind, but a ring system slides easily.

Suspending things. Hardware stores are full of hooks, wires, rods, buckets, bars, and so on, but you almost never really need anything but nails—and even nails can often be replaced by a hole. If, for instance, you want to hang up something in a wooden cabinet, you can drill little holes in it, run strings or wires through the holes, and knot them inside. You accomplish three things by such an alternative to the conventional hook or whatnot: You liberate yourself from the standard way of doing things, you keep ugly chrome-plated or plastic junk out of your house, and you save money. You imagination, once liberated, may lead you to do quite beautiful things: braiding colorful strings to hang up paper towels or toilet paper, using pieces of tree branch as coat hooks, building special little racks of driftwood or scrap wood for spices or candles or writing materials, planting small plants in the cavities in rocks or driftwood, hanging pots and pans from twisted pieces of very old rusty metal, and so on.

Rod supports (for curtain rods, shower rods, towel-roll rods, etc.). Make V-shaped supports by tacking two small pieces of wood to the wall, or driving three or four nails in a U-shape.

5. Fix heating problems.

Owners of rental dwellings are obliged by law to provide reasonable heat, and if you don't get it you can file a complaint to the city authorities or deduct from the rent the cost of heating the place yourself. But if you don't want to go that route, you may be able to improve the heating situation a little by yourself.

Air leaks around windows. Before cold weather comes, if possible, fill up the cracks. From the outside, where they are exposed to weather, the best thing to use is some kind of putty or sealing compound. (In cold country, some people just cover the whole window area with sheet plastic.) From the inside, practically anything will do—torn up newspapers soaked in flour-and-water glue and tightly forced into cracks, then painted when dry; rags dipped in some old paint and stuffed into cracks. Tack weather stripping around doors so they close tightly.

Radiators that don't heat up enough. Hot-water radiators sometimes fill up with air; then the hot water can't get into them. Get a valve key from a hardware store (or the landlord) and open the valve, so that air hisses out. When mostly water comes out, close it again. This may have to be done often, and if so only an automatic valve will permanently cure the problem.

Steam radiators also have a valve, which may be clogged. Turn off steam at the main turn-off handle. Unscrew the valve and clean out its little hole with a piece of fine wire (a very thin hairpin or a needle may work). Blow through or shake it, to get the water out. Steam radiators also have to be leveled just right. If they have just one pipe coming to them, they should slant down toward it just a little. You need a level to make sure, since the whole building may be tilted. Two-pipe radiators should slant toward the return pipe (the one without a turn-off handle). You can stick thin pieces of wood, linoleum, etc., under the legs to get them at the right angle.

Gas heaters that don't work. The most common trouble with wall or floor heaters is that their pilot-light thermocouple (which generates current to run the thermostat and safety cutoff) is shot. Replacing it will cost money, but it is not a complicated job, and hardware stores have recently begun to sell replacements. Turn off the gas at the meter, then remove the thermocouple and take it along to the store to be sure you get the right replacement.

Electric heaters. Electricity costs far more than gas for a given amount of heat. But an electric heater may be justifiable if you want to heat one small room and leave the rest of the apartment or house cool. Secondhand heaters can easily be found in good condition or with easily repaired defects, such as dust collected in the thermostat.

Kerosene and other room heaters. There are cheap kerosene heaters that are attractive in an old-fashioned way, but they have two disadvantages: Even if you use deodorized kerosene, the heaters still smell, and since they don't have vents, they tend to fill your room with polluted air. You can really only use them like the old potbellied stove: They're OK for drafty rooms when you are sitting right next to them. But you can't rely on them for regular heat; to use kerosene for that, you need a bigger heater vented through the wall or roof.

Turning on stove to give heat. When all else fails, you can use an ordinary stove to heat at least your kitchen. The best way is to turn on the oven and leave its door open, with the broiler door open a crack. But you also get quite a lot of heat if you turn on several burners *and put big pots of water on them.* This has two effects: The sides of the pots become "radiators," and the water vapor from the boiling raises the humidity, which makes the air feel warmer, as in a steam room. (You don't want to do this too much in a tight room, as excessive stream may loosen plaster.)

The healthiest temperature for human beings is around 65°F (18°C), but most Americans find that chilly. Many American houses are kept around 80° or even 85°—temperatures so high that they dry out your nasal passages. Oddly enough, people tend to overheat the most in cold climates—in New York, for instance, you may come in from zero weather to a blazing hot apartment where you immediately break out in a sweat.

Rather than overheating your home, put on a sweater, or wear two shirts, or even wear long underwear. This will also cut down the shock of going outdoors into the cold. You will conserve surprising amounts of energy and, if you are paying for your own heat, you'll save a great deal of money, because those extra degrees of heat are very expensive.

A thermostat not only helps keep the temperature steady, but also saves fuel. Whether you have a gas heater, a kerosene heater, or a furnace, it should be on a thermostat. Then keep the thermostat set between 65° and 70°F (18°–21°C). Turn it down even lower at night.

6. Respect the limits of materials.

The wise craftsperson does not try to make materials do things that are not within their capacity, but works along with their capabilities, studying their strengths, and designing around their weaknesses. Stone and concrete have great compressive strength; wood has tensile strength and also resists bending. Steel and other metals have great tensile strength (as does glass in fiber form), but do not resist bending unless they are heavy.

The means by which parts can be connected also have their limitations. You should not try to drive screws or nails into the end grain of wood—they will quickly pull out. (If a fillet or other way of attaching is not possible, consider doweling.) You should not drive nails through thin pieces of wood—they will split, especially if the piece is also narrow. Glue can hold only if the joint offers a large-enough surface considering the weight or force that may bear on it; otherwise, even if the glue itself holds, it will tear off the surface layer of the wood. Nonporous materials such as glass are hard to glue, even with epoxy or silicone-rubber glue, even if you clean the surfaces scrupulously. Any joint that is not firm and tight is hard to glue, because slight wiggles during the time the glue is drying will prevent a solid bond. (In gluing a loose chair rung, you can wrap a thin piece of glue-soaked cloth around the part that goes into the hole; this will decrease the play.) When clamping a joint isn't feasible, you can probably put a light nail into it, either permanently or just to hold it while it dries. Glue is usually not only neater but cheaper than screws or bolts.

Nails are best at holding boards together against shearing or twisting stresses; nails driven at an angle have some resistance to pulling (especially in pairs), but if you need to hold two pieces together against forces that try to pull them apart, it is better to use screws, and best to use bolts. In soft woods or where large forces are involved, big washers will spread the stress better.

In attaching parts to one another, the principle of triangulation is important: Whenever three points are fixed, they create a rigid shape. This is why houses and other heavy structures normally have diagonal frame elements—otherwise they would need very heavy joints to prevent swaying. A flat membrane like a piece of plywood will also stabilize a structure if it is attached at a number of points.

7. Be your own plumber.

Plumbers don't actually make the stupendous wages people imagine (much of their bills are for the same kind of overhead every business charges you for), but calling a plumber is bound to cost quite a lot. Most plumbing troubles are essentially simple and can be fixed without spending more than a few cents.

Clogged sinks. Sinks and washbasins have a "trap" underneath in which a little water is retained to keep sewer gases from backing up through the drain into your house. But these S- or P-shaped traps also trap grease from dishwater or hot fat that gets poured down the sink. When the grease hits the cold pipes, it tends to solidify and then pick up small pieces of food, etc. When it does get clogged—and every sink will, sooner or later—you'll need to borrow (if you don't have one) a "plumber's helper": a rubber bell-shaped thing on the end of a wooden stick. Put it over the drain, making sure it seals well, and work it up and down briskly. You will hear gurgling noises in the drain; that means it's working. Stop and see if the water is going down. If it isn't, or is going down very slowly, do some more "plunging." When it does get running better, turn on the hot water very hot, and run that for a while.

This is almost sure to work. If it doesn't, there are two possibilities: Either the trap is so clogged with old material that the sucking and pressure of the plumber's helper won't loosen it (as might be true if your sink has drained slowly for a long while) or the obstruction is somewhere below the trap (so that you or your downstairs neighbors may have noticed leakage elsewhere in the house drains). The trap may have a clean-out opening that comes out when turned with a wrench, but chances are you will have to remove the trap. This requires a large pipe wrench, some rags or tape to wrap around the nuts to prevent scratching them, and two replacement rubber gaskets to keep the trap from leaking when you put it back again. (Measure the diameter of the drainpipe, and go out and buy these gaskets before you start the job. Most hardware stores carry them. On old traps that have been scratched or bent, these gaskets may not seal; so it is wise to have some silicone cement handy, or at least some pipe compound, as backup.) Rings or silverware that fall down the sink can also be retrieved by removing the trap.

Backed-up toilets. There are few things as depressing as sewage floating around in your bathroom. Unfortunately, toilets easily get clogged by tampons, sanitary napkins, pencils, "disposable" diapers, pieces of cardboard or plastic, and other things that children like to flush. On a fishing boat I once saw a sign that read "Don't Flush Anything Down This Toilet You Haven't Swallowed First," and although this rule reflects the stringency needed to keep a boat toilet in working order, it's a good reminder that the toilet drainpipe is only about three inches across, and the pipe through which sewage flows has many joints that are not perfectly smooth inside. In short, a toilet will satisfactorily carry away only things that dissolve quickly in water.

When your toilet backs up, first try the plumber's helper. Get it well set in the neck of the toilet bowl before you start plunging up and down with it. Most often the obstruction is within the toilet itself, not down in the drainpipes, so you have a good chance of dislodging it. More stubborn obstacles can be removed with a "snake" or long, thin, flexible cable, which you gently twist and wangle down through the toilet. This must be lightweight or you will damage the toilet, which is actually a huge piece of crockery and quite crackable as well as scratchable.

Running toilets. Toilet tanks contain a valve that is operated by a float. Theoretically, when the tank has filled up, the valve shuts off the water. If it doesn't, look inside the tank. The most likely trouble is that the rubber tank stopper (way down at the bottom, where the water runs out to go into the toilet bowl) isn't fitting into its seal properly; it's allowing a little leak, and thus the water level never gets quite high enough to shut off the valve. These ball-shaped stoppers get tired, flabby, and don't fit tightly anymore; new ones are cheap, and screw onto the end of the wire that holds them. (Don't be finicky about working inside the toilet tank with your hands; the brown deposits you may see are deposits from the clean, incoming tank water.) Once you have put on a new ball, the thing should work OK. If it doesn't, the wire holding the stopper may be bent so it doesn't slide easily through its holder. Float balls may be waterlogged (replacement balls are easily obtainable) or their support rods may be bent. A little oil can't hurt, where the valve-action levers are supported. The valve itself is seldom at fault.

Clogged shower heads. All water supplies contain minute quantities of minerals and other substances, and as the water runs through fine holes, some of these get deposited. Take off the shower head and poke the holes open with a needle. (While you're at it, install a flow-restrictor disc, which will save you a surprising amount on your water-heating bill.)

Leaking faucets. Faucets contain little rubber disks called washers that press against a round seat to stop the water from flowing. These washers slowly wear out, causing the faucet to drip, and must be replaced. But before unscrewing the packing nut at the top of the faucet, be sure you have turned off the water—either at the shut-off valve under the sink or basin, or at the main house water-supply valve. Chances are that you will not be able to tell what kind of washer is needed until you get the faucet apart. Hardware and plumbing-supply stores sell little bags of assorted washers. When you replace the packing nut, be careful to get the handle part screwed in right, and don't tighten the nut more than is needed to stop seepage around the faucet stem.

When a faucet starts to leak, don't take to twisting it shut with force and violence. That will just wreck the poor washer and possibly its seat as well, which means real trouble. Fix it—and any others around the house that are dripping—because even a slow drip can waste an astounding amount of water.

Banging noises in the plumbing. Hammering noises signify that something is seriously wrong, which will tear the plumbing apart in time. Tell the owner about it and mention that real plumbing trouble is likely if it isn't fixed. Chattering in the pipes may be caused by worn or loose washers.

Incidentally, the single-handle faucet is a fine example of the kind of technological "progress" we get from our housing industry: It looks fancy and streamlined, and is expensive—but it's very hard to adjust to give the temperature and amount of water you want, and if anything goes wrong with it, you may have to call in a plumber.

Chapter 10.
Find It Yourself.

Just as you don't have to depend on others to furnish or make repairs in your home, you also don't have to depend on others for information. In fact, you will do much better to find things out for yourself, since, if you settle for other people's answers, you get answers only to *their* questions, and not to the questions that are important to you.

There are two major reasons for finding out things for yourself: for entertainment, and for self-education. But the more you enjoy learning, the more this distinction becomes happily blurred.

Nobody can possibly remember all the information needed to confront life's nasty little problems. In fact, a good education chiefly equips you with tools for locating information when and as you need it. (Most of the information you memorized in school is hopelessly outdated.) One basic information source is the library—but except for those which provide telephone reference service, you have to go there to use the resources.

A. Learn to use the telephone.

With persistence and some imagination, you can track down much useful information on the telephone, thus saving much walking, bus fares, and car rides. Don't hesitate to phone a store and ask if they have something you are looking for. If you are trying to find out something that a governmental office might be able to help with, look under "United States Government" in the phone book; you'll probably still have to phone their information number and ask for help, since many agencies are listed in confusing or obscure ways, have just changed their names, or are not listed separately at all; most big cities have far more federal offices than you would suspect. If you get nowhere this way, phone the office your congressional representative maintains in your district; it has a staff of people who know about what the government does or doesn't do in your area, and may be able to give you individual names of people to call. The same goes for city councils; your representative needs your vote, and maintains a staff that is supposed to keep you happy and thus get that vote; make them work for it!

A special information service for toll-free numbers is maintained by governmental agencies and many corporations: 800-555-1212. Try it if you need to contact one that doesn't have a local directory listing.

B. Learn to use informal channels.

If you are interested in some special field, you will soon find that there are two kinds of information-providing machinery. One is the official channel of printed publications, brochures, lectures, books, etc. This serves well to disseminate information widely, but it is always fairly slow. Consequently another, unofficial channel develops. Among scientists, for example, personal exchange of drafts of papers, telephone calls, and personal letters or faxes constitutes the real, living means by which people keep up with what others are doing. By the time a paper reaches actual publication, it's stale news. And in every field, networks of active workers exist, tied in to each other by these informal means. To be abreast of the state of the art, therefore, find some way of tapping into these circuits. This is not easy unless you have something to contribute that the people in the network will find attractive and interesting too. There are now computer services through which you can communicate with kindred souls, but they are unedited and thus offer a lot of junk along with a few brilliant thoughts. One is the WELL; for information, phone 415-332-4335.

C. Read periodicals and newspapers.

A taste for reading magazines quickly gets expensive. You can, of course, simply stand at magazine racks reading them for hours at a time until you get ousted, and this is a great and cheap pleasure. But you should also find out about the periodicals room of your library, where recent issues of many well-known and obscure magazines are available—often with comfortable chairs to read them in. (Sometimes they can't be checked out of the library, at least not the brand-new issues.) You may not realize it, but there is probably a magazine devoted to any subject you care about, from films to fortune-telling. Some are popular, with information ranging from the intensely useful to the purely commercial (never trust a magazine that carries a lot of big ads from manufacturers in its field). A visit to a big university library periodicals room is an exhilarating experience: row upon row of magazines, newsletters, journals, in many languages.

Since it takes about a year to publish a book, new information, especially of a technical or political nature, usually first appears in magazines. The *Reader's Guide to Periodical Literature* indexes most of the major magazines, and can tell you which ones have printed articles in the last year on jet engines, capital punishment, food alteration, Albert Einstein, or Susan B. Anthony. A reference librarian always has the *Reader's Guide* handy, and can show you how to use it, along with more specialized similar guides in the arts, social sciences, and other fields.

Some people love newspapers and couldn't get up in the morning if they knew the paper wouldn't be there; others find newspapers unbearably depressing, and read them once a month if at all. American newspapers are certainly not getting any better; in most cities, the biggest paper has managed to wipe out its competitors and is getting fat from having all the advertising to itself. As a result, small, independently owned community papers have grown up; these are oriented toward cultural events and political issues the big papers wouldn't consider, and often print new writers with something trenchant and original to say. (They also tend to have useful classified ads.) Besides printing news from a generally radical viewpoint, they also have interesting features about local happenings, plus advice columns on health and other practical matters. It has also become much easier to obtain the *New York Times* in remote parts of the country, which (despite the *Times*'s own failings) gives you some check on the performance of your local trivia purveyors.

Newspaper coverage may not be unbiased, politically reliable, or complete, but it is immensely more complete than television news: The material presented on the television news could fit into a couple of columns of a newspaper. Oddly enough, however, the television networks do produce some special documentary programs that are more politically informative and critical than anything you will read in newspapers. Unfortunately, you cannot find out about them more than a day in advance.

D. Read Books.

When television came in, and Americans began spending huge portions of their waking time staring at it, technology mongers told us that the book would soon become extinct—or at least that we would begin to read even less than we had in the past. For reasons nobody really understands, this has not happened. Although some Americans still read nothing but newspapers and popular magazines, as a whole we are reading far more books (both in total and per capita) than ever before. One cause may be that more people have now had at least a year of college. Another may be the stupefying boredom of most television programs. At any rate, many people have discovered that nothing is as endlessly entertaining, mentally stimulating, hassle-free, and inexpensive as just plain reading.

Indeed, as our mass-media culture (including mass-market paperbacks) is increasingly controlled by giant multinational corporations, it will probably become ever more stuporous—which will make even more intriguing the crazies and geniuses who persist in writing personal, passionate books. A real writer is not the paid employee of some network, but an individual—probably a rather crotchety individual, with something to say—and not just filling in time until the next commercial. Nobody bleeps writers out. When you read, you are getting what truth the writer may have to utter, as straight and unconstrained as possible—especially if you seek out works published by small firms and university presses, which are still run by people who have eyes for more than "the bottom line."

Thus no matter where in the world you live, if you have access to a library or a bookstore, you can contact the finest minds humanity has produced—people seldom seen on the tube. You can match your wits against truly original persons whose thoughts put the "information" we are barraged with into a much clearer perspective. And you can escape the dead hand of network-approved "controversy"—it is in print that you can find really dissident, really critical opinions. We read to survive; we read to find out what is really going on; we read for pure pleasure. In fact, with new millions of people now literate, the world is going through an explosion of reading.

1. Avoid textbooks.

There is nothing like a textbook to take all the life out of a subject. One of the greatest and simplest reforms that could be undertaken in our schools (and our colleges and universities) would be to abolish texts entirely. This would throw teachers back on their own ingenuity and intelligence in organizing and presenting their material. Many teachers would develop new and ingenious approaches to things students need to know.

If you're a parent and your child has trouble in class, take a look at the textbook. Mark the passages that are dull, unclear, inaccurate, biased, prejudiced, sexist, or just plain impossible for an average rational reader to understand. Take it in and talk to the teacher about it; or write a letter about it to the state superintendent of schools, whose office is probably responsible for approving the texts your local school is forced to use. And if your child happens to get a good text once in a while, make a point of praising it to the same people.

But the main problem for students is to get out from under these pseudobooks. The way to do this is to learn how to use libraries, where the real books are. If a history text raves about what a great hero Cortez was, you can find books that tell what Cortez actually did—which might lead you to conclude that he was a white European imperialist interested in nothing but gold and power. If your civic textbooks tell you how governments are supposed to operate, there are many books that tell you how they operate in fact. And if the attitudes expressed in your texts seem outdated or just plain stupid, you can find many books in your library that can open up your mind instead of closing it off.

2. Read while waiting in line.

We usually think of time spent waiting as "lost." But in actuality, if you prepare for waiting time, you can put it to some kind of use, and will probably be less irritated as a result. Make a habit of carrying a paperback book with you; carry some paper to make notes on; learn some exercises that you can do unobtrusively. (Isometric exercises, which involve the pushing or pulling of one set of muscles against another, can be done without anybody noticing at all.) Don't be afraid to be talkative; strike up conversations with other people waiting who look interesting. Most of all, seize the occasion as a rare opportunity to *think*, away from the confusions and pressures of your interpersonal or job relationships. Standing in line can be almost as good for thinking as taking a long solitary walk. Address yourself to some problem or concern in your life. Examine it carefully and systematically, pros and cons and maybes. Consider whether there may be ways to approach it that you have been in too much of a rut to really think about. After a while, when the subject has gotten thoroughly established in your head, try to let your mind go blank about it, which might give new ideas the chance to surface.

E. Learn to use libraries.

Ironically enough, you can learn much more in a library than you probably will in school. The library may easily be the single most important educational resource you can have, and it will help you throughout life. You could never remember everything you may need to know; so you need to know how to find things out. Moreover, a library is just a good place to know about. (The atmosphere created by a large collection of books is unique.) And once you know how to find things in a library, you open up gigantic new frontiers of both knowledge and feeling—for in books is distilled the entire mental and emotional history of the human race. Whatever you might want to know, the chances are excellent that somewhere in your library is a book that can tell you.

But how do you find it?

Walking into a big library can be a forbidding experience. Many libraries were built to look like train stations or government offices, with huge pillars and lots of marble. But they are public institutions, open to all. And inside every library you will find pretty much the same kind of arrangement, so that once you are familiar with its parts, you will be able to use not only your own library, but libraries in other sections of the city, nearby university libraries, and so on.

Information desk. This is usually near the entrance. Someone there can explain how to get a library card so that you can take books home, and can help you find things or figure out how the library system works.

Reference room. The chief purpose of the reference room and reference librarians is to help people "look it up." The reference room contains encyclopædias, atlases, almanacs, directories, guides, bibliographies, and other books useful for tracking down information. It may have telephone books from many cities or even other countries. If you want to know how many sheep there are in New Zealand, or the address of a company in France, a reference librarian can show you where to find out. If you want to find some bibliographic information, the reference department can tell you where to look. It's absolutely amazing how much sheer information is packed into the reference room of even a small city library. (But usually only the main branch has a special reference room or reference desk.) You can obtain information from reference librarians over the phone in many cities, and sometimes even after ordinary library hours.

Card catalog. The heart of the library is its catalog, once on cards, now usually stored in a computer system; if you're nervous about computer terminals, ask for help in learning how to use them. Usually there is one category arranged alphabetically by the names of authors, and another arranged by titles of the books; look in whichever is more convenient. Sometimes catalogs also include a section arranged by subject. That way, if you are interested in clocks, or cars, or revolution, or music, you can find a whole collection of books that may be useful to you.

The call number, which also appears on the spine of the book itself, is your guide to where the book is located; write it down, along with the author and title, on a piece of scrap paper, or on a checkout card if the library uses them. Show it to a librarian and ask where the book is located.

Some smaller libraries have open stacks—that is, all their books are arranged on shelves open for browsing. This is a lovely way to spend time, and not nearly as dangerous for your pocketbook as browsing in a bookstore! As you wander around finding your own book, you will come across books that you would never have thought of looking for, and that will give you whole new areas to think about. Take the books you want to the check-out desk, where they record your borrowing of them. Some books you can keep for a month, some for shorter periods. The date by which books should be returned will be indicated on the card in the pocket on the inside cover of the book. Return books on time, or you get fined. (The library is the essence of communal sharing.)

Really huge libraries generally have closed stacks, where you hand in a call slip or check-out card, and then wait until someone retrieves the book from the stacks for you. In such libraries you'll be given a number, and when it lights up on a board over the sign-out desk, that means your book has come out. (It may take ten minutes, sometimes even more.) Then the people at the desk will check it out for you.

Libraries often have a special section for records and CDs, which can be checked out and taken home just like books. There may be a children's room, where books and records especially appealing to children are available. There may be an audiovisual department from which you can borrow films, slides, projectors, even videotape cassettes. There may even be a place to borrow tools. Magazines may be kept separately in a periodicals room; when they're about a year old, they are bound in heavy covers and stored in the stacks for later reference use. Newspaper rooms are also common—a useful place to check ads for jobs or places to live.

Books are the central means by which our society stores and preserves its culture. People talk about information retrieval and computers and other electronic wonders, but except perhaps in a few easily organized and super-specialized scientific files, the place to find information is still going to be libraries, as far as we can see ahead. The stock-in-trade of libraries has been described as a "compact device capable of storing up to two million bits, serially arranged but capable of rapid searching by the human eye either unaided or aided by an index, transmissible through the mails at low cost, storable indefinitely without deterioration, reusable without accessory machinery, and remarkably inexpensive; sometimes referred to for short as the B.O.O.K."

But what is most important about books is that they are the repositories of the best (and some of the worst) that human beings have felt and thought over centuries. They come from every culture and every continent; they have been written by saints, scientists, dictators, criminals, poets, visionaries, bankers, chefs, revolutionaries, musicians, and madmen (and madwomen). They contain, for better or worse, the wisdom of the species. Knowledge is power, and libraries are where knowledge is.

F. Learn to read maps.

Maps are both fascinating and useful. But you have to get the hang of reading them—it's a totally different process because it's visual: The map is essentially a picture. Children beginning to use maps have a lot of trouble with this concept—to get the idea of how a map corresponds to its territory is a great leap of imagination. It helps to think that you are a super-tiny ant crawling around over the map, which is a kind of copy of the world. Once you have really grasped that this little inch of wavy line pictures ten miles of wandering river, and that the red line crossing it "is" a highway, you're ready to read maps. After you've read enough of them, you'll be making automatic interpretations, and also having fun.

There are map freaks who can lie on the floor with a big atlas for hours, the way other people do with the Sunday paper. It's incredible what you can find out from a map, even of an area you think you know pretty well: roads or streets you never knew were there, strange poetic names of places, little hidden towns. Besides, if you move around a lot, you'll have to know how to use a map quickly and accurately; if you live nomadically, or if you're in a hurry to get through some strange territory, you've got to be able to read road maps. If you're hiking or camping in the wilderness, you've got to be able to read topographic maps. One useful tip: Lay out the map so it's oriented right (so its north is toward the real north)—then you can imagine you are actually walking or driving on it.

You're probably most familiar with road maps, put out by oil companies who want you to be able to get from here to there because you'll have to buy gas to do it. These are, as you'll discover if you get into maps, relatively uninteresting, because all they show are roads and a few other main features like cities and big rivers. (The only highway maps that are really good are the ones issued by the American Automobile Association—free to members.) But they'll do to start with. On them you can learn how to read:

Scale. Somewhere on the map there ought to be a little ruler-like scale that tells you how big things are on the map.

Key. Decent maps include a key to the symbols they use—what mark stands for a big city, how a marshy area is indicated, what kinds of lines are used for freeways, main roads, country roads, dirt roads.

In a library you can check into some real maps. There are several good atlases that contain very carefully prepared and beautifully printed maps; ask the librarian to help you find a good one. Such maps will show, for one thing, the altitude of a place, by a system of different colors for different elevations (there's a key to the colors somewhere on the edge of the map). By using different sizes of type for names, it will tell you how big towns, villages, and cities are. It will show major mountain peaks and tell how high they are. There may be special maps that will show which areas are forested and which are bare. The best atlases around are *The Times Survey Atlas of the World,* the *Rand McNally World Atlas,* and the *Reader's Digest Great World Atlas.* All these are expensive, but decent libraries will have them.

A map that provides a good representation of the physical features of your region—its river pattern, mountains and valleys, cities and agricultural areas—

will begin to give you an idea of your bioregion, and how your life fits into the overall pattern of that region. This can help you to feel truly "at home" where you live.

For the ultimate in maps of the United States, you want the series of superdetailed topographic maps put out by the U.S. Geological Survey. These mostly cover very small sections of territory, only a few miles across, but they will show (in the country) literally every house, what the vegetation is like, how high contours are (essential for hiking), whether streams are intermittent, whether roads are passable in winter, and so on. You can buy these from hiking equipment stores, special map stores, or by mail from the U.S.G.S. (They have an index map that shows which maps you need to order.) If the U.S.G.S. isn't listed under "U.S. Governmental Offices" in your phone book, write to the U.S.G.S. Distribution Center, Washington, DC 20242, and ask where their nearest regional map distribution office is.

G. Write away for things.

One of the keys to enriching your life without spending much money is knowing how to reach out into the world and find out about or get things. For things that exist locally, you can do this by telephone, but writing letters is often necessary too. Many people feel awkward about writing letters. There's no need to. Half the letters by which the nation's business is carried on are full of misspellings, bad phrasing, and so on. Don't worry, therefore, about getting everything perfect in order to write a letter. Just bat it out. The important thing is to write it so that it will work: bring back the information you want, or get the response you want.

The first thing you need to know is to whom to write. If what you're after is information about a product, most corporations have customer-relations departments to answer inquiries, or else their sales departments deal with inquiries. If you don't know who really ought to deal with your request, address it to "Office of the President"; executives have secretarial staffs who route letters to people who can deal with them. It's a good idea to send *all* complaints and letters of outrage (which can be great fun to write) to the president's office; that way they may conceivably do some good. In writing to government offices, all that matters is to get the name of the office right; no one can figure out exactly whom to send things to.

Make sure you phrase your question clearly. Generally your reply will be coming from a clerk of some kind; so try to write your question in a way that invites simple, clear answers. If you have a number of interconnected questions, put them in a numbered list. Whenever you're asking about something you may want to buy, ask for a price list and information about ordering. Most companies and organizations have a file of ready-made catalogs, booklets, flyers, and so on. Whenever you are after some information that is probably too precise to be included in that kind of scattershot publication, you'll have to ask for it very specifically.

Write your full name and address and zip code anywhere at the top of your letter. Otherwise no reply can be sent to you. If a quick reply is important, you may get one by enclosing a postcard on which you've written your own name and address—that way the clerk who answers you only has to jot down a reply on the card and toss it in the mail.

There are many things you may want to write for. Government agencies such as the departments of Agriculture, Health, Education, and Welfare, or Interior put out many free pamphlets, and some thicker ones that they charge a quarter or so for. Bureaus in your state and local governments also issue useful items. Companies sometimes offer free samples if you write to them enclosing a coupon from some ad. Publications will often send you a sample copy in hopes you will subscribe. Organizations offering services or seeking your support will often send you materials describing their work.

H. Find free or cheap education or resources.

In recent decades new types of educational activity have proliferated in our urban areas. Somewhere in the shadows of most universities you will find a "free university" or education exchange of some kind. These organizations are basically coordinating and advertising entities to connect people who want to teach or study some subject. The classes offered range from highly technical matters like auto repair or computer programming to esoteric religious doctrines. The teachers who volunteer to teach them range from brilliant, innovative, restless souls to totally incompetent idiots: You are strictly on your own—you pay your money (most of which should be refundable after the first session if you decide to drop the class) and take your choice, without benefit of accreditation machinery. The material offered may thus be far ahead of traditional university fare, or garbled and out of date.

Community colleges are being asked to bear an increasing part of the load of educating students who have modest resources or do not wish to go to college away from home. They are not, of course, immune to the financial pressures that are grinding away at private and state colleges. But they cater to an interestingly varied student body, including people of different ages, work backgrounds, and motivations. Many courses are oriented narrowly toward direct job qualifications, but you can also continue your general education through a community college. Today, with jobs in top universities scarce, the staff at such colleges may be university-quality people.

Universities with budget problems have been expanding their extension divisions. These offer night and weekend classes in a wide variety of subjects;

some of them are identical to university classes and are available for academic credit if you wish. They are taught by people with good academic credentials, who have the same range of quality as professors generally (teaching extension courses is a way for underpaid academics to make a little extra money). Extension divisions usually have correspondence courses available too, if you can't attend classes or don't want to. These are, of course, on a higher level than those offered by private correspondence schools, some of which are accredited and some not.

Many high schools, despite budget squeezes, still offer night school or "adult school" classes in vocational areas like auto shop or business and language skills, as well as regular academic classes you can take to finish high school if you dropped out to work. A few of them are still able to offer craft and hobby classes.

I. Educate yourself.

The objectives of the official curriculum are defined and carried out in ways that prevent or inhibit students from using their minds to deal with the real issues and needs of their lives. Nonetheless, it is still possible to learn a lot in school, and for any student who is going to be confined there for many years, it is senseless not to put it to whatever advantage you can.

Many essentials of survival with any kind of style are left virtually untouched by the schools, and it is up to us to learn about them from other sources. This book provides a basic orientation in certain areas, and indicates other sources you can turn to. Try writing out your own list of what you think you must know in order to get by decently in modern conditions, and see whether your school offers help toward some of it. This might include a certain amount of technical information that is only taught, at present, to boys (and a few enterprising girls) enrolled in shop courses; how to use basic tools and work safely, how household electricity works, and what to do when it doesn't work. You may feel a grounding in "home economics" (dismal term!) is vital: how to cook basic nourishing foods, how to mend and sew, how to recognize frauds in stores, and how to figure unit prices of items. Your list might include social skills: how to find out about abortions in a hurry, how to complain to city hall, or file in small-claims court, how to react to police harassment, how to defend yourself—martial arts, handling firearms. We all need to know how to drive a car, type, and so on. We need food-providing skills: how to garden, fish, dress game and poultry. Educators worry about "mere" skill training, forgetting that it is in learning how to do something useful that we practice the real essentials of education (analyzing situations, using our minds and their knowledge of reading, mathematics, physics, biology) and that attempts to teach such things abstractly are doomed to dullness, failure, and resentment. Thus a course in martial arts, for instance, requires an understanding of all the principles of mechanics (levers, forces, momentum) taught in physics courses—but how much more directly and personally!

Our education is strangely abstract and word-limited. It has no poetry in it, even when English classes analyze poems. The care of our bodies is almost a taboo subject: When discussed at all, it is taught in special classes, often segregated by sex. Most teenagers pick up a great amount of gossipy lore about skin care, sexually transmitted diseases, and so on, but few know much about first aid—despite the fact that automobile crashes are a constant feature of American life. Our schooling helps conceal from us that the human body is a vulnerable and delicate organism: It can drown, bleed to death, suffer heart attacks, and experience many other dangers that quick help might greatly alleviate. Yet only a handful of people have real experience and training, and school first-aid courses are almost a joke. Schools should make sure that everyone knows how to administer sensible simple first aid—and not only knows how, but has practiced it. Imaginative schools should stage "accidents" on the grounds and in hallways, to give kids practice in emergency situations.

But it is not only in danger situations that we ignore the needs of our bodies. Massage, for instance, is a great aid and pleasure to people whose lives make them tense and physically rigid, and who don't get enough exercise. Reducing salons, physical-culture gyms, and massage parlors are all busily making money from massaging people. But massage is something that everybody ought to know how to do well, just as they ought to know how to make decent coffee and swim. It's not something you can learn out of books, either.

Perhaps worst of all, our schools do not teach us how to relate to each other in responsible, helping ways, but only in impersonal, competitive ways. Our education trains us for a life of alienation, conflict, loneliness. People brought up in prisons behave like inmates; they have been taught to. If we can achieve smaller schools, and if students can have a strong voice in running them, so that they develop a sense of responsibility toward each other, we may yet turn back the awful tide of anonymity and unconcern. And if in our friendship networks, extended families, and social and political groups we can practice direct care for each other, we may be able to develop the kind of direct personal solidarity that used to be found in large families, where everybody is educated by everybody else.

J. Find sources of free amusement.

It's amazing how much goes on in our cities that you can attend free—but most people never hear about it; so they end up watching television. Here is where to find out what's going on.

Newspapers. Sunday papers, community or special-interest papers, and some dailies have listings of museums, special exhibitions, political meetings, lectures, plays, free or low-admission concerts (sometimes you can get student ticket rates or get in free by ushering—call the house manager at the theater), dances, movies, court sessions, city council meetings—all of which are either free or very cheap.

Bulletin boards. These can be found in libraries, around universities and colleges (which have the best informal communications of any of our communities), sometimes in government buildings. Announcements of many coming events will be posted here.

Posters. The poster as a commercial art form had practically died out, but the use of arty posters to announce rock concerts in San Francisco led to a new flowering of the art poster. Some cities are belatedly following the European system and providing kiosks where posters for concerts, plays, and other cultural events can be displayed.

There are also many free amusements that do not get listed in any of these places; you have to find out about them on your own, depending on your tastes and ingenuity. For instance, many transit systems offer an all-day or all-weekend pass; with it you can travel anywhere on their lines, especially way out to the ends, where the parks, beaches, and other interesting places are. Or you can ride around the inner city and get to know it better. Coastal and river cities have ferries that are cheap and fun; in general, anything that exists for everyday purposes can lend itself to inexpensive amusement.

Parks. You can visit all the parks in your city, large and small; it's likely that some of them are really beautiful and interesting. For instance, a botanical garden usually has a fantastic variety of exotic plants you'll never see elsewhere. Or there may be a rose garden, or a monster greenhouse where tropical plants grow and the air smells damp and strange. There may be a park with a lake where you can rent little boats and paddle around, or where you can swim in the summertime. There might be a harbor park where you can walk around and look at the elegant boats—which is a way I have spent many a lovely (or rainy) afternoon. Walking or bicycling around a park can be both restful and relaxing.

Many cities have free facilities that few citizens are aware of. There may be free tennis or handball courts in your neighborhoods. There are probably shuffleboard courts, and in parks with buildings there are probably table-tennis tables. Most cities have at least one public swimming pool with a small admission charge.

Neighborhoods. You can also get a lot of pleasure out of your city just by walking around in places you don't usually go. In fact, that's one of the original appeals of cities: There's a lot going on that you can see in a compact area; many possibilities open up to you nearby. Don't confine yourself to the areas you are familiar with, though of course you should use judgment (and if necessary make some inquiries) before venturing onto turf where you might encounter hostility. Some of the most interesting areas are those inhabited chiefly by people from foreign lands: Chinatown, with its strange groceries and imported tourist goods; districts where there are Russian bakeries with mysterious cookies and pastries; black neighborhoods with African or Caribbean restaurants; Italian districts with extraordinary resources of pasta and delicatessen foods. As the years go by, more and more of the world's inhabitants are living in the same colorless, timid, bland, middle-class way. It is chiefly in our cities that we can see remnants of the more vigorous and varied cultures from which our ancestors came.

K. Find cheap visual entertainment.

On the whole, the less time you spend in front of a T.V. set, the richer and fuller your life will be—because you'll find other things to do with your time. But there are two ways to use a T.V. set without becoming a couch potato.

Buy a VCR and rent movies. Even when you spread the cost of the VCR out over time, and add in rental costs, movies seen at home are much cheaper than in the theaters. (They *should* be, since their visual quality is so inferior.) Besides, you can make better popcorn, save money on theater refreshments, and invite friends to join you. Try to find a video store with really extensive stock—old films, documentaries, even experimental films. Old Hollywood films, which are largely made up of "two-shots" in which a couple of actors mouth lines at each other, don't suffer as much on the small screen as do films with more visual intricacy and grace; it's probably better to see the wonderful old Hollywood fare on video than not to see it at all. But for real movies, try to find a repertory theater (it probably has a monthly calender). Many cities now have them, and college campus groups or museums also show a wide variety of fine films. Film is a subject that can be thought about, argued about, and enjoyed endlessly. Your library has a few books on the subject, and serious critical magazines like *Film Quarterly*.

Get cable. This is a substantial expense, even without subscribing to any pay channels, but if you are a heavy consumer of visual material, it may be a good choice for you. Cable greatly expands your access to video news (though it still doesn't match printed news for most kinds of stories) and sports, as well as MTV. Cable will improve your T.V.'s image if you have reception problems. Films are shown on some cable channels without commercial breaks, which can be an immense relief.

Chapter 11.
Take Care of Your Family.

A. Try living together.

Since the sixties, more and more couples have been living together without marrying, either because they are opposed to the institution of marriage as we have known it (which usually meant inequity toward the wife) or just because they don't feel like it, at least not with the person they happen to be involved with.

However, if you continue such living arrangements very long, problems may result in economic areas, and there is currently a trend toward having an explicit agreement, sometimes on paper, when people move in together. The Lee Marvin case, settled in 1979, indicated that a woman does *not* gain a right to half of her live-in partner's income as she would in many states if she married him, unless there is a written contract to that effect. Equity-minded couples, therefore, as well as women wishing to be sure they will not be exploited, might well put down on paper what will happen to money and other assets that come in while they are together. There is no need, of course, to make such contracts follow the lines of marriage; they could specify a total separation of resources, down to separate jars of peanut butter in the cupboard, if the partners felt that was the right way to go.

When people start living together, they often feel uncomfortable tendencies to revert to traditional patterns of family life, and a contract can also be a useful way to stave these off. If it is openly and jointly agreed that shopping, housework, and home maintenance work are to be shared equally, old patterns have a harder time reasserting themselves, and can be more easily choked off if they do.

In thirteen states, if a couple live together for along time and present themselves to the world as married, their relationship may become a "common-law marriage," and the state's rules for the sharing and inheritance of property come into play, along with possible provisions for child support, alimony, etc., in the event of separation. A lawyer's advice should be sought by couples who contemplate or find themselves in a live-in partnership of more than a few years' duration.

B. Enter into marriage with open eyes.

Marriage is a contract among three parties: the two spouses and the state. Depending on your financial situation and where you live, marriage may have economic consequences you do not desire or intend. Sometimes these can be modified by premarital contracts, which have a long and solid legal history. Now that more than half of all marriages end in divorce, it is important to be clear about your situation *before* you marry, so that in case you too divorce, the separation can be carried out with as little confusion and likelihood of legal combat as possible. Prospective spouses should expect each other to make full disclosure of their properties and debts, if any, before marriage. If your plan for living together involves one partner going to school and the other working to provide support, and this partner is to be repaid later by having a couple of years free (for childrearing, creative projects, or a well-deserved vacation), it is wise to put this agreement in writing.

In Arizona, California, Idaho, Louisiana, Nevada, New Mexico, Texas, Washington, and Wisconsin, known as "community-property states," everything a couple acquires during a marriage is joint property, no matter how it was paid for or who earned the money. If they split up, this property gets divided equally between them. In the other states, which are called "common-law states," the situation is complex. Property and possessions held in the husband's name, no matter where they came from or who earned the money for them (even if they belonged to the wife before the marriage), are considered his. In a divorce, the judge has discretion in dividing the property.

Marriages require a marriage license that costs a couple of dollars (at city hall or county courthouse), a blood test (to check whether either partner has VD), and sometimes a waiting period of a few days (during which you have a chance to cool off and think it over). In my opinion, it is much too easy to get married and much too hard for childless couples to get divorced. Marriage is a legal contract for the protection of children and spouses in the sharing of income and property. If no children are contemplated, sharing on the economic level can equally well be handled through a private contract—with a time limit, and provisions for renegotiation from time to time.

For some people, getting married signifies an emotional commitment to a partner that they cannot maintain without benefit of marriage; for others, getting married signifies an unacceptable degree of restraint and loss of personal independence. Many compromises and experiments are currently being tried: women choose to retain their name; partners maintain separate bank accounts, or question the importance of monogamy. For the vast majority, however, the act of getting married signifies a willingness to become more like your parents—to pass into the "parental" generation, whether or not you intend to have children. This self-definition, clearly, is not something to rush into lightly, especially as it has, statistically, only a fifty-fifty chance of surviving.

In attempts to make sure that their marriages work the way *they* want, and not the way society or parents suggest, many couples nowadays prepare written marriage contracts. It is often useful to have the help of a trusted but not too close person (a lawyer, clergyman, or marriage counselor), since working out such a contract inevitably raises difficult issues.

Money matters are not only critical, but particularly complex. How income is to be spent has many ramifications itself. Should the couple attempt to build up savings for some common purpose? Should accounts be separate, or joint, or a combination of both? How much discretionary spending money should each partner have? How much accounting should the partners expect of each other?

Issues connected with children are also crucial. Some couples specify the number of children they agree to have, and their spacing; others agree not to have any at all. If there are strong religious differences between spouses, the religious upbringing of the children must be clearly agreed upon. Since the rearing of children will affect the employment availability of the parents, plans to alternate working with staying home should be worked out in advance. How children will be named may also be an issue requiring thought. Many people also attempt to use marriage contracts as a way to establish guidelines for their sexual lives: whether they expect monogamy, and if not, what the ground rules are for sexual contacts with other persons. Others specify in their contracts requirements for the division of domestic duties.

Courts tend to take contracts seriously only when they involve money. Couples should therefore confine their "official" contract to matters that are financially serious (property, income, children) and may therefore become legal issues in case of divorce. A lawyer should help in preparing such a contract. Other more intimate and less "measurable" items should be handled in a second agreement that is intended as a serious personal commitment but not a legal document.

C. Experiment with extended families.

Throughout most of human history, the couple has been a relatively minor part of the family structure, and the nuclear family as we know it—two people and their children, if any, often living at great distances from other relatives—was virtually unknown. In the long sweep of human history, the nuclear family will probably be seen as a very brief aberration, brought about by the special needs of industrial capitalism and the isolated suburban living made possible by cars, but insufficient for nurturing and supporting human beings. It is certainly in steep decline—only about a third of American households now fall into the old pattern—but it is not yet clear what will take its place.

My own hunch is that in the long run—meaning several generations—we will probably move toward some new form of extended family—groups of say, six to fifteen people living together, bonded by ties of different kinds, sometimes by blood relationships, as in earlier extended families, sometimes by religious convictions, dietary practices, and so on, and sometimes by old established friendship connections. In such forms we will approximate the ancient groupings our species has relied on for survival: small bands whose variety of strengths and talents give great resilience against outside threats, and whose interior psychological life is rich and complicated enough to challenge its members' developmental potentials.

These extended families will help to reduce the present isolation and separation that characterize so much of American life. They will give children a secure world to grow in, but one with much more personal variety in their surrounding adults—to study, understand, and model themselves upon. They will relieve young parents from the severe emotional strains and practical stresses of trying to manage demanding babies or active young children entirely on their own; in a household or group of adjacent dwellings containing ten adults, baby-sitting or child-care exchanging works out much more naturally. Extended families give a warm surrounding support system for couple relationships, and reduce our present tendency to put all our emotional eggs in one fragile romantic basket. They will give older people a continuing role in the social structure, and make caring for them in the home during times of weakness more feasible, rather than shunting them off to an isolated life in some institution. In turn, this will help them to maintain a productive orientation to life throughout their years.

Higher rents and higher costs for other survival necessities will, as the years pass, increase the advantages of living with other people—or immediately next to them, so you can share cooking, appliances, child-care, cars.

From experiments made so far—many of which have been at least as successful as marriages now are, on the whole, in our society—it seems clear that extended families must be based on very strong ties and specific discussion of rights or responsibilities of each individual, not on just a vague idea that living together would be a good thing to try. Most groups successfully practicing shared living have either strong religious or philosophical convictions, or an economic life that ties the members together. (In emotional life, too, necessity is the mother of invention; we learn to live together happily and productively when we *have* to.) But some people have banded together on the basis of old friendships, and in some families brothers and sisters who would once have lived far away from each other are making it their business to live closer, sometimes buying property together, joining their friendship networks, helping to raise each others' children, looking after their parents, and so on.

Groupings of this kind have quite a different character when children are present than among people without children, since children constitute a great additional responsibility for the adults involved. In attempting to develop an extended family—a "family of choice"—for yourself, this factor needs very careful attention.

D. Pay attention to children.

Children are a heavy responsibility—both a moral and a practical one. But children are also among the most interesting people you can meet, if you bother to get to know them (your own or other people's). A lot of children are simply more fun to be with than most adults: more cheerful, more ingenious, more playful, more affectionate, more open. It's no accident that saints, artists, and other wise people have always paid attention to children—they know that you can learn as much from children as children can learn from you. Children are naturally free; they are full of energy we all might have if adult life did not wear us down so fearfully, and they are full of mystery and surprises because they are not imprisoned by adult ideas and words and habits. Our children carry within them the only literal immortality we have: DNA molecules bearing our genetic information, which will be passed on from generation to generation. But they also carry the immediate potential of the human race, so that in all our little acts of dealing with them we are helping create the freedom or the bondage of the next generation.

In earlier American life, children were considered an inevitable feature of almost everyone's existence. Even childless unmarried aunts and uncles participated in the lives of their nieces and nephews. It was a rare married couple that had no children, and large families (sometimes up to a dozen children) were common. With the availability of contraception, and the dawning realizations that children are expensive and that their presence sharply limits adult activities, birthrates in most sectors of the population have fallen. We are not yet to the point where our population has started a gentle decline, thus permitting less pressure on our resources, but we will probably reach it soon.

E. Adopt or foster-parent children.

Children available for adoption are no longer in oversupply, and indeed a sort of black market has developed, in which babies are sometimes "sold" even before they are born. Normal adoption, however, is a legal process, and one in which the state takes a proper interest on behalf of the child's welfare. A court must approve adoptions, usually on the recommendations of social workers who have interviewed the prospective parent(s) and checked on the home situation. Retaining the services of a lawyer is usually a good idea, and you will certainly need one if you are single, over 45, of a different race than the child, and so on. The tendency in recent years has been toward evaluating the actual psychological and social characteristics of the people wishing to adopt, rather than relying on traditional notions of "normalcy." In some areas, even single men (including gay men) able to provide a good environment for a child have been able to adopt.

Many older children are in need of foster homes—whether because of deaths in or dissolutions of their biological families, incompatibility with parents or stepparents, or emotional difficulties. Our society includes an astonishing number of people—some but not all with strong religious orientations—who undertake to provide good homes for these young people. Such relationships obviously make demands on both parties that go beyond the usual stresses of parenthood, but they sometimes offer unusual rewards as well. In addition, foster children placed through government agencies bring with them substantial child-support funds, and foster-parenting thus makes economic sense for some parents. It is certainly not, of course, anything to enter into lightly, or just for the money.

"Surrogate" births, in which women sign contracts to produce babies for other people (usually by artificial insemination) have a dubious moral and legal status, and should be avoided.

F. Make childbirth as positive as possible.

For knowledgeable people, there has been a notable improvement in birth conditions. Hospital delivery rooms and labor rooms have been revamped as tolerable human environments; medical attendants have grown in understanding of the birth and nursing processes; the dangers of drugging mothers during delivery are known; the possibility of rooming-in arrangements facilitates satisfactory beginning of nursing. In a few hospitals, quiet, low-lit surroundings are provided to give the baby a relatively comfortable first experience of life in the outside world. Sometimes the Leboyer warm bath immediately after birth is available, with dim lights and little noise or commotion. And in some areas midwives are available for home deliveries; in Britain and Holland, they have a better medical record than our hospital deliveries.

Unfortunately, however, these advances are extremely spotty, and even parents living in relatively enlightened communities may have to work hard to find and use facilities that seem decent to them. Many obstetricians are still obstinately noncooperative with women who wish to give birth without anesthetic, by a "natural childbirth" method. Some will promise to cooperate and then renege—which the father's presence in the delivery room may be able to prevent. (His presence is, of course, highly desirable for other reasons! This is especially true of the Lamaze method, where it is generally the father's role to lend support, time contractions, and generally monitor and facilitate the labor process.) Contrary to common belief, the number of drugs being given to women in gestation, labor, and delivery is rising. Episiotomies, though not required in many deliveries, are done as a matter of routine. Caesarian deliveries have been rising sharply in frequency, even though research has shown they are often not necessary. As with episiotomy, the motive seems to be legal prudence—protection against possible malpractice suits rather than medical prudence.

The drugging of mothers during delivery can affect infants during the first years of life, causing losses in IQ and motor development. Sometimes of course, an anesthetic is truly needed for delivery, and may well be the only reasonable procedure. But medical and public policy should attempt to minimize it.

Moreover, though no one quite knows why, babies who have protracted close contact with their mothers in their first hours after birth (rather than being snatched away by nurses) turn out to have significantly higher IQs at age 5. Attention from fathers also leads to calmer, happier babies.

Actually, hospitals are unpleasant places to be in under any circumstances, and especially for a joyous event like a birth. Home births allow the entire family to participate in the birth. This is one of the strangest, strongest experiences a human being can have—reminding us where we have all come from, and putting us in touch again with the biological basis of our being. A birth ought to be a happy human occasion, and not treated as a medical "problem" or emergency. An expectant mother should have the right to have her baby where she pleases, providing that she makes proper arrangements.

Home delivery should be considered only under carefully arranged conditions:

(1) proper prenatal care and examinations by an obstetrician or trained and experienced midwife who can tell whether the baby is in position for normal delivery;

(2) normal labor (not over twenty-four hours, no bleeding, fever, or other unusual factors);

(3) supervision of the birth by a doctor, ideally the same one who has supervised the pregnancy;

(4) definite arrangements with friends for immediate and rapid transportation to a nearby hospital in the event of complications;

(5) faithful participation by the mother and father in natural-childbirth training procedures.

Generally speaking, these conditions can be met only in cities where there are sympathetic, sophisticated doctors and easily reachable hospitals, which are especially necessary for mothers having their first baby, who may panic in a hard labor, even with the best preparation and greatest devotion. It is also desirable to have the support and advice of experienced friends, who can help prepare for birth. Since two lives may be at stake, childbirth is not a matter where heroism is to be considered more of a virtue than caution. If you have trouble, head for a hospital.

Generally the mother should take it easy for the first twenty-four hours after the home delivery, getting out of bed only to go to the bathroom. On the second day she can take a shower and begin to resume her activity gradually. It helps to have a woman friend around who has a couple of children and whom you trust to have both good instincts and accurate information.

Many mothers find it difficult to begin breast-feeding a first child in the hospital, where the atmosphere may be discouraging and where some nurses disapprove of breast-feeding. Here again, the help of reliable friends is your best defense.

The next best thing to having your baby at home is to have it in the hospital, but go home twenty-four hours later. Some doctors actually encourage this practice. Even if yours doesn't, there's not much he or she can do about it, since you are free to leave at will.

Babies born at home need to be examined (by a pediatrician if possible) within twenty-four hours at the latest.

If you are thinking of getting pregnant, check your medical insurance policy; most employee health plans now cover pregnancy care and delivery.

G. Take good care of infants.

There seems to be primordial urge to wash a newborn baby, but this should not be done for at least a week; the baby is born with a coating of grease on its skin, which is necessary to its protection. After a week, sponge baths are OK, but all-over wetting should wait until the belly button is healed.

Newborn babies are often covered up too heavily by worried parents. So long as the room is reasonably warm, they need only light covering. (Too much may give them heat rashes.) A diaper and a lightweight blanket is all the "clothes" a newborn baby needs; after a couple of days you can add an undershirt. If the weather is warm, new babies can be taken outdoors—but as with adults, a few minutes exposure to direct sun is enough.

Mothers and fathers used to feel tied down to the house with a new baby, but in fact young babies are more "portable" than older ones. You can carry them easily; they sleep a great deal of the time; and as long as the breast or bottle is handy, they will be happy.

There are important biological and psychological advantages to breast-feeding, though bottle-fed babies also develop well. Breast milk contains substances that cut down the risk of infections. Moreover, breast-feeding frees the mother from all the paraphernalia of bottles and sterilizing; besides being the natural way to feed babies, with the best milk they could get, it is handy. But propaganda for bottles as a "modern" method prevailed in this country for several decades; so many women have not learned from their mothers or friends how breast-feeding is done. The better hospitals are helpful to new mothers about it; and pediatricians (baby doctors) are too; if yours isn't, you should change to one who is. A new mother's greatest worries about her baby usually center on feeding. There is nothing more terrifying than the thought your baby may not be getting enough to eat—and it's your fault. Luckily, however, few mothers are truly unable to breast-feed; the human breast and the baby it feeds are ideally adapted to each other, or the species would have died out long ago. The only other thing a young baby needs is an occasional few drops of vitamins.

It takes a couple of days to get the nursing going well. If you encounter problems your experienced friends can't help you with, or your doctor can't help you as you think he or she should, get in touch with the local La Leche League—an organization of experienced nursing mothers, who help each other with any problems. Don't be afraid to ask for help. It's too important a thing to give up on easily. And then you'll be able to show your friends or your daughters how it's done. (As an added bonus, it is a great and surprising advantage of breast-feeding that the feces of breast-fed babies smell sweet until they begin to eat solid foods.)

H. Buy only necessary baby equipment.

There is no question that having children is expensive. But the amount of money spent for nonessentials, especially for babies, is staggering. Inexperienced parents who wander into a baby-supplies store are likely to come out with a ton of pink or blue junk that neither they nor the baby need. One of the great virtues of Dr. Spock's *Baby and Child Care* is that he explains inexpensive ways of providing things that salespeople try to push but you really don't need: pillows, booties, bath thermometers, and so on.

Here are the essentials:

Bed. Vaudeville family children slept in their parents' traveling trunks, but trunks and suitcases are OK only if they can't accidentally flop shut and suffocate the baby. Dresser drawers, big wood or cardboard boxes, and many other things will serve—all they really need is four sides and something soft but flat (not a regular pillow) on the bottom. Since being able to rock the baby helps when he or she is fussy, it's nice to suspend the sleeping place either by ropes or from some kind of bracket, like the beautiful old-fashioned cradles. And a simple cradle can be made out of any box by putting rocker pieces at each end. With any of these ideas, you can attach a string to the thing and run it over your bed; many times a baby who wakes briefly can be lulled back to sleep with a few tugs on the string—without your ever getting up. Since getting enough sleep is the number-one problem of new parents, such a device will richly repay the little trouble it takes to rig up.

If you are building your own cradle, you should know that traditional side-to-side rocking is *not* what babies like best. Rocking in the head-to-foot direction makes their innards gurgle better and keeps them comfortable; so plan your rocker pieces accordingly.

Babies wet a lot, so their mattress needs covering with something totally waterproof. You can buy pieces of crib-size waterproof sheeting that has flannel on both sides; it's washable, comfortable for the baby, and saves a lot of trouble. You also need some sheets (diapers will work fine when the baby is small) and a couple of blankets. Make sure you have at least one very light blanket. Several light knitted or loosely woven layers are better than one deadweight heavy one.

Changing table. Since you'll be changing the baby's diapers constantly for two years or longer, you need a changing surface that enables you to do it smoothly, efficiently, and safely. The best is a dresser that is kitchen-counter height; if it's table height, you have to sit down, which is awkward. The area should be big enough that an active older baby can't easily roll off of it. (All the same, you should never turn your back on any baby who can roll over, when you've laid him or her on such a raised surface.) Pad the top with rags or cotton batting, and tack a heavy plastic covering over the whole thing; on that, for comfort, you can lay a diaper or other washable cloth. Your supply of diapers and rubber pants should be stored right near the changing surface along with other clothes. Make an out-of-reach place to lay the diaper pins while they're off the baby, so you don't panic when one disappears and you think it's been swallowed. Sticking them into a bar of soap keeps them in one place and makes the pins easier to slide through the fabric. Keep some cotton balls handy, for cleaning bottoms, and ointment for diaper rash, which most babies get sooner or later. The diaper pail should be next to the changing table; get a big one with a tight fitting lid. (This is one case where plastic is best; urine is corrosive.)

Cloth diapers are better than disposable ones for the ecology, and are also much cheaper to use. Use disposables only when traveling.

Bathtub. A big dish pan makes an excellent bathtub, and you can use it on the changing table or on the kitchen counter. A kitchen sink and a washtub will also work fine. Keep the water slightly warm, not hot.

Clothes. In warm weather and in heated houses, babies don't really need much of a wardrobe. A couple of light shirts, a warm shirt or sweater, several sleeper coveralls (which come in terry cloth and can be worn day or night, leaving the child free to move but also warm), and maybe also some sleeping sacks (nightgowns that have closed bottoms, and are also good for going out in cold weather) are all you really need. But parents get a great deal of joy from dressing up their babies, and anything that leaves the baby free to move and not too hot will probably strike him or her as tolerable, and you as charming. A wool hat is a good idea for wearing outdoors in cold weather, since babies don't have much hair.

Transportation. Because your baby will go pretty much everywhere with you for the first months of life, you should pay a great deal of attention to how you plan to carry him or her around. If you live in a flat city area and have an elevator, a standard baby carriage may work fine. (The bigger the wheels, the easier to manage—try to find an elegant old-fashioned or foreign one.) If you plan to get into and out of cars or buses a lot, or have to go up and down stairs, a light, fold-up stroller is probably the best solution.

It is now mandatory to use a baby car-seat that straps onto the adult seat; otherwise, even in a small accident, your child is likely to hurtle through the windshield. Rear-facing models are best.

Maneuvering even a light stroller through doors and up steps is no fun, for either you or the baby. Many parents have begun adopting papoose-style carriers that strap onto their backs like a camping pack. The baby sits there, looking around at the world, yet with the immediate comfort of the parent's contact and motions. (For babies who can't yet sit up enough for these carriers, there are belly-sling affairs that carry the baby right up against the parent's chest; these are especially convenient for the first few months of nursing, since the baby is right at the mother's breast.) It takes a bit of practice to get used to carrying weight around, but if you like to be on the move and don't intend to let your baby tie you down, it's well worth it.

Young babies will usually sleep pretty much anywhere, but some parents like to get them in the habit of sleeping in a small sleeping bag. This adds to your flexibility when children get older, because they will usually sleep happily anywhere, so long as they're in their familiar bag.

Miscellaneous. The first thing a doctor asks when you phone in about a sick baby is his or her temperature; so you need a rectal thermometer. You also need some cotton swabs for nose cleaning (babies don't learn to blow until after they can talk).

That's it, if you're breast-feeding. You need no bottles, sterilizers, warmers, nipples, bottle brushes, strainers, bottle caps, funnels, and so on. In fact, all you need is some vitamin drops, which will be prescribed by your pediatrician. If you are nervous about weight gain, a scale is reassuring. Breast-fed babies normally gain more slowly than bottle-fed ones, and people may try to alarm you about this; make sure your doctor has plenty of experience with breast-feeding, because doctors unfamiliar with the process may lack the information they would need to be supportive.

I. Find adequate child care for your toddler.

Prospective parents sometimes blithely assume that ample child-care services exist, and that they will easily be able to return to work soon after having a baby. In reality, it is very difficult to find adequate care for very young children in most cities. "Official" institutions, though slightly more numerous now, are often cold and impersonal environments, with frequent staff turnover. Many home-based child-care operations are disorganized, lack basic necessities, or have tense and threatening atmospheres.

Keep in mind that the first several years of life are extremely important in a child's psychological, mental, and linguistic development. If you turn your child over to others during these critical years, he or she will be partly "their" child. This may not necessarily be a bad thing (you may recognize that you are not an ideal parenting figure in some ways, for instance), but think it over carefully. No matter what arrangements you make, having a child is a full-time responsibility ethically, and if you don't feel comfortable about the changes in your life that will bring, think again whether you really want to be a parent.

In evaluating a possible child-care situation, the first and most important thing is to honor your own psychological reaction to the place and people. If it feels comfortable and reassuring to you, it probably will to your child; if it makes you anxious and uncertain, it will probably make your child feel the same way. This overall sense is more critical than details, but you should also check out certain things about how children are handled. Make sure you visit long enough to notice, for example, how conflicts between children are treated. Are they suppressed instantly with great show of adult authority? Are they allowed to run on for a while, but interrupted if things get too serious? Are they given total free reign? You should be comfortable with the general pattern. For babies, you'll also want to observe how toilet-training questions are dealt with. If you believe in a relaxed approach, you don't want a child-care situation where a great deal of pressure is applied.

Of course, you will want to know what kinds of food your child will receive, since this will influence your own meal planning. Children love sugared foods, but a responsibly run center will minimize them, and will provide enough protein. Officially licensed facilities must meet state requirements for safety, and so on, but if you are dealing with a small private operation, make sure the children do not have access to dangerous streets, stairwells, balconies, or other lethal hazards. Check on T.V. policy; harassed child-care staff sometimes plunk children down in front of a T.V. for long periods. A good child-care program need not have a lot of expensive or complicated toys around, but the environment should be arranged to encourage free physical activity with a variety of objects. Nor is "organized activity"—games, dances, and so on—essential; given the chance and materials, children organize a great deal of activity by themselves.

You may choose not to send your child to a regular child-care service, for economic or other reasons. (If one parent's wages are low, the expenses of child care plus taxes, job transportation, clothing, etc., may entirely eat up that parent's wages. Be sure to carry out this calculation as part of your decision process about child care.) It is important nonetheless to develop cooperative arrangements with friends or relatives, so that you do not feel confined to full-time child care yourself. Develop exchanges with your friends from an early age on, so that your child gets used to the idea of being taken care of by other people. You will, of course, want to have some baby sitting in the evenings—and maybe you will even want to set up a formal baby-sitting pool, where people keep track of the hours they owe and are owed, with a rotating secretary to make appointments, and so on. But it is daytime child care that is the most crucial to your welfare; you need to develop a series of relationships with other parents with whom you can do informal exchanges so that, without any money changing hands, you can all gain important freedoms—and add to the variety of your children's lives as well. Sharing care of each other's children will also bring you closer to your friends. You might even consider starting a child-care service yourselves—it could bring in some income, and help to meet a pressing social need.

J. Improvise the best toys.

Children follow a very simple rule about playthings: They are programmed to imitate you, in big things and in small—that's how they learn to be human. And that's why you should keep your pots and pans down on the lowest shelf where a baby can easily reach them, together with a lot of other household utensils—you'll occasionally have to spend a minute hunting for something, but you'll save lots of minutes through having the child amused without special planning or attention. Give older children free access to the ordinary objects of the household; they'll invent plenty of fantasy things to do with them, and get a big kick out of imitating whatever it is you do with them.

The basic stock of toys that children need is simple, and you can improvise most of them or pick them up secondhand.

Balls. The simple fact that a ball rolls makes it entrancing to a baby. It makes little games possible for a two year old. And older kids can play a thousand games with a ball, any ball—a tennis ball, a ping-pong ball, a golf ball, rubber balls small or large, blown-up plastic balls. Big ball bearings make interesting noises as they roll.

Dolls. Actually "dolls" is a bad word; it has tended to mean only pretty little female dolls with wigs, made for girl children to play mom with, although today both boys and girls can play with both male and female "anatomically correct" dolls. In most cultures, dolls come in a huge variety of types. There are hunger dolls, demon dolls, protector dolls; parent dolls and children dolls and ancestor dolls; the child's mind is the home of many fantastic figures besides mommy and daddy! If you are handy with sewing, you can make rag dolls and rag animals that will give your child a greater range of play fantasy than store-bought dolls. Some people are good at wood carving, and can make special heads for dolls. Remember that children are "savage," compared to adults—their minds have not been cramped and confined by a lifetime of "education" and training for routine jobs. They regard life in a much more direct and human way than most adults—they deal with its joys and its terror in a far more immediate sense. Don't restrict your child's doll play to those cutesy miniature-adult dolls sold in stores.

When children get older, they are sometimes interested in puppets (the hand or string variety) or in putting on dramatic shows with costumes. It helps in such play if you can string a curtain across a corner of the room to make a stage area. Then watch the shows they put on. Two kids who really enjoy this can do things that will astonish you. Thrift shops are an excellent source of dress-up clothes, costume jewelry, feathers, bits of fur.

Blocks. The best blocks my daughter had were a set I made out of hardwood scraps from the saw table of a nearby lumber yard that specialized in exotic hardwoods—mahoganies, walnut, birch, ash, maple, and so on. I left them in curious irregular shapes, and just sanded off the sharp corners. Each block was different, and just right for some special purpose in a child's imagination. And I liked them too, because the wood was beautiful; it felt and smelled good; and the blocks made a good sound when my daughter banged them together. There's no need to spend money for blocks; any lumberyard or millwork shop should be willing to give you boxful of scraps for nothing, especially if you tell them what you want them for. Besides being more fun to build with than standardized blocks, they begin to give your child a sense of the variety and subtlety of natural materials.

Play shelters. Children of all ages like to make little houses and tents for themselves—a kind of imitation of adult houses. They can drape sheets or blankets over chairs and tables; they can lean things against ropes you run across the room just above their head height. Later on, when they can handle a hammer and nails, make sure there is scrap lumber around, so that they can build more substantial huts, outdoors. (In Scandinavia they have "junk playgrounds" where children, when given lots of stuff to work with, build entire miniature villages.) Tree houses, if you have a good tree, are one of the best parts of childhood, and some parents build big play sculptures in their yards out of driftwood or salvaged timbers—you can let your imagination go, and the result will serve as a castle, a tower, a house, a store . . .

Tools and utensils. Children as young as two-year-olds can use simple tools, and toy stores sell sets of simple wrenches and nuts-and-bolts that can be a lot of fun. A child of four or five begins to be able to use real tools—

hammer, pliers, saw, though probably not a screwdriver. Make sure both boys and girls learn how to use tools. It's a good rule never to buy kids junky tools or utensils that you would never use yourself; buy decent tools that really work, provide a good place to store them, and begin to teach your child how to care for them. An old wooden crate makes a good workbench, and a small vise can be attached to it.

Art and craft materials. Children like to make things, and it gives them a sense of pride and competence. So you should help them learn how to cut and paste and draw and paint, and work with materials that are easy to handle: paper, cardboard, styrofoam, soft wood. Here are some basic materials that are useful:

- a good scissors (if you worry about the pointed ends, file them round—those little "children's scissors" won't cut worth a damn);
- white glue;
- odd pieces of paper and cardboard (save grocery bags, shoe boxes, and anything else that looks like fun);
- three or four tempera (poster paint) colors and brushes;
- a big set of crayons;
- cellophane tape and mending tape; and
- a big sheet of oilcloth or plastic to lay over a table or on the floor for kids to work on. (Remember that getting messy is half the fun of artwork.)

Modeling clay is rather expensive; you can make dough clay for practically nothing, and it can be dried and then painted: Just mix flour and water and a little salt. When kids get big enough to handle them, probably around five or six, buy some good watercolors (beautiful, intense colors, though they are expensive); crayon coloring is never very satisfying because it's hard to get really bright colors from crayons. Oil-tempera stick colors, though they are brighter, break very easily.

Games. There are many expensive board games in the stores, but most of them don't interest children for long and don't interest adults at all. You should find games that *you* like to play too—otherwise playing them with children is just duty. Children learn to play active neighborhood games without any instruction from you (football, baseball, soccer, and so on), but it's nice to develop "family" games.

Incidentally, many store-bought toys are dangerous for young children. Toy ovens and plastic- or lead-casting devices get tremendously hot and also pose shock hazards. Dolls and stuffed animals contain pins. Putties and glowing substances may be toxic. Noisemaking rattles have sharp inside parts. Toys with glass parts may break. And keep in mind that babies may try to swallow small parts that come off things.

K. Travel safely with children.

Even children as young as two begin to be bored with what they can do around their own house, and parents commonly meet this situation by plopping them down in front of the T.V. It's usually much better, for parents and children both, to get out of the house instead: to go visit friends, take a walk, go to a park or even the store. You don't really have to have a destination: Small children are endlessly curious about everything; so any change of scene will intrigue them. One advantage of raising children in the country, of course, is that you can allow them to extend their "range" naturally: The bigger they get, the greater the territory they cover. A house in the country is usually surrounded by fields and woods where children can roam freely; in cities and suburbs they have to be restricted because of traffic and other hazards. Since the country is quiet, parents can count on hearing them crying if any disasters occur, whereas city parents can seldom let small kids out of the house unless they are in the care of an older brother or sister. (Middle-class parents are usually unwilling even to do that—so they have to trot along with kids whenever they leave the apartment. Small families could learn a lot from large families about how children can learn to be responsible for their smaller brothers and sisters.)

Small children who get used to being taken around with their parents learn how to deal with other small children; they get used to a variety of people and settings and situations. Carrying children around with you tends to break down the segregation that surrounds the young in our country; they get to see how adults behave and what adults expect of them.

By the time children are two-and-a-half or three, they need more activity and stimulation than even the most single-minded parent can provide, and you need to bring them into plenty of contact with other children—in a child-care group or a nursery school, or just by exchanging them with friends who have kids about the same age.

L. Educate your own children.

One reason America's school situation is so tragic is that the problems we are asking the schools to solve can hardly be solved once children have reached school age: A child's basic mental capacities and attitudes toward life are well-formed by the age of three. Thus, a child who is going to be curious and alert about how things work will be that way on his or her first day of school; a child who is going to go through life without ever figuring out what is going on will usually be that way on his or her first day too. What we are doing, really, is asking the schools to salvage the latter type of child as much as possible, and to give the former whatever encouragement they can.

The fundamental tasks of education must be begun by the parents, and they begin as soon as a baby is born. Though they never slack off entirely, they diminish by the time a child is four or five. When a child actually reaches school age, his or her "educational character" is largely formed.

It is within the immediate grasp of every parent to attend to the preschool education of children. This doesn't mean giving them lessons; it doesn't even necessarily mean teaching them numbers or the alphabet. What it essentially means is to show them how to use their minds. And there is only one way to do this: Show them how you use yours. Children learn, like adults, chiefly by example. Here are some ways you can try to put this principle to work without beating your brains out trying to "be a teacher." (Remember that children only pick up on things they see are fun; if you go into some kind of agony trying to do something *to* them, they will actually perceive it as a bum trip.)

1. Talk to them as if you were "talking to yourself." If you talk to yourself while you're doing things, this will be easy. If you don't, just try thinking out loud to them, whenever you're dealing with them or when they're hanging around: while you're doing housework, while you're fixing something, while you're laying out some food. It doesn't matter if it's a complete explanation or just a word here and there. What counts is that you're telling them what is going on, and why, and how. (Especially how.) You'd be surprised how many basic "educational" lessons this will get across. For instance, if you talk to your child (even a child of two or three) while you mix a cake, he or she will learn (1) that pleasant things like cake can be made out of things that don't look terribly impressive, like flour and water; (2) that making a cake requires a certain sequence of steps in order to work; (3) that you use special tools or utensils or appliances to accomplish things, like mixing and baking the cake; (4) that processes take time, like waiting for the cake to get baked; and perhaps most important and subtlest of all, (5) that you can act upon things in the world and get them to respond to your desires—that if you understand them, you can control them, and that you can do them better or not so well depending on your understanding.

2. Get them to help you. If you're an efficient type, this takes a lot of willpower, because small children's "help" often seems like interference unless you are willing to pay close attention to what they are trying to do, go along with it to some extent, yet still carry them along on your own project. But it can be fun, if you relax about it. Try it when you have plenty of time, and on projects that don't have any deadline or urgency—you don't want a child around if you're trying to stop a water leak that may flood your apartment! But if you're just putting a wheel back on a tricycle (children love to see you fix their own things, of course), by watching you and helping you, your child will learn (1) that tools have special names—ask for things and point to them when you need them; (2) that different tools have different purposes; (3) that there are causes and effects—the wheel fell off because the cotter pin broke, and a piece of wire in its place will hold the wheel on again; (4) that things have parts, and these parts are related—to replace the wheel, you have to remove the hubcap; the cotter pin or wire holds the wheel and the axle together.

3. *Read to them.* Having books, magazines, and newspapers around the house will show your kids that the printed word is important and interesting. Get children's books from the library. Take children along to the library as soon as they can walk around and look at the books there. Get them used to the idea that there are mysterious and fascinating things to be found out through reading.

4. *Cut down on T.V.* It's not so much that the contents of T.V. programs are bad for kids (though some of them certainly are). The real problem is that kids who spend most of their time watching T.V. don't get the chance to develop ingenuity by inventing games with other children. They get used to being entertained by others—to sit and wait for things to happen, rather than making them happen. So it's a good idea to pay attention to how much T.V. your children watch, even if you can't bear to pay attention to what they watch. One hour a day is certainly plenty—it's probably more than your child spends directly relating to you. (A handy way to keep your kids' minds off T.V., not to mention your own: Throw an attractive piece of fabric over it whenever it is not in actual use.)

5. *Teach them to write.* Let your children watch when you have to write something—a letter, a list of things to buy at the store. Let them play with your pencils and paper. Get them to tell you stories and write them down (sometimes their drawings have stories in them). When they get old enough to read a bit, write down notes and stick them up on the wall.

6. *Teach them names of things.* Our world runs by words; if your child becomes curious about words and good at using them, it's an immense advantage. See if you can make up rhymes or word games with the names of things around the house or in picture books.

7. *Numbers.* A child who sees parents using numbers will know what they are used for—adding up a budget, seeing how much an installment plan will cost, planning the dimensions to make something, how to measure and mark the parts, reading prices in the store on shelves and cans, and so on.

8. *Teach them to draw.* Most young children naturally like to draw. If they are given any chance at all, they will draw themselves, their parents, their pets, their street, their house, and so on. They will also draw their dreams, imaginary stories, and strange fantasy scenes. Unfortunately, most schools have limited facilities and allow little time for drawing. Only a few good teachers understand that through drawing a child can come to understand and learn just as well (or maybe better) than through other kinds of learning. So at home give your children plenty of paper, crayons, pencils, and even paints if you can afford them. The cheapest kind of paper you can buy is called "news-

print"; an art-supplies store or a large stationary store will sell it. The easiest-to-get free paper is computer printout paper, which any friend who works in a big office can probably get for you. It has numbers on one side, but is big and great for drawing.

9. *Teach them to use reference books.* For older children, one of the most important things you can do is to keep books of various kinds available in the house. And there are two special kinds of books every household needs, for children and adults both:

Dictionaries. Anytime you put something important on paper—a letter, a petition, a plan—you'll need a dictionary to check spellings and meanings. Besides, a dictionary can be a fascinating kind of reading. Get a good big one. The *American Heritage Dictionary,* available in paperback, is the best I have found at present: It has good design and printing, and beautiful illustrations; its handling of usage standards is very complete, and it frequently gives derivations of words. Many special children's dictionaries are available; check with a children's librarian for recommendations.

Encyclopedias. Never buy an encyclopedia of any kind from a door-to-door salesperson, no matter how sweet the deal sounds, no matter how beautiful the encyclopedia, no matter how good it might appear to your children! You will end up paying many hundreds of dollars for the set, much of it in interest and carrying charges. But you can phone a couple of used-book stores and find encyclopedia sets, probably of the identical edition, for modest prices.

Before you spend money on encyclopedias, however, drop in at your public library and talk to the children's librarian (or reference librarian, if you're thinking of a set for yourself). They know which encyclopedias are satisfactory and which are junk; ask their advice, and look through the sets they recommend to see if they suit you. Many households, even intellectual ones, are well enough served by a single-volume job, the *Columbia Encyclopedia,* which can be bought easily secondhand. It is authoritative, fairly complete, and so big and heavy that it's much better than telephone books for seating kids at the table.

M. Own pets.

Amid the alienation, loneliness, and despair prevalent in our society, many a dog is its owner's literal best friend, and many a cat is the chief source of grace and calm in a harried life.

A relationship with a dog can be as demanding and intense as one with a child; moreover, dogs often serve as emotional lightning rods through which families discharge emotions just as well not discharged on each other. People also get dogs for protection; remember, though, that training a big dog to be under your control is a major commitment (and a severe test of your firmness of character!). But above all, having a dog gives you a window into the life of another species; if you let your dog have a natural social life (which many cities prohibit through leash laws) you can observe clear territorial rules, and the sexual rites that make canine life, if freely led, so much better than a "dog's life" it is often imagined to be.

Through our dogs we may also get in touch with a neglected—in fact largely taboo—aspect of our own emotional lives. Sexual attraction in humans, as in other animals, is directly connected to the sense of smell. Hygiene handbooks never mention it, much less cosmetic ads, but the fact is that some people's smells makes us feel good and some make us uneasy. Smell, though no one lists it as a factor in marital compatibility, may indeed be more important in how people get along than physical appearance, religious beliefs, or politics. We never get used to smells that don't please and reassure us.

Usually the sense of sight is thought to be our dominant sense. But sight is rather impersonal and neutral, and it is connected to our brains through an intermediate sifting-out circuit. The nose, however, is plugged in directly; its signals affects us, directly and overwhelmingly, though not so subtly as a dog's. Sooner or later, wise people realize that they have to relax and trust their sense of smell.

But such sensibilities can, of course, be cultivated without the presence of a dog; and we can't avoid the ethical questions involved in keeping pets. Subjecting other animals to human wills is a dubious proposition generally (including raising them to eat). Keeping large dogs, who need to run around in wide open spaces, in a cramped city apartment or house is no kindness to them.

If you decide to keep a pet, understand that it is a serious and lasting responsibility, both psychologically and financially. Inoculations for rabies and other diseases are essential; vet bills can run high. Spaying, which is the only way to prevent your pet adding to an already bulging population of unwanted puppies and kittens, is expensive. And food for a pet, even if you feed it mostly table scraps, will cost a surprising amount. Dry foods tend to be cheaper than canned ones. Accustom your pet to them from the beginning.

Humane societies and animal shelters are full of healthy, well-trained animals available for adoption; check your phone book.

N. Be civilized if you must divorce.

In recent years, uncontested divorce has become much easier in many states and do-it-yourself divorce filing is common among people separating relatively amicably and without significant property to divide up. However, when children or property are involved, legal assistance is always necessary and desirable. Unstable economic conditions make separation and divorce agreements more complex financially; expert tax advice may also be needed. When spouses plan to remain partners in holding property, the consequences of various contingencies need careful exploration, so that risks and benefits are shared fairly. It is tempting, in a divorce, to try and get everything settled quickly, so that you can be rid of the whole mess. Many people make very unwise settlements when they are in this frame of mind. Remember that divorce may be quick, but its consequences may be with you for the rest of your life. And once a divorce agreement has been approved by a court, it will be impossible to alter, except sometimes for child-support payments, which can be changed if financial circumstances change (for the better or the worse).

Child-support payments are often set on an escalator basis. So are alimony payments, which are now relatively rare, but do exist—for ex-husbands as well as ex-wives. (Sometimes quasi-alimony lump-sum payments may be won when people have lived together for substantial periods without marriage.)

In backward states, where "fault" must still be proved even for a divorce that is really uncontested, a lawyer is essential. Unfortunately, getting married is cheap, but divorce can be very expensive. A wise society would arrange things the other way around: Getting married should be difficult and expensive, and uncontested divorce should be available simply by filling out a form and paying a filing fee. Marriage is, after all, a contract, and it ought to be dissolvable by mutual consent like any other contract, except where the state has a legitimate interest in the welfare of any children involved.

O. Get help if you're a single parent.

That supposedly "normal" nuclear family of the past (father works, mother stays home with two children) is now a small minority of American households—less than one-sixth, in fact. "Blended families," including stepparents and stepsiblings, are increasingly common—since most divorced people remarry, often with other divorced persons who may also have children. At current rates, two out of five children will spend at least part of their childhood or adolescence in single-parent homes.

Single parenting thus is an overwhelming reality of American life, but we have not, as a society, developed satisfactory ways of dealing with it. In many communities, some stigma still attaches to divorce, especially if children are involved, and divorcing parents' friends may express unwarranted and counterproductive pity. In fact, as various careful studies have established, children after divorce do at least as well emotionally as children whose unhappy homes have remained "intact." Nor do children of divorced parents have higher rates of juvenile delinquency, school problems, or sexual identity problems; they can become warped by two unsatisfactory parents as much as by one! Most children and adolescents recover from the pain and confusion of divorce fairly readily, unless one or both parents configure it as a matter of lasting and earth-shaking trauma. If the parents establish satisfying lives for themselves, and do not fall into patterns of conflict over the children, the children may even experience positive benefits from the divorce—for example, in receiving more and higher-quality attention, especially from the father. Single-parent children may have high verbal skills, and they may be more socially mature, doubtless because of greater closeness to the parent. If you are a single parent and your child is having some kind of emotional difficulty, don't leap to the conclusion that it is due to your status as single parent. All children go through developmental stages that give them some trouble. Read a child-development book, or check with other parents, before you convince yourself that something is terribly wrong. Watch out for unconscious—and unjustified—feelings of guilt.

It is obviously critical for ex-spouses to transcend their grievances, and establish fair and healthy visitation schedules or child residence-sharing. In recent years, many couples who parted on relatively good terms have found joint legal custody an attractive arrangement (though many older judges still view it with distaste). It establishes shared responsibility for the child; it symbolizes that both parents still love and will care for the child. Instead of having the child live entirely with one or the other parent, it encourages more extended living (summers, or alternating months, when ex-spouses live nearby) with both parents. Contrary to earlier fears, many parents who could not get along while living together can cooperate quite decently toward their child's welfare once they are separated. Custody is also given to fathers much more frequently today, and is sometimes the best solution. A court fight over custody is expensive and almost certain to be harmful to both children and parents. (Most children of divorced parents who *do* have serious emotional disturbances have parents unable to agree on how the children should be raised, with consequent inconsistency and quarrels.)

The greatest hazards of the single parent are isolation and poverty. Single mothers especially sometimes find themselves isolated from their friends or other steady adult contact—and prolonged exposure to nobody but children can drive you off the deep end. Some newly divorced parents embark on a sexually open life-style, as if to make up for the time they lost while unhappily married. They may segregate their sexual lives from their home lives, so that their sexual partners are not real participants in their or their children's lives. This is unwise from both your standpoint (since it doesn't help your general isolation) and your children's (since it gives them no adult life to learn from). Your reality is that you are both a parent and a sexual person. This is a reality that children can accept, and accept better than they tolerate concealment or deception.

But no matter how you manage them, sexual relationships alone cannot constitute a healthy social life. You need to pay conscious attention to building up a solid, sustaining friendship network. You can start with other single parents, for which churches and other organizations have special groups. But make sure that you pursue genuine interests of your own, as well as seeking company; you are most appealing to other people when you are following up things that really mean something to you.

Consider joining forces with one or more other single parents, and living together in one household, or in adjacent apartments or houses. In this way you can provide each other regular moral support, exchange child care, cut down on everybody's cooking and laundry chores, and generally make your home life more interesting. It's important, of course, to explore beforehand your basic ground rules about rent-sharing, overnight visitors, housekeeping responsibilities, and so on, to avoid surprises later.

Since most single parents are women, they are generally economically disadvantaged. (The average single father makes twice what the average single mother makes.) Despite better computerized tracking of fathers who try to escape their child-support payments, many divorced mothers are left on their own. Mothers who work full time may have incomes so low that they qualify for welfare; don't be ashamed to look into it! Extensive training programs exist for single mothers; inquire about them at the state employment office. There are also "earned income credits" for women who earn below a certain amount. And, of course, AFDC welfare programs apply to divorced, abandoned, or never-married mothers.

P. Get legal help with wills and probate.

When people die without a will, their property is passed on to their relatives according to state laws. Often some goes to their spouse if he or she is still living, and the rest gets divided up equally among the living children. This applies both to "real" property such as a house and to "personal" property such as a car or mobile home, boat or clothes.

If for some reason you don't want your property to be given in the state's way, and many people do not, you can sometimes accomplish this through a will—though your spouse will get half of it, anyway, in community-property states. (This is one reason why legal marriage agreements clarify your thinking and can prevent later trouble.) You can also provide for guardians other than grandparents for your children if you wouldn't want them to fall into your parents' hands.

A will can name an administrator (usually your lawyer or an old family friend) to manage or sell your property on behalf of your spouse or children.

If you make a new will, prevent possible confusion by destroying all copies of your old one.

When a relative dies and leaves you something, there is sometimes a court legal process called "probate" that verifies the will and sees that its provisions are carried out. Generally this requires the services of a lawyer in the place where the relative died. Most lawyers are glad to handle probate cases, because there is a good deal of money in them. Some crooked lawyers will suck practically all the money out for themselves; so it is important that you or the family find an honest one.

Q. Accept that dying is a part of life.

Seeking to avoid recognition of our temporary status as living organisms here on our lovely Earth, we relegate the process of dying to the social shadows. It happens "offstage," presided over by impersonal, professional, hired "others." Though more conscious attention has been directed toward it recently, dying is still a taboo subject for most of us, and hence we are often unable to deal with people for whom it becomes an imminent reality. But this means cutting ourselves off from an important aspect of our lives—an aspect that then operates only subconsciously, if no less powerfully, until aging or disease or accident forces us to confront it.

Counseling services are now available for families and individuals who are facing death. The process of recognizing and preparing for our own death is obviously an overwhelming challenge to our psychological resources, and we should not be ashamed of needing help. Nor should family members or others close to a dying person underestimate the severity of the strains they will be under.

Costly funerals are intended to make the survivors feel better. In fact, they are often authorized even when the dead person has specifically asked for a simple burial. The reasons why family members will buy a costly funeral are complex. It reduces guilt they may feel at having treated the dead person badly; it softens the unconscious sense of relief at still being alive while somebody else is dead; it gives a dramatic focus for the expression of grief—a chance to weep, to feel desolate, to feel the loss (both to yourself and to others) that a death may entail.

Only the last of these reasons—providing an occasion for true mourning—is a decent and humane reason, and it ought to be the overriding concern behind our ways of handling death and burial. Mourning requires no pomp and circumstance, and certainly not the presence of a gussied-up corpse. It requires only the gathering together of people who truly had feeling for the dead person and who wish to express it in each other's company. They can arrange a relatively formal event, religious or otherwise—or they can simply, like the Quakers, sit quietly and reflect on the life of the dead person, some individuals wishing to say something and some remaining still. Perhaps because flickering light and the immaterial, enduring quality of music seem magically appropriate, people often play music on such occasions and light candles. In many cultures which are less shy about the fact that life must go on, a wake is customary later—a drunken feast that gives expression to the life-force remaining and transforms grief at death into joy at living. We might do well to experiment with this example.

People should feel free to invent ceremonies that suit them and disregard commercial funeral practices. Death is a powerful emotional experience for those who live on; its impact ought not be distorted by the vulgar tastes and sordid commercialism of undertakers.

In America today most people still die in a hospital surrounded by chrome-plated equipment, hooked up to pumps and needles, watched over by dials and meters, sedated and isolated from their families and friends. The intention is humanitarian—to prolong life. But the effect is often to make a person's last days a nightmare of medical desperation, so that one dies like a medical phenomenon and not like a man or woman. In many ways it seems preferable to die at home amid your family and with your own things, thinking your own last thoughts about the adventure of life in a setting you love and feel reassured by. But this takes a great deal of strength. Also, doctors generally dislike it, and of course for some terminally ill people the care needed in their last days can be provided only in a hospital or in a "hospice," a home-like but medically equipped environment. Even the medical and insurance industries are now recognizing the benefits of home care; so you may be able to secure the services of professional nurses and other care-givers who will attend to your family members in your home.

What people need most when somebody has just died is practical help, moral support, and friends who are sensitive to their feelings. See whether you can pitch in with concrete assistance; don't wait to be asked. Children probably need to be watched, fed, comforted. Families may be swollen with relatives from distant places who need to be fed and housed. Mourners need to be kept company and, if they feel like talking, listened to. And, in all of this, it is important to preserve a sense of ongoing life—not to distract people from grief, but to give them the security they need to express their grief and thus transcend it.

As a reaction against the excesses of the undertakers, various types of funeral societies have been created across the nation. (You can get the address of one near you from the Continental Association, 6900 Lost Lake Rd., Egg Harbor, WI 54209-9231; phone number 1-800-458-5563; or the Neptune Society, phone number 415-771-0717.) You join these in advance for a small fee, and when the time comes they carry out the instructions you have given them. This saves your family and friends from having to confront undertakers at a time of grief and weakness, and can save very large sums of money. You will decide about these essentials:

Embalming? No religions commend this practice, though state laws used to require it. It means pumping the corpse full of preservatives and making it look "life-like" for viewing in the elaborate funeral services on which the undertakers make their big money.

Casket? A "container" may be legally required to transport bodies, but it may be surprisingly difficult to obtain a traditional and honorable plain pine box, without expensive handles or other "extras."

Burial or cremation? Both ground burial and cremation are very ancient customs—though cremation has become common in America only in recent years. Burial returns a body to the earth from which it sprang. There is a certain poetic and ecological rightness in this, especially for people who have a strong attachment to the region they have lived in, or in a family whose members have customarily been buried in one spot. On the other hand, buying a cemetery plot can be very expensive.

Cremation, the burning of a corpse until it is reduced to a small boxful of ashes, has two aspects that appeal to many people. First, ashes can be scattered, which, like burial, seems an appropriate return of our mortal substance to the earth. Many legal obstacles used to obstruct this practice, but they have been struck down in most states. (People could easily circumvent them anyway, claiming to be taking ashes "back home" for interment.) Second, the fact that ashes can be scattered means that you don't have to buy a cemetery plot or an urn and a niche—for which cemeteries charge almost as much for as plots.

There are two alternatives. One is bequeathing your body to a nearby medical school, where it will help train doctors. This is the only way to die without costing your family anything at all, in either money or trouble. Unfortunately, some medical schools are not interested, but it may be worth a phone call to find out. The other is do-it-yourself burial. The idea that people can be buried on their own or friends' land without any participation by undertakers is discouraged by every means of propaganda and law at the funeral industry's disposal. But until 50 or 100 years ago, almost everybody was buried by either church or family. It can still be done, except where city ordinances prohibit it, but there are permits to be secured, and advance planning would be obligatory. In this, as in other areas, our undertaking laws are one of the major insanities of our society, but they can sometimes be circumvented, and sooner or later must be directly challenged.

Social Security pays a death benefit that may cover a funeral managed by a funeral society. Unions, credit unions, and lodges or similar organizations may also pay death benefits, and Workman's Compensation insurance may also apply. Veterans theoretically can be buried free in national cemeteries, but most of these are full (check with the Veterans Administration).

Chapter 12.
Make or Repair Your Own Clothes.

Our recent ancestors made all of their own clothes. Recapturing their skills will free you from the tyranny of fashion, fads, and retail stores.

A. Learn to sew.

All you really need for sewing, of course, is a needle and thread and some scissors. But an old straight-sewing machine can be picked up cheaply, and it should last forever. The fancy zigzag models cost a great deal more and are essentially designed for virtuosos. They also have extremely complex works, and if not used and oiled just right may give trouble. So get a work-horse type, then relax and enjoy it. Unless you like to make salespeople squirm (and don't mind coming away empty-handed anyway), stay out of the shops that advertise "fantastic repossession bargains": These are bait-and-switch ads, and the advertised machines somehow never are there.

You'll also need a tape measure, a piece of chalk (for marking cloth), a good supply of straight pins, and an assortment of different colored threads. It helps to have a sewing box or basket with compartments to keep things in, as you will begin to accumulate buttons, zippers, snaps, hooks, and other little objects. Also, thread comes in so many lovely colors that it's a pleasure to collect them.

It's unwise to try anything fancy at first—stay away from items with turned-down collars, pockets, and other complications. Go to a fabric store and look for patterns marked "easy to sew," which have very complete and precise directions. Follow them slowly and don't cut any corners, literally or figuratively; there really *is* a reason for everything!

You can learn to work up your own designs by moving from the very simplest designs to more complex ones. You can start with the cloak, poncho, or serape, basically just a big piece of fabric with a hole for your head.

The next simplest item is a kimono or robe, which fits a bit more closely, but also requires no cutting except chopping pieces off a length of cloth. Sew the sleeves onto the main part, and then sew the sides together, and you have a pullover kimono; to make it a wraparound type, split down the front and hem the edges.

Full skirts that pull in around the waist with elastic can also be made in a few minutes. Make a large cylinder of cloth, run a wide hem around the top, and put a piece of elastic through it. Try it on, hem the bottom at the length you want, and that's it.

Shirts are complicated if you do tailored collars; so stay away from them. A super-simple blouse can be made just from one piece of cloth folded over, like the top part of a kimono. Sew the sides together from the armpit down to the bottom, cut a slit for the neck hole and hem its edges. In cold weather such a garment may not keep you warm by itself, but it can be worn over some kind of turtleneck or other close-sleeved shirt.

All conventional clothes can be thought of as sets of tubes attached to each other. The body has a tube, the arms have tubes, the legs (in pants) have tubes. Since you can make a tube shape simply by sewing a piece of cloth up both sides, everything else is refinements: tucks, gores, linings, bindings, buttons, pleats, and so on. As long as you stick to clothes that drape rather than hug the body, you can exercise your ingenuity freely. Best of all, you can wear fabrics that may not be widely used in ready-made clothes.

One of the nice things about draped clothes, incidentally, is that they lend themselves to decoration: fringes, laces, rick-rack, frogs (fasteners you sew on, without buttonhole making). Sewing stores and secondhand stores are sources for thousands of such curious additions.

B. Dye your own fabrics.

If you ever come across clothes that appeal to you in every way but their color, they can often be dyed. Hideous pinks can be turned into almost any dark color; pastels can be covered up. You can't entirely obliterate flowery printed patterns, and you can't turn a dark color into a light one, but there are a vast number of interesting transformations you can work on clothes. It is also pleasant to give some color to items that are normally white, like men's undershirts.

The dyes available in dime stores are seldom used by weavers and other craftspeople who know good dyes; they are not available in subtle shades, they don't take well, and they run onto your other clothes in the wash. To get dyes that perform well in these ways, you have to write away just like the weavers do to a company such as W. Cushing Co., Dover-Foxcroft, Maine; ask for their color book and price list. Their dyes are slightly more expensive than the dime-store brands, but well worth it. There are also many natural dyes: marigold and acacia flowers produce oranges and yellows, so do onion skins; coffee gives a reddish brown. Generally a lengthy soaking is required to extract color, and then the fabric must be simmered for an hour or so.

Cotton and wool take dyes better than the synthetic fabrics, but you can dye rayon, acetate, and most other synthetics. Remember that all fabrics, but especially the synthetics, dry a good deal lighter than they look when wet. You can save the dye mix until your clothes dry; if they're not dark enough, put them in again.

Follow directions carefully. Afterward, rinse the garments carefully and repeatedly—and handwash separately the first few times.

You need a large pot, such as an enameled one made for canning, which can take stove-burner heat. Don't use galvanized buckets or washtubs. A roasting pan is usually big enough. Make sure you've cleaned it thoroughly. The goods to be dyed also need to be clean; otherwise irregularities in color result. There are creative techniques for using irregularities—usually caused by dribbling wax onto the fabric—to make random patterns in fabric, but if you want even color, the fabric has to be clean.

Tie-dyeing is a fascinating special form of dying. If you bunch parts of the fabric together and tie them up tightly with string or elastic bands, little or no dye can get into the tied up parts; thus they come out lighter. Since the whole thing involves many variables, you can't predict exactly what the results are going to be. This is the special fascination of the process: The generally symmetric vaguely circular motifs are always different, always subtle.

You can't really re-dye army surplus camouflage or olive-drab, because dyes used in army goods are excellent. To get rid of them requires a process known as "digestion" that can be done only by a commercial dyeing plant; even then it doesn't get rid of all the underlying color, which tends to shine through the overlay of new dye.

C. Learn to identify fabrics.

In recent years fairly strict regulations have been issued by the Federal Trade Commission to control deception in the garment trade. New goods must carry labels stating the types of fibers in the goods, their percentages, and washing and drying requirements (or if dry cleaning is necessary). Stores may no longer remove these small labels or conceal them so you can only see the bright, fancy advertising-type labels that don't have to meet standards of truthfulness. Of course, by the time the goods reach the secondhand store, all their labels except the store-name label have usually disappeared. You must, therefore, develop some expertise in recognizing fabrics.

Although small pieces of yardage don't come with them attached, larger pieces of fabric must also be accompanied by labels telling what's in them and how to care for them; fabric stores must supply these to you upon request.

Study cloth. There is sleazy cloth and there is sound cloth, and you can get a feel for the difference. Good material is essential for clothes you can love; they have to feel right. If your reaction to something is "Well, it might be all right for some occasions," take that as a danger sign. Really good clothes will make you feel right on practically any occasion: You can work in them, play in them, even sleep in them.

Cloth where the colors are woven in rather than printed on afterward is usually superior in other ways as well. And in general, cloth with a fine, tight weave is superior to cloth with a loose weave (unless the looseness is desirable for some special reason, like coolness in hot weather). Hold the cloth up in a strong light and look at it very closely on both sides, seeing how the threads run. Sunlight is best, since it shows true colors.

It is no mystery what determines the qualities of cloth—an enormous amount of research is done by the army and by private textile manufacturers to find out. The basic factors are as follows.

The warmth of a fabric depends on how much air it can trap within and between its fibers. Both thick and thin cloth are 60 to 90 percent air, and it is this air that keeps you warm. Wool, which has numerous tiny curly fibers, is the warmest, though some curlable synthetics are fairly warm. Warmth also depends on how well the fabric enables water vapor to evaporate from your body; there again wool is best. For outdoor garments like winter coats, a wind-resistant outer layer over a thick, soft inner layer is the best combination. This can be achieved, for example, by a sweater and jacket, a quilted coat, or a zip-in lining coat.

The feel of fabric on your skin depends upon several factors. If the fibers are hairy, like wool, it will feel warm. If the fibers are slick, like silk, rayon or nylon, it will feel cool. If the fibers are thick, the fabric will feel scratchy, as in coarse wools. If the fibers are fine and tightly woven, the fabric will feel smooth, as in good cottons and some synthetics. Ironing makes cloth feel cooler because it squashes down the fibers, so that your skin touches more of them.

The drape of fabric depends on how fine the yarns are (the thinner they are, the softer the fabric and the more subtly it will hang). It is also influenced by the type of fiber; linen is used in tailored dresses and suits precisely because it is stiff. Sizing, water repellents, and other chemicals may also stiffen cloth.

(Remember, in buying fabric by the yard, that the sizing will come out in the wash, leaving the fabric somewhat thinner and softer.)

The water repellency of a fabric depends on how "wettable" the fibers are—how fast they conduct water from the outside surface to the inside. Both wool, which is naturally slightly oily, and some treated synthetics shed water, but they are never entirely waterproof. Entirely waterproof things, like plastics, are unbearable to wear for very long, because they trap perspiration inside and you are soon clammy all over; in really cold weather they are downright dangerous—they can lead you to freeze to death at temperatures in which wool clothing would be quite comfortable. Chemical water repellants don't usually last through a dry cleaning. Fabric treated with them also gets dirtier, since the repellants attract dirt.

One approach, unfortunately quite expensive, was to use fabric of super-close-woven cotton, which can sometimes be found in very costly hunting and Arctic gear. In the parts that stay dry it breathes, but in the parts that get wet, the fibers swell, closing off their pores so tightly that water cannot pass through.

But for general use the problem seemed basically insoluble—until the invention of Gore-Tex fabric. This is a system of coating fabric with a film that has microscopic pores—pores so small, in fact, that air molecules can pass through them, but water can't; so the fabric breathes, and you stay dry and warm. Gore-Tex is now used in camping equipment as well as garments. It requires careful handling, since the film is easily damaged, and seams must be resealed after a year or so of use.

Cotton. Washable, durable, easily ironable. Takes mending and patching easily. Available in every color conceivable; after long use the colors fade to soft, beautiful, subtle hues. Especially after some washing, cottons drape softly and are extremely good-feeling on the skin. Some cotton garments are now treated with resins that make them wrinkle-resistant and cut down on ironing, but the formaldehyde-based resins used in treating some permapress cotton are currently being tested for carcinogenic effects. Also, cotton burns rapidly; be careful of it around stoves and fireplaces.

Wool. More expensive than cotton, and usually woven in heavier fabrics, wool can be either in plain or "worsted" form; the latter has more tightly twisted threads and wears much longer. Wool is also woven into loose-knit fabrics called jerseys, flannels, and cashmeres. Good woolen cloth is springy when you squash it and hard to wrinkle. Unfortunately, wool has to be either hand-washed or dry-cleaned.

Labels in new goods that read "virgin wool" mean that the wool has never been used before. "Reprocessed wool" has been used before, but not in clothes. "Re-used wool" is taken from clothes.

As wool takes up moisture from body evaporation, it appears to generate heat. The oil on natural wool is lanolin, incidentally, and adds to its heat-trapping abilities. And wool is made fire-resistant with chemicals, which fill up its pores and make the cloth breathe less.

Many wool articles, such as sweaters, can be washed very carefully with mild soap in lukewarm or cool water; lay them out afterward on a towel to dry, making sure you dry them in their proper shape and size. (Wet wool can stretch badly, and heated wool will shrink disastrously.)

If you have something ruined by a cleaner or get into a dispute over charges, contact the Better Business Bureau. There is so much trouble with cleaners that the BBB will probably have an arbitration panel to which you can complain and perhaps win out. Suing in small-claims court might be worth it if an expensive garment is ruined.

Incidentally, it is almost never worth dry-cleaning a rug. Hang it up and beat it with a broom, or scrub it off with mild soap and lukewarm water (Oriental and other wool rugs too). Most rugs will shrink or discolor if dry-cleaned.

Synthetics. Chemists have produced a large number of synthetic fibers, some derived from renewable biological sources and some from petrochemical sources. Because they have slick fiber surfaces, where natural fibers have many little crooks and branches and protrusions, they do not hold water well and generally dry quickly.

Acetates and rayons are derived from cellulose, which comes from wood and cotton. They are generally strong fibers, and may be used as reinforcing mixed in with cotton or wool. They burn and melt. Some forms need dry cleaning; others can readily be washed; check the labels. These fibers may sometimes be woven to look shiny and have a chilly plastic feel; they can, however, also be woven to resemble wool ("jersey"). Even in tight weaves, they tend to stretch (especially when wet) and do not hold stitching well. Since they are cheap, they are very widely used.

Acrylics (like the others below) are petrochemical products. Orlon is the best-known acrylic. It is soft, reasonably warm, and lightweight, dries quickly (also burns and melts rapidly), and is machine-washable.

Nylons come under many different trade names. Nylon is the strongest fiber available (in thicker strands it is used for fishing line). It was the first drip-dry synthetic to be widely used in clothing. It usually has a clammy plastic feel, but nylon can be woven into soft, bulky forms suitable for light sweaters, or into jersey-type material. These tend to stretch, and take stitching badly. Nylon is useful chiefly in combination with other fibers, to add strength. It deteriorates in sunlight, and burns and melts.

Polyester fibers, which include Dacron, Fortrel, Polar Guard, and others, are strong and wrinkle-resistant. Dacron is used for sails because it is strong and never soaks up water. It tends to be stiff and uncomfortable in tightly woven fabric and often feels plastic. Polyesters are widely used blended with cotton; the resulting combination fabric can be machine-washed and needs little or no ironing. They are also blended with wool for slacks, suits, and other hard-wear items that need dry cleaning. In the infamous "polyester doubleknit" form, they tend to droop and look sleazy.

Various other synthetics have been devised: Spandex, which is quite elastic; olefins (polypropylenes), which do not absorb water and are used in carpeting and upholstery; sarans, which are weather- and flame-resistant.

Many of these synthetics are useful supplements to the natural fibers, but they are seldom if ever as comfortable. In some garments, such as women's panties and panty hose, synthetics are positively undesirable, since they are not absorbent and concentrate heat and moisture.

D. Make patchwork.

The patch is an ancient and honorable device and by no means a sign of disgrace. An honest, forthright patch is not a disfigurement, and can be a decorative addition. Keep bright-colored pieces of cloth around, even if they're small; you never know when a shirt or skirt or pair of pants may wear through. Don't forget that patches can be laid over patches, too—and patches can be round or square or oval or oblong or star-shaped.

"Iron on" patches don't stay ironed on forever, and they're dull and standardized besides. Use strong, honest cloth, and sew it on carefully. Sew around the outer edge of the patch (turning it under neatly) and then also around the edge of the hole or rip, so the fabric is firmly attached to the patch.

You can adopt the principles of our grandparents' patchwork quilts and make large pieces of cloth out of patches—big enough for curtains, quilts, furniture covers, car seats, tents, who knows what. You can often find beautiful fragments of cloth in the rag bins of secondhand stores. Let your imagination have free rein. The best patches are the boldest patches.

When patching can no longer save the knees of pants, cut them off and turn them into shorts. Since most American cities have tropical summers (which may get hotter from the greenhouse effect), the wearing of shorts is desirable for practically everybody.

E. Repair your shoes and sandals.

Like all clothes, shoes are a highly emotional subject. Some people enjoy shiny shoes and take a great deal of pain to preserve their leather. Others wear suedes, which can go for years with only an occasional brushing (you can never polish them).

But there are some things to look out for in shoes. The worst is a tendency to produce deformed feet. In the natural shape of the human foot, the toes stick out straight from the attached foot bones. The wearing of conventional shoes of the pointy-toed variety (and there are plenty of these around, especially in boots and in women's shoes) gradually deforms the foot until the toes get curved and compressed. This makes the foot less efficient as a weight-bearing device, gives work to foot doctors, produces corns and calluses where the foot rubs against the shoe, and makes the foot ugly when, at intimate moments, it is removed from its casing. You should, therefore, wear round-toed, square-toed, or open-toed shoes. Most running shoes have to be designed with a functional fit in mind, so that they are healthy for your feet, though models momentarily fashionable may not be healthy for your wallet.

Shoes that fit loosely, like clogs, increase serious foot injuries; and the higher the heel, the greater the likelihood of twists, sprains, and strain.

Unless you are always working around things that may drop on or scrape your feet, or in mud or slime, sandals have many advantages for everyday life. They allow the skin of your feet to breathe normally; they allow your feet to function as feet evolved to function; they allow fungal infections to dry up.

Sandals and sandal lacing lend themselves to inspired designs that you can work out for yourself—always better than a factory-standardized style. Their history goes back to Greek and Roman days; their elegance has been appreciated for millennia. You can also wear tabis (thongs), the Asian rubber sandals that are the cheapest footwear yet devised.

Even in cities, some young people today experiment with going barefoot. In my country boyhood, nobody wore shoes from the time school was out until it opened again, except on compulsory formal occasions. City pavements are harder on the feet than country dirt, but many foot doctors believe it is far more harmful to wear shoes all the time. The real danger with bare feet in the cities is glass: There is so much broken glass around that you really have to keep alert, even if your soles are quite hardened. You will also be unwelcome in certain stores or restaurants, where managers will tell you that bare feet are dirty.

Do sandals give your feet support? Some doctors think that "support" is necessary, considering modern conditions, and some don't. In a general way, you can assume that if your biological structure needs something, it's got it; your feet turned out to be feet rather than hooves or webs because that was the most useful to your ancestors over a period of hundred of thousands of years.

There are various tricks by which the life of shoes can be stretched. One is the old newspaper or cardboard trick: When a hole wears in the sole, you lay a piece on the inside. This is good only as a stopgap, however, because the hole will continue to grow. Leather soles and some hard composition soles can be made to last longer by putting a layer of duct tape or Mystik cloth tape over the holes. Surprisingly, a double layer will often last for months, especially if you also lay paper or cardboard inside the shoe and don't wear the shoes when it's wet outside. There's not much you can do for crêpe rubber or soft-rubber soles.

You can reheel your own shoes if you have patience and a little skill with tools. You have to find a piece of old rubber tire, a knife sharp enough to cut it to shape, and some short, small nails. Remove the worn heel, before the sole under it begins to wear away, by prying it off (try to find the bent-over nail ends inside the shoe and straighten them out, which makes it easier). Carefully carve out a piece of tire rubber of the exact heel shape. Then putting the shoe upside down over a block of wood, nail the new heel on and crimp the nails inside; then replace the inner sole.

If you want to get a little more professional, which is always satisfying, you can glue on a new sole that will last something like a year. You may be able to find resoling kits at a big dime store, or you can just buy the sole material (Biltrite makes some that have pebbled texture) from a shoe-repair shop; it comes in sheets that give enough for two or three pairs of shoes, and costs about 20 percent of what a resoling job will cost you.

The trick is in gluing the sole material firmly onto the old sole. Best way: Clean the old sole carefully with a stiff suede brush or dry scrub brush. Cut off a piece of sole material bigger than the shoe. Then slop on a layer of silicone glue, not too thick, not too thin, and press the sole and new material together, driving out the air bubbles. Then lay some small stones or other small, heavy weights on top of the shoes; if the soles still curl up at the toes or sides, lay the whole business on top of some heavy rags to support the new material near the edges. After the glue has dried (allow plenty of time), trim off the excess sole around the edges.

If the sewing that holds the top parts of a shoe together has begun to come apart, you may be able to sew it back. To do this by hand, you've got to get some strong "button" type thread and get the needle to go through the old holes. This takes time, but the shoemaker would charge you many dollars to sew a shoe back together.

It's impossible, without special shoemaker's equipment, to sew back soles that have separated from the uppers. When that happens, a shoe is beyond your powers of redemption, and good only for puppies to chew on.

F. Replace zippers.

If zippers stick or don't run free, the tape on the back may be binding in the slider; sometimes you can iron it to stay out of the way. Dry cleaning can make a zipper run hard; sometimes a little soap on the teeth will lubricate it. Although the zipper is one of those rare modern inventions that is a real improvement over its predecessor (the button), zippers do jam, they do pull off in time, they do sometimes lose teeth; and then they need to be replaced. It is not as hard to replace a zipper as you may think, but you must get one that is the exact length of the old one. As you carefully remove the old one by clipping the threads with a small knife or scissors, pin the new one in as you go—that way it'll be in place and ready to be sewn on when you get rid of the old one.

An alternative to zippers is the Velcro sticky-strip kind of fastener that is sometimes used by commercial garment makers; you can buy it in sewing stores. It is especially useful for fastening things like headbands and bicycle-light straps that need to be adjustable.

Chapter 13.
Improve & Protect Your Health.

Traditional medicine tends to isolate us from the functioning of our bodies and to put responsibility for curing disorders onto a doctor's shoulders. (Responsibility for *preventing* disorders is not considered part of medicine; that is classified as "public health," and about one-fifteenth as much is spent on it as in conventional curative medicine—despite the fact that such advances in our general medical welfare that have been achieved are almost entirely due to public-health measures.)

In reaction to this pattern, recent years have seen a great growth of interest in nonconventional healing and preventative systems, from acupuncture (whose biochemical mechanisms were elucidated only in 1979) to biofeedback, herbalism, hypnosis, massage, iridology, etc. Experience with and evaluation of these techniques have not yet demonstrated their value, but many people have found them effective, and certainly the atmosphere in which they are administered is generally itself a support for the body's own healing energies. The doctrines involved are complex; some have long traditional histories; some are likely to prove susceptible to scientific analysis in the near future, others not. The literature on these doctrines is extensive, and of varying quality.

I believe that many of these disciplines are useful for maintaining good health and for dealing with certain kinds of chronic conditions, but persons facing an immediate and serious health crisis should first, or also, consult a traditional doctor—many of whom are beginning to understand some aspects of holistic medicine.

It is noteworthy that "folk medicine"—the lore on which most humans, in industrial or nonindustrial societies, actually depend for their day-to-day health care—has never forgotten that "disease" has nutritional, psychological, and environmental components, as well as microbial, physical, and chemical aspects. In a sense what we need is a new look at folk medicine, adapted to our conditions and incorporating what "scientific medicine" has discovered. The holistic-health movement is heading in that direction.

A. Know about psychotherapy or its equivalent.

The best way to deal with your mental health, as with health in general, is to prevent problems before they occur or get hard to handle.

1. Get help from friends.

Most people who have "nervous breakdowns," "flip out," "go crazy" for a while, or "can't cope" are driven into it by their situations in life—although, of course, early experiences influence how they deal with those situations. As a neighbor of mine once remarked, "Everybody has the right to be crazy in their own house." Harmless strangeness is a right, not a crime. But what can be done if a person behaves so strangely that family and friends can't take it? If you or someone close to you begins to have serious upsets, the first thing to do is to look at the situation. Serious emotional trouble, as shown by suicide attempts, persistent depression, wild behavior or talk, and so on, is often connected with serious real-life problems—it isn't "all in the head"—so help from friends is what is most needed. People who have breakdowns are seldom dangerous, unless severe depression or rage are obvious; indeed, the difference between "crazy" people and "sane" people is not as great as you might think— we all have some craziness in us. And most of us, if we can get some help from our friends or family, manage to get through our crisis somehow.

Here are some basic things to think about.

Is there trouble between members of the family, which is bearing down hard on the ill person? (It is partly because our mental anguish is often connected with our families that friends are usually more of a help than immediate family members.)

Is he or she going through difficult changes with authorities, on the job, or in relationships?

Is the economic situation rocky? Is he or she living a solitary life, so that a lot of time is spent brooding alone, without any warm contact with other human beings?

Has he or she lost touch with good friends or favorite relatives? (A person who needs friends should change environments, if that's what's needed to find some.)

These things, if they have gone bad, can sometimes be put to rights by concrete actions: a vacation, a change of scene by going to visit people you are fond of, or contact with old friends, ministers, or relatives who are under-standing. Most Americans have mental and emotional difficulties at one time or another in life; it's nothing to be ashamed of. Nor is it something to be terrified of: Most people, after a time, learn to cope with their problems fairly well. A good therapist can certainly help people work through their problems. On the other hand, people without therapists usually get through their crises too. And a relationship with a therapist requires careful management, so that it does not slip into long-term dependency. If you feel you need a therapist, try to find one heartily recommended by friends who have been his or her patient. (There are, unfortunately, some very unhelpful therapists out there.)

2. Get help from public institutions.

In the past, often people could be locked up quite easily—and once you get committed to a state mental hospital, it can be very hard to get out. In most states now, however, it is harder for relatives to put you away. A hearing must be held in court; psychiatric examinations of a more than routine nature must be held; and you can get a lawyer to defend your rights. Furthermore, mental hospitals are now so overcrowded and understaffed that they are anxious to keep a rapid turnover of patients—so they too have largely resorted to tranquilizers, and after a month on pills they send you home. Mental hospitals probably create more mental illness than they help, but they do scare some people into getting better. In most mental hospitals you seldom see a psychiatrist, and when you do, it'll be only for brief periods. They are basically custodial institutions, and depressing besides. Stay away from them if you can, and if any friends get put away, help them get out and re-establish as normal a life as possible.

Some other smaller places can sometimes help mentally ill people. Medical schools usually have Suicide Prevention Bureaus in many major cities. They maintain a 24-hour telephone switchboard that people can call and talk to when they feel at the end of their rope. (You can find them in the phone book.) Any community medical center is a good place to ask for information about mental-illness treatment.

Medicare, incidentally, covers up to one hundred days in a mental hospital, on a lifetime basis. Health-insurance policies often have mental-illness coverage. Health maintenance organizations have increasingly extensive psychiatric facilities.

Fortunately, recent progress in pharmaceutical research has led to the development of new types of medication that have been successful with some severe cases of mental illness. Various antidepressants are being widely used, and lithium treatment has been effective in some types of schizophrenia. However, using these powerful drugs is as serious as having a major operation; you would be wise to obtain a second opinion before going ahead with them.

3. Try the Twelve Steps.

The rapid spread of "Twelve Step" programs during the last two decades has made the equivalent of group psychotherapy freely available to all who want it. If you or any relative or friend have any sort of problem with substance abuse, compulsive behavior, or family dysfunction (and that covers about 95 percent of our population), you can attend Twelve-Step meetings for free, and gain new friends, endless emotional support, and many valuable resources for self-help.

Alcohol is by far the greatest American drug problem. We have many millions of alcoholics—people whose lives are dependent on alcohol, and who drink so much that their health is seriously endangered. Our death rate from alcohol-induced cirrhosis of the liver is staggering. And alcohol takes its toll on every level of society: in the executive suite, behind the facade of the suburban home, in the working-class neighborhood, as well as on skid row. A large proportion of our 55,000 auto dead each year is due to alcohol, along with hundreds of thousands injured or maimed. The judgment of most medical researchers directly familiar with drug use is that alcohol is a more dangerous drug than marijuana. It is especially hard on the liver, may help cause malnutrition, and doesn't do your head any good either. However, in small quantities, it promotes conversation—and even digestion (there is a dedicated band known as the Medical Friends of Wine).

Alcoholism, like addiction to other drugs, is a mental-health problem. Some states have a drying-out program in their state hospitals. But to really get off alcohol requires a total reorientation of one's life, and can be accomplished only with a lot of help. Alcoholics Anonymous, the originator of the Twelve Steps, is listed in the phone book, has much experience in coping with alcoholism, and seems to offer the most successful "treatment" so far.

There are about a million alcoholic American women of childbearing age, and their number is increasing, especially among teenagers. Maternal alcohol consumption can lead to brain deficiency in babies. Women who drink heavily should avoid pregnancy, and pregnant women should avoid alcohol.

B. Avoid known causes of cancer.

Despite many decades of expensive research, the biological process of cancer development is still not understood. Treatment success rates have improved somewhat, through surgery, radiation, and chemotherapy; so early detection (through regular self-exams, doctor exams, and mammograms) is even more desirable; it may literally save your life. Still, vast numbers of Americans continue to die of cancer.

But we *do* know some things that help cause it, and can be avoided. Smoking causes not only lung cancer, the most fatal and untreatable type of cancer, but also bladder and pancreas cancer (in addition, it is implicated in a host of other disorders). High consumption of any kinds of fat, and low consumption of fiber, are associated with cancer of the digestive tract and possibly other parts of the body. Rates for various other kinds of cancers have gone up and down over the years, for reasons that are not clear; so reasonable ways to minimize them are also unclear.

It is not true, as some people conclude in despair, that "everything causes cancer." Environmental pollution probably contributes to some types of cancer; certain states with very low pollution, like Alaska and Hawaii, also have low cancer rates. Tragically, a substantial part of our working population is exposed to toxic substances, which may often be carcinogenic, in their places of work. Such exposures ought to be eliminated through legislation and regulation, and government budgets for testing new chemical compounds need to be expanded— or the manufacture of the compounds prohibited. In the meantime, you can try to minimize your exposure to pesticides, herbicides, and all mysterious ingredients and additives in foods, cosmetics, cleaning products, etc.

It is one of the sad ironies of our time that smoking a little marijuana, which decreases nausea from chemotherapy and pain from cancers, is illegal—though your doctor may be able to prescribe pills containing its active substance.

C. Get enough exercise.

Exercise should be looked at as a potential pleasure, rather than as a duty or a necessity: It *feels* good to use your body's remarkable physical capacities at something near their biologically intended levels of performance, rather than letting them moulder away through inactivity. Muscles that have some tone will not only look better, get you around better, and do your work better than flabby muscles, but also just plain feel better. Heart and lungs in shape to cope with substantial physical exertion are also in better shape for less strenuous activity; they give you a generous back-up capacity, which you can then happily and confidently call on if you feel like exerting yourself by running upstairs to catch the phone, or going dancing, or making love. Getting plenty of physical exercise also, of course, keeps your weight under control, generally improves your skin, keeps your digestion in order, and makes you a more attractive and energy-filled person all around.

It does not, of course, earn you money, which is probably a major reason Americans have traditionally paid so little attention to it. (Even now, only 15 percent of us get any serious exercise—a major cause of our bad state of national health.) But it doesn't need to cost you anything to speak of, either. The best activities for general conditioning are swimming, brisk walking, and active dancing. You can probably find a public pool, or a river or lake or ocean, in which you can swim free; for walking your only expense (but it is an essential one) is a good pair of shoes. You can dance anywhere there is music.

Swimming. More muscles are brought into play by swimming than in any other type of exercise, and the cardiovascular system is also given a good workout if you swim seriously for 20 minutes or so. Learn a variety of strokes, so that you don't get bored. The key to successful and relaxing swimming is learning to breathe properly, which also reduces fatigue. If you don't know how to swim, take lessons at your YMCA or public pool. Swim fins sometimes are so much fun that they convince people that swimming is for them, and of course they are especially useful for snorkeling, for swimming long distances, or for use in rough ocean water. For swimming in chlorinated pools, small eye-goggles are available.

Walking. You don't need to run, or even jog. A half hour of brisk walking three times a week will keep your cardiovascular system tuned up, your cholesterol reduced, and your weight down. Begin by a serious program of walking—not just strolling—and work up to develop your heart and lung capacity. If you have worries about your heart, a stress test can be arranged at most hospitals, after which you will be given a range of pulse rates to keep within; this is easy, and indeed in time almost automatic.

Dancing. Courses in "aerobic dance" exist throughout the country—in athletic clubs, on videos, on television, etc.; you go through minutely planned routines, like the dancers in musicals, which are contrived to give you strenuous cardiovascular exercise. You can achieve most of the same results by continuous active dancing at home, by yourself or with friends. A large mirror helps you to see possibilities for movements that will loosen up or use neglected muscles. The movements in exercise books, or practiced on television, can be turned into dance movements with a little ingenuity.

No matter what kind of exercise you like (and there's no reason, of course, to confine yourself just to one kind), the key is regularity. An exhausting burst of activity every two weeks is probably worse than nothing. What you need is a steady level of activity that you pleasurably keep up without feeling it's an obligation. Look for ways to incorporate exercise into your regular daily life: Walk to the post office to mail that urgent letter, take the stairs instead of the elevator, use a hand lawnmower instead of a noisy, gas-powered one, experiment with more physically fluid and active lovemaking (start out by dancing, and resist the temptation to jump right into bed!).

In any kind of exercise, it is important to learn to open up your chest and throat, which are often tight and constricted from stress and anxiety. This permits air to enter and leave freely, and thus improves your oxygen intake and your body's general physiological efficiency. Various stretching exercises (like lying on a bed with your head and arms hanging down over the edge) will help. So will the simple effort to breathe more deeply and deliberately.

If you get more ambitious about physical activity, there has been a resurgence of interest in participant sports, as opposed to spectator sports, in this country. Groups and facilities abound for volleyball, racquetball, squash, track and field events, softball, touch football, etc. Many such sports involve little expense and provide opportunity for socializing and making friends, as well as getting necessary exercise.

Don't deceive yourself that a little exercise will negate the bad effects of eating a high-fat diet or heavy cigarette smoking. Regular vigorous exercise cuts your heart-attack risk by some 35 percent, whereas stopping smoking cuts it by 30 percent. Why not do both?

If you are interested in burning off large numbers of calories, the best activities are jogging, jumping rope, cross-country skiing, and squash or racquetball.

A good deal of active exercise is necessary for children also, and you can no longer assume that urban children get it naturally, because so many of them spend so many hours sitting at school desks, watching television, or being driven about in cars. (Many children also have bad dietary habits, which give them high cholesterol levels and tend to make them overweight.) Make sure your children get at least a half hour of really vigorous activity three or four times a week. Sports with relatively intermittent energy output spurts, like baseball, don't count. Basketball played *seriously* is good and so is soccer; tennis is only good for really skilled players. If an activity doesn't involve a lot of running, it probably doesn't give the heart and lungs a truly aerobic workout, which is what you and your children need.

D. Take care of your eyes.

Comprehensive prepaid medical plans of health maintenance organizations include eye care—the checking of your vision every couple of years to make sure you are seeing all right, checking for glaucoma or other problems, examination for glasses if you need them, and provision of low-cost glasses. Medical schools and some universities have optometry departments where you can get eye care free or at low cost; they can usually direct you to a source of inexpensive glasses.

Elementary schools usually have vision-testing programs, but parents are the best persons to spot any vision defects a child may have. If you notice squinting or head craning when a child looks at T.V., reads, or tries to see something across the room, it is a sign that something may be amiss. Headaches can also be caused by vision difficulties.

The most common types of vision problems are easy to correct with glasses. Nearsightedness, or myopia, is when you can see things clearly only close-up. Astigmatism makes things a little blurry at any distance. Generally only older people are far-sighted.

You may be able to find glasses that fit in happily with your personal style. If not, contact lenses are the kind of luxury it may be worth a good deal of economizing to indulge in. Teenagers can now get contact lenses prescribed by some optometrists. In recent years there have been great improvements in contact lenses (soft lenses, lenses that "breathe" better), so even if you were once told you couldn't wear them, you might check into it again.

Eyes that have been exposed to heavy dust, chemicals, tear gas, Mace, or other irritating things should be washed with water. Lie down and run it gently over the eye for at least five to ten minutes. Then keep the eyes closed for a while until they feel OK again. Severe exposure to Mace or tear gas can require medical treatment.

Eyelashes and bits of flying dirt will sometimes wash out, or you may be able to see them in the mirror yourself—use a clean handkerchief, and dab it against the object, which will usually stick to it and come away from the eyeball. Any really painful object in the eye may scratch the surface and needs a checkup by an eye doctor. In such cases, be especially careful not to rub your eye, since that could damage it severely.

E. Learn to give and get massages.

Giving a decent massage ought to be as elementary a social grace as the ability to make good coffee or tea. Most people in "advanced" industrial civilizations go around in chronic states of tension and stiffness; we need all the help we can give each other in loosening up. A one-day workshop will teach you the essentials: a series of simple massage strokes, easier to learn than dance steps, which give pleasure and relaxation. You will learn how to soften the knots that form around the base of the skull, often connected with tension headaches; how to limber up the tight places in shoulders, neck, and back; and effective strokes for arms, trunk, legs, and (most subtle of all) feet. Having mastered the basics, you may then want to go on into more arcane disciples: shiatsu, polarity, deep-pressure massage. . . .

A massage workshop teaches you a good deal about the body's internal structure, which you can explore and refine with your own hands. It will thus give you new understanding of, respect for, and confidence in your own body as well.

Some people arrange massage groups: They share a light supper, quiet talking, the opportunity to work on unfamiliar bodies. (It's also pleasant to have two people massage one, which produces very complicated sensations.) Especially if a hot tub or swimming pool is available, these simple sensual delights can be very invigorating and yet soothing. Massage can, of course, be sexual, or the sight of happy, naked bodies may simply fill you with mellow feelings and happiness.

F. Beware of drug misuse.

Millions of Americans with heart trouble, diabetes, and other diseases depend on drugs for their very lives, and millions more need drugs to combat serious illnesses. But Congressional investigations have made it clear that Americans are being robbed by the drug companies. They overcharge fantastically on brand-name drugs that do no more than the same drug in a plain package with no fancy name. (Whenever your doctor gives you a prescription, ask whether it is for the cheapest reliable type of the drug—the drug companies spend about $6,000 each year on each doctor to brainwash them into prescribing their drugs rather than cheaper brands.)

What can you do? Here are some ways you can save money without jeopardizing your precious health.

1. Ask your doctor to prescribe "generic."

The same drug substance with Lilly's name on it may cost three times what it does with another manufacturer's name on it. Your pharmacist is a trained professional; ask for the cheapest satisfactory brand of the drug you need. If your doctor gives you problems about prescribing generically, you may be wise to find another doctor, especially if your health situation requires a lot of medication; it could cut your drug costs in half.

2. Ask your doctor what effects to expect from the drug.

Many doctors believe "patients want pills," and will prescribe something or other thinking it will make you feel better. (The more honest ones prescribe a "placebo," which is a pill with no active drug in it at all.) If you are asked to pay a stiff bill for some pills that might or might not make your sniffles go away, you'd probably like to know that's all you can expect—and save the money.

3. Compare prices.

Phone a couple of different pharmacies and read the prescription to them; ask them to tell you how much it will cost. If you are too shy to say you are checking prices, pretend you're not sure you have enough money. Pharmacies connected with prepaid health-plan clinics or unions usually have the lowest costs. There are also low-cost mail-order pharmacies, usually serving groups like the American Association of Retired Persons. Three available sources are Pharmail (800-237-9927), Medimail (800-331-1458), and Action-Mail Order (800-452-1976).

4. Don't buy non-prescription drugs.

People waste a great deal of money on tonics, laxatives, iron pills, tranquillizers, sleeping pills, wake-up pills, pep pills, and so on—which are either useless or distract you from taking action to improve your diet, your exercise patterns, or your life-style so that you don't need the drugs. If you eat right and get enough exercise and sleep, you should need no drugs except if you actually get sick. Stay out of drug stores except when a doctor sends you there, and spend the money you save on eating better.

a. Laxatives. If you eat a good diet with plenty of fiber in it (grains, vegetables, fruits) and get enough exercise and sleep, your bowels should move normally, and you will seldom or never need a laxative. Some people have a movement every day; some people several times a day; and some only once every other day or so. Any of these natural patterns is OK. But many different types of laxatives advertise to the contrary, hoping to get your dollars.

True constipation is rare except in very old or sick people. (If you have constant constipation, stop and ask yourself whether bad diet or living habits may be causing it.) But many people get "addicted" to laxatives, and get their bowels used to having them, and then they don't work normally anymore.

You can taper off from laxatives, using less and less, by adding lots of fluids (like water, hot tea, or moderate quantities of unsweetened coffee—avoid carbonated or sweet drinks), and by eating laxative foods such as dried prunes, raw fruits and vegetables, and whole-wheat bread. Walking or other exercise helps too.

Mild laxatives are the only ones you should use unless a doctor tells you otherwise; these include: milk of magnesia with several glasses of water, or a three-grain cascara tablet. Camomile and other natural herb teas are more organic.

Never use laxatives when you have abdominal pain, nausea, vomiting, or other appendicitis symptoms.

b. Sleeping pills. These are both more dangerous and less effective than either patients or doctors realize, but they are the most commonly prescribed medical drugs in the world. Careful research shows that, particularly when used for more than two weeks, the pills don't control insomnia. Moreover, barbiturates are strongly addictive, and are lethal in overdose, especially when combined with alcohol; alternatives such as flurazepam (Dalmane) and related drugs such as Valium and Librium are also addictive. By-products of Dalmane remain in the body for a long time; so you can build up concentrations that dangerously diminish alertness and coordination.

But the most striking research finding about insomnia is that in fact the sleep of most people who complain of insomnia (and seek sleeping-pill prescriptions) is barely different from those who think they sleep normally. Sleeping pills are dispensed in hospitals as a matter of routine, and this seems to carry over into doctors' office practice, reinforced by constant sales pitches from the drug companies. Try to live a less stressful life, and you will sleep better. Be willing to lose some sleep once in a while; it's not a life-threatening problem, and if your mind keeps racing it is probably telling you to slow down.

c. Vitamins. A good diet provides the vitamins you need. However, evidence has been building up that taking additional vitamins C and E may be beneficial, along with a substance called beta carotene. C has various positive effects (though it probably won't have much effect in preventing or shortening colds—nothing will) and the other two are "antioxidants" that may be helpful against cancer processes.

5. Check on the side effects.

Laws require pharmacies to remove from certain drug packages the full-information folders placed there by the drug companies. Until these laws can be changed, as they have been in other advanced countries, make a point of asking your doctor which side effects your prescribed drug will have, or if it will react badly with another drug you are taking. Common side effects can be unpleasant or dangerous: drowsiness, dizziness, jumpiness, addiction, and so on. But some drugs, in some people, have far more drastic effects, both mental and physical. Report to your doctor anything unpleasant or suspicious that happens after you start taking a drug; don't assume it's another symptom of your disease.

6. Treat virus infections sensibly.

There's a doctor's joke about the patient who comes in with a bad cold. The doctor tells him that if he gets sleep and rest, it will go away, but nothing else can be done for it.

"But what if it turns into pneumonia?" wails the patient.

"Ah," says the doctor, "*that* I can fix!"—because pneumonia is a bacterial disease. If it affects your lungs, the doctor can give you an antibiotic that will kill the bacteria; unless you are old or in an otherwise weakened condition, that will probably cure it without any trouble. A cold, on the other hand, is a virus disease, like polio and even measles. Once you get them, no pills or shots will help.

Many people go to doctors for colds or flus that are viral diseases, for which your own common-sense care is the only remedy, and are surprised when the doctor can't do anything about it; they whine for antibiotics, which may be not only useless but dangerous, causing anemia and other dangerous reactions, killing the useful bacteria that live in your intestines, and leading to the development of resistant strains of bacteria. Viruses—and there are many different kinds that cause colds, flu, and similar annoying illnesses—are not sensitive to any antibiotics. They must be fought off by your body's natural defense mechanisms. Viruses, in fact, are very strange things. They are not even quite "alive" in the same way that bacteria are, although they can and do reproduce by the millions within your body cells. The way to help our bodies fight them is to make sure we get plenty of rest and sleep, don't get over-tired, and eat well.

7. Don't overuse aspirin.

Scientists don't yet understand how aspirin works, but it is the most widely used remedy for headaches, colds, and miscellaneous aches and pains. In addition, a quarter of an aspirin per day keeps your blood "slippery" and aids against stroke and heart attack. Buy the cheapest aspirin you can find, for there is absolutely no difference in brands—they are all the same substance, acetylsalicylic acid. To get the lowest price, buy the "house brand" in drugstores, supermarkets, or health-plan pharmacies. Don't let name brands like Bayer's or Squibb's impress you. Aspirin is just aspirin, no matter what name it carries.

Many highly advertised and high-priced aspirin-based pills are around—Bufferin, Anacin, APC, and so on. They are all a waste of money. Some of them contain caffeine; some of them contain supposedly stomach-soothing drugs; but if you get sleepy from aspirin, have a cup of coffee; if they upset your stomach, try a glass of milk. (Milk is a good idea with aspirin anyway, because aspirin—especially when consumed with alcohol or citrus-fruit juices—tends to make the stomach lining bleed slightly.)

Aspirins in large quantities are dangerous; they can be fatal to small children. Baby aspirins, which are flavored to make them appeal to young kids, usually come in tight safety-cap bottles that are hard for small fingers to open. But keep them locked up in a high cabinet anyway (along with all the other dangerous drugs and substances you have around). Don't call them "candy" to get your kids to take them; they'll take them gladly, because they taste good. (A child who has swallowed a lot of aspirin needs prompt hospital attention.)

Don't over-rely on aspirins. If you find you're having persistent headaches or other aches, see a doctor. Some headaches come from temporary stresses, overtiredness, the coming on of a cold, or other temporary causes, but can also come from eyestrain and serious threats to your health.

If you have had reactions to aspirin, there are alternatives called ibuprofen and acetaminophen (such as Tylenol); they're expensive, but easier on your stomach.

G. Don't just do something; sit there!

Americans are busy a lot, always rushing around doing things. We still suspect that if we aren't engaged in productive activity, we must be doing something wrong. This busyness not only enables us to ignore our own and other people's feelings (because stopping to pay attention to them would interfere with "getting the job done"), but also enables us to get through life without ever noticing the fundamental realities of birth, growth, decay, death. We do not pay attention to ourselves in any serious way, and we do violence to the natural order and our fellow animals because they stand in the way of our "work."

Sitting down and doing nothing is, therefore, an intensely purposeful and difficult thing. For many Americans it is literally impossible; they get twitchy if they try it, and soon jump up to do something or turn on television. This is why religions prescribe various rites for meditation that help you to focus on your own being and cut out extraneous distractions: yoga exercises, the lotus position, breathing exercises. There are various forms of meditation that you can read about or learn about from members of Zen groups and other organizations. If organized groups do not interest you, you can still use meditation or contemplation as a private, personal defense against pressures that throw you off center. Many of our difficulties in confronting modern life arise because our sense of self is dissolved in the roles we must play: employee, student, soldier, consumer.

Sit down very quietly, and become conscious of your biological existence; hear your heart beat, your breath go in and out. Pay attention to your immediate surroundings: the surface you are sitting on, the wall in front of you, the pressure of your clothes upon your skin, but try to empty your head of thoughts. If you can carry this far enough, a great feeling of pure being comes over you—it's not really describable in words, but you feel at one with your body and the universe. By contrast with such a state, even if you experience it only briefly, the ordinary worries and tensions of daily life seem trivial and petty; when you return to the world of doing, you are likely to find your energies more concentrated and free-flowing.

H. Pay attention to your posture and alignment.

The eyes may be the "windows of the soul," but we have learned from the work of bioenergetics therapists that posture *is* character. Actors have always known this: Attitudes and feelings are literally "bodied forth." But so are deep-laid childhood patterns, including neurotic behaviors, which constitute our fundamental orientations toward the world.

However, we *can* change our posture. Posture is a matter of daily habit; by retraining, ideally with the help of a bioenergetics mentor, we can reshape our bodies, unlocking our "body armor" so that our energy flows more freely, allowing better connections through the common blockages at neck and shoulders or pelvis. Many practical and pleasant postural improvements can be done in your daily routine. Avoid locking your knees into a rigid, vertical stick when you are standing in line, for example; this keeps the whole body more flexible and energized. Keeping shoulders and neck muscles loose (friends can help here with massages) helps your breathing to become unrestricted and deeper. Avoiding the T.V. slump (remember, your body is built both to sit up and to lie down, but not to do both at once) avoids deleterious pressures on internal organs, and minimizes the passivity of body and mind that T.V. induces.

Yoga, dance, and various other disciplines are also helpful in paying decent attention to your body's needs and capacities. Exercise alone is necessary, but not sufficient; to achieve the grace and comfort your body is capable of, you need to understand its muscular workings in some detail. Your body's welfare is just as important as your mind's, and indeed the two are intimately connected. It is a sad thing in our society that so many people do not make any serious effort to know their bodies, and hence cannot appreciate their extraordinary capacities for pleasure, agility, strength, endurance, and beauty.

I. Lose some weight.

Three-quarters of all Americans are overweight, at least a third of us seriously so. Obesity is not the only cause of our high rate of heart disease (cigarettes are another major cause), but it certainly does no one any good.

Being fat is ordinarily a long-range problem; it comes from a group of eating and living habits, and it can only be overcome by a great and serious effort—just like smoking. The first thing you must be clear on, therefore, is whether you care enough about it to make a real campaign to be thinner. Formerly heaviness was looked down upon less than now—it was a rare person who could get enough food to grow fat. We still sometimes hear it said that a fat child is a healthy child, but this just isn't true—in fact, fat cells developed during childhood can never be gotten rid of. Children and teenagers can be obese just like adults. In general, of course, fat people suffer a great deal, especially from being unattractive sexually. But if you really don't care how you look, relax and enjoy it; be fat with style like Falstaff, although of course your health will suffer.

The great fact about reducing diets is that most people can't stick to them, however mild they may be. This is why fortunes have been made with "magic" reducing aids (few people can stick to them, either). But there is really only one way to reduce: Eat less (especially fatty foods) and be more physically active. Trick diets, shimmying machines, and other panaceas have no lasting effect whatsoever. (Amphetamines—reducing or appetite-depressing pills— are "speed" and fairly addictive, and it's probably better to be fat than a speed freak.)

The only reliable and healthy way to get thinner is to be more active, regularly, every day. Neither a body-building course nor taking up a sport is necessary, unless you happen to go for that sort of thing. It just means *using* your body for something other than a bag to store your guts in. You can burn up stored fat by making love (or masturbating, for that matter), by driving nails, by running, by doing sitting-up exercises, by scrubbing floors, by chasing children, by riding a bicycle, by walking around your office, by shopping. In the end, it usually comes down to walking. Walking briskly one-half hour every day is better for your health and your weight than occasional frantic exercise (which may actually do you harm if you're not in shape for it). So try to find some way of getting this into your daily routine. Can you walk to the store instead of driving? Can you pick up your children on foot instead of by car? Can you walk up and down stairs instead of taking the elevator? A daily half-hour of active walking (not just strolling) means, for most people, that you have turned the tables and will begin getting slowly thinner instead of slowly fatter. Don't be in a hurry; just keep at it.

Of course, it's lovely if you happen to be interested in dancing, hiking, swimming, table tennis, tennis, or some other activity that involves bodily action. Home carpentry, scavenging, and many other activities use up a lot of energy. So do manual jobs and many semimanual jobs, of course: I was never as fit as when I was a book runner in a library.

You may worry that exercising more will also cause your appetite to grow to the point where it cancels your hoped-for weight loss. Luckily, this doesn't happen. As a moment's calculation will show, if it did, anybody who was physically active would grow indefinitely fat. In reality, your eating can never catch up with your exercising if you are active. It only catches up when you are sedentary, spending most of your waking hours at a desk or in front of a television. It has recently been shown that sedentary men average about 20 percent heavier than active men, though the active men eat 600 calories a day more. Sedentary women are 30 percent heavier, although active women eat 570 more. The moral is plain: If you are really more active, you will be able to eat more and weigh less!

Incidentally, people sometimes forget that alcohol is a drug that has a lot of calories in it, as do the dips, chips, and nuts that often come with it. Cutting out booze may in itself cut down your calorie intake enough to send your weight down.

J. Quit smoking.

It is now solidly established that cigarette smoking is self-destructive behavior, leading not only to lung cancer but also to heart disease and other maladies. It increases skin wrinkling and reduces blood circulation in the skin, probably leading not only to smoker's pallor but to reduced sensitivity, including that of sexual organs. It costs society, not to mention the individuals involved, huge sums in medical bills, lost work, etc. Each year, almost 100,000 people die from lung cancer, 80 percent of which is due to smoking; only 10 percent of lung-cancer patients are saved. And, new evidence indicates, it harms nonsmokers exposed to "sidestream" smoke from other people's lighted cigarettes, and may pose genetic dangers to smokers' offspring. (Cigar and pipe smoking, like the use of chewing tobacco, cause cancer of the lips and mouth, rather than lung cancer.)

Nicotine is such an addictive drug that its use will probably never be completely eliminated. But the extent of its use, and the fact that it is capturing large numbers of adolescent users, must be laid to two major factors: the heavily financed advertising campaigns of the tobacco companies and, paradoxically, the very fact that smoking *is* dangerous. Smokers, a good deal of evidence suggests, tend to be rebellious sorts who do not enjoy being told what to do, even when it means their own survival. (Some of them also simply manage to disbelieve the overwhelming evidence.) Many people seem to smoke to assert their independence, their belief in their own physiological immunity, and their determination to continue their own gratification no matter what anybody says about it. Smoking for such people plays somewhat the same role as dangerous sports like skiing or hang-gliding. There is also a strong economic factor: Lower-class people, whose lives are severely deprived, may literally feel they have less to live for than middle-class people, and are thus less motivated to try to extend their lives if it means giving up immediate pleasure.

Most smokers come from families where the parents smoked. An additional motive for trying to stop, therefore, is to protect your children from believing the habit is natural and desirable.

There is some evidence that a vegetarian diet and the avoidance of alcohol give the body a more alkaline balance, which somehow helps to counter the desire for nicotine. Especially alkaline foods are molasses, lima beans, raisins, dried figs, beet greens, spinach, yeast, almonds, carrots, soybeans, sweet potatoes, and tomatoes.

K. Take care of your teeth.

Because so many parent bug their children about toothbrushing, a lot of people neglect their teeth when they finally get away from home. Young people today usually get a great deal of soft, practically pre-chewed food (pizza, milk shakes, cake), and their diets when they start living on their own often lack essential nutrients. They also stop brushing their teeth and going to the dentist, feeling that such concerns are depressing to their newly liberated states. They go along fine for a few years and then lose a couple of teeth, which shocks them back into toothbrushing and flossing, and also flattens them with a huge dental bill.

Like eyes, ears, noses, breasts, penises, and other parts of the human body, teeth vary a lot. A few people have stupendously strong, beautiful teeth that last until they are ninety with nothing more than daily brushing. Others have teeth that rot away even under the finest dental care. Unfortunately, you never realize how wonderful it is to have good teeth until your teeth or gums begin to go bad. Any kind of toothache or prolonged sensitivity to cold or hot is a sign of potential serious trouble—have a dentist check it out.

There are ways of getting dental work done for very little money—sometimes none at all. There may be a dental school with a clinic attached to it nearby; check with the Dental Society office in your city.

Dental techniques are now virtually painless. But many patients still dread going to the dentist, and they transmit attitudes of fear and resistance to their children. It may help you feel better to have a friend go with you who doesn't mind dentistry. And certainly, when your child first begins to go (a first preliminary checkup is needed around the age of two or three, to make sure the teeth are coming in correctly), make sure the person who takes him or her regards it as a tolerable experience. Kids have no innate distrust of dentistry, and rather enjoy all the machinery the dentist has to play with. A dentist who is kindly and sensible will always explain to the child just what is going to happen and why it's necessary. With novocaine, the worst discomfort you feel in the dentist's chair these days is in the initial prick of the novocaine injection. And some dentists use "laughing gas" (nitrous oxide) for its pain-deadening properties; it gives you a delicious and altogether legal high.

Your dentist probably has gruesome charts and pictures that can explain what tooth decay is and why it is important to fill cavities when they occur. Gum troubles, which are much better understood now than in earlier times, are especially important to watch for when you get into your thirties and forties (they can cause you to lose teeth, literally).

False teeth are expensive, hard to chew with, and a general mess; you should try to keep your own teeth as long as you can, even though it takes time and trouble. It is important to have tooth abscesses, especially, attended to. A rotten tooth just sitting there is a little infection factory that sends bacteria all through your system, and can cause a breakdown in your general health. If you have a serious toothache, don't try to kill the pain with medicines; see a dentist, for the pain is a biological signal warning you something is wrong.

The main things you should do to take care of your teeth are:

1. *Get in the habit of using dental floss (or waxed dental tape) before you brush.* Flossing gets out food particles stuck between your teeth. Then brush regularly, after each meal if you can, but anyway in the morning after breakfast and at night after supper. Toothpaste is no particular necessity; it's the toothbrush that does the job. Find a brush that's stiff enough to work, but not so stiff it scratches your gums. People spend a great deal of money on fancy-tasting toothpastes and powders whose sole advantage is that they may encourage you to do more brushing (a tiny dab is enough for this purpose). Stay away from toothpastes that claim to "whiten" your teeth—they are dangerously abrasive, especially for people over thirty-five.

Incidentally, it's surprising how many perfectly intelligent people don't really know how to brush their teeth. The most important part of it is the scouring, twisting wrist motion whereby you bring the bristles from the gum area sliding over the teeth—thus massaging the gums and digging out particles from between the teeth. Even if it makes you feel like an idiot, ask your dentist for a refresher course in toothbrushing.

2. See a dentist twice a year, and get your cavities fixed.

3. Eat a good diet, with plenty of nutritious foods and also chewy foods. Your teeth partly depend on your general state of health. And the reverse is also true: Neglected teeth can cause medical trouble.

4. For your small children, **ask your dentist to give you a prescription for** **fluoride pills** if the water in your city is not fluoridated. Taken while the teeth are developing (which they do until they actually come through the gums), fluoride markedly cuts down on the tendency to cavities. The pills costs very little, and you will be repaid many times in lower dental bills, even during childhood. Women should take fluoride pills during pregnancy in unfluoridated areas, since some tooth enamel is laid down before birth.

L. Beware of sun light.

Because of our use of CFCs for refrigeration and various industrial processes, the protective ozone layer at the top of the atmosphere is steadily thinning, so that more dangerous ultraviolet rays are reaching the Earth's surface. Nobody knows how far this process may go, but already levels in populated areas far from the poles (where "ozone holes" were first observed) have become worrisome. There is no need to panic, at least not yet, but it is wise to minimize your exposure to sunlight. Wear a broad-brimmed hat whenever you will be in the sun for more than 15 minutes (there are lots of stylish hats around, and most people look great in them). Use the heaviest-duty sunblock you can find. Clothing doesn't entirely protect you; still, cover up with light, loose shirts and pants. Wear sunglasses treated to keep out ultraviolet. (Driving, incidentally, is not hazardous, because your car's windows themselves filter out ultraviolet; so if you use sunglasses only for driving, UV coating is unnecessary.)

Ironically, we have come to feel that a tan is a sign of glowing good health. But today it is mainly a sign of overexposure to the danger of skin cancer. Scientists also suspect that high UV exposure may damage immune systems; it is known to lower the productivity of rice and soya-bean plants.

M. Avoid sexually transmitted diseases.

Disease primarily transmitted by sexual contacts have been with us throughout human history, but in recent decades the appearance of AIDS has made the situation far more frightening. AIDS has been greatly affecting sexual practices, among both heterosexuals and homosexuals. But you need to know about, and protect yourself against, many other diseases as well.

AIDS can be transmitted by ordinary heterosexual sex, and millions of young heterosexual Americans are now infected, though the greatest concentration of cases has been among gay males and intravenous drug users, who get the virus by sharing hypodermic needles. Protecting yourself against AIDS means never engaging in sex without a condom, unless you have taken the time to get to know your partner and his or her sexual history very well; your life may depend on it. (An AIDS test result only guarantees freedom from the HIV virus up to six months *before* the date of the test.) Condoms can be fun; they come in many shapes and colors and tastes, and if you and your partner take a playful attitude about them it can be very sexy. For more information you can call the AIDS-HIV Nightline at 1-800-273-2437.

Monogamous sexual relationships are on the rise, largely because of AIDS; think through your feelings about monogamy, and see whether it may be the best course for you and your partner. Some people are also experimenting with "group monogamy," where a number of people who know they are disease-free sleep with each other but absolutely nobody outside the group; this takes a great deal of mutual trust.

Gonorrhea in males causes a discharge from the sex organs, itching, burning during urination, etc. It is unpleasant and worrisome; because it is hard to spot in females, it may linger and damage reproductive organs. Too many people let it go, hoping it may not be real or that it will just go away. It won't. Drop in at a clinic and get the necessary pills, which will cure it in a few days, and notify any persons with whom you have had sexual contact in the past three weeks.

Syphilis causes sores, either on the sex organs or at other places on the body. Syphilis can be cured readily with proper treatment, but it can be a very serious disease if not treated—leading in its last stages years later to a nasty kind of insanity and death. Again, alert anyone with whom you have been sexually involved recently.

Herpes was formerly rare, but has now reached epidemic status in some metropolitan areas. It is related to the virus that causes cold sores, and its small, fluid-filled blisters resemble cold sores. They develop into shallow, moist sores, generally around the neck of the penis, on the lips of the vagina, or on the skin between the genitals and anus. They can also occur unnoticed on the cervix. Sometimes there is swelling in the genital or groin area, painful irritation, or vaginal discharge. Some persons experience hypersensitivity, itching, or burning on the skin of their buttocks, thighs, legs and heels before blisters appear.

The first outbreak of herpes is generally the worst, since it may last from three to six weeks; recurrences usually last less than ten days. The herpes virus remains in the body after the blisters have healed, and can break out again because of various factors, including stress and fatigue.

Herpes is highly contagious and can be transmitted by oral, anal, or genital contact. The discomfort from herpes can be minimized by cool baths, local anesthetic ointments, and pain medication. Keeping the infected area clean and dry is necessary to prevent secondary infection.

Herpes is especially unpleasant and dangerous for women. It increases their risk for cervical cancer, and can cause miscarriage or premature delivery; if a woman has sores at the time of giving birth, a Caesarean delivery is necessary.

To avoid getting herpes, avoid sexual contact with anyone who has blisters or sores, or who has had them recently. It can, of course, be embarrassing to discuss such things at tender moments, but the risks of infection are far worse than even a great deal of embarrassment. The use of a condom provides protection only if the sores are located on the penis and completely covered by the condom, or if they are inside the vagina; and even then, great care is required; the virus can live in hands and mouth long enough to be passed from one person to another. It is dangerous and irresponsible to engage in sexual activity with someone when you are having an outbreak of herpes.

If you do contract herpes, get to know what triggers recurrences for you and try to avoid them. Also, avoid tight pants and nylon underwear, which keep the genital area overly warm and moist.

Human Papilloma Virus (HPV) affects only women, but can be carried by either sex. If untreated in women, it can cause uterine or cervical cancer.

The symptoms of most sexually transmitted diseases are harder for a woman to spot than a man. This means that early detection is primarily men's responsibility. If you find you have a disease, be sure to tell all the people you have recently had contact with, since one or more of them probably gave it to you, or you may have given it to them, and you ought to visit a clinic for tests and treatment; otherwise they will give it to you (and anybody else they sleep with) again. Detection, by the way, may require several tests.

Although not a disease but rather a small parasite, "crabs" can be treated at a VD clinic. The symptom is intense and persistent itching in the hair of the pubic area; if you are sharp-eyed, you can spot the little beasties themselves. A related skin parasite, scabies, is caused by a mite so small that it is invisible. They live only *outside* the pubic area, and cause persistent itching on stomach, legs, hands. Like crabs, they are readily dealt with by means of an ointment.

N. Keep your home clear of pests.

Some parasites live on our bodies (like lice); but there are other creatures that just like to live near us, eating our food and sharing our shelter and heat. It has been estimated that there are as many rats in cities as there are people (though nobody has ever taken a complete rat census).

Because rats, roaches, flies, and other pests live on your food, the only lasting way to get rid of them is to stop feeding them. You can trap them (cheese won't work, by the way), poison them, swat them, and so on—but as long as their food supply remains, each dead one will soon be replaced by a thriving younger one, and you will have to spend more money on traps and poisons.

1. Be careful with pesticides.

If you have household pesticides, keep them stored in a high, safe place away from children, especially if they are in spray cans, which kids love to play with. Follow the label directions carefully, and remember that farm workers have died from exposure to these substances. Never let the spray get on dishes, utensils, or pets. If it does, wash it off immediately with plenty of hot, soapy water and rinse well. If it gets on food, throw the food away. If it gets on your skin or clothing, wash it thoroughly as soon as possible. Never breathe insecticide spray or let it touch your eyes; keep the doors and windows open if you have to use it. Keep it away from aquariums (it kills fish) and pet food or water. If you use poison baits against rats, make sure children and pets can't get at them; many children die from rat poison each year.

2. Get rid of rats and mice.

Rats live in woodpiles and bushes around fancy suburban homes just as happily as in slum basements and sewers. Some rats and mice live wild, eating natural foods, but they will sometimes come into houses, through holes or open doors. Rats seem to enter sewer systems through roof vents; sometimes they try to come up through toilets and drown.

Close off all the holes by which they can get in. Holes in plaster walls are best filled with spackle wall-mending mixture spread over some wire mesh, or steel wool dipped in spackle or plaster. Stuffing holes with paper or cardboard just gives the rats chewing exercise. Holes in baseboards or wooden walls that you can nail into are best closed by nailing on a piece of metal—a flattened tin can or a piece of roofing or whatever's handy. Make sure doors and screen doors shut properly. In summer, make sure open windows have screens—rats are just as capable of climbing up or down a fire escape as people are. (If the owner won't provide screens, nail on any old piece of wire mesh.) If there are big cracks under your door, nail a board along the bottom to make the crack too thin for a rat to pass under. Don't be discouraged about keeping rats out—anybody with a hammer can prevent rats from getting into a living space.

Second, store your food in containers that rats can't gnaw through. This is a good idea anyway, because food keeps better in airtight containers. Put your rice, flour, bread, cereals, and other loose-packed foods into painted snap-lid coffee cans, big pickle jars, a tin bread box, or at least a ratproof cabinet with a tight-closing door latch on it. Rats and mice are busy, active animals and need a lot of food. If they can't get it, they will go away to other places where they can. Also, you should try to get together with your neighbors and building owner to get rat-proof garbage cans, for many rats survive solely on garbage. A neighborhood clean-up campaign to get rid of junk piles and other trash will help too. Rat infestation is grounds for breaking a lease, if done soon after you move in.

3. Get rid of cockroaches.

Roaches are always looking for a good place to hide through the day. If you don't give them too many places, you'll have fewer roaches. Sometimes they live in cracks that you can close off or stop up; they may live under shelving paper in kitchens; sometimes they live under cabinets or other furniture that you could raise off the floor on bricks, to let the light in.

They also like damp places—bathrooms or under leaky sinks. Shaking boric acid (buy it in a drugstore) into their hiding places is the cheapest and safest way to kill roaches, but it costs money, and here again, the real answer is to stop feeding them. They quickly become resistant to pesticides. Boric acid takes a day or two to work; then you wipe it up. Although it is not a carcinogenic chemical poison, boric acid is dangerous, even fatal, in large doses; so keep it out of the reach of children.

Unfortunately, it takes very little to keep a cockroach alive. It will eat small crumbs of food that you can scarcely see—so if you have children, you may have to get used to sharing your house with a few roaches. They will be, in effect, cleaning up the tiny shreds of cereal, toast, baby food, and whatnot that the children spread around a house. You may feel better about it if you take the time to look at cockroaches carefully; they're really quite marvelous creatures, superbly adapted to their way of life. Their smell is actually the worst thing about them.

You can keep cockroaches off tables by setting each leg in a tin can that's been carefully washed to get rid of the label and all the label glue (cockroaches can't climb a slippery metal surface). People sometimes hire exterminators to come around and poison the roaches in their apartments or houses, but as long as the food supply remains, the roaches will come back to live off it. The best single way to keep down cockroaches: Wash the dishes and take the garbage out after supper (cockroaches feed at night).

4. Keep ants under control.

Generally ants come into your house for the same reason as roaches—to eat the food you have provided for them, in the garbage, the sink, the food-preparing area, or in cans or jars left open. The way to control them is to stop feeding them. There may be a few around from time to time, foraging and looking for food you've missed, but you can probably stand that. It's better than going the expensive poison-spray route, which can poison you and your children. Never spray a vegetable garden to control ants, for some vegetable roots will take up the poison and you'll eat it. In some cases, ant stakes driven into the ground around a house will control the ant population fairly effectively. If you have a real ant problem—they're eating up your trees or biting your children—call your local public health department and get some advice. Otherwise it's easiest to regard ants as nature's way of cleaning up your garbage and returning it to circulation in the biosphere.

5. Get rid of fleas.

Fleas live by sucking blood, and if they can't get enough from your pets, they will bite you. There seem to be two ways to get rid of fleas: by killing them on the pet (with a bath and dip, a flea collar, or flea powder) and/or by spraying them in the furniture and on the floors with an insecticide. Unfortunately, flea collars are dangerously poisonous, both to pet and children who might touch them. Some flea powders work; others don't; evidently some breeds of fleas have become resistant to them. Call your local Humane Society or veterinarian and ask what they use (many flea powders are dangerous to cats and puppies). It is unwise to begin spraying poisons all over your house just to get rid of fleas. In cases of bad infestation, it's better to take the infested rugs or furniture outside, beat or vacuum them thoroughly, and leave them outside for a week, away from passing animals or humans the fleas could feed on. This should interrupt their life cycle without spraying. If you are forced into spraying, move to friend's place for a few days, until the pesticide has become less dangerous.

6. Get rid of flies.

Wherever there is a lot of manure, garbage, other decaying matter, or food lying around, there will be flies. If the manure is from your own animals, try to collect it and put it in on your compost pile, where the temperature (and the black plastic cover you should use) will keep flies away. Wet manure breeds many more flies than dry; arranging your animal pens so manure falls on straw helps dry it out fast. As with rats, securely closed garbage cans are a big help against flies. Screens and screen doors are your basic defense; usually they are required by the local housing code, so the owner of your building should provide them. You can trap flies on flypaper or similar chemical devices, but remember to keep these well away from food-preparing or eating areas—otherwise you may poison yourself more than the flies.

7. Get rid of bedbugs.

They are very hard to get rid of, and spraying seems to be the only sure way. They are often resistant to some insecticides; so you have to use sprays containing deadly malathion—or pyrethrum, not so dangerous, but it needs to be applied several times. You must get the slats, springs, and bed frame thoroughly wet; so working outside is best. Spray the mattress separately—get it wet but don't soak it; be sure to get spray thoroughly into crevices and tufts. Spray the baseboard all around the bed, cracks in the wall or floor, and any place nearby where the bugs might hide. Let the sprayed mattress dry thoroughly before sleeping on it; double sheets might not be a bad idea either, for a week or two.

O. Cut down on noise pollution.

Our organisms evolved to be very sensitive to noises, since we needed to hear the approach of predators or other dangers in order to survive. If you manage to spend any time in a wilderness area that is not overflown by airplanes or helicopters, you will probably be astonished (and perhaps alarmed) at your ability to hear tiny cracklings of twigs or rustling noises, which your mind may transform into rattlesnakes or marauding bears.

This delicate sensing mechanism is overwhelmed by the intensity of sound to which we customarily subject it, especially in cities. Transmission of sound in the inner ear involves microscopic hair cells which in many people are damaged by loud noises. This is the mechanism by which truck drivers, rock musicians, and heavy-industry workers habitually exposed to loud noise become deaf. But this damage begins at sound intensities around 85 decibels—a level often achieved by a vacuum cleaner, power saw, lawnmower, or motorcycle. Noise pollution is thought to be a substantial contributor to deafness rates and to hearing losses in the high-frequency ranges.

But noise pollution probably has far worse effects on our general health and well-being. Evolution has also given us a superb "startle response" to loud noises: Hearing the saber-tooth tiger's growl, our ancestors leaped out of the way, insulin charging their muscles instantly, heart rate surging, breathing rate shooting up. When you are lying in bed asleep and a truck goes by at a sudden 100 decibels, your body (which is never entirely asleep) reacts as if the truck were a tiger. Once a night or so, this might not be so bad; but if you live on a busy street, it may happen hundreds of times a night. Your sleep is disturbed; your vital organs and systems are stressed; your irritability increases.

It behooves us, then, to cut down when we can on this onslaught. Make sure your own muffler is in good shape; driving with a noisy muffler is like wearing a big sign on your forehead saying "asshole." If you have neighbors with noisy mufflers, tell them politely that they're waking you up with them, and point out that a new one can be installed for surprisingly little at a muffler shop. If you are outraged by a noisy (or smoke-emitting) vehicle, turn in its license number and description to your local cops, though it's doubtful they will do anything about it.

Air conditioning and other mechanical systems in buildings often contribute low, unnerving humming noises that cause tension and distress. Many household appliances contribute annoying and erratic noises, though under the EPA's new noisyness-rating labels their levels should decline. And of course air traffic, with its deafening jet roar, is not only unpleasant but demonstrably dangerous: People living under airport-approach patterns enter mental hospitals far more often than similar people living elsewhere.

How can you defend yourself against noise? First, of course, attempt to avoid noisy environments in your daily activities—try not to live on heavy-traffic streets; try to work in buildings with natural ventilation (and with silent incandescent lights, or humless electric-ballast fluorescents). When possible, drive with windows closed, using air vents for fresh air and cooling. You may, in particularly noisy but otherwise desirable situations, want to try blocking out sound. Double windows, especially of heavy plate glass, will cut down sound from outside substantially. Double doors, if sealed around the edges and sills with weather stripping, can reduce noise from hallways or between rooms. Using sealant to provide a tight gasket around metal-frame windows can stop the surprising amount of noise that can enter through very small cracks. (Use waxed paper, to which it won't stick, if you want to keep the window openable.)

Some people also use white-noise generators—devices that produce a kind of neutral hiss, made up of all frequencies in the sound spectrum—in hopes of masking undesired noise. A small recirculating water fountain (using an aquarium pump that's submersible) produces white noise and also helps humidify your air. It is also possible to play records of surf noise, rainstorms, and so on—though generally these are best played at very low volumes, and therefore don't have much masking effect.

And you can, of course, resort to ear plugs. Waxy types fit themselves to your ear passages and are quite comfortable. Hearing protectors, which look like studio headphones, are also being rated by the EPA, and are advisable for anyone who works in an industrial environment that is uncomfortably noisy.

P. Apply for Medicare and Medicaid.

Practically everybody who is over 65 is eligible for medical benefits under Medicare; apply two or three months before reaching 65. The cost goes up if you delay, and you may miss out on some benefits. Though Medicare has been able to help older people without much money, it pays only a part of their health costs, because there are deductibles and limitations of benefits, and they have to pay for drugs used outside a hospital. Disabled people under 65 may also be entitled to Medicare.

You apply for a Medicare card at the Social Security office. Take along something that will prove how old you are. This card enables you either to have your doctor send part of his bill directly to Medicare, or to get back part of the money if you pay the whole bill yourself and apply for reimbursement to Medicare. In general, it is better to have the doctor bill Medicare directly, since you then don't have to put up the money and wait to be repaid. (You are supposed to get a complete record of the costs in either case, incidentally.) Also, you risk less in case the doctor is overcharging, and Medicare refuses to pay its share of the total bill.

Medicare does not pay all of any medical bill. You still have to pay quite a bit yourself. There is always a deductible you have to pay yourself on hospital bills, plus the monthly charge you have to pay (or have deducted from your Social Security) for coverage of doctor bills, plus the first $100 of coverage of doctor bills each year (not each illness), and so on. Because of skyrocketing costs, you are therefore likely to be only a little better off than you would have been before Medicare. However, by the same token, it's now almost essential for any elderly person to have Medicare, because otherwise medical costs are simply ruinous.

The Social Security office has a booklet on Medicare that explains how it works. Make sure you get one of these when you are approaching 65, so that you are familiar with the program.

Medicare coverage extends to most kinds of hospital care (including psychiatric, up to one hundred days' lifetime total), operations, doctors' office calls and house calls (if you can get them), nursing, drugs, laboratory tests, nursing home and physical-therapy treatment, some care at home after being in the hospital, chiropractic, osteopathy, dental surgery (if related to the jaw or facial bones), and some drugs. Ambulance service is covered only if it's a real emergency, and only if you go to the nearest hospital or clinic. Emergency-room treatment, splints and casts, lab tests, and so on are covered, but eye examinations and glasses, hearing examinations and hearing aids, false teeth, orthopedic shoes, and immunizations are not.

Members of health maintenance organizations (group health plans) generally do not have to bother with filling out claim forms; the plan applies for repayment directly to Medicare, and you only have to worry about those few services that are not covered by the plan.

Whereas Medicare is a federal program and operates everywhere on the same basis, Medicaid is administered through the states (except for Arizona). You apply for it at the welfare office, and will generally be eligible only if you are also eligible for welfare, but states' rules vary. People over 65 and the blind are also eligible, and some children. Medicaid will sometimes cover expenses that Medicare fails to cover, and it pays for many kinds of doctor and hospital services, sometimes even for dental and eye care.

Both programs are massive: 11 percent of the population is covered by Medicare, and almost as many by Medicaid programs. If you think you may be eligible, check into it.

Chapter 14.
Be Safe, Not Sorry.

A. Be prepared for disasters.

City people are used to having specialists handle a large number of tasks that rural people generally perform for themselves: everything from domestic plumbing repairs to dealing with the consequences of storms. When services are not provided in the way they think fit, they feel helpless to do anything about it—except maybe to vote out some politicians, as happened to the mayor of Chicago when the city failed to clean up the snow one winter.

We need not only to cultivate the all-round resilience of country people who are accustomed to pitching in and improvising, but also to give definite thought to possible disaster situations and how to prepare for them.

- Have a household meeting to discuss what should be done if there is a power blackout, earthquake, or crippling snowstorm.
- Keep a flashlight with good batteries in some place where everybody can locate it, along with candles and matches.
- Be sure you know where the cutoffs are for your household water, gas, and electric supplies.
- Make a policy of keeping enough of some kind of basic food on hand, such as rice or bulgar wheat, so that you could survive on it for a couple of days.
- Most of all, get to know your neighbors, since in emergencies collective action is almost always essential.

B. Prevent fires.

Of all household dangers, fire is the most terrifying. Anyone who has come back into the house to find it full of smoke (as I did once, when kittens had dragged a pillow over a floor heater) knows the fear it brings. Some 300,000 dwellings burn in this country every year.

If there is fire in your house, even a small one, get the people (children and old people first) out of the place before you do anything else. The fire may be bigger and worse than you think. Fire can spread with lightning speed, blocking off exits or moving into new rooms. It can spread over spilled cooking oil, paint, kerosene, and other flammable liquids.

Then see whether you can reasonably do anything to stop it—either by pouring water from pots or hose, or by using a fire extinguisher, or (for small stove-grease fires) by pouring sand or salt on the fire. When a fire has gotten bad, don't be heroic and rush back into it, unless there are people to be saved—get out and call the fire department on a neighbor's phone.

Most people don't think seriously about fire, any more than about auto accidents—they think it can't happen to them. But you might save your children's lives by taking a little thought beforehand, as I learned from an uncle who was a fireman and had an eagle eye for hazards.

1. Establish emergency exits.

Look around the house to see how to get out of it in a hurry. If a fire starts at one end, can you get out the other—through another door, or a window, by climbing out on the roof and jumping down? If a fire appears in the hallway, how can people in the rooms get out? On upper stories, the landlord or landlady is supposed to provide a fire escape, besides the main entrance. If this hasn't been done, you may need to get a heavy knotted rope to keep near some window, so that people can slide down it to safety. (Find something solid to tie it to, if necessary screwing a big eye-hook into a wall stud.)

2. Keep fire-fighting supplies on hand.

Look around to see what you have handy to put out small fires with. Is there a bucket or really big pot always near the kitchen sink? Are there garden hoses that could stretch inside the house if needed? For electrical fires, grease fires, or burning liquids, can you afford a small fire extinguisher that won't spread the fire? Are there blankets to use for smothering fires in clothing or people's hair?

3. Eliminate hazards.

Check through your place for unnecessary fire hazards: piles of old clothes or rags (especially greasy ones), woodpiles surrounded by dry grass, cluttered collections of stuff under the house or in the attic, anything burnable above or around a furnace, heater, water heater, or cookstove.

4. Install smoke detectors.

These devices save thousands of lives each year. Mount one or more on the ceiling where smoke is likely to rise. When the device starts beeping to tell you the battery needs replacing, make it a top priority.

5. Teach children fire safety.

Teach your children fire safety from a very early age. Children seem to be practically pyromaniacs around the age of four or five—they just love to light matches, and many fires, both in houses and in forests, are set "by accident" by children playing with fire, usually matches. Keep all matches up high, out of sight. Show your kids how fire spreads, perhaps by setting a small, controlled fire. Teach them by example not to drop a match, even after it's out, on anything else that can burn. (Don't throw matches into wastebaskets or garbage cans, which they may set on fire.) Let kids burn their fingers a couple of times, to learn by experience that fire is painful. You may even want to practice getting out of the house in a hurry. Many lives are lost when fires occur at night, and sleepy people don't move fast enough in getting out before it's too late. Remember that many fire deaths stem from being overcome by smoke. If a room or hallway is full of smoke, drop to the floor and crawl. A damp handkerchief or washcloth over the face will also help filter some smoke, but move *fast*.

Television sets sometimes catch fire; keep them away from drapes and other burnable things, so the fire can't spread.

One of the few drawbacks of draped, loose-hanging clothes (kimonos, gowns, bathrobes, etc.) is that they may be a fire hazard—you can catch a sleeve on fire over a stove, and some cottons and synthetics burn very easily. The best thing to do if your clothes (or hair) catch on fire is first to scream for help, and second to smother the fire—by rolling up in a big coat or soft rug or blanket. Fire needs air to continue burning. If you get badly burned and some of the fabric adheres to the burned skin, don't try to pull it off. Get to a doctor for treatment immediately. Never smoke in bed; you will incinerate yourself if you drowse off and the bedclothes catch fire.

C. Beware of household hazards.

Many recently developed cleaning and polishing substances are dangerous, especially to children.

- Dishwasher detergents may contain TSP, a caustic that can painfully damage eyes and digestive tracts.
- Furniture polish in spray containers, which children may squirt at each other, can cause blindness.
- Cleaning liquids may be colored and packaged to be "attractive," and children may swallow them, with lethal results.
- Simplify your supply of cleaning products to a few necessities, and keep those in a locked storage place if you have small children.

Here are some other items which irresponsible manufacturers produce that endanger their users.

- Some color T.V.s give off dangerous radiation—don't sit closer than ten feet from one.
- Some vaporizers used to make steam for coughs contain boiling water which will scald you if the vaporizer is tipped over.
- If small rugs lack nonskid backings, sew on jar rings.
- Gas floor heaters, whose grates get extremely hot, brand waffle patterns on tender children's flesh; if you have a baby just beginning to crawl, build a fence of some kind around the heater. Teach the baby about moderately hot things by letting him or her touch them and saying "Hot!" at the moment of contact. You will later get real attention when you say "Hot!" about something really hot.
- Children's cribs and playpens with wide-spaced slats allow children to stick their heads through and get stuck.
- Fireworks, even though supposedly illegal in most states, still cause many injuries each year.
- Ladders are often rickety from bad design or age; when you use a ladder, make sure it's solidly placed.

D. Beware of poisons and children.

Children seem to be more foolhardy than animals—at any rate they gobble up poisonous (and often foul-tasting) stuff surprisingly often. (The manufacturers are partly to blame, because they make poisonous stuff look like milk, strawberry soda, or other goodies.) The most common causes of child poisoning are cosmetics (permanent-wave neutralizer and polish remover are especially bad), pesticides, petroleum products such as kerosene, cleaners, disinfectants and deodorizers, polishes and waxes, and lye or other corrosives (such as Drano). These substances should not be accessible to children in a sensibly run house.

Never leave medicines on a bedside table or bathroom sink where children may find them and imitate you by taking them.

Inflammable, corrosive, or poisonous substances should be stored in tight-closing containers on shelves or in cabinets far above the reach of small children. Teach children by your example that foul-smelling liquids are to be shunned: If you use ammonia for cleaning, make a face when you pour it out.

There are antidotes for many poisons, but stomach pumping is also sometimes necessary. If you think your child has eaten or drunk something poisonous, immediately call a doctor or hospital and explain what it was. In some areas, "Poison Hot Lines" have been set up. (Take the container to the phone with you, so that you can read to the doctor from the label if asked to do so.) Then get the child rapidly to the hospital or clinic.

E. Beware of spray cans.

An international treaty has outlawed CFC-containing cans as a menace to the ozone in the atmosphere. But spray cans of any kind can be a menace to you, and you should keep them out of your house (and especially out of your car). They can explode like hand grenades if they get hot—as they will in a glove compartment, or just on a windowsill in the sun. They tempt kids to play with them for fun—so they may give themselves or each other a dose of deadly insect spray or paint. Even innocent-looking hair spray is a menace—if you use it in a small room or carelessly, you'll breathe it in, and it may coat so much of the inside of your lungs that their oxygen-absorbing capacity is cut down. Several other kinds of lung damage have also been caused by aerosols.

When a liquid absolutely has to be sprayed (which is probably a lot less often than you've been told by the advertisers), get it in a spray bottle that you work with a finger-pump. Keep it well away from your face, and if possible use it quickly and get out of the room until the tiny droplets suspended in the air have a chance to settle.

F. Learn first aid.

Training in first aid can help you save lives, especially in auto crashes, and may even save your own. It can also save unnecessary doctor bills. There is no shortcut to learning first aid; so you need to pick up knowledge and experience wherever you can. However, since situations arise where even a little information is better than nothing, the following recommendations might help in emergencies when no fuller information or better treatment is available. They have been condensed from authoritative sources (chiefly the Red Cross booklet *First Aid*) and checked by doctors active in first-aid training. *First aid is not treatment.* Any serious injuries need the attention of a doctor as soon as possible.

Head wounds, chest wounds, belly wounds, very dirty wounds, and wounds that can cause severe bleeding or shock require more than immediate first aid. You must just stop the bleeding and then get the patient to the hospital immediately, no matter what the consequences.

Head wounds often cause bleeding that's difficult to stop. Because of the danger of a fractured skull, all head injuries beyond a simple bump should probably be seen by a doctor, who can check for fractures. Any period of blackout, confusion, stupor, or loss of memory means at least that a concussion has occurred, and possibly worse. Head injuries can have extremely bad aftereffects.

Chest wounds may interfere with breathing. If air is being sucked in through the wound, smear heavily with vaseline and bandage heavily, to prevent air getting into the wound. A hand will do in a drastic emergency. Then get the patient to a hospital immediately.

Belly wounds can be severe, even if they don't look bad on the surface, because there may be internal bleeding. Shock, pain spread out over the belly, and rigid muscles when touched are signs of serious trouble. Back pain, vomiting, bloating of the belly, and general poor condition are also possible danger signs.

Here are a few of the things about which you should learn more in a first-aid course. (The American National Red Cross gives free courses—look them up in your phone book. Community organizations and schools also give training.)

When somebody has been hurt, try to find out from observers or the hurt person just what happened. Above all, keep calm as you inspect the situation and decide what to do. It helps the patient actually to get better, and avoid the dangerous condition called shock, if you can reassure the patient that you know what you're doing. If possible, send someone for a doctor or ambulance, while you check:

Breathing. Learn to do mouth-to-mouth resuscitation. This is basically breathing your own breath into the other person. You must keep it up until he or she begins breathing again. Sometimes this takes a long time—even up to twenty minutes. Don't give up.

Heart. CPR courses teach a kind of heart massage to help the heart resume beating.

Bleeding. The best way to stop bleeding is by pressing on the wound firmly with a sterile bandage, folded clean handkerchief, piece of underwear, or any other handy clean cloth. Do not try to use a tourniquet; they do more harm than good. Keep pressure on for at least fifteen minutes, and bleeding will almost always stop. Then apply a clean bandage, plenty thick to keep a light pressure on wound. Don't pour on liquid antiseptics—they may burn the wound. If the wound is not terribly bad, and delay would not mean serious extra loss of blood, you can clean a dirty wound by washing it with clean water and mild soap before pressing on it to stop bleeding. This greatly lessens danger of infection.

Shock. Anybody who has lost a significant amount of blood must be treated for shock. Medically, "shock" means that because the body has been hurt, its blood vessels expand, and thus there isn't enough blood to go around in all of them; the brain gets starved of blood, and the patient may pass out. Trying to prevent this, the heart pumps faster, and the skin blood vessels clamp down to send more blood to the brain. So the signs of shock are very fast pulse (like one hundred per minute); skin pale, sweaty cold; patient very nervous or even unconscious.

If you see signs that as much as four cups of blood have been lost, the patient may need a transfusion, and should be taken to a hospital emergency room as fast as possible; it is a question of life or death.

A patient who seems to be in shock but has only slight injuries can be laid down with feet four to six inches off the ground and head flat. People who have merely fainted will quickly recover within a minute or two.

In mild cases of shock, without large blood loss, the patient should be put in bed to rest, watched carefully, and made to drink large amounts of fluids. If he or she has been taking fluids, but doesn't urinate at least two cups every four hours, the kidneys may be damaged, and a physician should be consulted.

A related and potentially fatal condition is hypothermia, or severe chill brought on by immersion in cold water, by severe winter exposure, or by wind chill—which can be dangerous even at seemingly mild temperatures. The body must be warmed gently, and kept protected from wind and further chill, for example, in a sleeping bag.

Infection. A normally healing noninfected wound has a little rim of red, tender skin around it. Dangers of infection occur when a wound develops an abscess, like a giant pimple; a large red, hot, tender area spreads out around a wound; or red, tender lines appear in the skin around the wound. A fever is usually a sign of infection. Any of these conditions means trouble that can result in death; a doctor should be seen as soon as possible. The usual treatment prescribed for infection is to soak the area in warm water four times a day for ten to fifteen minutes, and if the wound is in an arm or leg, to keep it raised as much of the time as possible. Antibiotic treatment is only sometimes desirable.

Deep dirty wounds can result in gangrene or tetanus, both extremely dangerous diseases, and a doctor should be seen after first-aid treatment. Black, dead, bubbly, or foul-smelling flesh around a wound is a sign of deadly gangrene, a life-or-death matter. To guard against tetanus ("lockjaw") after a puncture wound, go to a doctor and ask for a tetanus shot.

Aspirin (two tablets every four hours) will help dull mild pain. Patients who are terribly nervous—and not in shock or danger of shock—can be given one shot of liquor (never more). Pain is a biological danger signal; do not dull it until you are sure you know what is causing it.

Fractures. The signs of a fracture are swelling, tenderness, misalignment of bones, and pain when moved. Broken bones should always be checked by a physician, who will usually take an X-ray and then "set" a break. Don't try to walk on a possibly broken leg, or use a broken arm. If you can feel or see a break in a rib, or suspect one, the patient should not be moved except by trained ambulance people, because of the danger of lung puncture.

First-aid supplies. Every household needs a first-aid cabinet with a collection of essentials in it, though obviously you can improvise for many requirements like bandages.

- Aspirin (hundred-pill bottles); buy the cheapest you can find, and keep away from children.
- Sodium bicarbonate (for "heartburn" or indigestion); cheaper than brand-name products with added ingredients, but works just as well.
- Calamine lotion (for bug bites, poison ivy, etc.).
- Adhesive bandages ("Band-Aid" brand is usually more expensive than others).
- Ice bag (for headaches, hangovers, injuries to joints and muscles—do not use a hot-water bottle or heating pad on such injuries!).
- Thermometer (if you have a baby, get the rectal type).
- Tweezers for removing splinters.

Other problems.

- To stop a bloody nose, pinch the nose and hold for several minutes; this works better than cold packs or other remedies.
- If someone is bitten by a dog or wild animal, try to catch the animal for examination by a vet and check of rabies records; otherwise a painful series of anti-rabies injections may be necessary.
- For frostbite, do not rub the frozen part with snow or ice, since doing that may damage the tissues; cover it with woolen cloth, and once indoors, soak in body-warmth water (not hot); a warm drink (not liquor) may help too. Don't put the frozen part near a stove or on a heating pad or on a hot-water bottle.
- For rattlesnake bite, experts differ on whether to attempt suction over a small criss-cross cut, or simply to run water over the bite and get the victim to a hospital. If you are way out in the wilds, the suction treatment may help; but be careful of arteries, muscles, and tendons in your cutting!

- Bites and stings from scorpions, spiders, bees, and wasps can cause intense pain; packing with ice, or soaking in cold water, is helpful. Incidentally, those huge tarantula spiders that look so deadly are actually harmless to humans, though a few people may have allergic reactions to a bite.

Burns. Cold water is a good immediate treatment for any burn. Light "first-degree" burns (as bad as a bad sunburn) usually need no further treatment (though a really bad sunburn can give headaches, nausea, and extreme tenderness of the skin). Blistered, deeper "second-degree" burns, and charred, twisted, no-feeling-left "third-degree" burns need to be treated immediately by a doctor. Face and hand burns may require special surgery, and may heal badly. Burns can result in serious shock and fatal infections. If a severe burn has clothing stuck to it, don't try to remove it yourself; the skin may come with it.

There is much evidence that a heavily negative-ionized atmosphere decreases the pain due to burns. If you have a household ionizer, you might put it and the burned person in a small room together.

The American Medical Association Encyclopedia of Medicine (Random House, 1989) is a good all-around source of medical information; very well illustrated.

G. Use the county hospital if you must.

Nobody likes county hospitals, because they are huge, impersonal places where you feel lost and wonder whether anybody will bother to take care of you. But actually their medical work is reasonably good these days—most of the staff doctors are young and are working in the hospital because they see it as a way of helping humanity rather than getting rich quick. Outside medical experts who have investigated medical care in big county hospitals in Los Angeles and Oakland have found that it's acceptable, although conditions are crowded, nursing staffs are short, food is terrible, etc. The worst part is dealing with all the applications, offices, and the endless waiting. Before going to a county hospital, try to get the name of a doctor who works there and call for advice; then ask for him or her when you get there.

Try never to go to a county hospital without a friend who can go to bat for you, keep you company, get you snacks, and generally help you out. Clinic outpatient services are far less good than hospital services—and sometimes very expensive if you have to pay for them.

County hospitals must treat anyone who comes in, whether he or she has any money, health insurance coverage, or any other resources. Some privately run hospitals in a county are used by the police to take emergency cases to, and you can go there under your own power too. But unless you can prove you're able to pay the bill, or are in clear and immediate danger of death, many hospitals will refuse to help you.

If you are without money or insurance coverage, therefore, make sure that whoever takes you in, waits around to see what happens—it may be desirable to take you to the county hospital rather than wait for often delayed city ambulance service.

If you have any income at all and are not on welfare, the county hospital will bill you, at possibly far more than regular doctors' rates!

Chapter 15.
Live Well in the City.

Admittedly American cities have been hellish messes, and American young people often think about "going back to the land"—taking their inspiration from the original Indian inhabitants. One of the main advantages to living in the country, of course, is that you have more opportunities to use your natural ingenuity on shelter and food problems; so you can live very cheaply there. You may not have the city's advantages, but you escape the disadvantages you would suffer by living at the same income level in a city slum, and you live in closer contact with the natural order and in a less stressful life-style.

But rejection of the city is a peculiarly American phenomenon; it doesn't occur in European countries whose cities are pleasant places, and where active, intelligent, future-thinking people find cities a congenial and stimulating environment. Not only that, but many wholesome activities directed toward self-reliance can be carried out in urban situations as well as in the country. It is possible to spend healthy time outdoors in city parks or on city waterfronts. City dwellers can learn to be conscious of the lives of their neighborhood trees, plants, birds, and insects just as country people can: In any city vacant lot there may be fifty separate species busily surviving. Community gardens often provide a springboard for a neighborhood to revitalize itself biologically, through planting trees and flowers. Every city window and balcony and roof can support luxuriant plant life. Once you start looking at your city environment as more than just concrete and glass, you may be surprised at the possibilities.

The cost and aggravation of suburban commuting have become so great that many people realize they can afford stiff city rents or housing prices and still lead a better life—cutting down their dependence (and expenditures) on cars. With this resurgence of middle-class interest in the central cities, piecemeal regeneration is improving the quality of life in all kinds of neighborhoods. Blighted waterfronts are being restored as parks and shopping areas; sometimes pollution control is even able to make bodies of water safe for swimming again. Far from being just the dying end product of a decaying industrial civilization, cities have been the crucial element in human development since the very beginning of history. Jane Jacobs in her study *The Economy of Cities* (Vintage Books) suggests that even the beginning of agriculture came from the early neolithic cities.

Certainly in our world, the city is not only where the vast majority of us now live, it is also the source of most ideas (scientific, artistic, political, and philosophical—including environmental and back-to-the-land ideas). It is the source of jobs, money for development, political power. Most of all, it is in the city that people have the characteristically urban human opportunity to mix with a great variety of others: to talk, to argue, to dream, to make contact with those whose minds fit with theirs, to plan, to scheme, to buy and sell. Our real problem is not to get away from or eliminate cities, but to transform them into ecologically and humanly satisfying places to live.

Romantic dreams about the easy satisfactions of rural life are usually espoused by people whose ideas of country life have been formed by brief vacations financed by city earnings. As a person who lived there twelve years, I can certify that country living is pleasant and soul-satisfying in many ways, but intellectually stimulating it is not. Living in the country tends to be harder materially than in the city; people are poorer, work longer hours, have worse medical and dental facilities, and even eat poorer diets.

A. Organize your block.

Neighborhood committees and block organizations are useful in bringing people together on a human basis: for cleanup campaigns, to bring pressure on the schools, to fight City Hall for better services, money for parks or stop lights, and so on. They are also a way to combat the depersonalization of American life, the atomization that locks each household up by itself, isolated from its neighbors. In recent years they have been springing up by the thousands all over the country, in all kinds of neighborhoods, oriented to many different types of concerns.

To get started in neighborhood organizing, you need to find a few friends who want to help. Go around and talk to some likely-looking neighbors, and find out what they think needs to be done, what people will be organizable around. Try to put up a street bulletin board where people can pin up announcements, for-sale notes, and whatnot. When you get going, plan some kind of fun event (a picnic, potluck, etc.), and print a leaflet to drop off at each apartment and house—also including your ideas about neighborhood organizing.

Neighborhood organizing should be undertaken not as a duty but because it can improve your daily life and bring you into contact with new friends nearby.

B. Keep your friends.

In an alienated and fragmented society like ours, with the family faltering and love relationships (or even marriages) increasingly tenuous and often temporary, our friendships become all the more precious. Yet, curiously enough, few people give any systematic thought to their friendship patterns. A healthy friendship support network can help us through life's worst crises, and can make everyday life more interesting, varied, and productive. Sometimes, on the basis of well-established friendships, we can enter upon living experiments with other people, in joint or neighboring households, to help fill the void left by the disappearing nuclear family. In these new situations, we can establish new enterprises, or undertake challenging adventures, that we would never have been able to manage alone.

The emphasis in American society has always been individualistic, leading to our familiar national posture of "looking out for Number One." But now that there is no more frontier to escape to, or open road to flee on, we must come to terms with living with each other. Our psychological literature is full of books on solving internal personal problems or the problems of our couple relationships. It is time to turn this narcissistic focus outward, toward our friends and our interrelationships with society. It is largely through our friends that we cling to our particular ecological niches in the world. We need to pay attention to our friendships and to nurture them; they are one of our chief survival mechanisms.

Romantic love and friendship are in some ways opposing values, as people discover who fall madly in love and find themselves abandoning their friends— "well lost for love." The romantic tradition implies that passion should suffice for happiness, that the ideal state of human life is continual enchantment with a beloved. But enchantment is transitory and founded on fantasy. Unlike friendship, it can not long survive the realities of day-to-day life; unless love is founded on friendship, it is doomed to be temporary. Moreover, the friends we abandoned yesterday turn out to be badly needed when our lover abandons us. We are better off, thus, to regard the qualities important in friendship (trust, loyalty, equality, mutual regard) as the foundation of our lasting relationships, to which passion is an occasional delightful ornament.

C. Celebrate your own holidays.

Our traditional holidays are actually debased versions of very ancient festivities. Christmas goes back to the Roman festival of Saturnalia, and beyond that to pagan celebrations of the winter solstice—the time when the sun reaches its lowest point and the days are shortest, after which we can look forward to the coming of spring. Easter is our spring festival of rebirth, falling about a month after the spring equinox. Midsummer Night's Eve is still celebrated in Scandinavia; it is the summer solstice, or time of the longest day and highest sun. In prehistoric times, and indeed up to the Middle Ages, our Western European ancestors celebrated these pagan holidays as periods of fertility rituals, sometimes sacrifice, and often sexual license.

The sexual side of traditional holidays has been diverted in our times mainly into two other kinds of excess: eating and buying, both of which tend to become unpleasant obligations. At Thanksgiving you are expected to eat too much; at Christmas you are expected to give too much; on New Year's you are expected to drink too much—and pretend to be happy, when in fact you may well be feeling pretty dismal. (In actuality, the winter holidays are the heavy suicide season.) We need to recapture the original ceremonial meaning of our holidays: their celebration of the phases of our yearly cycle here on earth. We depend on this eternal cycle just as our forebears did, from the agricultural standpoint, though few of us are actually engaged in planting and harvesting. A certain gratitude to Earth and Sun would seem to be as much in order for us as it was for our ancestors. Surely we can be inventive enough to devise some new expressions of it.

Here are some examples of other traditional holidays we might want to revive or rehabilitate or reemphasize.

Iroquois Indian Dream Festival (mid-January). During this festival people were thought to be out of their minds and thus not responsible for their actions; they went around masked, smashing things, and generally evening up old scores.

Valentine's Day (February 14). This was originally much sexier than our commercial greeting-card version—on this day birds and animals were thought to choose their mates; so humans did likewise, by magic or games of chance. If you want to take the risk they took in Rome, the first person you see on this day will be your true love, or you can draw names out of an urn.

May Day (May 1). This is a double-faced holiday, one side sex and the other politics. For the sex part, you needs lots of dancing around a maypole and much nearby grass and woods for the celebration of fertility rites. For the political part, you need to remember that the tread of thousands of parading workers' feet has often struck terror into the hearts of bosses, raising the specter of general strikes and the revolution.

Dragon Boat Race (early June). This is in honor of Ch'u Yuan, a dissident Chinese scholar of the third century B.C. When his proposed reforms of a corrupt court fell on deaf ears, he jumped into the river. This festival commemorates the search for his body—with gaily decorated boats, drums and gongs, and a lot of racing back and forth. However, there is no goal and no judges, so the day becomes an occasion for picnicking, drinking, and assuring that yin and yang are in balance.

Bastille Day (July 14). In 1789, the French people stormed the hated Bastille prison and destroyed the records of the police, as oppressed people have done since and will do again. In France, celebrating begins the previous evening with music and dancing in the streets, followed by fireworks and more dancing the next day.

Day of the Dead (November 2). In Mexico and other cultures where wakes are regarded as an occasion for showing that life goes on, it does not seem strange to celebrate the dead. This day in Mexico is a picnic day; people stream to the cemeteries, long before sunrise, with candles, flowers, and food. For the dead (though the living eat it) they bring candy, cakes, and so on—made in the shape of skulls—and poets and musicians write and sing of death.

You may also find some of the traditional religious holidays to your taste. Modern religions tend to be bland, commercialized, and banal, and they try to make their holidays pretty much like everybody else's. If you want holidays with more guts, you'll have to find an old-fashioned religious group that still takes rituals seriously. They exist. One of the best current resources on holidays is Aidan A. Kelly, *Religious Holidays and Calendars: An Encyclopedic Handbook* (Detroit: Omnigraphics, 1991), since it lists the holidays of more different kinds of religions than any other available book.

D. Organize parties and celebrations.

The best parties are focused around some activity other than drinking, but they do need some kind of focus, and this seldom comes about automatically. If you happen to know musicians, live music gives a beautiful center for a large party; dancing to a band is always more exciting than using records. Providing food gives people a chance to relate to each other by relating to something real, especially if you either arrange a big potluck with lots of surprises or have some special treat like a big fish to cook. Even work parties tend to be better than shapeless parties: It's pleasant to get together with friends to paint an apartment, assemble a newsletter, or do some other chore that's time-consuming but doesn't interfere with socializing. It's true, of course, that sometimes a very good party happens spontaneously—a combination of people drop by who relate well to each other, good things come up to do, and everybody ends up feeling warm and loving.

You can also organize parties around celebrating something: a birth or birthday, a marriage, a new apartment, a discovery, a departure or return, a success of some kind. At any such gathering, good music is important, because dancing is a basic human way of celebrating and marking important occasions, and because it does away with a lot of needless talk. The cocktail party is basically an opportunity for trying to impress others, but we hardly need more of that in the contemporary world. What we need to create are opportunities for touching each other, for responding to and expressing basic feelings, and for taking our lives and friends seriously. A good party is an occasion for celebrating and enjoying collectively these important needs.

E. Try potlucks and communal cooking.

Sharing regular potlucks with people you like is a good way to escape the grind of your own solitary food preparation, even if you are not up for communal living arrangements. It's also great fun to give an occasional big eating party. Eating together is a much better way of cementing basic human contact than drinking together.

Neighbors who are friends sometimes set up arrangements to share cooking. If five families participate, each one has to prepare the meal for all just one evening a week. This makes possible putting some extra effort into the planning and cooking, and usually makes the meals into more festive occasions with gourmet aspects you might not undertake just for yourself. It also tends to save money as well as time, and gives you the feeling of eating out without having to spend a lot of money on restaurants.

F. Plant some trees in the city.

Wood for habitations and furniture is one of our most beautiful and satisfying materials. Trees are also a major force in making the Earth a habitable planet. Trees in cities have an important role to play in helping to make them healthy and pleasant, and a new field of "urban forestry" has been developing in response to this need. A treeless suburban tract is something like 15 degrees hotter than an old neighborhood with big trees. (It's even hotter if, as is common, the tract devotes a larger proportion of its surface area to asphalt.) Trees increase property values in residential areas, and will become an ever more important source of fuel wood; eventually urban woodlots may serve dual park and energy-production purposes. Wasteland areas of cities slated for later development can be put into quick-growing tree species so that they don't simply remain totally unproductive. And most city backyards could support an extra fruit tree or two. (Dwarf or miniature varieties are readily available if your yard is small.)

Trees help provide oxygen for the atmosphere. They absorb and diffuse sound and thus cut down on noise pollution. Their decaying leaves add humus to the soil (don't burn them—compost them!) Trees are a chief ally in the process of resisting erosion by wind and water. Their beauty and peace, their very stolidity, give comfort in a world where everything else seems to move too fast. Planting a tree is not only good for the earth, but also good for your soul. And, since trees usually grow slowly, seeing your tree grow will give you a link to the next generation, which will enjoy its shade and beauty long after you are gone.

In some situations you can obtain tree seedlings free; check with your city or county. Even if you have to buy them at a nursery, small trees are surprisingly inexpensive. Go to your library first and check out a guide to the tree species that grow in your region. If you are thinking of a tree on the street, check with your city street department; it probably has restrictions on what trees you may plant, but it may also have free or low-cost trees available, and may give you advice or even assistance in digging the hole.

Digging a big enough hole is the major problem in tree-planting. Allow plenty of time for the job, and get a good shovel. The hole needs to be about *twice* as far across and deep as the tree's root ball or can, so that you can surround its roots with good, soft earth. (Be prepared to mix some compost material in with the dirt you dig from the hole.) Then water the tree strictly according to instructions. A tree's first days and weeks in its new home are perilous—though once their roots have become well established, most trees fend for themselves with very little further care.

Always consider carefully the impact the tree will have, when full grown, on the sunlight situation. Though trees can be pruned and shaped, you don't want a dense evergreen to shade your sunny balcony where you want to take sun baths; if your yard is small, you won't want a tree that ultimately will occupy all of it. Generally, deciduous trees are best on the south side of a dwelling, since they provide shade in summer but let sunlight reach the building and warm it in winter. If you are in doubt where you want your tree, remember that a tub three feet square and two feet deep can, with proper care, support a tree twenty feet high; you can enjoy the tree while it grows, and plant it permanently later.

Acre for acre, trees produce more useful food or fuel than any other use of the land (as Native Americans knew who lived basically on acorns). Don't neglect the possibility of planting nut-bearing trees (or olives, if your climate permits) that will produce food as they beautify your environment.

Chapter 16.
Find Work—or Survive Anyway.

A. Hunt for jobs efficiently.

At some point in your life, you'll find yourself in the "job market" trying to sell your labor power, talents, and energy. Like basketball, job hunting is a statistical game, and your chances of success are improved if you can manage a lot of shots. Here is a brief summary of the rules.

1. Don't panic.

If you are desperate and take the first thing you can get, you'll probably soon regret it and be looking around for something else. Therefore . . .

2. Hunt jobs when you don't need one.

The worst time to hunt a job is when you are desperate; like everything else, jobs are easier to find when you really don't need them. If you have been laid off, don't delay going to the unemployment office to apply for your benefits. You can also save yourself some money and therefore buy yourself some time by moving in with family or friends if you suddenly find yourself out of work.

If you have a job that will end in a few months, use up some sick leave or vacation time in hunting for other jobs, long before you're actually laid off. When you don't need a job right away, you can talk relaxedly with potential bosses. (On the other hand, a totally blasé attitude turns bosses off; they want somebody who is good enough not to worry about being out of work, but who is eager to do the right job well.) Once you really need a job and haven't found one, you tend to get more depressed and anxious every day. It is supremely important to try and fight this, because it tends to make you seem less "employable" to interviewers. Hunting early also solves the otherwise difficult problem of whether to take the first job that's offered or to take the chance of telling the employers you want to look into other possibilities (which may lose you that job). If you're still working, potential new employers know they have to give you something better or they can hardly expect you to make a change.

3. Make deliberate, planned use of your network of friends.

Since most people work at something or other, practically everybody you know is a source of potential job information. Moreover, the really interesting jobs seldom get advertised; they're filled by word of mouth by friends of the people who already work there. So when you are job hunting, sit down and systematically phone everybody you know, letting them know you are looking, and asking them to pass on leads to you. Don't be shy about it: Everybody needs a job sometime! Ask friends if they know anybody else you could call who might have job leads. Write down everything so you can come back to it later. Don't forget your relatives, and if you live in a city that still has a working political machine, get hold of your precinct captain and see if he or she can help you out. If you belong to any churches, ethnic groups, clubs, hobby organizations, etc., try to get the word out through them too.

4. Concentrate on what you have to offer.

The awful question "What can you do?" terrifies most beginning job seekers, and a lot of pretty experienced people too. Employers often take the view that if you haven't already done whatever it is they want done, you can't possibly do it; and it's very hard to counteract this attitude. But it may help a little to sit down, before you get into the actual action of seeing possible employers, and outline your capabilities as you see them (not as you think some potential boss should see them). Many people who fear they "can't do anything" are extremely capable, but just not in ways they connect with jobs: You may be extremely good with children, or an ingenious con artist, or super neat and orderly, or love to talk with people. The problem is to find some kind of job where some of your capabilities—the things you really like doing and do well—can be put to use. (Otherwise you are just selling your soul and your time.)

5. Know what the company or organization does.

The atmosphere of a place is strongly influenced by its products, and it is good to work for a company whose output you respect, or at least don't consider a menace to society.

6. Case the prospective job place.

Sometimes it is possible to look the place over before applying, and maybe even talk to some of the people you'd be working with. Coffee rooms and cafeterias are semipublic; walk in and have a cup. Don't be afraid to tell people what you're doing—they're usually glad to open up and give you some pointers. That way you can get a pretty good idea of what the atmosphere is, and you can stay out of jobs that would be real grinds. You may even be able to find jobs in places where you like to spend time anyway—as a waitress or waiter in a coffee house, a clerk in a specialty store or bookstore, a guide or guard in a museum, a boat repairer in a yacht harbor, and so on. It's worth a lot to work in a place where the other people are interesting to you, and where the nature of the work and the supervision are such that they don't constantly rub on you: Do the supervisors monitor you by watching or listening to your calls? Can you physically move around without having to get permission? Are the supervisors or fellow workers mostly narrow-minded types or more loose and tolerant? Every company has its own "climate," and you should stay out of those that are unpleasant to you.

7. Make Up Résumés.

In most any kind of work, you need a résumé—a sheet listing your name, address, and phone number at the top, together with what kind of job you're seeking, and then detailing your experience in previous jobs and your schooling. Unless you've worked steadily, it's best to arrange your jobs by categories and leave off the dates (you can mention these during the interview). Arrange your schools in order, showing what you concentrated on. You should type up the résumé very neatly and make copies. It's useful to leave some with influential friends, send some to companies that might have a job open, submit some to employment agencies, and so on. It gives you something to hang onto when you walk into an unemployment office.

8. Be Prepared.

Applying for a job takes time, and you have to be ready to spend it, or don't bother applying. Remember it's part of the statistical game. You'll have to fill out each company's forms, whether you present them with a résumé or not. You'll have to answer each interviewer's questions about why you left your previous jobs (don't bad-mouth other bosses—sound loyal but discouraged about prospects, etc.), what you did with your time in between jobs, why you want the job with this particular company, what you plan to do with your life, and so on. Follow directions—that's one of the basic requirements for any job. You may have to take aptitude tests, typing tests, psychological tests. You'll have to give references, too: either previous bosses, teachers, or other respectable people who will give you a good plug if asked. (Make sure you check with them first, and don't be afraid to ask whether they would give you a good recommendation—nobody needs false friends in job hunting.) If you are hunting a new job while still working at your old one, be careful: The prospective boss may ask whether your present boss knows you're looking, and if not will worry that you might leave him in the lurch too.

Always carry a working pen with you when you are job hunting, both to fill out forms and to jot down things that might be useful later. Keep a record of your interviews and contacts in a notebook or on file cards, so that you don't get mixed up as to what you or the interviewer said.

9. Dress for the part.

You are seeking a role in a game, and only certain costumes are allowed. The president's son or daughter may wear pants, ruffled shirts, and a velvet coat, but except in advertising, films, and a few other "creative" industries, the safe bet is to look conventional-American; suits for men and women in status jobs, and plain, attractive, though less formal wear for others. (If you really want a job in a certain company, find out how its employees dress by dropping into the company cafeteria or watching them come out after work.)

10. Know what a personnel officer is.

It may make you less nervous about interviews if you remember that the personnel people in most companies are only screeners—they sift out the applicants; supervisors actually make the real decisions. Personnel departments are often staffed by people who couldn't make it in the production departments and have been sent to pasture in personnel, where they can't do too much damage. They still have the power to turn you down if you come on in some way they don't like, but they aren't geniuses who can read your mind. Offer a firm handshake, talk to them in a lively but businesslike way, not deadpan. Sit quietly in your chair, look them in the eye as much as you can, don't smoke unless invited to, and be two or three minutes early for interviews. It is not a bad thing to be a bit nervous in interviews. If you're too cool, they may decide you don't really need the job.

11. Develop a credible explanation for your job gaps.

Employers were once very suspicious of anybody who didn't have a continuous job record. If you had an unexplained three-month gap, they'd figure you must have been in jail or something, or were unreliable in some way. Now so many folks are in and out of school, traveling around the country, taking special training, setting up small business enterprises for themselves, and whatnot, that there is no need to be embarrassed at explaining what you were doing when not working. So write down a job history and develop stories for any gaps in it. Use your imagination—work it all out in detail; give it reality in your own mind, and it'll have reality when you tell the personnel interviewer about it. Stick to the truth where possible, obviously—if you went back to school or got specialized training, say so, even if it isn't relevant to the job you're asking for.

B. Make cautious use of employment agencies.

It's a good idea to try employment agencies before you get too desperate for a job—don't treat them as a last resort. Check the want ads and find agencies listing your kind of job. When you go to an agency, put on your job costume and behave as if they were employers.

Racket agencies sometimes list juicy imaginary jobs in the papers, and then push you off onto other jobs when you show up. Don't deal with agencies that charge a "registration fee" or other fee before they get you a job; legitimate agencies get paid only if they place you. Try to avoid agencies that demand exclusive representation—you may want to have several agencies try to help you. When you register with an agency, they will make you sign a contract. Read it very carefully. Especially check for penalty clauses; sometimes these allow the agency to charge you even if you find a job yourself, or even if some other agency finds it for you. Sometimes they obligate you to pay a huge fee if you accept a job and then don't show up, or if the job turns out to be intolerable and you quit or are fired. Do not sign such a contract, no matter how much you need a job, or how "nice" the agency people are. (If they were really nice, they would delete these clauses from the contract, and put their initials next to yours in the margin.)

An agency that is on the level will set its fees as a percentage of your future earnings, like 50 percent of the first month's pay. But generally these fees can be paid in a series of installments, so that you have something to live on while you're paying them off. Make sure the interest rate on these installments is clearly specified—agency fees can be deducted from your income tax at the end of the year.

Some employers in effect use employment agencies as their personnel departments, and pay the fees involved. Watch for their "Employer Pays Fee" ads, but don't neglect the other agencies.

Agencies are especially handy if you are looking for a job while you still have your old one, because that way you can't possibly answer an ad and have it turn out to be your own company. Using an agency may also save you a certain amount of duplicate filling out of employment forms.

After an interview with a possible employer, phone back to the agency and tell them what happened.

For anybody who wants to work less than steady, full-time, year-in-year-out grind, temporary job-placement agencies can be very useful. Working through such agencies can be especially attractive to older people, who may have top abilities but find employers unwilling to hire them on a regular, full-time, long-term basis. Some agencies specialize in providing accounting services or other special skills, but most deal in a wide range of office jobs for both men and women; they also offer manual and labor jobs, mainly for men but occasionally for women too. Temp agencies exist in every city. The pay is about equal to that for jobs you could get directly yourself—but you don't get tied down to one job.

When you work through one of these agencies, you are actually an employee of the agency, and they rent you out to businesses—for a day, for a week, for a couple of months; when that job is done, they will send you on to something else. Considering how boring most jobs are, this gives you some delightful variety. And somehow it's not so bad doing menial work if you're not the boss's regular "property." You can tell the agency approximately how much of the time you want to work (be careful in thinking about this, and settle on a realistic figure); they won't consider you suspect if it's only half-time, or only the first six months of the year, or only the summers.

Your pay, withholding and Social Security taxes, unemployment taxes, and so on are all handled by the agency. When you go on the job for them, you are not required to fill out forms, wring your hands in an interview, or worry—you just go to work.

Shop around to find the best agency in town. The agency should pay once a week and should have an upwardly sliding scale depending on your skills. Frequently the smaller, local temporary agencies pay better than mammoth chains. Avoid any agency that tries to charge you a fee.

Since the agencies are now highly competitive for workers, many are offering benefits of different types. You can opt for health insurance at certain agencies. Others give vacation time after you've worked a set number of hours for them within any given year. One agency has a "three-day weekend" bonus, where, if you work the Friday before and Tuesday after a three-day weekend, you get paid for Monday.

C. Try self-employment and supplemental jobs.

One drawback of ordinary jobs is that you are at somebody else's beck and call. Even if your boss is a perfectly decent person, you may not like this aspect very much. There are ways to create a job for yourself as an independent operator, even without having to find a lot of capital and "set up in business." The possibilities in every locality are different, but here are some kinds of work that are needed almost everywhere:

Typing. A good free-lance typist can make the equivalent of normal wages, and can work at home any hours. Around universities and in big cities there is lots of typing to be done. All you really need to get started is a word processor and some cards to stick up on bulletin boards or hand out to people. It's also useful to advertise in student newspapers.

Child-care. Since so many parents now work, there is a serious shortage of good child-care services. Operating government centers costs almost as much per child as paying the parents welfare to stay home, so it seems unlikely that government-run centers will expand to any significant extent. If you love children, therefore, you can certainly find children in your neighborhood who need care, and at going rates a half-dozen kids bring in enough income to support you in a modest way. This is a kind of work that men are undertaking more often. Many American children living with their mothers have little contact with nurturing men, and such contact is extremely valuable. It's best to work with one or two other child-loving people you get along well with; you can then contemplate a better site, and perhaps develop into a full-scale nursery school. Be prepared to encounter hassles with city officials or neighbors; find a lawyer who knows the local situation to advise you and deal with trouble.

Juice stands and other refreshment places. You don't have to have a fixed place of business; you can rig up a truck or even a push cart. By finding out where large crowds of people gather, you can do a brisk business if you offer a really fine product. People have especially good luck these days with good, cold drinks—the ordinary food stands sell such chemically concocted junk that a good glass of real lemonade, orange juice, apple juice, or other cooling drink will sell fantastically at fairs, at outdoor concerts, in parks, and just on hot city streets. Ice-cream wagons, of course, are an old city standby. But you can sell hot pretzels, candy, fruit and a variety of other goodies—so long as you buy a business license from the city and scrupulously observe cleanliness requirements.

Teaching. If you know how to do something well, you can find students who want to learn it. People live by teaching tennis, English, computer programming, music, swimming, reading, foreign languages, and so on.

Data processing. Because computerization has so many complexities, organizations often get into binds where they need outside help on an emergency or short-term basis. There are also many research projects and students who must use data processing but don't know how to handle it. If you happen to understand computer languages and like to be creative with them, you can make money by helping people who don't and aren't.

Caretaker and apartment-manager jobs. There are many kinds of properties around the country, often located in remote places, which need watching: abandoned mines, summer estates, hunting or fishing clubs, unrented factory buildings, properties being contested in will settlements, and so on. Any property that is either economically valuable and might burn down or suffer other damage, or which is hazardous and might cause legal liabilities, is a candidate for a caretaker. Usually these jobs include live-in facilities, of course, but in some the conditions may be primitive. Metropolitan newspapers, and newspapers in the areas where the properties are, run caretaker job listings too. When applying for such jobs, it pays to look responsible and carry along respectable references.

The urban counterpart is the apartment manager's job, where you get a free apartment (or reduced rent) and sometimes a part-time salary in return for taking care of a building. This means renting vacant apartments, fixing things that get out of order, keeping up the gardening, and so on—a pleasant and not very time-consuming sort of work. It can get a bit sticky if you have to collect the rent.

D. Apply for unemployment.

Unemployment programs usually provide a subsistence income and sometimes more for up to half a year. However, even a little money can be made to go a long way; and your benefits are not affected by any other family or group income that may be available.

Since employers help finance the fund that pay these benefits (by a tax they have to pay on your earnings while you work for them), bosses are not eager to lay you off—they would rather make things difficult, so that you quit instead. If you suspect such a plan is afoot, and layoffs are in the wind, be careful not to give them any excuses for firing you, and don't quit. A good-hearted boss, however, can usually be counted on to certify that you were indeed laid off—which he or she will have to do after you apply for benefits.

Apply at the state department of employment; do so as soon as you are laid off, because it takes several weeks to begin getting checks. You will be expected to continue actively looking for work; find out exactly what this means—sometimes just phoning five companies a week to ask about job openings will suffice. You may have to go into the office for an interview every few weeks to prove you are still around and looking. If they line up a job appointment for you somewhere, you must go to it.

Obviously, however, when jobs are in short supply, the employment people will not likely find you a job during the eligibility period unless you do some kind of work that does have openings, like clerical jobs. If you have a skill in a category where jobs are scarce, it is almost impossible for them to place you. (In most states they cannot force you to take a job outside your category or at a lower salary than you got before.)

One of the advantages of working intermittently, rather than part time all the time, is that you may be able to find some jobs that you can tell will not last long. You can then count on a cushioned period after you get laid off if you arrange your life right—and save some money during the period you're working.

Most states also have some kind of disability insurance, which provides benefits if you get sick or injured and cannot work. (Worker's compensation provides only for disabilities that arise from your job, but the state programs go beyond that.) A doctor's certificate of disability is required, and periodic checks are made to see if your condition is continuing. Sometimes applications for disability payments can be made by mail from the hospital or from home; call the employment department to find out.

E. Apply for welfare.

Right-wing politicians like to spout off about "welfare cheaters," and a few people do manage to abuse the welfare system. Most people on welfare, however, are ordinary people who have had serious misfortune in their lives, just as we all may. A majority are white; few stay on welfare long; most have children. Welfare payments are your right if you are in a situation that qualifies you for them; don't be afraid or ashamed to apply.

The most common form of welfare is AFDC: Aid to Families with Dependent Children. In many areas it is, in effect, the only kind of welfare there is, except for a few occasional cases of desperate unemployed fathers who qualify for extremely small grants; GA (General Assistance) emergency relief may occasionally be granted (depending on the county regulations) to people who cannot get unemployment, "supplemental security income" through the Social Security system, or AFDC. However, by a familiar Catch-22, it is generally very hard to get an emergency grant unless you also qualify for AFDC.

Many mothers who qualify for AFDC have been married and divorced. Unless their ex-husbands are very well off and provide alimony as well as child support, they will be obliged to work, no matter the age of the children, unless they can get AFDC. And if they do work, their wages may be so low that they are still entitled to welfare support.

States must now provide AFDC for anyone, without a residency requirement such as still applies to other forms of welfare. You can thus move to a different state and be eligible immediately. States vary widely in their welfare programs, and so do counties. Generally poor and backward areas are, as you would expect, less generous, but the pattern is unpredictable, and information has never been assembled into compact form; people pass tips among themselves.

To receive welfare you must generally dispose of any substantial liquid assets you possess. You may be able to retain your house, and sometimes a car if it is not worth much. But you do not have to let welfare workers make uninvited visits to your home.

When you go in to apply for welfare, make sure you have the whole day free. Go in early and take a book along with you while you wait. The social worker will want to know whether you have any income or property at all, where the father of your children is, where you live and who else lives there, where your parents are, and other information. If you believe you are eligible and are refused welfare, you can ask to see the supervisor, or come back another day—with another worker you may have better luck, since some judgment is involved.

Welfare departments are under constant pressure to save money, and they will turn you down if they can. (Some states, in fact, have deliberately flouted federal welfare regulations.) It pays, therefore, to learn whatever you can from friends who have had contact with the local welfare program, from people in the waiting rooms, and from talking with sympathetic welfare workers.

F. Apply for food stamps.

If you're trying to live in low-income style, you may very well be eligible for food stamps along with millions of your fellow citizens. The stamps can also help on those occasions that many people face at least once in their lives, when they're really totally out of resources—the food-stamp program is supposed to provide stamps quickly, so you don't starve, after a single interview. Though the program has often been regarded as hostile to students, in principle if you are available for 20 hours of work per week, you are eligible.

Eligibility is determined basically by your income, from which you deduct certain standard items like Social Security payments, child care, and excess rent. You cannot possess cash, savings accounts, stocks or bonds, or other liquid assets in excess of a certain amount; people over 60 get an allowance that is almost double. If you have an expensive car, some of its value may count as a cash asset.

Food stamps may be used only to buy food—not household supplies, vitamins, or foods intended to be eaten on the premises, such as at a lunch counter. In states with sales tax on food, food stamps may be used to cover such taxes. When checking out at a supermarket, be sure to separate your food items from nonfood items, and inform the checker you will be paying with food stamps; otherwise the whole checkout may have to be repeated.

Your local welfare or unemployment office is the best place to begin inquiring about possible eligibility for food stamps. The program is run by the Department of Agriculture's Food and Nutrition Service, which has regional offices in major cities.

G. Apply for apprenticeships.

Many highly skilled trades are still learned by apprenticeship—a system that goes back to the Middle Ages, when boys were legally "bound" to master goldsmiths or weavers or whatnot for the years it took them to learn the trade. Skilled workers make more money than semiskilled, but the real advantage of learning a complex trade and becoming a printer, machinist, carpenter, plumber, auto mechanic, electrician, electronics-repair person, and so on, is that you can then find work anytime, anyplace, in any town or city in the country. You are good at something; you probably have a union card to prove it; you can always find a job, even in a full-scale depression. But you are not compelled, like many white-collar workers, to work full time all the time, or to be nervous about keeping a boss happy. Some jobs are partly seasonal, like construction carpentry. Others are short term, and when a project is completed you can lay off for a while if you feel like it. Part-time work isn't easy to find, but if you're good, you can sometimes work that out too, in small auto shops or other independent operations.

As automation spreads, skilled workers are needed more, not less—to build and service the machines used by unskilled and semiskilled workers. Skilled workers tend to get jobs with more variety and challenge. And if you move around on the job, as many repair crews do, you get a fair amount of down time when you drink coffee and socialize. You have a strong union to back you up in disputes and protect wages and working conditions. (Many craft unions are racist, sexist, and undemocratic, but all are under strong pressure to take in minority apprentices and women and be open to new members, generally for public-relations reasons if nothing else; so it pays to keep pushing.)

Being an apprentice is not much different from holding a regular job. You work a full eight-hour day, alongside experienced workers who are supposed to help you pick up on how to do things. You get paid much less than they do during your first six months or year, but it's still well above a subsistence wage; and after that (on a pre-arranged schedule) you get periodic raises until toward the end you are making nearly what they make. Some apprenticeships last two years, some last up to four; in printing some last six. You have to take night-school courses too, between two and six hours per week. In theory the contract obligates both you and the company to carry out the full program for the prescribed number of years, but in practice you can quit if you wish; the company, however, can be held to its obligation.

The country has a chronic shortage of skilled workers, but there are less than 260,000 apprenticeships, and they are hard to get. The biggest apprenticeship possibilities are in the building trades. Neither the giant corporations nor unions have traditionally put much energy into apprenticeships. The companies often prefer to train semiskilled people to run just their own machines at lower wages than all-around skilled workers would earn; and the unions often prefer to keep down the number of members, so that high wages can be secured.

Apprenticeships are generally set up by a company-union agreement, and there is an actual contract that both sign, together with the apprentice (and the parents if the apprentice is a minor). To apply for an apprenticeship, you should first collect a number of character-reference letters, including at least one from a union member (more if possible). The best way to be sure of getting into an apprenticeship program is to have friends on the union committee so it pays to do a lot of preparatory sniffing around to meet the right people. You should have finished high school, or at least two years of it; and you should be in good physical condition. Generally aptitude tests and a physical exam are required; many trades also require good school grades, since "working with your hands" takes more intelligence than many white-collar jobs. Age is not necessarily a barrier; some trades will accept you over age twenty-four.

There are some fake "apprenticeships" set up by companies to get young people to work for low wages. States have apprenticeship agencies where you can check out a program, as does the U.S. Department of Labor. Some companies (and nonprofit organizations) have "intern" programs where you work at low wages, or sometimes none at all, to learn what you can and perhaps worm your way into a regular job. This can be a useful way to find out if you really like a field.

Information on apprentice programs in your area can be found at the state employment office.

H. Be cautious about migration.

Most people move to another city or region chiefly in hopes that finding a job will be easier there—and they tend to go places where they have relatives or friends to whom they can turn for help in learning the ropes. Unfortunately, many of the rumors you hear about plentiful jobs in other places turn out to be false; the country as a whole has a surprisingly inefficient distribution of jobs— there are whole regions that have serious unemployment problems (such as California and Oregon) but keep attracting new people anyway. If you are contemplating a move, try to get some reliable information on jobs by visiting your library and asking the reference librarian for help; also, write to the department of employment of the state you are considering, and ask what the situation is there. They will probably be glad to reply, for states are anxious not to add to their unemployed.

Another good way to find out about both jobs and other aspects of life in a city you might move to is to subscribe by mail to their local newspaper. Besides studying the want ads on jobs, houses, and so on, you can get some feel of whether the style of the city might suit you.

I. Apply for social security.

Until 1935, when the Great Depression had brought the country to the verge of revolution, the United States had no social insurance program of any kind— lagging behind most other industrial countries. It was strictly dog eat dog—and when old age came, die dog die.

Social insurance is like private profit-making insurance, but is cheaper and is democratically controlled by Congress. It operates by spreading the risks of life among a huge mass of people. During the working year, employees and employers (and, through the IRS, self-employed people) pay Social Security a percentage of their paychecks. This money goes into a special trust fund. When earnings drop or stop, because of disability or death or retirement, monthly cash benefit payments go to the worker or the surviving family. Because benefits have been increased, and because a greater number of retired people are coming along, Social Security deductions have grown steadily and in time may rise higher. But the system is a deeply rooted major part of American life; so don't believe scaremongers who say you won't get anything out of it.

Most older people have checked into Social Security and know what their benefit payments will be when they reach retirement. But actually, Social Security insurance covers many other situations, including those that can affect young people. Long before retirement, you or members of your family may become eligible for Social Security payments. To find the Social Security office, look in the phone book or ask at the post office. Here are the times when you should go around to the local office:

To get a card. When you first get a regular job, the employer will ask you to get a Social Security number; employers are obliged to take Social Security deductions from your pay, and contribute an equal amount themselves. All your deductions, accounts, and benefits will be handled under this number, even if you marry, divorce, or change your name. (If you happen to get two cards, it will cut down your benefits; go to a Social Security office and get the situation straightened out.) Your account information is held under your number at the Social Security Administration, Baltimore, MD 21235, and you can write at any time to get an accounting from them. Your benefits will depend on how much and how long your contributions have been, so it's important to keep the record accurate; especially if you change jobs often. Be sure none of your deductions go unrecorded, penalizing you later.

When there is a death in the family. Survivors' insurance payments are due to children, widows (and sometimes dependent parents and divorced wives), and dependent widowers of deceased workers who have had Social Security deductions from their pay in recent years. Recently, benefits became payable to ex-spouses in cases where marriages lasted ten years or more, even if the former spouse has remarried. Moreover, widows and widowers no longer forfeit their benefits if they remarry—which will probably decrease the number of unmarried elderly people who have been living together. Children are now eligible when either parent dies. Even if you think you may not be eligible, go and check on it; there's a lot of money at stake. First, there are outright death payments, which should cover burial expenses. Second, there are monthly benefits to the survivors— indefinitely for adults, and up to the age of eighteen or graduation from high school, whichever comes latest, for children.

When somebody is disabled (meaning they can't work or expect to work for twelve months). Not only the disabled person, but other members of the family may be eligible for payments. Disabled children become eligible if a parent dies or begins to receive retirement or disability payments. It is important to go to the

Social Security office and apply for benefits as soon as it appears someone is disabled for a lengthy period; this will avoid the possible loss of benefits. Curiously, it's easier to qualify for disability benefits when you're young than when you're over 31. Handicapped and mentally retarded people are often eligible for substantial benefits.

When you are nearing retirement. Men are eligible for full retirement benefits, and Medicare coverage, at age 65. Women are eligible at 62. (These ages will rise slightly in the future.) If you postpone retirement, your benefits when you do retire will be somewhat larger. And if you return to work after retiring for a while, your added earnings will usually boost your retirement payments when you stop working. If they wish, men can retire at age 62, and widows at 60; the monthly checks are somewhat smaller; nevertheless, depending on your circumstances and style of life, earlier retirement may be preferable. However, you should go to the Social Security office to apply for benefits several months before you actually reach retirement age. The precise date at which you officially begin retirement may raise or lower the benefits received in your first "retirement year" by several thousand dollars. It will save time and simplify the application procedure if you take along your Social Security card, proof of age (such as birth certificates) for yourself or your children, and your last year's income-tax form.

People receiving retirement payments under Social Security can also work, but their payments will be reduced somewhat. You can earn up to a set amount per year (it tends to be about a third of the average yearly wage) without any reduction in Social Security payments. Above that, however, $1 of benefit payments is withheld for every $2 you earn ($3 if you're 65 or older). "Substantial" employment (more than 45 hours per month) can cut your benefits irrespective of what you actually earn. Income from savings, investments, pensions, royalties, or insurance does not count as work income; so the situation isn't quite as bad as it seems. Nonetheless, it clearly pays retired people to avoid ordinary paid work and instead use time to produce things for themselves—or to make transactions by barter or other informal methods; since no money is involved, this will not cut down your Social Security checks.

The total sums involved in Social Security are often large, even though the payments, on a monthly basis, may sometimes seem meager. In general, widows, widowers, and children receive far more than could be gotten from any insurance policy they could afford. Social Security is one of the few undeniably good things in American life. It gives huge numbers of workers a guarantee of minimal subsistence in old age, and under the pressure of inflation (in an increasing elderly population) it is constantly being liberalized.

It is to your advantage to make sure Social Security deductions are taken from your pay even for short, low-paid, or part-time jobs. Some benefits depend not on the total money deducted, but on whether any was deducted over a three-month period. Domestic workers, especially, often neglect to have Social Security deducted from their already pitiful wages. But you can be "currently insured," as the term goes, if you've earned as little as $50 in three months, so long as Social Security deductions were taken out by your employer. (This qualifies you for disability and survivor payments you may desperately need.)

Not only wage earners but also farmers and other self-employed people can get Social Security coverage. And self-employed people—which includes a lot of artists, musicians, writers, inventors, travelers, and other ingenious souls, as well as people with small farms and more or less regular businesses—can get credit for a whole year of coverage if they have a net income of only $400. Farm workers can also get a whole year of coverage if they make $400. You get to be "fully insured" when you've run up a total of covered years that depends on your age; the minimum is 1-1/2, and the maximum is 10 years. You get maximum benefits if you've been working at high-paid covered jobs in recent years, so that your average covered income is high; but an averaging process is used, so that a couple of lean years can often be left out of the calculations. If you work partly for tips, it may not be wise, in the long run, to underreport them; you'll probably lose far more in Social Security benefits (because your reported average wages will be lower) than you'll save from income tax.

If you are operating something that might qualify as a business, get all the information you can on income tax and Social Security. Often enterprises that show virtually no profit on paper can be very useful to their operators, and run up Social Security credit besides. The paperwork is not very difficult, because for small incomes you don't have to itemize expenses. Social Security offices have a special booklet for farmers that might give you some interesting ideas.

It is now possible to receive Social Security payments abroad, but the decline of the dollar means that you must find a low-cost country. Make arrangements at your local Social Security office.

Service in the armed forces counts as covered employment.

Aged, blind, and disabled people may qualify for "supplemental security income" in addition to or in place of Social Security payments.

The present Social Security system favors spouses who stay home over spouses who work (and thus contribute to the Social Security fund, but get no more benefits). It also penalizes married couples in which both husband and wife work (since they pay double contributions, but actually get *less* benefits than one-earner couples).

Oddly enough, since getting Social Security cards is a simple matter that requires no proof of your identity, they are often used for identification. It is no particular trouble to get a new card with your new name on it, if for some reason you change your name. But make sure Social Security knows you are the same person, or your earlier credit toward benefits will be lost.

INDEX

flea collars, cautions, 239
flea markets, 12
flea powder recommended by Humane
  Society or veterinarian, 239
fleas, getting rid of
  killing them on pets, 239
  removing infested rugs or furniture
    from house for a week, 239
flies, getting rid of, 239
  compost and cover manure, 239
  flypaper caution, 239
  screens and screen doors, 239
  securely closed garbage cans, 239
floor heater, gas, hazard, 246
floors
  cleaning, 142
  unusual coverings, 111
  wood, restoring, 111
flossing, 233
fluorescent light bulb, 147–148
fluoride pills, taking
  during pregnancy, 234
flurazepam (Dalmane),
  long aftereffects, 226
food
  basic supply for disasters, 243
  buying in appropriate quantities, 14
  buying small quantities
    for single people, 15–16
  chewy, for good teeth, 234
  coupon specials, 15
  fads, avoiding, 42
  fast, avoiding, 43
  growing, 127–136
  healthful, 25–40
  in bulk, 5
  inexpensive, 127
  labels
    irradiation symbol, 16
    reading, 16
    requirements, 16
  leftover, at institutions, 9
  pre-packaged and pre-measured,
    avoiding, 15
  processed, avoiding, 43
  scavenging for, 8, 9
  shopping for without children, 15
  storage, 45
  supermarket specials, 15
ood dislikes, 25
ood poisoning, 32
  avoiding, 45

food processor, 139
food stamps
  applying for, 270
  eligibility, 270
  use of, 270
food stores, small, avoiding, 13
fooling around, xiii
forks, stainless steel, 153
Fortrel, 212
foster homes, why needed, 186
foster-parenting, 186
"four food groups, " 25
fractures, 250
freezer
  upright, heavy energy use, 137
  use, 46
French Intensive gardening, 129
friendship, 255
  single parents, 202
frogs, catching, 17
frostbite, 250
frozen food, care of, 46
fructose sugar, 36
fruit, 34, 43
  buying, 14–15
  canned, avoiding buying, 15
  drying, 129
  juicing, 139
fruit ices, 29
fruit soup, 23
fruit trees, 128
frying, avoiding, 22
fuel-injection nozzle, furnace, 144
fuel wood from trees, 258
full disclosure, premarital, 182
funeral
  commercial practices, 205
  costly, reasons for, 204
  societies, 205
  wake, 205
furnace, maintenance, 144
furniture polish, hazard, 246
fuse replacement, 158
futons, 122

GA (General Assistance), 269
gambling, 49
games
  active neighborhood, 195
  board, 195
garage sales, 12
garbage, emptying, 44, 238